THE SHERWOOD ANDERSON DIARIES, 1936–1941

THE

Sherwood Anderson

DIARIES

1 9 3 6 – 1 9 4 1

Edited by Hilbert H. Campbell

The University of Georgia Press

Athens and London

The Sherwood Anderson diaries in this volume © 1987
by the Trustees of the Sherwood Anderson Literary Estate.
© 1987 by the University of Georgia Press
Athens, Georgia 30602
ALL RIGHTS RESERVED
Designed by Barbara Werden
Set in Linotron Sabon at The Composing Room of Michigan, Inc.
The paper in this book meets the guidelines for permanence and durability of the
Committee on Production Guidelines for Book Longevity of the
Council on Library Resources.

Printed in the United States of America
91 90 89 88 87   5 4 3 2 1

LIBRARY OF CONGRESS CATALOGING IN PUBLICATION DATA

Anderson, Sherwood, 1876–1941.
The Sherwood Anderson diaries, 1936–1941.

Bibliography: p.
Includes index.
1. Anderson, Sherwood, 1876–1941—Diaries.
2. Authors, American—20th century—Diaries.
I. Campbell, Hilbert H. II. Title.
PS3501.N4Z47 1987   818'.5203 [B]   86-19311
ISBN 0-8203-0908-7 (alk. paper)

British Library Cataloging in Publication Data available.

*The frontispiece is Sherwood Anderson at Ripshin, January 1941.
(Walter Sanders, Black Star.)*

For

MARVIN O'NEILL MITCHELL

An Extraordinary Teacher

Contents

Preface

The daily diary which Sherwood Anderson kept from January 1, 1936, to February 28, 1941, a few days before his death, is preserved in the extensive Anderson manuscript collection at the Newberry Library in Chicago. The diary consists of six small bound volumes, "desk diary" type books with a dated space provided for writing on each day of the year. Anderson obtained these books from the Hawkins Insurance Agency of Marion, Virginia, which gave them as advertising at Christmas to preferred customers around town. The volumes for 1936 through 1939 all measure about 3 5/8 × 6 1/2 inches and provide a full page for each day's entry except that the book for 1939 has Saturday and Sunday together on one page. The volumes for 1940 and 1941 are larger and thinner, both measuring about 5 1/8 × 7 7/8 inches and providing only one-half of a page for each day's entry. Anderson invariably wrote in ink, using his pocket fountain pen, and commonly filled up the space allotted for each day. During his increasingly frequent periods of illness during these years, he sometimes wrote very little in the diary; but only three spaces (for February 3, 1936; February 4, 1937; and December 1, 1938) are left completely blank during the entire period of more than five years.

Although Anderson's diary provides important information about the last stage in the life of a seminal American author, it has heretofore been largely inaccessible to students and scholars. To read it, one must travel to the Newberry Library in Chicago and gain access to the rare book room. That accomplished, it is likely that the handwriting will appear to most readers almost entirely illegible. Anderson's handwriting, bad at best, is at its worst in the diary. Like most diaries, furthermore, Anderson's is replete with private or obscure references which call for explanatory notes.

I attempt to provide here both an accurate transcription and reasonably full annotation. In transcribing, however, I have been less concerned with total "purity" of the text in a bibliographical sense than with readability. For example, Anderson's characteristically poor spelling I have unhesitatingly corrected, since I have been unable to convince myself that retaining the botched spelling would add anything to the flavor, the authenticity, or the usefulness of the diary. His erratic punctuation I have reproduced largely as it exists in the original, but I have modified it without comment when clarity and coherence seem substantially enhanced by doing so. Although I have subsequently corrected a large number of my own initial misreadings of Anderson's difficult hand, at least a few others must certainly remain. In a few places where I remain utterly baffled, I have used [?] to indicate a word I simply cannot read, or even guess at intelligently; and I use [word?] for a few words or spellings of names which are guesses. In order to avoid an even larger number of explanatory notes than already burden the pages, I have in several places entered into the text in brackets first or last names of persons where Anderson uses only one or the other and where the reader's ability to follow the meaning readily is enhanced by giving both the first and last names. Also, I have without comment spelled out some names in instances where Anderson jots down in haste only an initial or initials. Finally, I have omitted from the text a very small amount of material, the publication of which might prove painful or embarrassing to living persons. These slight omissions (a total of 146 words altogether) should in no way inhibit the continuity or usefulness of the diary. I have indicated the location and length of omitted passages in footnotes.

I have added explanatory notes identifying persons, organizations, places, events, and literary works mentioned which would probably now be obscure to a reasonably literate reader. I have, however, avoided including notes to identify persons whom the same reader will certainly recognize (e.g., Gertrude Stein, Henry Miller, Frank Lloyd Wright, John Steinbeck). A few persons whom I would like to identify I cannot. Among the people who have been helpful to me in the course of this project, I am especially grateful to John S. Anderson, Patricia F. Campbell, Arthur Eastman, Virginia Fowler, Elise Friend, Loris Green, Elizabeth Hance, Diana Haskell, Charles Modlin, Walter Rideout, Marion ("Mimi") Anderson Spear, Welford D. Taylor, Kathryn Weindel, and Vanessa Williams.

Among published sources, the ones which have been most useful to me are *Letters of Sherwood Anderson*, ed. Howard Mumford Jones and Walter B. Rideout (1953); *The Buck Fever Papers*, ed. Welford Dunaway Taylor (1971); *Sherwood Anderson's Memoirs: A Critical Edition*, ed. Ray Lewis White (1969); *Stark Young, A Life in the Arts: Letters, 1900–1962*, ed. John Pilkington (1975); and *Sherwood Anderson: Selected Letters*, ed. Charles E. Modlin (1984). I appreciate the many courtesies received from the Newberry Library and the Virginia Polytechnic Institute and State University Library. To the many other librarians, authors, and friends who have contributed directly or indirectly to the project, a blanket "thank you" will have to suffice. Finally, my greatest debt is to the late Eleanor Copenhaver Anderson, Sherwood Anderson's widow, for her unfailing kindness, generosity, and encouragement over a dozen years, and for permission to publish her husband's diaries.

Introduction

When Sherwood Anderson started keeping a daily diary on January 1, 1936, he was fifty-nine years old and in the third year of his marriage to Eleanor Copenhaver of Marion, Virginia. For the remainder of his life, he routinely recorded in the diary each day where he was, weather conditions, what he was working on, whom he associated with, and how he was feeling. Although individual entries can be fairly pedestrian, taken together they provide an interesting record of the patterns and routines of his life and work, his triumphs and failures, satisfactions and dissatisfactions, healths and illnesses, during the last five years and two months of his life. The most constant thread running through this record is his love for, trust in, and dependence on his wife Eleanor. She was the rock in which he hid his soul in the face of many professional and personal frustrations, the unfailing anchor of his stability. When Eleanor was with him, he consistently wrote such notes as "E grand," or "E very lovely." When they were apart, he frequently found himself writing, "Very lonely for E." On December 26, 1936, he wrote in his diary of Eleanor that "She remains the best one, of all living people I have known."

This was Anderson's first sustained attempt at keeping a daily diary. He had, however, kept a kind of diary while in France in 1921; and he had compiled a "letter-a-day" file for Eleanor during 1932. Actually, Anderson's almost daily letter writing during much of his life represents a diary-like record. Just why he started keeping a more systematic daily record in 1936 is uncertain. Eleanor had begun to keep a diary at least sporadically after their marriage in 1933; and perhaps he was following her example. Anderson had always been a nomad, and he remained during this last stage of his life a restless wanderer. Loving to drive his automobile over long distances, he continued to seek out new scenes and new acquaintances while at the same time renewing whenever and wherever he could his associations with people whom he had known and loved for many years. His fascination with observing common people and listening to them talk never flagged to the day of his death. Eleanor remarked in her own diary in 1936, "Certain, alas, he will not go where he cannot talk with people in little dumps." At the time of his death in March 1941, while en route to South America, he was looking forward eagerly to living for awhile in the small towns of Chile and Argentina; and he had spent a great deal of time in the year before his death trying to master the Spanish language.

Wherever he wandered, however, the coming of June each year found him back in Marion making preparations to open the house at Ripshin, his Grayson County, Virginia, home. Anderson had built Ripshin in 1926, of native stone and logs, employing local craftsmen, and lived there during the warmer months until his marriage to Elizabeth Prall collapsed in early 1929. He had made a few dispirited attempts to sell the house in 1929 and 1930; but after his marriage to Eleanor in July 1933, Ripshin became once more, graced by her presence, his pride and joy. Between 1933 and 1941, Anderson's happiest times were the summers at Ripshin. Here he could have Eleanor with him for a few months, not entirely absorbed in the work of her own busy career with the YWCA; here he could play gentleman farmer, conferring with his farm caretaker and good friend John Sullivan; here he could work on his writing each morning in the cabin beside the creek and play croquet in the late afternoons and evenings with whoever dared challenge him; here he and Eleanor could entertain a stream of summer guests, favored old friends whom they both enjoyed.

As summer began to decline into autumn, Anderson inevitably fell into a mellow mood of happiness mixed with regret. Eleanor wrote in her diary on August 18, 1938, "Sherwood came up from his cabin this morning wistful and in a glow. Why couldn't everything like this last so perfectly? But of course everything has to end. Why can't we hold the now?" Not long after his birthday each year, on September 13, Anderson would begin preparations for closing the house and moving back to New York, or perhaps for an interim period to Marion, before going on to New York in October.

The small southwest Virginia town of Marion, where Anderson had edited both the *Smyth County News* and the *Marion Democrat* from 1927 until 1931, lies about twenty miles north of Ripshin in Smyth County. Marion was both the home of his wife's family and the home of his son Robert Lane Anderson, to whom he had turned over the editing and principal ownership of the newspapers in 1931. Anderson and his wife had a bedroom and a study at Rosemont, the handsome Copenhaver residence in Marion; and he spent considerable time there, with or without Eleanor, when life in New York or on the road grew unbearable. He and Laura Lu Copenhaver, Eleanor's mother, were especially close friends; and Anderson was hurt deeply when Mrs. Copenhaver died in December 1940, not many months before his own death. He makes frequent reference in the diary to Mrs. Copenhaver and to other members of Eleanor's family, including her father B. E. Copenhaver, her air force doctor brother Randolph Copenhaver, her sister and brother-in-law Mazie Copenhaver Wilson and Channing Wilson of Baltimore, and her sister and brother-in-law Katharine Copenhaver Van Meier and Dr. Henry Van Meier of Stillwater, Minnesota. "Aunt May" Scherer, unmarried sister of Laura Lu, lived with the Copenhavers and was a favorite with both Eleanor and Sherwood.

Anderson's son Robert Lane ("Bob") had by 1936 become an established and influential citizen of Marion, married and not only editing the newspapers but also becoming much involved in local and state politics. Bob's younger brother John, an artist, moved around but frequently managed to spend time with his father in Marion or during the summers at Ripshin. Anderson's daughter Marion ("Mimi") and her husband Russell Spear were editing the *Madison Messenger* in North Carolina. Mimi sometimes brought her children to visit at Ripshin in the summertime, and Anderson visited her in Madison whenever his travels took him to that vicinity.

Much of Anderson's typical year during the period from 1936 to 1941 was spent in New York, where Eleanor's YWCA work was headquartered and where they usually stayed with their friend Mary Emmett at 54 Washington Mews. In New York Anderson worked at his writing; consulted with his literary agent or with Maxwell Perkins, his editor at Scribner's; dined out frequently; went to baseball games and Broadway theaters; and kept up his contacts with old and new friends. Among the most valued of these friends were Paul Rosenfeld, Lewis Galantière, Alfred Stieglitz and his wife Georgia O'Keeffe, and Anderson's painter brother Karl, who lived in nearby Westport, Connecticut. Anderson was fond of leaving New York to spend days or even weeks at a time at the Hedgerow Theatre near Philadelphia, where the proprietor Jasper Deeter was only one of many friends and where the dramatic version of *Winesburg, Ohio* had been playing in repertory since 1934.

The New York winters were, however, hard on Anderson's sinus condition and his vulnerability to colds and flu and, beginning in 1935, he sought relief by going south with Eleanor for part of each winter. They spent January and February of 1935 in Corpus Christi and Brownsville, Texas; February and March of 1936 in Tucson, Arizona; and early 1937 in Corpus Christi again. A visit to Mexico in February and March of 1938 proved to be the last of their leisurely winter trips south, however; for Eleanor was promoted in 1938 to the position of Head of the Industrial Department of the National YWCA and was thereafter simply too busy for such trips. After 1938, Anderson made a valiant effort to spend the winters with her in New York but found it hard going. Discouraged by the gloomy weather and by continual bouts with colds and flu, he began to spend more of his time in Marion or in making journeys, by himself, to New Orleans and other places in the South.

There were other reasons, too, for Anderson's continuing to travel extensively. He frequently accompanied Eleanor on trips to the South and Midwest related to her YWCA work; and they made a protracted trip to California in late 1939. Occasional lecture engagements took him to several states. He spent the period of July 26 to August 11, 1937, at a Boulder, Colorado, writer's conference. An enjoyable three-week stay at Olivet College in Michigan during January 1939 led to some lasting friendships and three more trips to Olivet in 1939 and 1940. As an interesting byproduct of the drives to Olivet, Anderson renewed old associations in Springfield, Ohio, and in his boyhood home of Clyde. He remained fond of revisiting Chicago and New Orleans, both cities with rich associations and memories for him; and groups of loyal old friends in both cities were always ready to welcome him.

With the exception of his marriage, Anderson's closest personal relationship during the years of the diary was his relationship with Mary Emmett, widow of Burton Emmett, the wealthy advertising man and collector who had lent Anderson the money in 1927 to purchase the Marion newspapers. After Emmett's death in 1935, Mary continued generously to assist Anderson, making him regular gifts of money and inviting Sherwood and Eleanor to live for several months of each year in her New York home at 54 Washington Mews. Although Anderson appreciated her generosity, her constant presence and emotional dependence came near to smothering him. Although he frequently recorded in the diary his irritation and his determination to take no more of her money and to live no longer in her house, he never really solved what he called "the Mary problem."

The word "work" as used by Anderson in the diary almost always means "writing"; and he continued to work religiously at his writing wherever he happened to be. He published three books and a large number of stories and articles between 1936 and 1941. By the time of his death, furthermore, he had largely completed his posthumously published *Memoirs*. But with the exception of parts of the *Memoirs*, a handful of short stories, and some characteristically high-level journalistic writing, Anderson did not do his best work during this period. For the most part, he engaged in a succession of projects, enthusiastically begun but eventually dropped, which survive today only as fat stacks of unfinished, unpublished manuscripts at the Newberry Library. His own realization that both his creative impulse and his reputation were on the decline in the late 1930s led to ever more frequent periods of depression and discouragement.

The details of Anderson's later life are fairly well documented outside the diary, partly because more of his letters have survived from this period than from earlier periods of his life. After her marriage to Sherwood in 1933, Eleanor, with an eye to posterity, frequently had Anderson's letters copied and filed before they were mailed. Thus, even when the originals have been lost, her file copies have survived. Nevertheless, the diary provides an indispensable supplement to the record in the correspondence. Anderson wrote the diary for himself, not for the eyes of a correspondent, and hence created a record here which is, if sometimes more mundane, also more personal and hence frequently more revealing of the smaller details of his private life and of his inner feelings. Anderson's diary thus represents an essential part of that record of his life and work which the late Eleanor Anderson devoted herself so faithfully to preserving in the years between her husband's death in 1941 and her own death in 1985.

THE SHERWOOD ANDERSON DIARIES, 1936–1941

1 9 3 6

Ugly night. Doped myself to sleep. Dreamed that Malcolm Cowley was leading troops into battle.

In the morning, Jan. 1, wrote to E—having spit out poison at her.[1]

Deep snow—the land very beautiful. Came yesterday from Dr. Jones.[2] Head better. Jones getting rich.

Mother very beautiful.[3] The dog thing exaggerated in my mind because the essential thing too hard to get at.[4] The man to man project getting more definite.[5]

Great stir in the house. Mother to go to the hospital for x-rays. Was to go to Charlotte with E but roads too icy. Yesterday outlined my man to man letter, addressing it to Dreiser.

Went to Funk to make preparations for racking off wine.[6] It is raining, washing away the heaviest snow I have ever seen in Marion.

Made notes for the Civil War,[7] read and went to dine with Wyse, County road man.[8]

Heavy rain all day, taking the snow away. Worked on Kit.[9] Wed.—2nd[10] —evening with Jap and Hedgerow crowd at Bristol.[11] E, John, Mary— heavy fog home.[12]

Sat., Jan. 4
[High Point, N.C.]

To Mimi and Russell.[13] The roads clear. Went by 58 to Martinsville. Streams rough—in the hills clear—in the valleys muddy. Snow gone. Mimi's house and babies both lovely. There is something established. Drove on to High Point in the night, thinking of the Dreiser letter.[14]

Sun., Jan. 5
[High Point, N.C.]

Knocked out all day by my sinus. In hotel by station—High Point, N.C. E particularly lovely and kind. Went to doctor and found him the usual fake. Worked little and drank a good deal.

In evening with E and working girls to dine in Greensboro. Found girls very fine, sensible, alive. The talk very good. They ready to receive any thought, not prejudiced. They seemed to me much more alive than most of those who try to teach them.

Mon., Jan. 6
Charlotte

Raining. Partly recovered from nose trouble. Drove here from High Point, N.C., last night. Wrote yesterday about Kit's lie to Tom about doctor.[15]

The trouble with any sort of physical pain is that it not only slows you up in work but also turns too much attention to self.

Yesterday one of the odd days when all other humans seemed peculiarly far away. Read Jernegan on the American colonies.[16]

Tues., Jan. 7
Charlotte

A lost day. Went out in the damp to a big fire in the evening. Have been going too much on whiskey. Finished Jernegan on Colonial America. Wrote Roger yesterday and worked on novel.[17] Will be lucky if I can get down a few pages today.

E very lovely. How she keeps on wanting to live with me is sometimes beyond my understanding.

Wed., Jan. 8
Marion

The day spent driving—Charlotte to Marion. Rain all the way. Letter from Dreiser. Heavy fog over Fancy Gap.

When I got to Marion, raised hell about pack of books, for autograph, from some college professor. Really my own fault. Not nice about it.

Thurs., Jan. 9
Marion

Unnecessary quarrel with E in bed. My fault. She unhappy. What a bastard I was.

Wrote a letter to Gene O'Neill. Have had the feeling that he has separated himself too much from the rest of us.

The weather cold and wet. E a wreck from last night. I seem able to be a son of a bitch and pop right out of it as gay as a lark.

Fri., Jan. 10
Marion

E off to N.Y. last night. We had a very happy day. I did a little work on Kit—not much. Sun came out in the late afternoon and it is a clear morning. The night sky was beautiful. Wrote to Gene O'Neill and Erskine Caldwell. Had a rather sleepless night—too high with unfinished works.

Sat., Jan. 11
Marion

Half-clear morning with some fog. Birds singing. Worked on Kit. Went to Abingdon tobacco market with John and Dave.[18] Market good. Good feeling among farmers.

Man who preached from truck—Holy Roller.

Dave's scepticism. To J. Birchfield to drink.[19] Home to Copenhavers to dine. Cards.

Extraordinarily beautiful sky coming home from Abingdon.

Sun., Jan. 12
Marion

Cold and clear. Long walk and talk last night with Andy. Discussion of why men like Culbert go to pieces, become drunkards, in small town. Discussion of Burt, Bob, etc.[20]

Why E. T. blackballed A. F. in Masons.[21] The failure of masonry.

Wrote Randolph.[22] Sent stories and an article to agent.[23] In the late afternoon worked on Kit.

The long walk in the cold night brought sound sleep. Sky again very lovely.

Mon., Jan. 13
Marion

Grey cold day. Dined yesterday at Bob's and then to Ripshin.[24] Road from Troutdale worst I ever saw. Stuck twice.

Finished chapter of Kit. Read "The Irrepressible Conflict," by Arthur Schlesinger and Dixon Fox.

To Burt's with Funk in evening. The day, yesterday, very sunny and beautiful. Letter to Dreiser.

Tues., Jan. 14
Marion

Hemingway's "Green Hills of Africa"—letter about it to Ralph Church.[25] Pop C. and Texas steers.[26] Cold. The day however, overhead, bright and clear.

No more work now on Kit until I get settled.

Made outlines Baltimore and Chicago speeches.

Love of E very strong all day.

Evening with Funk. We both too masculine.

Wed., Jan. 15
Marion

Sunshine part of the day. Took Mother for a long drive. Unable to work much. Wrote to Ralph Church about Hemingway's *Green Hills of Africa*. Book leaves a curious bad taste.

In the evening to Funk's house to rack off my wine. Will have about 35 gal. pretty good table wine. Nose some better.

Thurs., Jan. 16
Marion

Grey and foggy. Am starting to Richmond newspapermen's meeting with Bob and Jim Birchfield.[27] Couldn't work yesterday. Wrote to Jap. It rained nearly all day and my nose bad. Walked about and renewed relations with men here. Pretty much wasted day.

Fri., Jan. 17
Richmond

Drove with Bob and Jim Birchfield from Marion. Fair weather. Feeling half dead. Discussion in Pat Collins' room in hotel. Real niceness of Frank Lemmon.[28] Triumph of women. To office of Times Dispatch. Bob and his dogs.

Sat., Jan. 18
[Richmond]

The day spent in Richmond. To hear the much-heralded Jap Christian.[29] Not impressed. To Mark Ethridge for cocktails and then to press dinner. Vic and Annabelle in Bob's room. Talk of women authors. Disappointed with Maverick's speech.[30]

Sun., Jan. 19
Baltimore

Drunk last night. Took it out on Maurice Maverick. Will write him letter.

Took train to Baltimore. Getting over drunk. Didn't sleep until after 3 a.m. the night before. Big night with Mark Ethridge. Dopey on train. Channing and Mazie at train in Baltimore.[31] Spoke at production of play—Mother. Rotten play.[32]

Mon., Jan. 20
Marion

Big night at Baltimore. Tell story of Fagin and gorgeous wife.[33]

Remember always the long drive over ice—Mary driving.[34] Wrecks along road—the tenseness—man who with wife went into river. Heroism of truck drivers . . . in the night.

The crowded car—risk . . . reality of the day and night.

Tues., Jan. 21
On road—Marion
to Chicago

The day at home—in Marion. The great beauty of the day. Again a bit too much drinking. The loveliness of E and also Mary. Thoughts about Mother.

The death of the fine dog Boy.

Remember impression of packing—the terrible predominance of THINGS.

Wed., Jan. 22
Lexington, Ky

Day of driving. Mary drove most of the way. Great cold at starting. Ice kept gathering on windshield. We went north by Cumberland Gap—in many places ice covering the mountains.

The day with no adventures, except the constant danger of skidding off mountains.

Thurs., Jan. 23
Sergels—Chicago

Terrible day—the wind a hurricane sweeping across the road—often blinding. We kept going, the storms of wind and dry wind-driven snow always more violent. Drifts forming, cars stalled. Thermometer falling. It got to 20 below. Stalled at Lebanon, Ind. Train to Chicago.

Fri., Jan. 24
Sergels—Chicago

Still very cold. Day spent in the house.[35] In the evening lecture—Friends of American Authors. No good, lousy feeling later. Roger and Ruth fine. Their house having a fine feeling.

Fire in the house later—tramping in of firemen. The bitter cold beginning to break.

Sat., Jan. 25
Chicago—Sergels

Downtown with Roger to get traveler's checks. Very cold yet and papers report it will get still colder.

I played pool and billiards with all the Sergels and beat them all.

We spent the evening with Roger and Ruth. The house has a lovely quality. It was a quiet good day. Read in Percy's book on Politicians.[36]

Sun., Jan. 26
Sergel—Chicago

The evening with Lloyd Lewis and Schevill.[37] Good talk—the Civil War. Still very cold.

Mon., Jan. 27
Sergel—Chicago

Frank Knight. Percy Wood and his novel. Sandburg at his worst—pompous, even pontifical.[38] Stayed in all day. Sandburg stayed over night. The last hour's talk—comradeship. Wrote Scribner's about Percy's novel.

Tues., Jan. 28
St. Louis

Driving through snow and ice. The trouble finding quiet room for Mary. The cabaret. The woman who eyed me—blonde.

Wed., Jan. 29
Claremore, Okla.

Will Rogers town. Fight with Mary over turn in road. Over Ozark. Big Piney—the delightful lunch place.

The job getting Mary to sleep.

Thurs., Jan. 30
Amarillo, Texas

The 1st day's long drive through the open plains West Oklahoma. Into Texas Panhandle at dusk. Mary slept and behaved well. In early morning came near upsetting car. I drove nearly all day. The sunset grand over the plains. The Packard car much less satisfactory than the light Chevrolet.

Mary's big morning in regard to tire. No skid—no bump.

E constantly writing.

Fri., Jan. 31
Santa Fe, New
Mexico

Mary drove in morning—about 60 miles on earth road, then 100 on pavement. I drove in afternoon about same. The country always more and more lovely—the afternoon the most inspiring drive I ever took.

Impression of Santa Fe as having become largely a sucker town. Many Indians and Mexicans on the street. 10 gallon hats everywhere. We went to dine at a Mexican restaurant run by two eastern college girls. Witter Bynner came to call.[39] I find myself easily exhausted in the high altitude.

Sat., Feb. 1
Santa Fe

To Taos—a beautiful drive over a long plain, snow-topped mountains on all sides. Then canyon of the Rio Grande.

Majal Claflin in the restaurant.[40] The drive through slush to the Pueblo. Then the old Spanish church.

In the evening to Witter Bynner's house. Lynn Riggs. Hunt. The bad poetry. The collection of jade. The extreme luxury of the house. Alice Henderson.[41]

Sun., Feb. 2
Las Cruces, N.M.

Got to this town at night. Start from Santa Fe after a rain. Drove over a high plain, surrounded by high mountains. No bad luck. There were some 30 miles of gravel road very good, the road dipping down into deep arroyos—the whole land a dry desert. Passed Indian pueblos. The town of Las Cruces, in Rio Grande river valley. We followed the river nearly all day.

Mon., Feb. 3

[No entry.]

Tues., Feb. 4
Tucson, Arizona

Arrived Tucson, Arizona. A lovely clear day. Mary drove 95 miles in 90 minutes. Tires expanded in rare air. One exploded. 2 hour wait. Man with consumptive wife. Mary's rudeness. Passion for minor successes—to be right. Day over high clear plains. Bisbee. The man from Omaha. Stop at tourist camp at Tucson. Mary's birthday. Formulation of letter to Mary.

Wed., Feb. 5
Tucson

The day spent in an excited rush of getting into quarters. Mary making most of excitement. She goes at goodness with a mad rush.

Got into Hotel St. Paul and Mary and I in a fuss . . . me wanting to settle and quit looking. Made her feel badly. Sorry. Went into her room and embraced her.

All this on Tuesday. In the evening lost at cards.

Thurs., Feb. 6
Tucson

Got back to the novel. Worked all morning—in a fine swing. In the afternoon in the car with Mary and E. Peace between us. Took fine drive at sunset toward mountains. Saw much strange cactus growth.

Greek running French restaurant. Won at cards.

Fri., Feb. 7
Tucson

Wrongheaded writing all day. Mary has become very charming. Every day here the bright sun. Will have to destroy all done yesterday.

In the evening to take pictures of the tall cactus. The evening sky gorgeous with blues.

To Solve in the evening. Walsh came in. To bed at 1 a.m.[42]

Sat., Feb. 8
Tucson

Another bright warm day. Last night smashed mud guard of Mary's car, getting out of parking lot.

Morning spent at work—good morning. My cold gone in 24 hours. In the p.m. we drove up into a canyon in the mountains and home in the fading light. Again the pristine glory of blues, lavender, and red in sky and mountains.

Sun., Feb. 9
Tucson

Up early and to work. Then with E, Mary, Solve and wife to Nogales in old Mexico. Dinner in the Cave. The floor show good. A singer very like Libby Holman.[43] Two fine Spanish dancers, heels clicking. Wanting to be such a dancer.

Home slow, in beautiful light, then to Paddy Walsh for drinks and more food.

Mon., Feb. 10
Tucson

Got settled for little white truck. Work did not go well. Got Paddy and sat in little saloon, drinking gin and soda.

Took Mary for long drive, looking for lost earring. We had good honest talk. In the evening to bed early but did not sleep well. Read story of John S. Mosby.[44]

Tues., Feb. 11
Tucson

The work didn't go well. Read Dodd on Lee and Lincoln. Also Adams letters, edited by Ford.[45] Mary left early for Palm Springs.

We gassed the little white scooter and went off to the cactus forests, the first cloudy day we'd had here. In the evening to an Italian restaurant where I overate.

To bed early.

Wed., Feb. 12
Tucson

Showers. Reading in the Adams Civil War letters—very good and intelligent.

Went with E out a new road and we laid on the sand in the desert, the sky wonderful.

Went in the evening to Paddy Walsh, who told stories. Conversation never did get started.

E looked tired.

Thurs., Feb. 13
Tucson

Cold cloudy morning. Again I got back into Kit. Still reading Adams letters. Also read "Lincoln or Lee," by Dodd.

In the early evening a long walk with E in Mexican quarter, she with pain in side. The Mexican quarter curiously beautiful in evening light. Talk and drink with Paddy. In the evening to boxing match.

Fri., Feb. 14
Tucson

A bright warm day. After work took a drive—E lying in desert.

To cocktail party at Solves—big crowd—mostly college people. Got Walsh to cash check.

In the evening E with pleurisy.

Went to boxing match.

Sat., Feb. 15
Tucson

The first day of big rains. Worked well on novel. Went out in car but rain drove us in. Saw Chaplin's new movie—he using only old stuff.[46]

Read Adams letters again. To bed early and long sleep.

Sun., Feb. 16
Tucson

Another beautiful day on the desert and the finest sunset we have seen yet. After a morning on the Civil War, E and I went to lie in an open place among hills. She walked away up into the hills while I stayed below reading. The whole country was so beautiful it hurt.

In the evening a walk through the Mexican quarter and dinner in a Mexican restaurant—tongue—in the Mexican way—very delicious.

Mon., Feb. 17
Tucson

Work in the morning and then a trip up a mountain road. View of the great plain in which Tucson lies below. We found many desert flowers in bloom up there.

Saw and talked with the man from Massachusetts—shoe manufacturer—very lonely. His explanation of the mysteries of shoe manufacture.

Tues., Feb. 18
Tucson

Felt rotten but worked. To the desert but the day cold and blustery. In the
evening a walk with E in the Mexican section of town. The wishing well.
Boys flying kites. Beauty of Mexican woman with child.

Read in Jefferson Davis, Rise and Fall of the Confederacy.

Wed., Feb. 19
Tucson

Good day. Went with Kit through killing of Wyagle by Alfred—[47] tense.
To lunch at Rotary Club with Paddy. Howell of government. Single tax
man. Man from Danville.

Long walk with E in Mexican section. The two young whores.

In the evening with the Walshes to dine. Good Mexican food. Red and
white wine. To the Walsh house listening to sad old Irish songs.

Thurs., Feb. 20
Tucson

A big day. Got through stirring chapter of Kit. In the afternoon we went
to the Rodeo—Indian day. The field, out in the desert, grey sand, Indians
very serious and strange.

The games much more lovely than that of the circus cowboys.

The Indian women in lovely colors and the runners and riders very
lovely.

Fri., Feb. 21
Tucson

A clear beautiful day. Went to see the big parade. The whole town out in
cowboy outfits. Many bands.

In the afternoon with E into the desert where she climbed a high mountain while I stayed below and admired.

Afterwards by a long dirt road, through tall cactus til dark.

In the evening to see boxing.

Didn't work.

Sat., Feb. 22
Tucson

Fine morning of work on novel. Then to rodeo grounds—to sale of pure bred livestock.

Then to Rodeo—the ropers very beautiful to see. The wonder of the trained ponies. The neglected man with rope and Monte Montana.[48]

Went later out new road into desert and to Paddy's in evening.

Two men with banjo and guitar. The grey haired, positive and nervous man and his children.

Sun., Feb. 23
Tucson

Work in morning. In p.m. drive with Paddy Walsh and wife to Nogales, by a new and long route over high mountains. There is a high plateau with fine pasture and scrub oak, very beautiful and park like. We went by Sonoita and Patagonia. It was one of the most beautiful countries I'd ever been in.

Picnic lunch with wine by a little river.

Mon., Feb. 24
Tucson

The day being sick—probably intestinal flu. Unable to work. Read Memoirs of Gen. Phil Sheridan. Day fair and warm.

Tues., Feb. 25
Tucson

Another day of illness. Spent the day reading a life of Seward. Weak from intestinal flu. Made a good many notes on the Civil War. Much of the day in bed. It rained in the morning but the afternoon fair.

Wed., Feb. 26
Tucson

Ill all day—a dull day. Read life of Sumner. Did no work.

Thurs., Feb. 27
Tucson

Better. A bright warm day. Got outdoors. Finished Sumner—made notes. Wrote on constitutionism and why poor whites fought in Civil War.

Got back to Kit. Took E out into desert. Took walk in Mexican district and got stung, buying red shirt from fat Jewess.

Fri., Feb. 28
Tucson

Floyd Olson[49] arrived and Paddy and I went to find him a house.

Got new upholstering for car. Took E for a long ride. Day almost hot. Worked on Kit. Read Sherman. Went in evening to basketball—University of Arizona against University of New Mexico—very pretty game.

Sat., Feb. 29
Tucson

Nogales, Mexico—Sonora, with Matthews—of Star—and wife.[50] Wife a bore—Matthews fine—the wistful thing found in so many successful Americans. Venison dinner with good wine. While E and that wife went to shops, Matthews and I walked through streets of the town, both trying to get out some expression of what might be American manhood in our day. Liked him.

Sun., Mar. 1
Tucson

Good day with the novel. Saw—with Paddy Walsh and wife—fine polo game. Man of 74.

Went in the evening to Mikes.[51] The girl in black and middlewestern waitress. The bitter Irishman.[52] Visit to houses. Did not get home until 2 a.m.

Mon., Mar. 2
Tucson

Not so good. Not enough sleep. Still worked well. There was a dust storm. Went to desert in late afternoon . . . the sky all heavy with dust. To bed early and heavy sleep.

Tues., Mar. 3
Tucson

Knocked out. Did not work. We drove to Casa Grande, an old ruins of early Americans, made of mud and said to be 2000 years old. A very curious place. We came back through Florence over a grand road, under the mountains.

Wed., Mar. 4
Tucson

Did not work. Went over the mountains and took a desert ride. In the evening to Solve—Paddy and wife there.

Did not sleep.

Thurs., Mar. 5
Tucson

Rotten. No work. Took E and went to Sasabe, a town on Mexican border—through very beautiful cattle country. Town nothing. Took dope and slept.

Fri., Mar. 6
Tucson

Good day. Got at final chapter of Kit. We went to Oracle, up 4500 feet— lovely country. Then to desert where I made buttons for E. Evening to Paddy and Mims. Story of Roberts, the entertainer.

Sat., Mar. 7
Tucson

Good morning of work—on Kit. Many letters. In the evening to a party of University men. Much singing. The party degenerated into a contest of dirty story telling. Little or no wit. I finally said, "Hell, when you get drunk there is no difference between you and a lot of drunken advertising men."

Sun., Mar. 8
Tucson

Did not get home until 2. Drunk on beer. Went off with E and Mr. and Mrs. Walsh for afternoon and evening in desert. Drank dry California wine and felt better toward evening. Very lovely moonlight. Have a growing affection for Paddy and his lady.

Mon., Mar. 9
Tucson

Not so good. However, worked. Went in the late afternoon with E to the desert and sat making her buttons for a dress out of the wood of cactus bushes. To bed early.

Tues., Mar. 10
Tucson

Mary came at 3. We went to the mountains. To bed fairly early. No work.

Wed., Mar. 11
Tucson

Only one more scene of Kit to do. Mary came from California. To desert and mountain in the p.m. To Paddy and Mims in evening. Good day. Very happy. E curiously beautiful in the evening. Picnic among the tall cactus.

Thurs., Mar. 12
Tucson

Drove, after work in the morning, with Mary and E to Nogales, via Patagonia. We dined in the Mexican town, and E and Mary both bought glass. Mary tried to get hers through but failed because she had brought goods in but 2 weeks before.

Fri., Mar. 13
Tucson

Stayed at home while Mary and E went to Nogales, Mexico, to get Mary's stuff we couldn't get in. They went on into Mexico—to the town of Magdalena in Mexico. Got home at 6:30.

We went in the evening to Solves. Solve not attractive—professor with middle class mind. Mary had E all tired out. The conversation at Solves not so good.

I worked while E and Mary were gone, getting up Civil War notes.

Sat., Mar. 14
Tucson

Packed to leave and loaded truck. Mary bought me insurance, in case I killed anyone going east. We went to Casa Grande to Indian rodeo but there was none.

Beauty of Indian men. Women—fat and stubby. The men who wouldn't answer when asked about show.

E sentimental about Mrs. Paddy's desire to see Old Maid—getting us to go. Mary bought tickets. Show bum.[53]

To Paddy's house. His niceness. Hat.[54] Mrs. Paddy's niceness.

Sun., Mar. 15
El Paso, Texas

Left Tucson at 7 after very little sleep. Too many dissipated nights. Mary got up to see us off. She planning to go to Guaymas, Sonora, Mexico. Cold morning. Drive over high deserts—partly earth roads by a 90-mile cut-off.

Got to El Paso at 4:30. To Mexican town Juarez. Shine. Platters. Whores.

To bed at 9:30.

Mon., Mar. 16
Alpine, Texas

Got here at 6, after leaving El Paso at 10. Had 2 punctures in 10 miles. A strong Texas rain storm all day. It rained sand, wind-driven.

The last 80 miles wonderful, among high mountains, always up and up.

Toward the end of the day the air cleared of dust. We picked up big nail then, in 10 minutes big staple—2 tires gone through.

Tues., Mar. 17
Del Rio, Texas

Left Alpine at 6 a.m. Over beautiful upland mountains, at first softly rounded. Very cold. Saw herd of deer.

Then rough rugged country. Towns from 50 to 60 miles apart. No houses to be seen. The landscape constantly changing. Got here early and went to Mexican town Villa Acuna. Got some flowered bowls and an Indian bracelet for E. Walked around Mexican town. Everyone poor and nice. American who sold Mexican candy. Cold wind all day.

Wed., Mar. 18
San Antonio

Short drive from Del Rio, on the border here, through sheep country— town of Vice President Garner[55]—the rough, uncultivated, half desert country, slowly changing to farms.

Stayed at Hotel Menger. Saw Alamo—full of bad poetry. Took a walk in Mexican district and dined on fish. No work.

Thurs., Mar. 19
Orange, Texas

We did not leave San Antonio until ten a.m. Intended to drive only to Beaumont, Texas, and stay in tourist camp. Dark when we got to Beau-

mont. Went into town to get White Rock and ice.[56] Decided to find camp
east of town. None there. Only swamps. We drove on to Orange and
stayed in hotel. All day amid the broad black fields of East Texas. Men
with big tractors and 4 or 6 horse teams plowing. Day beautiful but
windy.

Fri., Mar. 20
New Orleans

Again a clear day with high winds. We got into a watery land, in contrast
to the desert, out of which we came. Grass luxurious but, oddly, the cattle
miserable. The last 50 miles into New Orleans miserable roads. Went
over new bridge, over Mississippi.
Dined with Marc and Lucille; and Jimmy, Julius, Elise and Elma came in.
Julius looks very ill.[57]

Sat., Mar. 21
New Orleans

To the seed store to buy garden seed with Lucille. Then to a little bar to
drink beer. Played slot machine. To lunch with Jimmy. Talk of humanities.
In the late afternoon, after writing letters, to Marc and Lucille. Talk of the
theatre. To Julius and Elise to dine—good dinner. No drinks. Harvey and
Dorothy Perkins there.[58] Good talk. Dorothy Perkins very lovely, also E.
Too many children stories. They bore.

Sun., Mar. 22
[New Orleans]

To visit the Group theatre building. Hunger for stage returning. With
Marc, Lucille, Elma and Italian man to levee below city. Young Italian
communist school teacher. Very didactic and immature—as usual. In the
beginning nice, fresh, alive—then a bore.

   In the evening to Jimmy and Dorothy. Dorothy very beautiful.[59] Jimmy
much improved. No work. Myself quiet all day and evening. Getting
ready for work again. Talked all evening with Julius. E looked ill. She had
a headache.

Mon., Mar. 23
New Orleans

Very hot. Worked on revision Kit. To dine at Elma's where I spent the
evening quarreling with a young communist. He is an Italian—about
28—school teacher, very superficial education, didactic, self-centered. In
person quite charming. He has great physical charm and vitality so the

women cluster to him and are sorry for him when he is attacked. They are perhaps thinking of being in bed with him. He may be quite clever there.

Tues., Mar. 24
New Orleans

Revision work on Kit. Hot and sultry—finally a drizzle of rain. Went to dine alone with Jim and Dorothy—E working. Much talk of Sergel and philosophy.

Went afterwards to a cabaret. E coming, very lovely. Julius and Elise there.

In the afternoon with Lucille to buy E a ring. Couldn't sleep. Had to take amital.

Wed., Mar. 25
New Orleans

Hot and sticky. Got on well with Kit. Went to ball game in afternoon with man who is in slot machine game. Cleveland versus New Orleans. Cleveland won.

To dine with Marc and then to play—"Kind Lady." Miserable rot.[60]

Unpleasant incident later. Pretty rich woman sore because I wouldn't go off after play to sit in restaurant. Let her go to hell. Wanted to sleep. Did.

Thurs., Mar. 26
New Orleans

Still very hot and sticky. Worked on revision Kit. Jimmy to lunch. Ophelia Godchaux.[61] To dine at Julius' mother's. Julius' food being weighed out to him.

Went to hear Julius talk on the approach to understanding of history. Talk good but figure of Julius pouring himself out to the Jeffs and Lillians not so good.[62]

Fri., Mar. 27
New Orleans

Suddenly cold and rainy. All day in room, struggling with last two chapters Kit. Not satisfied with them. After all day struggle had to put them aside, still not satisfied.

To dine with Marc and Lucille. Lyle Saxon,[63] Dr. Freedman, Jimmy, Dorothy, Jeff, Lillian, Becky.

E and Dorothy most beautiful women. Talk rambling—not so good.

Sat., Mar. 28
New Orleans

Didn't work. Wrote letters. Got Elma Godchaux's novel.[64] Went to lunch with E and Wittenburg gal. Little communist secretary—O.K.

In the evening to Jimmy's big party. Saw Hallie Flanagan[65] and took her [to the party]. Slot machine man telling stories—automobile industry. "If you put the nickel in the slot, who gets the gum?" Jewish man, grand natural story teller. The Flanagan nice. Will see her again.

Sun., Mar. 29
New Orleans

Packed. The day at Feibleman's—Jeff and Lillian. Perfect day with everyone nice. The Feibleman house some 50 miles out of New Orleans on a quiet bayou. There is a big swimming pool and we all swam. It was one of those days when many conflicting personalities all seem to blend, something bigger, nicer than any one person in the air. E very beautiful.

Mon., Mar. 30
Laurel, Miss.

We got here at 3. Had one puncture. Dirt and gravel roads most of the way. Very hot. The dogwood in bloom. We had breakfast in New Orleans with Marc and Lucille. Lucille gave me a beautiful bottle of bay rum. Everywhere along the road the riot of spring and flowers.

But it was hot, hot.

Tues., Mar. 31
Birmingham, Ala.

Started from Laurel, Miss. at 12—here at 6:30. A day of dogwood, the newly green woods all spotted with the lovely trees.

There were many other blossoms not known to me. Got out of the piney woods and into forest of trees of every variety. In the evening, in Birmingham, E and I dined in style, with a big sizzling steak each.

To bed early—no thoughts in my head.

Wed., Apr. 1
Birmingham, Ala.

Bad, rotten day. Half-ill, I think with life. Roger disappointed me—expecting him here.[66] Went to see the Yanks play the local team—good game.

Man who picked me up. The thunderstorm. Lawyer walking with his two farmer clients. E lovely. Outburst to her about the South.

Thurs., Apr. 2
Macon, Ga.

At Aaron's house.[67] The drive over from Birmingham quite lovely. E curiously beautiful and fine the last few days, during my gloomy time.[68]

Aaron's house quite charming. The Doctor Pepper man who read the newspaper and then slept. The bluff put up by wife. She fine. The young man with sharp voice. No one got really acquainted. The negro woman Viny—14 children. Her figure. Her story. It turned bitterly cold.

Fri., Apr. 3
Macon

Aaron's house. Bitter cold but I worked after a hard sleep, then went to town. Viny, the negro cook, told me the story of how she and her husband lost cow, mule, and hog. Read [Erskine] Caldwell's "Kneel to the Rising Sun," terrific book. With Aaron and Sue[69] to meet lady author.[70] She like woman with first baby, very vain and struggling to conceal it. A rather unhealthy looking female. Long walk through town seeking negro phonograph records. No luck.

Sat., Apr. 4
Macon

Aaron's house. A bit warmer and a blustering wind. Worked on Kit.

Went to town at 5 and tramped about. A big party in the evening and a lot of drinking—the party notable for a Mrs. Bernd-Cohan—as lovely a woman as ever I met.

Sun., Apr. 5
Macon

The day in a kind of drunkness from the party on the night before. Slept in the afternoon. Steady rain. The wise-cracking authoress left. Talked in the evening with Fletcher McCoy of Duke.[71] Charming wife. Dined with the Dr. Pepper man and Kansas wife.

Was sleepy and a bit irritated so tried to irritate others by saying things against the South. Drank coffee—like a fool—and couldn't sleep.

Mon., Apr. 6
Macon

Aaron's house. Another cyclone near here. One destroyed the town of Cordele. This one Gainesville, Ga. Sultry hot and threatening rain all day.

Did not sleep Sunday night. In bed reading most of the day and in the evening to party—all men but Sue. My suspicions two or three of the crowd homo.

Tried to work but too stupid and gave it up. Will be glad to get back to the house at Marion.

Tues., Apr. 7
Macon

Last day here—a day of rain and threatened flood. Worked. In the evening went to the country to Bernd-Cohans and made an ass of myself by my arrogance. Talked of things about which it is best with most people to keep your mouth shut.

Wed., Apr. 8
Charlotte, N.C.

The day on the road—300 miles Macon to here. Cold and grey.

Myself not in good shape. Have been drinking the Georgia moon and my stomach not hardened to it.

On all sides flooded rivers—one I just could cross—the water up to the bridge floor. To bed early.

Thurs., Apr. 9
Marion

A miserably bad day of driving in the rain. It rained all the way. Soaking wet. Was to have stopped to see Mimi but didn't. Arrived Marion just ahead of E.

Fri., Apr. 10
Marion

The 1st beautiful day of the Spring. Spent the day getting things in order after long absence. Heavy mail.

Sat., Apr. 11
Marion

It turned cold and rainy again after a perfect Friday. Worked on accumulated mail. In the afternoon had a long talk with Funk, first in his office and later in cellar wine drinking. My getting his slant on all the human and political goings-on during my absence. The evening at home, card playing.

Sun., Apr. 12
Marion

Rather a cold gloomy day spent with E and full of love for her.

Went with her to her father's farm.

Afterwards took Mother for drive to Sugar Grove. Cold outside and spitting rain. Very little sign of spring here. The new lake, built by government, is going to make all the country about Marion lovelier.[72] E left for New York.

Mon., April 13
Marion

Went to [Ripshin] farm and found everything in much better shape than I expected. Some of walls down.

Like a damn fool stayed in cold house too long and caught a half cold. Didn't sleep well. Got story Nice Girl off to New Yorker. Several stories off to London.[73]

Tues., Apr. 14
Marion

Worked some in the morning but no good—fighting cold. Work wouldn't go.

Went and sat in Funk's back yard and watched him try to beautify it. It is going to be very bourgeois but lovely. In the evening rode with him and had long and very human talk.

Wed., Apr. 15
Marion

A fine day and after working, again trying to get right on the last chapter of Kit, to Ripshin—taking Miss May.[74] Arranged to change the water pipes. The new bridge O.K. Log cabin not hurt by floods—flowers blooming.

In the evening to ride, 1st with Emmett Thomas—then with Funk.

Thurs., Apr. 16
Richmond

Drove to Richmond by back way (58). Morning rewriting last chapter Kit. Got in very tired. 325 miles 11 to 7—beautiful drive.

Met 3 very literary ladies in dining room hotel.[75] Sat at next table.
Conversation about self overheard. Boom exploded. After much talk they
recognized me and were much embarrassed.

Fri., Apr. 17
Hedgerow
Media, Pa.

Pleasant drive from Richmond—arriving at 3. Roads bad after winter.
Came by Baltimore and Washington. Sun and drifting clouds.

In the evening after seeing Liliom,[76] long talk about Ruth, Joe, and
Tony with Adrian, Katy and Jap. Jap in fine form. Feeling that this is the
one place in America I feel at home.[77]

Sat., Apr. 18
Hedgerow

E arrived from New York at 4:38—30th St. Station, Philadelphia. Rose
went with me to get her. Cold grey day. We dined at Hedgerow House and
went to see the Hepburn play, "Behold Thy God."[78] Went to see Sean
O'Casey's The Plough and the Stars. Very lovely play.

Sun., Apr. 19
Hedgerow

Slept late. Went to Wharton's to dine. Wharton in New York. Eat with
Letty and Pussy.[79] Brought Letty over to Hedgerow to see Hepburn's
"Behold Thy God." Dress rehearsal. Didn't like it. Took Wharton and
Letty to room. Letty makes you sad. E very lovely. Cold grey day.

Mon., Apr. 20
Hedgerow

Up at 7 to take E to Penn Station at Chester. Worked on play. Went to
help Katy and Mims plant cabbage. A very lovely warm spring day. After
I took E to train, back to hotel and slept for 2 hours. In evening took
Harry,[80] Katy and Mims to drink beer in little tough beer hall outside
Chester. Good talk.

Tues., Apr. 21
Hedgerow

Spent the day working. In afternoon drove with Jap to West Chester
where we dined. Play by Dick Hepburn opened but stayed in cellar, under

stage. There was birthday—13th—party at theater house but was unsocial and ran away.

Wed., Apr. 22
Hedgerow

See how to do play. E came—more lovely than ever.

We went to play. Didn't like it much. Play by young Hepburn, brother of famous actress.

Was very happy.

Thurs., Apr. 23
Hedgerow

Again at the new play. E and I to see Mask[81] —very beautifully done. Jap and I took E to train for Colorado Springs, dined. Went to 12th Night.[82] Was dull. Went home early. Can think of nothing but play.[83]

Fri., Apr. 24
Hedgerow

Feverish day of writing. Finished rewriting 2nd scene—play and got down the entire third scene. It was cold and clear outside. I keep dreaming of writing a story of a ball player and a prostitute and a play of family life.

In the evening to see St. Joan—of Shaw's. Shaw grows on me. Katy beautiful in the play. Even half-liked that final scene.

Sat., Apr. 25
Hedgerow

A good day of work. I work here because there is the spirit of work about. I mean so little of success, money, etc.

The room is pleasant although I do not like the nights without E.

Went with Katy and Mims to a German place in Philadelphia. Danced. It was hot and I took off my coat. They saw my brown shirt and cheered. They thought me a Nazi.

Sun., Apr. 26
Hedgerow

Drizzle of rain and then sun. The players rehearsed all day—a play—Kit Marlowe—like an English novel of the last century.[84]

Worked. Jap did a rehearsal of Triumph.[85] It was delicious. We laughed until it hurt. Later we felt like crying.

Mon., Apr. 27
Hedgerow

Worked until I was all in. I typed and read to Jap and Ferd[86] 4th scene.
Did 1st writing of 5th. Drank much beer. Saw The Plough and the Stars—
beautifully done. Got upset by wire from E—from St. Louis—had fever.
  Very tired. Slept hard.

Tues., Apr. 28
Hedgerow

Did not work. Day started cold. Jap, Robert and I to Philadelphia in car.
Bought new shoes. The shoe machine.
  Read Chekhov's letters—so much illness. He had real guts.
  Saw Liliom—again beautifully acted. Mims was very beautiful, also
Joe. All day thought about the last act. Miss E terribly.

Wed., Apr. 29
Hedgerow

Another exciting day of work, writing through the final scene of Hands
twice. Am not sure of it yet.
  The day was beautiful but I could not take it in. Mary Esherick[87] had
an unpleasant time with an exhibitionist. Went in the evening to see the
farce "Mask and the Face," by an Italian. Fun.

Thurs., Apr. 30
Hedgerow

An odd day. I worked, went restlessly about, finished last scene of play.
  Reaction as usual—the thing done seems so trivial. So much to be said
and so little said and so badly.
  I was sick, blue, could not bear myself. I took some amital and got into
bed.[88] Slept 12 hours. Wire from E at Colorado Springs. Mary's car is
smashed and she hurt.

Fri., May 1
Hedgerow

Sent the last scene of the play off. Thought out scene of comedy. Went to
Jap. We had long and involved talk on author and producer. Just the same
would like to try writing on subject.
  Wire from E, Mary hurt in car wreck. Began to clean up yard about
theatre house. Went with Jap and Robert to dine with Letty. Saw American Tragedy, beautifully produced.[89]

Sat., May 2
Hedgerow

Finished off [from] play and bowels. Went with Mims to Chester. Met wonderful man in restaurant—"My heart is breaking now—it is touched."

In the evening with several players to get John. We cooked our own dinner. Saw the play "Plum Hollow."[90] Sat at the Inn a long time drinking beer.

Sun., May 3
Hedgerow

With John spent the day at rehearsals of Kit Marlowe. The lines got me high. Saw and talked with the dreamer Oscar Ameringer.[91] It rained. Jap, John and I got high on rum. Took John to train, with Letty, at ten. In bed at one.

Mon., May 4
Hedgerow

Began work on the first scene of a comedy of family life. Put the idea into a long letter to Mother.[92] Was very lonely for E all day. It was cold and wet—in the late afternoon a cold sun. Went to work on yard.

In the evening saw a beautiful 12th Night.

Tues., May 5
Hedgerow

With Jap, Katy, and Rose to Jap's mother—one of the most remarkable women I have met. Something of Mother Copenhaver.

I have been self-conscious since my outbreak to the dreamer Ameringer.

The Deeter garden very beautiful. The drive both ways, beautiful. Saw Shaw's Doctor's Dilemma. Do not like it. To get at doctors he sells out the artist.

All day wishing for E.

Wed., May 6
Hedgerow

Began the long short story about the ball player and the two women. I also did a few pages on the comedy.

Went to the house and worked all afternoon, clearing the yard. Got

letter from Perkins who likes Kit.[93] Went to see the play Falling Leaves—
very beautifully done.[94] Very lonely for E.

Thurs., May 7
Hedgerow

Day of rain. Worked on the new long story. Stayed in and worked all day.
Got drunk last night. To bed early. Sound of rain nice.

Fri., May 8
Hedgerow

E came. Jap went with us to dine. We saw "Plum Hollow." Sat until very
late drinking. Fine talk. Very contented and happy, having E.

Sat., May 9
Hedgerow

Slept late. Breakfast in bed with E. We both happy. She was beautiful.

In the afternoon Jap read play by Duval—Prayer for Living. First act
wonderful. Jap read my new play. Can't tell yet how he feels. Bed early.

Sun., May 10
Hedgerow

Saw rehearsals of the play Kit Marlowe. Suddenly went into green room
and wrote an additional act for my play. It will improve it. E helped get it
in type. Mary came. Nice.

Went in the evening to more rehearsals.

Mon., May 11
[New York]

Didn't sleep. Went with E to see Jap rehearse girl in love scene. Didn't
work.

Mary drove off, to New York, at two and we left for New York at 6.
The evening with Mary, Eddie and Alice, and Millers, drinking beer.[95]

Tues., May 12
New York

Getting the new act coordinated with the rest of the play. I worked all day.
In the evening E and I with the Russian wife of Y. K. Smith, and much
talk of the revolution through which she went.[96]

Walk in Washington Square—among the crowds of people. On the
whole a happy day. Got inquiry for Danish edition Dark Laughter.[97]

Wed., May 13
New York

Worked again on play and went to see the people at New Yorker and literary agent.[98] It rained and I walked to town and back in rain, returning with E.

Went to Joe and Ann and got Carl and Leane. We all went to Cafe Royal.[99]

Got sick headache from cheap whiskey and had to sit up half the night.

Thurs., May 14
New York

A heavy stupid day, with nothing done. The day itself cold, clear and beautiful.

In the afternoon took E to go have cocktail with Perkins of Scribner's. It was nice to see them together, two really gentle people.[100]

Fri., May 15
Hedgerow

Jap appeared at 54 and rode with us to Hedgerow. He is not satisfied with the play. He spoke of it vaguely.

In the evening saw Liliom. Wanted E to see it. Joe and Mims fine. Jap not so good.

Went afterward to drink with E, Mary and Jap.

Sat., May 16
Hedgerow

The Kit Marlowe show in rehearsal. Nothing worth 10 cents except costumes. Author got E cornered.

We all went to Wharton's and dined there, coming back, after swell dinner, for Androcles and the Lion, very amusing. Best of Shaw.

Sun., May 17
Hedgerow

Restless day. Did two new scenes for the play. Kept driving about restlessly. Couldn't stay about Marlowe rehearsal without laughing. This no good for actors.

To bed early and slept. Mary and E to leave for New York.

Mon., May 18
Baltimore

A full day. Rewrote new scenes. Had long talk with Jap, over drinks. Drove to Baltimore and Mazie. Letter from Mother. Got $300 for Nice Girl from New Yorker.

Jap thinks the foundation for the play really laid now. Will lift the intimate scene and make one-act play of it.

Dr. Johnson came to Mazie's and stayed until midnight talking. Drove her home in the rain.[101]

Tues., May 19
Washington

In the morning, at Mazie's worked revising play. Took Mazie for a drive to look at house. Drove to Washington. Southern Club. Took John to Tobacco Road—Henry Hull.[102] Good work.

Wed., May 20
Washington

Devoted the day to John. Went to where he works. Puzzled about the central purpose of government in it all. None of the work seemed to me notable.[103]

Wrote a new last scene for play. Uncertain of that.

Went to the country—to two women friends of John. Lindeman—(big stiff). Man who can never tell anything straight.[104]

Thurs., May 21
Hedgerow

Had lunch and talk with John, about Bob and money.[105]

Left at 2 for Baltimore. Found Wilsons there. Suddenly decided to go on. Arrived Hedgerow after 1st scene. Saw two Mexican playmakers and talked until 2.

Fri., May 22
New York

Left Hedgerow at two. E and I went to see new WPA play, "John Brown"—not so good.[106] Saw Mary Morris[107] and many others. Play lacked conviction and force. Guests of Eduard Lindeman.

Sat., May 23
Valley Cottage,
N.Y.

Worked in the morning at the play and then drove to Valley Cottage.[108]
The country up Hudson very beautiful. Went by Washington Bridge to see
the new work for the skyway along the river. Had a quiet evening. E
sleeping on the couch while Mary and I played cards.

Sun., May 24
Valley Cottage,
N.Y.

Paul came and in the afternoon read the play aloud.[109] 1st act splendid.
The second act goes all to pieces—I think perhaps because I am trying to
state a solution to the inventor's problem. I will have to make it the simple
tragedy of the unusual man.

Mon., May 25
Valley Cottage

Spent the day alone at Mary's house, Mary going to city. Wrote letters
and began Jap article.[110] Was stupid. Read account of writing Of Time
and the River.[111] Got a bit straighter on play.

E came and we rode in evening to Haverstraw.[112] The river very beautiful. Headache. Couldn't sleep.

Tues., May 26
Valley Cottage

Conceived of an idea for a book—"The Good Life"—perhaps to be
worked on this summer. Went to the city and took Channing and Mazie
to dinner—very expensive. Went to a big vulgar place—Cafe Francaise—
at 50th and 7th. Manufacturers and visiting business men from the
provinces. Much bored and thinking of hungry people. E also sad. We
trying to be cheerful for the sake of Channing and Mazie. Nonsense.

Wed., May 27
Valley Cottage

Long talk with Mazie about Katharine.[113] I wrote a lot of notes on Good
Life to fix idea in mind.[114] Something like Stein's book but more honest.[115]

Drove to the farm with Mary. Hadn't slept. Channing and Mazie for the evening. Conversation with tired man. Tried the wine made here. Good.

Work on the Deeter. Mary and I went to ball game, Giants and Boston Bees—double header. Giants losing both.

Dined with Millers. B. Rogers there—minor man.[116] Saw the play the critics raved about, Bury the Dead.[117] It is second rate enough.

Got home early but E, Mary, and I sat talking and beer drinking until midnight.

At the ball game someone broke into Mary's machine and stole my typewriter, also razor and pajamas. Got up early and drove from 54 to farm. Spent the day getting detailed stuff ready for Good Life. Played cards. Wrote letters. Loneliness of Madge.[118] The country doctor.

Awakened by Mary Tate getting off—made fuss. Curious relationship.

The day cold and cloudy, road about Mary's place filled with weekenders. Pain in stomach. Worked on Good Living and Deeter. Lunch at house. Mind very active. E lovely.

Went to Henri and Jean Mouquin and saw Jean's garden. Had bottle of very fine French wine. Talk of the mystery of communication. Went to restaurant where E and Mary ate big steaks while I drank wine. Slept well.

Ill—the day ugly, made ugly by Mary. Ate nothing—attack of nervous indigestion. May have to really challenge Mary.

Lovers in the grass.

Tried to work. No success. In the evening played cards.

Mon., June 1
New York

At 54. Still ill but ate a little. Read a cheap detective book. Slept in p.m. Thinking all day of situation as regards Mary. Dined in a charming outdoor place—on 9th Street. E lovely. Had bottle of wine. Slept.

Tues., June 2
New York

A curious neutral day. Hot. Worked on the Deeter article. Prepared a statement for Mary which I must think about. Went to office of fashionable doctor. Left without seeing him. Went to ball game, Yanks and White Sox. Sox won.

Went with Paul and E to dine. E a bit high—very lovely. Talk with Paul—the American landscape—trying to get his meaning. He very gentle and nice. Sat in Square until 12.

Wed., June 3
New York, 54

Finished the Deeter. Wrote letters. A day of thinking— possessions, did they kill Burton Emmett?

To Dr. Stieglitz—and then to Alfred and Georgia.[119] To cocktail party—Calverton, gimme, gimme, crude wife. Max and wife. No drinks. Edmund Wilson. Talk of Paul's place.[120] Mary's pushing in—childishness, ugliness in me, loneliness.

The deeper left.[121]

Thurs., June 4
New York

Worked on the one-act play—Marriage. Made notes for Good Living. Karl[122] came and we went off to ball game—Yanks and White Sox. Sox won.

Went to Maud Fangel[123] to see the writer [James Norman] Hall—Mutiny on the Bounty. Hall all the flame now.

Mary took us to dine at the Brevoort—frog legs and a good imported wine. Karl in good mood. E very charming.

Fri., June 5
New York

The day spent largely with Jap Deeter, going over the profile, and in good talk. He is doing the new edition of Winesburg—the Barton dead of gas.[124]

Got new croquet set.

Dined with Stieglitz and O'Keeffe—O'Keeffe having done a huge painting of flowers for the rich Elizabeth Arden.

Jap told me of Wharton and Letty, and Wharton showed up at 54 but did not see him.

Sat., June 6
Valley Cottage,
N.Y.

Went early to Dr. Stieglitz to get stomach pumped out and general examination. Went to Mary's and worked on one-act play. Drove E about east side. Went to dine with [John] Dos Passos and wife, Edmund Wilson, E and Paul.

Drove to Mary's at Valley Cottage, beautiful moonlight night. To bed at one.

Sun., June 7
Valley Cottage

Slept late. Made final revision of Deeter. Spent most of day reading bad book by Gene Fowler.[125] The day beautiful.

Mon., June 8
Richmond

Got up early. We—Mary and I—drove to Hedgerow. E went early to New York. Jap said new Winesburg fine. Heard of Barton's death, by suicide. Drove to Richmond. Discussed religion with Jay.[126]

Tues., June 9
Marion

Fine drive, by 58—grey day. Got to Marion 324 miles from Richmond at six. Had talk of John with Bob. Tired. To bed.

Wed., June 10
Marion

Day at Ripshin, getting settled. Garden fine. Mary worked hard all day. Got cabin ready for summer work. John Sullivan has done good work.[127]

Thurs., June 11
Marion

To Ripshin with Mary. She all day in flower garden. John started work on bridge improvement. Got settled in cabin and had three hours of work.[128] Home by old road. Caught in rain. Mary very nice. Day good.

Fri., June 12
Marion

To Ripshin where I worked on The Good Life. Mary worked on the garden. There was a slight shower and the world very beautiful. In the evening played cards.

Sat., June 13
Marion

Big day. Opening of park.[129] Very angry because E didn't arrive and no letter. Stayed in town. Mary, May, and Mother with me on porch playing cards. A week of too much women. It leads me to go off and write anti-feminist stuff.

Saw Funk in evening. Unable to sleep and took amital.

Sun., June 14
Ripshin

Up early at Marion and the truck packed. E arrived. Find I only half live when she is not about. Had Mr. and Mrs. Copenhaver for big steak dinner, the house very beautiful. In the evening May and George Cook's daughter arrived. Looked into Fagin's book on the short story.[130] To bed early after putting lettering on car.

Mon., June 15
Ripshin

Elenore's birthday.[131] Began the third of the short plays for an evening to be called Short Stories.[132]

Went to town and to Funk's for wine. Mother had got up a fine birthday dinner for E. Talked with Bob about the park situation. Enjoyed the drive home to Ripshin in dark. E very lovely. Incident of the locked car— Mary and the key.

Tues., June 16
Ripshin

Stayed at home—began and worked on the one-act play, Tobacco Market.

In the afternoon helped Major[133] haul stones for the new wall by the bridge. Went to Grant[134] to get hams and bacon. To bed tired with out of doors. Good day.

Ripshin Farm.
(Greear Studio, Marion, Virginia.)

Wed., June 17
Ripshin

Worked on Book of Days[135] and then off to town where I did many errands and racked off my share of wine made with Funk. Got 240 pint bottles.

Drove home at night, the road very silent and mysterious.

Thurs., June 18
Ripshin

Word came of the death of Gorki and I wrote of him for *Soviet Russia Today* and Tass Agency. Many of his stories have moved me deeply. He had a full rich life. I have always felt tender toward him.[136]

Mary working like a horse all day. Went to town with E. Brought pipe for the new plan of getting water to the lawn. A song sparrow has built a nest over the door of my cabin. Very dry.

Fri., June 19
Ripshin

The problem of Mary—whether or not to let her go. It in my hands. I did let her go. E cried.[137]

Advanced the tobacco play a little, the day dry and hot. Swam in the stream. Took Mary to train in Dave's car.[138] The country very beautiful. Mary very puzzled—a little hurt. Schmeling whipped the Negro Louis. Was it a bought fight?[139]

Home in the dark with E. She beautiful, sad, and puzzled.

Sat., June 20
Ripshin

Worked advancing Tobacco Market. Still very dry. Mary has invented us a water system. Wrote a long letter to Mary I won't send. Many thoughts of her. Went to Marion. Traded rugs with Mother. Came home, bringing E for the evening, first one alone together. To bed early and E had brought me some lovely new pajamas.

Sun., June 21
Ripshin

Up early and to work on both Tobacco and Good Living. In the afternoon drove to Marion. Got queer letter from Lynchburg woman about Republican lawyer. Went out to new state park at Marion. Many people in swimming. The day hot, dry and sultry. Gave Funk letter. Got indignant because no place Negroes to bathe.

Took E and Mother to Ripshin. Got ugly over game of croquet and was very childish. E seemed sad. Perhaps I made her so. She was lovely. Read Wilson's 2 Democracies.[140]

Mon., June 22
Asheville, N.C.

Got up early and took E and Mother to Marion. Much fuss about finding title to truck. Drive hot and dry. We went for a walk and I got the notion of doing an article to be called Tom Wolfe's Town. Very sensual all day. E and I went on a spree, eating a big dinner and drinking champagne.

Tues., June 23
Camp Merrie-Woode, N.C.

Caught a slight cold and nose closed. Felt pretty seedy. Worked in hotel room and left for E's camp at noon.[141] Went from Asheville via Candler and over Mt. Pisgah, 5800 ft. Heavy fog. Could see nothing. Took wrong road and came out at Canton almost where we went in. Went on to Sylva and cut across to Cashiers.

Turkish woman waiting. Conversation about life in Turkey.

Wed., June 24
Brevard, N.C.

Came here to see Hamilton Basso, the writer.[142] He had asked me. Did not feel the visit very successful. There was something cold and barren, a sense of futility. We walked and talked. I could not sleep. The house near Brevard, on the French Broad,[143] with a lovely view.

Thurs., June 25
Ripshin

Driving all day. Tired after sleepless night. Did many errands and worked until night. Had sick headache. Miserable night.

Fri., June 26
Ripshin

Painted chairs. Went to Marion and dictated to Helen. Did a lot of letters. Very hot. Still no rain. Took truck and brought home lime. Not worth the trouble. Did not try to write. The house very lonely without E. Cannot bear being away from her. To bed early and slept—headache gone.

Sat., June 27
Marion

No rain. Advanced the Tobacco play. Worked on Book of Days. Bought new Chevrolet. Took Flora[144] to Marion and stayed there. The whole country burned with the heat and lack of rain. Had grand letter from Jap about play. More proofs came of Kit. The evening spent with Funk, on the courthouse steps, in the darkness, talking of town people.

Sun., June 28
Ripshin

Marion—no work done. A long talk with Mother as she lay in bed. Rain threatening but it did not come. To park. Too hot.

To Ripshin at five. Bob and Mary. I beat Bob at croquet 3 to 2. We went down to the cabin and talked.

Mon., June 29
Ripshin

Vivid animalistic dream of K, the actress.[145] On a country road with a queer half animal figure. We began love making 3 times, were interrupted. She said she wanted a child by me.

Tues., June 30
Camp Merrie-Woode, N.C.

Very hot. Drove down to get E, at her camp. Picked up man who gave me new idea for man in Tobacco Market. Arrived at 4. Found the older women at camp rather dull. The factory girls were nice. The impression in the dining room, campfire—songs. Touch of joy. Touch of despair. Got them wrong end up. Counting the frogs' croaks.

Wed., July 1
Marion

Stayed in camp until noon. Brought a Miss Brown.[146] Got mixed up in roads. Beautiful storm in mountain above Bat Cave. Dined at Boone. Dr. B and his nurse. The night drive, E asleep on my leg. Got home at 10:30. Report of two beautiful rains.

Thurs., July 2
Ripshin

A slow delightful rain—lasting nearly all day. The whole world looking refreshed after the long drought.

Mimi and Russell arrived in rain, bringing children. Played croquet, between showers. Covered by bites of red bugs—very miserable at night.

Fri., July 3
Ripshin

House full of a new generation of Andersons. Russell, Mimi's husband, becoming more and more Rotarian, taking easy position on strike at Mayodan. I won at both croquet and cards. Mrs. Brown an odd creature. It rained all day. Took them all to Marion. The children quite lovely. Worked on proofs of Kit.

Sat., July 4
Ripshin

The house full—Mimi, husband and babies, a Mrs. Brown of Washington—husband a cowboy—afraid he [will] leave her . . . Miss [Helen] Gregory—Damascus—losing property. Sent to Funk. Reading proof . . . To Bob's . . . the dogs sexy . . . Mazie and Channing arrive.

Mazie to E—E sadness—fear for Mother.[147] The day thus full, running up and down scale of emotions.

Sun., July 5
Ripshin

A pest of people—too many—12 or 13 guests all day. . . .[148]

Worked on proofs of Kit. Bob and Mary came—seemed nice. Baby talk in the house—economics outside. Got fed up—bed.

Mon., July 6
Ripshin

Tired from people . . . feeling of piggishness. Took Knoxville working woman to banker—to get note renewed. Channing on socialism and communism. This is day-anniversary of marriage. Evening alone with E— she lovely. Great feeling of peace.

No work.

Tues., July 7
Ripshin

Worked on Rudolph . . . fine, bright, clear day. Later all sorts of small chores. Built couch for Paul. Painted and varnished pig's head, reset flowers. Was, on the whole dull, not up to much. In the evening stupid and to bed. In bed awake. Excited.

Wed., July 8
Ripshin

Did no work. Went to town in truck for couch. Channing and Mazie— also Mother and B.E.[149] came in the evening. We had big dinner and played croquet. Dave came to go with us to Media.[150]

Thurs., July 9
Hedgerow

Drove the entire distance in the day—the hottest I ever drove. The air coming into the car seemed coming out of a furnace. Got to the inn at Media at ten and dined. Dead—to bed.

Fri., July 10
Hedgerow

Day with the players Katy, Mims, Ferd, all as fine as ever. John came at 7. Big storm with hail. No audience for Winesburg.

The play remade and very, very beautiful. Everything gorgeous. Was very happy.

Sat., July 11
Ripshin

After driving again all day. Tree in road. Heat, sprinkles of rain. E very tired. Dave not good driver.

The beauty of the play made it all seem very unimportant. Got in about 10:30 and at once to bed.

Sun., July 12
Ripshin

Started introduction to Winesburg book, plays.[151] E to town to meet Paul [Rosenfeld]. The mess about Flora, she talking big and spoiling the relationship. Many women conferences. One time when Mother not nice. Inclination to run [i.e., control] by Mother.

In the evening Flora for her belongings.[152] Bad feeling in the house. Paul has a nice influence.

Mon., July 13
Ripshin

The Flora matter still making E sad. Doris came in evening with Helen—Helen to take dictation. Helen, Paul and I played croquet.

Worked all day on proofs of Kit.

The day hot and clear. Walked in afternoon with Paul and discussed John's letter, also a man's relations with sons. Made hay.

Tues., July 14
Ripshin

The day spent in dictating to Helen. Got through the revised Winesburg play. Got started on introduction. In the evening drove Helen to town, Paul along. Mazie and Channing came. Worked ten hours steadily. Had to dope myself to sleep. E very lovely.

Wed., July 15
Ripshin

Rather listless after the big day of dictation. E went off to Marion with Mazie and babe, leaving Channing. We mowed lawn and played croquet. Finished new version of Winesburg. Got Triumph ready for book.

In the evening, Paul, E and I played rummy on the porch. Channing went on to Marion.

Thurs., July 16
Ripshin

A new start on Cousin Rudolph—new conception. Good day.

The last batch of proofs to Kit came.

Went early to town in truck, taking Doris. E following in car with Paul. Dined with Mother.

Doris—the idea that she lies with any man, etc., built up by V. and E. The way the poor hurt each other.

Strangeness of drive home, in truck under the storm.

Fri., July 17
Ripshin

Long day of work on proofs of Kit. Feel pretty good about it. Channing and Mazie—Bob and Mary to dine. Mary to stay until Sunday. Political discussion—Channing and the rich men—property—fascist possibilities. E particularly sweet and lovely.

Sat., July 18
Ripshin

Rudolph—proof Kit.

The boys who swung the guns around. "I'll get you before you get me."

The dogs and the dog men. Dog talk.

The beauty of the rain.

The too sensitive man, unaware of hurts in others.

Working with brain, not feeling.[153]

Sun., July 19
Ripshin

Work on Rudolph. Fraley came from Norton. I was tired after work and slept. The day warm and dull.

In the evening Bob came for Mary. Took walk with Paul. Day made dark by continual talk of fascism.

Mon., July 20
Ripshin

The day very cold, with rain. Built a fire in the cabin. Worked on final revision of proofs Kit. Worked on Rudolph. Had to sit at work in big jacket and overshoes.

In the evening warmth coming. Played cards and annoyed Paul by winning all evening. He thinks me too cocky.

Tues., July 21
Ripshin

A sweet clear day. Worked on Rudolph. Paul, John, Major and self went cow trading over beyond Grant, a fine walk along an upland road—the whole country spread out in soft clear light.

Paul's accident at the bridge. Swept all before me at croquet. Reading Man of the Renaissance.[154]

Wed., July 22
Ripshin

Rudolph.

Clear fine day. Long walk with Paul and swim in pool below Swan house.[155]

Paul very tense and upset at games. Cannot bear to lose. I play with him at games, often cruelly, like a cat with a mouse. Even when he is 5 or 6 wickets ahead he is over-anxious. At the first threat of defeat he goes all to pieces.

Thurs., July 23
Ripshin

Good day with Rudolph. Took Paul to town—his application for Guggenheim—strange fussiness. E on edge, very high.

Took Paul and all Copenhaver family to dine in Hungry Mother Park—the evening lovely, sunset over mountain, new moon.

E more than usually lovely. Very much in love with her.

Fri., July 24
Ripshin

Adventures of Rudolph again.

In the afternoon, over Flat Ridge and down Ripshin with Paul and E. Bob Williams and Mazie to dinner.[156]

The day aside from work in thought of Paul—a kind of disappointment, in his lack of social sense, self absorption. Some suggestion that, freed of fear of what may happen to himself, as Jew, he'd be a fascist.

Sat., July 25
Ripshin

The day starting rainy. Had good time with Fred of Rudolph's book. Fred and Kate.

Wrote declaration to Paul—believe in him less. It may all be the result of the persecution of the Jews. In the evening cards, and he won. His terrible anxiety to win spoils games.

Wrote John, Mimi, Mother. Went for early evening walk to Swan House—with Paul and E.

Sun., July 26
Ripshin

Cloudy with soft rain but clear at noon. Fred's adventures. The red haired woman of Chilhowie. To Marion—Mazie's selfishness. The boy John. The lake. Bob's. John Lineaweaver.[157] Funk on Bob Williams. Paul—cockroaches and cancer.

Mon., July 27
Ripshin

Cary Ross, son of a rich Knoxville banker, for a 3 day visit—very gentle quiet fellow. Poet. To town with E, after working on Rudolph. Mother very high—much fun. In the evening music. Paul and the fiber needles. We took a drive, in the moonlight, up the mountain to Flat Ridge, down Ripshin road. The man with the rattlesnakes.

Tues., July 28
Ripshin

John and Major, with Roby Privett,[158] cutting oats. Went up the hill with John and sat, seeing the whole country, John telling me something about each farm and its owner. Very hot—the creek very low.

I have a desire not to talk with Paul. He is constantly bothered, I believe feeling guilty for his inclination to radicalism.

Wed., July 29
Ripshin

Rainy. Marc and Lucille arrived to live in the green house.[159] Rudolph's book marching.

John Lineaweaver came over with Marc and Lucille. We went up the mountain to see the snake man but got caught in a terrific storm and had to turn back. Mary and Bob came—Mary very beautiful in her pregnancy. Bob is getting a new mature quality.

Thurs., July 30
Ripshin

With Fred Wescott—his thoughts and troubles.[160] To Marion with Paul, E and Doris.[161] Dinner at Mother's, me rushing about on errands.

To Funk to talk over the political quarrel at Bob's house. His point of view on pension. The strange telephone call from Doris.

Fri., July 31
Ripshin

Went wrong on Fred. Have to kill what I did yesterday. Doris missing.

She appeared with a husband—handsome young farmer. Water in spring gave out.

Picture of Paul, on porch of tent condemning all proletarians—their hatred, etc.[162]

Myself winning at croquet and then at cards. The niceness of Marc and Lucille. Aunt May and E racing about. Goodness of Aunt May.

Sat., Aug. 1
Ripshin

A day of distraction, but it did not keep me from work. There was a big evening party plan—and E and Aunt May, with Ruby Sullivan busy all day. Doris, who was to come at 11 a.m. did not arrive until 3.

The party was a success but I thought Mazie's friends dull. This party was for her. Roger and Ruth Sergel came. For the next two weeks the house will be full.

E and Aunt May did a masterful job. The spring went dry.

Sun., Aug. 2
Ripshin

Paul left. Roger and Ruth came late Saturday evening.

There was a big, rather dull party—for Mazie and Channing—their friends.

The C's are right not to trust the B's.

Paul seemed to go off sad but having had a good time.

Bob came with Mary and John Lineaweaver. A fair warm day. Worked. Proof of Kit here for final reading.

Mon., Aug. 3
Ripshin

The house full of people. Certainly, for all his charm, the going of Paul takes off tension.

To Johnson City to see about pension matter and to get typewriter fixed at Bristol—Roger, Julie, Y.K. and me.[163]

E under too much tension but I do not know how to relieve it.[164] She is very beautiful these days.

No work.

Tues., Aug. 4
Ripshin

Some work on Fred. It stopped. There is, in the house an outbreak of proof reading—on Kit.

Went in the afternoon in 2 cars up over Flat Ridge. The house, just now, too full of people.

E very lovely.

Wed., Aug. 5
Ripshin

Didn't try to work. John came.[165] We took a walk, over to the hill by the Swan house. Marc made a beautiful color drawing.

In the evening, Funk and wife, Bob and Mary to dine.

Thurs., Aug. 6
Ripshin

Again on proofs of Kit. The whole crew to town, to swim in the lake, to
dine in the park—12 at table.

Have decided the present way of life is no good—too complicated. It is
too hard on E.

John here and very fine, as always.

Fri., Aug. 7
Ripshin

Mimi and Russell arrived. It rained . . . . [166] Party for John—
Birchfields[167] and Bob Williams.

Off to town with Roger. He and Ruth the healthier ones here.

No work. Doris suddenly left and we got a new girl—Virginia. Smith
lectured the crowd in the evening.

Sat., Aug. 8
Ripshin

Rain all day. Walk in the rain—Roger, Marc, Y.K. . . . consciousness of
Y.K.'s strange inner hurt. Mimi and Russell here—Russell self conscious.
In the evening Dave, who ate and slept by the fire.

A growing fondness for Roger and Ruth. Julie don't stand up. Marc is
first class.

Got back to Fred, having cleaned up on Kit. Some new John paintings.

Sun., Aug. 9
Ripshin

There is great joy in the Cousin Rudolph book. May call it an American
Comedy.

Lunch with Marc and Lucille. Man named Krock came from Washington with his wife—rich people.

Afternoon with Roger, the day warm and fine. At night my head full of
Rudolph in [?], his thoughts, adventures, etc. Unable to sleep much.

Mon., Aug. 10
Ripshin

The YK's a mistake. She is a vulgarian. YK a diseased man—no touch
with others. He might be splendid. He has been terribly hurt sometime.
Roger and Ruth healthy.

Went off, after morning with Fred in the beer garden, to drive with

Roger and Ruth. We went to Wilkesboro, N.C.—bad roads, mountains, mud, rain and a good time. E in Marion at work.

Tues., Aug. 11
Ripshin

Thinking, all day, of YK and his life with the older, greedy, second-rate woman. The strange forced laughter always ringing through the house.

Fred—and then a long walk in the woods with Roger. There is in him very fine quality.

Also Marc and Lucille—a fine summer.

The YK's sunk too deeply in something—unable to give, too old to learn the new generosity.

Wed., Aug. 12
Ripshin

Fred. Roger read it. I think not impressed.

Julie remains the same—a female pig, YK a diseased man.

It is good to see Roger and Ruth take to Marc and Lucille.

What a gulf YK opens up.

We all except the YK's to Marion. Mother and the English Major Raven-Hart to dine. The major tall, mild, pleasant.

Virginia leaving—love—the third this summer. Development of Ruby.

Thurs., Aug. 13
Ripshin

Not a good day. It was the end of a writing period. Roger and Ruth left in the morning.

The day bright and fair—same as always. There is something too unhealthy in the air—the folk thing going on[168]—the YK's. It will be good, healthier, when they are gone.

Fri., Aug. 14
Ripshin

In a writing slump. Rewrote the letter to Paul, trying to make my position clear . . . tried to make it less harsh.[169]

To town with Marc and Lucille and YK. YK much nicer away from Julie. His reactions to Kit seemed to me healthy and fine.

Engeman the newspaper man—Baltimore Sun—with his wife to spend the night.[170]

Read the plays "The Children's Hour" and "Paths of Glory."[171]
Could not sleep. Inner excitement unable to release itself in work.

Sat., Aug. 15
Marion-Ripshin

No sleep. No work.
Marc and Lucille left in early morning—YK and Julie in evening. Went
to see the Barter players—no good, too much hamming.[172]
Again a night without much sleep.

Sun., Aug. 16
Ripshin

Ferdinand Schevill arrived. Cary Ross, Eleanor [Hacker], John and Katherine Moutoux for the day and night.[173]
Again no work. In the evening there was a magnificent rainstorm.

Mon., Aug. 17
Ripshin

Knoxville crowd left in the morning. Dropped Fred and worked on the
Winesburg introduction. In the afternoon a long walk with Ferdinand.
The day very clear and fine after the rain.
Not a very good day for work.

Tues., Aug. 18
Ripshin

Switched to the Winesburg book. There was a heavy rain in the night . . .
the day extraordinarily fine and clear.
We went to town, taking May and Ferdinand. I wasn't very nice. We
came home by the back road from Atkins, Sheriff [Sam] Dillard in the
road—had a flat.
A night of distorted dreams. The Negro Louis whipped his man.[174]

Wed., Aug. 19
Ripshin

Worked on the Winesburg.[175] E, Ferdinand and I went for a walk among
the big trees back of Mrs. Anderson's house.[176] A quiet peaceful day.
Ferdinand turns out to be a real croquet player. We make a good
match.[177]
Still in a dull time, not much work being done.

Thurs., Aug. 20
Ripshin

Long letter from Mary. We went to town and I saw Andy Funk. We dined at the restaurant in the park, the guests of Miss May.

Ferdinand very charming. He is more at himself than when here last, just after Clara's death.[178]

I brought the truck home, loaded with phlox to go against wall.

Worked on the Winesburg thing. Mother came over to spend a few days.

Fri., Aug. 21
Ripshin

Mother at the house. I went forward with the Winesburg thing. In the evening Joe Wyse and wife came.

Ferdinand is holding me low at croquet.

We planted the phlox. There was a fine rain in the evening.

Sat., Aug. 22
Ripshin

Work on the Winesburg introduction—which got over into the Robin's Egg book. Not right.[179]

E went off to town with Mother. She [Eleanor] is ill from typhoid shots.

Ferdinand and I walked to where John is building the new road to the Swan farm. I finally got the best of him at croquet. Did not sleep well.

Sun., Aug. 23
Ripshin

I am having trouble getting the Winesburg book clear. Will have to make outline.

Ferdinand off. He is a treasure of a man. When he tells anything he elaborates too much. The most trifling explanation goes on often for a half hour. Full of cliché. A good man, with a fine spirit.

To town to dine at the Copenhavers. E sick from typhoid shots.

Mon., Aug. 24
Ripshin

Another try at the talk of the theatre.

Rain in the morning—the afternoon grey. For the 1st time this summer E and I alone together. I am constantly puzzled trying to get my work less personal and more outside self and objective.

Tues., Aug. 25
Ripshin

E off to town. Still struggling to get the Winesburg straight. John building the road to the Swan place—Major cutting brush.

I am in a half slump—trying to work my way out of it.

Wed., Aug. 26
Ripshin

The Winesburg introduction. In the afternoon to Marion. The whole day spent in thoughts of Lincoln Steffens.[180]

Had a discussion with Mother about democracy that came to nothing. Headache all day.

Bob and Mary to dine. Bob growing constantly nicer.

Thurs., Aug. 27
Marion

Half ill. Have been concentrating too hard, trying to really say something in the Winesburg introduction. In the evening Mother, Nick, Bob Williams, Evelyn and Mary Sprinkle to dine.[181] Went to Marion to sleep. Mother in great form.

Fri., Aug. 28
Marion

Up early and with E to Roanoke—to be examined for pension.[182] Ill all day. Home at 5 and at once to bed. Pain in stomach and violent headache.

Sat., Aug. 29
Ripshin

Ill, all day. It is nerves. Too much concentration. It has affected my guts and head.

E busy trying to get my mss., papers, etc. straightened out—making bibliography.

No one here. The day spent without work. Very cool and grey. Early to bed.

Sun., Aug. 30
Ripshin

Because I had been ill did not try to work. Wrote letters. E and I went to the Negro meeting on the mountain top—very few Negroes.[183] The whites have taken the show. Wyse, the road man, came with wife and a car load of children. Mr. and Mrs. Bill Wright came.[184] E very lovely all day.

It has turned cold but there is a bright sun.

Mon., Aug. 31
Ripshin

Letty and Pussy.[185] After work a long walk. In distress all day but kept going.

Tues., Sept. 1

Ill all day but kept going.

Wed., Sept. 2

Quite ill all night.

Thurs., Sept. 3
[Abingdon]

Still ill. E called Dr. [A. B.] Graybeal in the night and in the afternoon he came again. Took me to hospital at Abingdon. Talk of appendicitis.

Fri., Sept. 4

Not appendicitis. But quite ill—probably abdominal flu.

Sat., Sept. 5

Still at hospital—better.

Sun., Sept. 6

In spite of protest of doctors, better and went to Marion.

Mon., Sept. 7

Still ill but getting gradually better.

Tues., Sept. 8

Still ill.

Wed., Sept. 9

Still ill.

Thurs., Sept. 10

Ill.

Fri., Sept. 11

Ill.

Sat., Sept. 12

Better. Got up and walked about.

Sun., Sept. 13

My birthday. Mother gave me a suit. Still ill. Getting fed up on Mary.

Mon., Sept. 14

Eleanor left for New York. Mary in charge. She is hard to take. A lot better.

Tues., Sept. 15

Went to Funk's. Sat in cellar, for wine making. Had a setback.

Wed., Sept. 16

Not so well. Mary on my nerves.

Thurs., Sept. 17

Ill. Pretty sick of it all. Wish E here.

Fri., Sept. 18

Ill. In bed all day.

Sat., Sept. 19

Ill. In bed.

Sun., Sept. 20

Better. Still more fed up on Mary.

Mon., Sept. 21

Left town. Went to Knoxville to escape Mary—announcing I might be gone for weeks.

Tues., Sept. 22

Back to Marion. Decided to shake her off.[186] Much better, with her gone.

Wed., Sept. 23

Better.

Thurs., Sept. 24

Walked about. It rained all day. Much better.

Fri., Sept. 25

Went to farm. Clear cold day. Cleaning up over there. A lot better.

Sat., Sept 26

Went twice to Ripshin. Much stronger. Grand fall days. It is a grand relief to think of being free from impediments and living alone with E.

Sun., Sept. 27
Marion

Bright clear day. To Bob's to dine and a great deal of talk of dogs. Reading 3 James.[187] Finished reading new book Kit Brandon.[188] Forget it now.
   In the evening to supper at Funks. Quiet talk. Beautiful night.

Mon., Sept. 28
On Road

Got on the road at 8:30—a bright clear day and drove to Hagerstown, Md. Lunched at Winchester. At home all apparently well. It is great relief to think of being on my own—no Mary.
   Read Pat O'Donnell's book. Too literary.[189]

Tues., Sept. 29
Hedgerow

Arrived at Hedgerow about 2 p.m. Jap wonderfully nice. It was grand to see all there.
   In the evening, in the rain to see the Countee Cullen play "One Way to Heaven," Negro players—only Mims and Katy in cast. It was beautiful . . . a play of Negro life by a Negro. It opened up new vistas. Pretty well.

Wed., Sept. 30
Hedgerow

It rained all day. Sat about the theatre house talking with actors. With Jap to drink beer in the afternoon and listen to the 1st World Series game on radio. Eleanor came by train at 7:15. We saw "American Tragedy."
   Home and to bed but Jap got us up to talk until 1:30.

Thurs., Oct. 1
Royalton
New York

Left Hedgerow at 9 and drove to New York. Got grand big room in the Royalton, George Nathan's hotel. It is the biggest hotel room we've been in and very luxurious. $60 per month.[190]

I read Pat O'Donnell's novel, pretty dull and literary. The hotel is at 44 W44th—right in the heart of the theatre district. Hope to get back to work. E lovely but with very bad pain—neuritis in shoulder.

Fri., Oct. 2
New York

Began to work. Went to broadcast with Amelia Earhart.[191] Walked about, wrote letters.

E was cornered by Mary—who is all contrite. The whole thing, with my illness, has exhausted E.

Sat., Oct. 3
Paoli, Pa.

E and I drove to Wharton Esherick's house, to leave the car there, stopping to see Jap. In Media I left the key in car and locked it.

We spent the evening over the fire, at Wharton's in talk. Wharton the same. Pussy came from Philadelphia.

Sun., Oct. 4
New York

A beautiful bright clear day in the country. Wharton and I took a long walk in the woods. We played croquet. In the afternoon listened to the World Series ball game, Yanks and Giants.

Visitors came. We took a 6:30 train in the evening for New York. E very lovely all day.

Mon., Oct. 5
Royalton, N.Y.

Clear fall day. Got into Green Grass.[192] Karl came in. Went to be measured for new suit.

To see Max Perkins. Again impressed by his fineness. We went to drink and talk. New Editor at Scribner's.[193] Giants surprised by winning 5th game. Karl to dine. E tired but much happier in this way of life.

Tues., Oct. 6
Royalton, N.Y.

A long letter from Mary. Will see her on Thursday. To Joe [Girsdansky] and to lunch with him—his reckless driving. Saw a man killed by a truck in the street.

To the tailor for try-on of the new suit. Mother gave me the cloth. Eleanor better. The Giants lost the World Series.

Wed., Oct. 7
Royalton, N.Y.

Did thing for Scribner's Book Buyer.[194] Saw reviews Kit for Herald and Times—both fine.

Went to see New Yorker and to Scribner's to sign books for friends. Gave interview to Herald reporter—attitude of newspapermen toward papers.

Went to dine at Lüchow's with George Nathan.[195] Lots of talk. Much beer.

Thurs., Oct. 8
Royalton, N.Y.

Did a short thing I hope to sell to New Yorker. Call it "Small Towner in Town."[196]

Took walk by Hudson.

At 4 saw Mary—1st time since break. She quite changed and lovely. Read Nathan's book.[197] It, like Mencken's work, all of a tune.

Fri., Oct. 9
Royalton, N.Y.

Went over the Winesburg play and left it for George Nathan to read. Worked on Green Grass. Went to get my new suit. Went in the evening to see Joe Louis fight the Argentine champion Brescia. Knock-out 3rd round. Louis very cat-like and beautiful in action.[198]

Bad night, sleeplessness and coughing.

Sat., Oct. 10
Royalton, N.Y.

Caught a head cold, leaning out the window, in pajamas, watching the crowd, standing about Joe Louis's car, at stage entrance to Hippodrome. Blacks and whites all cheering.

Worked on "Green Grass." In the afternoon laid out.

Got new tan shoes.

Dined with Paul and E at Italian restaurant, 6th and 39th. Back to room and Paul and I talked of the early New England writers until 12:30 while E slept on a couch.

Sun., Oct. 11
Royalton, N.Y.

Very sympathetic and even glowing reviews Kit in both Times and Herald. E and I blew ourselves to big breakfast at the Algonquin.[199] Bought $1 worth of papers.

Wrote many letters. Loafed with E in the p.m. Went to Tommy Smith at 5:30—Komroff, Eddie Mayer and a dull woman.[200] Drank rum cocktails. Cold in head no better. Ate at Chinese restaurant. E very gentle and lovely.

Mon., Oct. 12
Royalton, N.Y.

At home—in the hotel room, nursing a head cold.

Went at lunch time to have lunch with Ben Hecht[201] at an expensive place. Ben the self I used to know when he was a reporter in Chicago. The conversation was mostly reminiscent but it was fine to feel the old Ben there.

Tues., Oct. 13
Royalton, N.Y.

Worked on a short thing called Brown Boomer.[202] Got a new pair of brown shoes. There is little use trying to work on the long thing here. Mary came and brought the ray lamp, also money.

Went with George Nathan to see bum opening new play. About artists and punks.[203] Sat a long time talking with George Jean Nathan—suggestions about Winesburg.

Wed., Oct. 14
Royalton

Still at work on Brown Boomer. E at home all day with bad cold. Swell review of Kit in Daily Times.

Went in the evening with Mary and E to place called "Gay Nineties."[204] Mary had a swell time. She was really charming. E lovely.

Thurs., Oct. 15
Royalton, N.Y.

Finished up the piece on the Brown Boomer. New Yorker turned down the small towner. Feeling rotten.

Lunched with Ben Huebsch[205] and called on [Harlan] Logan at Scribner's.

Went to dine at Longchamps—with John Cournos, wife and daughter.[206] Delightful evening with extraordinarily nice people.

Fri., Oct. 16
Valley Cottage,
N.Y.

It rained all morning and I stayed in bed, reading a tough detective story. Mary very very nice. In the early afternoon we played cards and then, the weather clearing, drove out. E came out on the evening train and again we played cards.

No work.

Sat., Oct. 17
Valley Cottage

To the doctor for my nose. Slept late. No work. Eddie and Alice Wolf came and were nice. The afternoon in talk. Drove into the city in the evening. Most of the talk of the coming election. The worker who is going to vote for Landon.

Sun., Oct. 18
Royalton

Again much bothered by the curious inadequacy of much of American criticism. It is, at any rate, now pretty generally admitted that I work sincerely—some however announce me naive—others too sophisticated. There is very little pointing of any path.

Mon., Oct. 19
Royalton

In my room and back to Green Grass. The head cold hangs on. Lunched alone and walked a little. In the evening went with E to see an old French farce, somewhat modernized—Horse Eats Hat—a kind of joyous slam-bang fun.[207]

Tues., Oct. 20
Royalton, N.Y.

Worked on Green Grass. Went to lunch with Luise Sillcox and Barrett Clark.[208] Went to Jerry Frank's office.[209]

Went to cocktail party at Studin's.[210] Went to Mary's—dinner there. Mary got drunk. Repetition. Cold still hanging on.

Wed., Oct. 21
Royalton, N.Y.

Finished a chapter of Green Grass. Amazingly fine review of Kit by Jim Rorty.[211] Went with E to get new hat made and to a meeting for Spain.

In the afternoon saw and talked with Pat O'Donnell and with Paul and E to dine and to the Empire—John Gielgud as Hamlet, Judith Anderson—the Queen, Lillian Gish—Ophelia. A strange new homosexual Hamlet. Gish fine in insane scene.

Thurs., Oct. 22
[Hedgerow]

The morning spent writing many letters. E has got to something—a giving off all the time of warm assurance of affection . . . that makes living near her always rich.

To Hedgerow by taxi from hotel. 2 fights, my man and others on the way. A very beautiful Winesburg. New and rich George and Reefy.

Fri., Oct. 23
Hedgerow

Staying at the inn. Bright clear day. Went with Mims to Paoli to get my car. Wrote letters. Worked a little.

Went in the evening to see an early Shaw play—"The Devil's Disciple." Bad second act. Scene of the trial the only really good one. The wit in all the other scenes, heavy.

Went to bed at 11:30. Cold not much better.

Sat., Oct. 24
Hedgerow

Worked in my room until 2. 2 to 4 drank beer with Jap. In the evening went to see Shaw's "Getting Married"—long and dull. It went well enough for the 1st hour but then got very dreary. The acting good. Was allowed pension $20 per month from Government.[212]

Sun., Oct. 25
Hedgerow

No work. Up late and to Wharton's. Spent the day there and returned for a Hedgerow session until evening—talk of organization and how to get more quality into the work. Jap at his best, as teacher.

Mon., Oct. 26
Hedgerow

With Jap, Mims, and Ferd to the University in Philadelphia where they arranged to do "Beyond the Horizon" later.[213]

To theatre to see "Cast Up by the Sea," riotous fun. A take-off on Shore Acres and Old Homestead.[214] It was a kind of circus.

After to the inn to drink too much beer. Talked until 3 a.m.

Tues., Oct. 27
Hedgerow

Dopey from too much beer last night. Wrote letters. Wrote article for New Masses. Saw the play Anchor's Weighed—very beautiful and beautifully done . . . strangeness and poetry.[215]

It turned very cold. Put alcohol in car. Sat with the actors at the house. Back to hotel at 1 p.m.

Wed., Oct. 28
N.Y.—Royalton

Drove from Hedgerow direct to Valley Cottage to leave car.

Got letter from Mary (nice about call-down). E very lovely. We tried to go to Ickes meeting but couldn't get in.[216] E swank in new coat and hat.

Thurs., Oct. 29
Royalton

Did thing for Masses. Anniversary number.[217] Went for cocktails to Norton[218] and then to Elmer Adler.[219] Dined with E and Mary. Mary took E's ticket to "It Can't Happen Here."[220] Big crowd. Play starts off fine and then blows off into second-rate melodrama. Too bad.

Fri., Oct. 30
Royalton, N.Y.

It turned bitterly cold. Was to do a stunt for New Yorker, in lower New York but so cold gave it up.

To lunch with Ernst and Lindey—to talk of New York production of Winesburg.[221]

Went to dine with Joe and Ann [Girsdansky]—their wedding anniversary. Wrote articles for Masses and The Writer.

Sat., Oct. 31
Royalton, N.Y.

Finished the thing for Writer which I like and will try on New Yorker.[222]

The whole town full of election, girls with cloth sunflowers, loudspeakers, etc. Went with E to work on 5th Avenue[223] and to see the mechanical show in Radio City.

We went to Saxe Commins[224] to dine and heard good music. Saxe being held up by his communist friends. Got from the musician's wife a terrible story of the position of the cultured Jew in Germany now.

Sun., Nov. 1
Royalton

Slept late. Beautifully soft warm day. The campaign at an end. Wrote on building house.

Went, in late afternoon to Mary's—good talk, Mary nice . . . then to dine at Ticino's—and afterward to Y. K. Smith's—saw fine portrait of Lucille [Antony].

Mon., Nov. 2
Royalton, N.Y.

Began a new thing—building Ripshin. It may do for Scribner's. Went to lunch with Libby [Holman]—very nice. She may do something about Winesburg.[225] Went to dine with the Millers—a grand evening . . . Mary hurt by article in the Villager. Heard Landon on radio—very bad. Did not sleep well.

Tues., Nov. 3
Royalton, N.Y.

Election day. John Emerson arrived.[226] Breakfast with him and Jane Grey—the actress. Went to see "Boy Meets Girl"—very funny—satire on movies.[227]

Dined at Barbizon-Plaza. Went to see the Follies—very bad.[228]

The sweep for Roosevelt was evident, even at dinner and all evening the majority piled up. Two states for Landon—Maine and Vermont. Great excited crowds in the streets. We stayed up until 2 a.m.

Wed., Nov. 4
Royalton, N.Y.

Charlie Studin gave a cocktail party for E and myself. Got two offers for Kit, from England. Took 120 pounds—Hutchinson.[229]

After the cocktail party, John Emerson, Jane Grey, E and myself went to dine with Whit Burnett.[230] Drank too much. Worked during day on "Build My House."

John Emerson arrived this morning from Hollywood.

Thurs., Nov. 5
Royalton, N.Y.

Knocked out. Too much drink. Went to lunch with engineers about the abundance play. In the afternoon to bed and then to dine at Mary's— Katy, Eddie, Alice, Thompson, Adler.[231]

Sorry Millers not there. Katy talk. Katy and John. Sat with John in Lambs.[232]

Fri., Nov. 6
Royalton, N.Y.

Took big chance of offending, by letter to Mary.

Up late and worked a little—the House thing.

Went with E to dinner for peace delegate going to South America, Harry Ward and Bishop McConnell speaking.[233]

Went to Henry Canby[234] to meet Thomas Mann's son and daughter, the German and a journalist from Serbia.

Sat., Nov. 7
Royalton, N.Y.

Got letter from Funk, telling of election celebration at home and the two Bobs.

Went with Alice to lunch and had long talk of Mary, and what may happen.

Went to book fair—amazing crowd. Stood up in big hall to talk for two minutes.[235]

Went with John Emerson to see St. Helena.[236]

Went to Cafe Royal to have dinner with John Cournos and wife.

The day rainy and cold. Got a little work done.

Sun., Nov. 8
Royalton, N.Y.

Up late so slept late. To Algonquin, to lunch with John. With Mary, E, and John to Karl at Westport. Big party. Lots of people—Mary behaved.

Got painting from Karl—his new work very beautiful. We drove home in rain—went to Cafe De La Paix[237]—drinks—In bed at one.

Mon., Nov. 9
Royalton, N.Y.

Worked until almost all in. To lunch with John Emerson—and a good talk—Algonquin.

Went home then for long talk with Mary.

E and I dined at Japanese restaurant and went to Mr. and Mrs. White, at New Yorker.[238] Sat talking until 11.

Very tired.

Tues., Nov. 10
Royalton, N.Y.

Not in the mood for work but got in. Many jobs started. Worked revising in Build My House. Wrote letters.

Went to lunch with Eugene Jolas[239] and had a long interesting talk— Paris, Stein, Joyce, Matisse, Picasso, etc. Joyce on new language a comedy.

E and I to the restaurant where we ate too much—had wine. Restless night.

Wed., Nov. 11
Royalton, N.Y.

Last day in town. Worked, pretty well. Went with Mary—Valley Cottage—to get car. Went to party for Max Eastman[240] . . . from there to Eddie Wolf to dine—E coming at 10. Left at 11:30 and took E home. Went to sit with John Emerson and Jane Grey. Bed at 1:30.

Thurs., Nov. 12
Baltimore

Spent early morning packing, left N.Y. at 12:30. Got to Hedgerow at 3:30. Short visit there. Went on to Baltimore—Wilsons—arriving 6:30. No dinner. New house. Got to bed at 10:30.

Fri., Nov. 13
Salem

Left Baltimore at 9:30—Washington at 10:45. Tried to get Morgenthau—out of town.[241] Went to Agriculture Dept. Went to see man in
Executive offices—President.

Hearst man—Ryan. Saw John. Left Washington at 2:30. Got to Salem
at 9:15. Spent the night there.

Sat., Nov. 14
Marion

Arrived at 10:30 from Salem. Spent the day cleaning up letters and re-
packing. Bob's daughter Margaret Lane born yesterday. The day warm
and fair. In the evening took a drive with Funk and had a long talk.

Sun., Nov. 15
Salisbury, N.C.

Finished packing, talked with Bob about his ear, took books to Funk. It
began to snow with a high wind. Backed car off driveway. B. E. declared
steering gear broken, radiator leaking. All false alarm. We got to Winston
[-Salem] and went to see Mary and her babe. No snow after Wytheville.
Speedometer—7600 leaving.

Mon., Nov. 16
Waycross, Ga.

We fixed Mother to lie down and sleep on the back seat. A bright clear
day. Cotton picking going on. We lunched at Greenville, arrived Waycross
9:15. Mother quite fresh. Most of this day's drive, from Greenville on,
new country to me.

8206 speedometer.

Tues., Nov. 17
Tampa, Fla.

Speedometer 8529.

Got up feeling rotten but drove all day. When Mother and I are together we always quarrel playfully about the South. I said, "You Virgi-
nians always see the whole U.S. in terms of Virginia."

She and E are alike in this. They are intellectuals of the finest sort. They
do not really see either people or nature.

Wed., Nov. 18
Tampa—A.F. of L.

Wrote letters I won't send. Went to A.F. of L., Frances Perkins[242] spoke well . . . Walked in Spanish section. Funny how prostitutes, making signs to me, arouse both abhorrence and desire. It's the same feeling you get when you watch the copulation of animals.

Went with Mary Vorse[243] and Charles,[244] E and Mother to Spanish restaurant—ate stone crabs—delicious. Good talk.

Thurs., Nov. 19
Tampa—A.F. of L.

An impression of something very sick in the labor movement. The life, with the absence of the Lewis faction, quite gone. Fat men drinking in bars.

Went with [Marquis] Childs—St. Louis Post Dispatch, Mary Vorse and man from labor relations to swim. Went to dine at Spanish restaurant. Spanish ambassador arrived. Saw picture of life in South Seas. Went to Tarpon Springs to see the sponge fishermen.

Fri., Nov. 20
Tampa—A.F. of L.

A swift day. Worked on Green Grass. Saw Mary Vorse. Went with her to labor temple. Little earnest Spanish cigar maker organizer.

Went to cigar factory—the ambassador, his daughter, manufacturer's daughter, foremen, union leader—little dark society girl—desire.

To A. F. of L. hall. With Doctor Franz to chief of police—sailors in jail—the talk with them.[245]

The petition—changing it. To the football game. The girl cheerleader. Dr. Holt of Rollins.[246]

Sat., Nov. 21
Tampa

Worked better. Left with crowd for beach at 2. Grand afternoon on the beach. We went in two cars.

Pat Jackson's story of Stark Young and Robert Frost.[247]

We went to Indian Rocks and dined, some 20 or 30 in a little hotel by the gulf. Great argument as to course of John L. Lewis. Home early. Got car fixed.

Sun., Nov. 22
Tampa

Went in the morning to Christian Church, Sunday School—men's class.
Banker from Texas. A. F. of L.—great humanitarian.

Christ, as A. F. of L. preacher. E. C. Nance and his book.[248]

To Spanish labor temple—ambassador and heard Isabel de Palencia.[249]
Sat at speaker's table. Pat Jackson's speech bad.

Went with party to Spanish restaurant. Sat talking until ten. Had night
of sex dreams.

Mon., Nov. 23
Tampa

Vital day at A. F. of L. Session until midnight. We 3 dined with Bill Mangold.[250] Impression, at A. F. of L. of everyone lying. Green, in final
speech, queerly suggestive of angry impotence.[251] Force got by shouting
and violent swinging of arms. Labor in a mess.

Could not sleep. Had again night of faces. In semi-conscious state they
kept coming—all women, all sad, all hurt. The faces, one after another,
seemed to draw very slowly nearer and nearer. Soft lips met mine. There
was a feeling of aroused sex. There was something very sad, very gentle,
very beautiful, felt.

Tues., Nov. 24
Tampa

In the room working until 1:30. Went to the beach with newspaper crowd
and then back to dine with Pat and wife and Palencia. Sat with her—a
very extraordinary woman. Went with her to a huge outdoor meeting
where she spoke with such force and eloquence that I sat in tears.[252]

We came back to the hotel to sit until nearly one a.m., de Palencia
talking with a group of us over drinks.

Wed., Nov. 25
Tampa

Dream of many young men, many young women, all running furiously
along roads and across fields.

Worked in late morning on Green Grass. Took Mother and E to Tarpon
Springs. Grey cool day. Dined with Palencia, Pat and Mrs. Pat, with oth-
ers.Took Palencia and Mother to train. Went early to bed but did not
sleep until after one.

Thurs., Nov. 26
Thanksgiving day
Tampa—Clearwater—
Tarpon Springs

Not a damn thing about official labor.

Went with some 15—grey, cold windy day—to Clearwater. Ate there. Went to Tarpon Springs—don't just know why. Everyone tired in spirit . . . the talk for the most part dull.

It is because all had seen too much of those in official charge of labor. Dreamed of being in a strike—fighting A. F. of L. No work.

Fri., Nov. 27
Tampa

No work. Tried to write letter (open) to Green. No good. Walk in Spanish and Negro residence districts. Multitude of prostitutes.

"Come in. Fix my radio."

"I've got a young one for you."

"Come back of the house. I'll frisk you for a quarter."

The unpleasant feeling that comes. Man's occasional half-formed desire for any woman.

To the convention in the p.m. and then with E, Mary Vorse, Childs and Little to dine.[253]

Sat., Nov. 28
Jacksonville

Left Tampa at 10:30 after hard effort to arouse Herb Little, Washington News—who was to ride with us . . . too much party for him last night. Drove leisurely route, by Daytona Beach, stopping at Herb's boyhood town. Took ten mile drive on beach—cool but clear. Smoke over orange groves. B Girl with lover in Washington. Bartender's tale of bottle drinkers.

Sun., Nov. 29
Charleston, S.C.

Drove with Herb Little (Washington News) to the North Carolina–South Carolina border, where he hoped to get a story about fingerprinting workers. No story. We left him at a little town, on the border.

Went in the evening to Josephine Pinckney. Dubose Heyward and wife there—terrible people.[254] Also rich Mr. Huntington, tale of Heyward's portrait. Josephine real.

Mon., Nov. 30
Durham, N.C.

Up at 7 and on the road at 8:30. A beautiful drive to Wilmington—dense negro life—swamps and pine forests with occasional glimpses of the sea.

Wilmington a disappointment.

After that a desolate country of sand, poverty and scrub pine. The country began to improve as we approached Durham. It is a light yellow tobacco country. Got to Durham at 4:30.

Tues., Dec. 1
Durham, N.C.

Very cold. In the evening snow that turned to rain and then froze. Icy pavements.

Dreamed at night of taking part in a long and ugly strike.

It was a day of gloom. Began Green Grass from a new angle. In sharp reaction to ugliness of labor meeting at Tampa. Went for a walk in icy streets. The streets full of negro cigarette factory workers.

Wed., Dec. 2
Durham, N.C.

Reread Thomas Burke's "Limehouse Nights"—found it stupid and cheap.

Worked on Green Grass. The day damp, cold and foggy.

Went to tobacco market—no sales. Weather too bad for farmers to come. Prices good.

Went with E to dine at house of Duke professor. Psychiatric man. Not much impressed.

The room hot. Could not sleep and when I did sleep dreams concerned with Edward of England and Mrs. Simpson.[255] Myself stupid.

Thurs., Dec. 3
Durham

Did a piece for E, on the A. F. of L. convention.[256] Wrote a lot of letters. Worked some on Green Grass.

It was a cold rainy day—slime under foot. Stayed in nearly all day and read John Cournos' Babel. Same material used as in autobiography with often the same words. There is a fine honesty but lack of invention. The prose rarely has swing and rhythm.

Dined with E and little hungry woman secretary . . . She, obviously, very hungry for a man. Slept well.

Fri., Dec. 4
Durham

A cool, sunshiny day. Worked Green Grass (Fred) and then to Mimi and Russell—80 miles by Reidsville. Stopped at tobacco house.

Mimi and Russell in new house—both babies strong—they depressed. They may well lose the paper and all their start in life. Thoughts kept coming, making me feel a little guilty that I had not devoted my life to money making. I stayed to dine and drove home in the dark, puzzled and upset.

Sat., Dec. 5
Durham

Worked on novel. In the evening to Dr. Howard Odum's house, at Chapel Hill—Russell, Green, and others.[257] Talk mostly of the South—its problems. Table set 3 short of the number of guests. No drinks. Odum a Methodist—but O.K.

We went later to Paul Green's house. Both he and wife [Elizabeth] very attractive—the house beautiful. His determined stand against Shirley Temple. Gone with Wind sort of thing. To bed at one.

Sun., Dec. 6
Durham, N.C.

Warm grey day with occasional sputters of rain. Worked on Green Grass. Went with E to dine at Paul Green's. James Boyd of Southern Pines there.[258] The hunting writer.

Found Green and Boyd both essentially sweet men, Green more puzzled than Boyd. Boyd, born rich, has escaped much of Green's puzzle.

The evening spent in a kind of sparring—each man trying to get at the other.

Boyd told of conversation with Tom Wolfe regarding myself. Wolfe booming in big voice that I would outlive all my detractors, etc.

Mon., Dec. 7
Durham

Green Grass.Rain all day. Lunch with E's Y W secretaries. At 3 drove to Green's and then on to James Boyd, at Southern Pines.

House lovely. Mrs. Boyd, ill-looking. Had written out proposal to Green and Boyd but didn't present it. Saw his great pack of fox hounds.

Home at 1:15 a.m. Very cold.

Tues., Dec. 8
Lynchburg, Va.

A fair bright day. Pat Jackson and wife showed up at breakfast. He just came from T. V. A.

The story of the struggle there—from Pat's angle.

Fine drive to Lynchburg. The car to be repaired. Thoughts all day, of possible project with Green and Boyd. E upset about her work.

To bed early. E very lovely but tired.

Wed., Dec. 9
Lynchburg, Va.

A dull rainy day with no real work accomplished. Wrote letters to Paul Green and Jim Boyd, making proposal for collaboration on book—artist's position in a capitalistic society. Read in Myers, "Great American Fortunes."[259] The rain continued all day. Walked some in the rain. A gloomy and unprofitable day.

Thurs., Dec. 10
Roanoke, Va.

Another futile day. No work. It continued raining. Reading "Great American Fortunes"—Myers. Much excitement about King Edward's abdication. Met government attorney and talked with him of his work.

Drove to Roanoke, from Lynchburg. Went on to Salem to sit in trial of two murderers . . . killed deputy sheriff. They claimed he killed and robbed brother.

Went, for the night to Lucinda Terry. Went to meet crowd of her relatives. Began reading life of Randolph Hearst.

Fri., Dec. 11
Marion

Still gloomy and rainy. Left Roanoke at noon. Sat in Mrs. Terry's house reading of Hearst, took the book away with me.

Bad road between Wytheville and Marion—road under construction. Still feel very futile and dead. Nothing in me sings. Can't really approach anyone. Got to Marion at 3 p.m.

Sat., Dec. 12
Marion

Writing letters. The hills, covered with a thin coat of ice, very lovely. Went in the afternoon to Funk, to try out the new wine. It turned out a disaster.

The wine tasted fine but not through working and I, foolishly, drank 3 glasses, giving me a miserable night of violent indigestion.

Got Winesburg off to Chicago.[260]

Sun., Dec. 13
Marion

A day of illness, the result of the new wine. Stayed at home most of the day. No work.

Went in the afternoon to Bob and he gave me a new red flannel shirt. At 8:50 E left for New York. The house very hot—filled with distorted dreams.

Mon., Dec. 14
Marion

Recovering from the new wine drinking. Revising the short play "Mother."

In the evening took a drive with Funk who told me the Leona Lincoln story.[261]

He also invited [me] to a goose and quail dinner.

Decided I'd better, for the time, let "Green Grass" go and devote myself to short plays and stories. Miss E terribly.

Tues., Dec. 15
Marion

Still dieting—living on orange juice and eggs. Worked, revising two short plays.[262]

Wrote letters. The house cold—something wrong with furnace. Went to work by stove in print shop.

In the evening to Funk's workshop where I played rummy with Andy Funk and Bob Williams.[263]

Wed., Dec. 16
Marion

Started a short story, called "Man to Man." Did 1500 words. Sick of the Myers book. Too much—the case too well-proven.

Dreamed I was a boy, my mother trying to get me a job in a factory—E my mother.

Went to Funk's. Bob Williams, Funk and I. We had limburger cheese, crackers, and beer. Played cards. Stayed awake reading until 3 a.m. but slept until 10.

Thurs., Dec. 17
Marion

Worked correcting plays; slept late. Beautiful day. Walked to Lincoln Hill. Miserable houses of the poor.

Very alive all day.

Went in the evening to Funk's, where we ate quail and pheasant. I won 3 games of rummy. In bed at 11.

Fri., Dec. 18
Marion

The house in disorder—Mazie very busy—baby ill. After work I went with Mazie for a walk, on B. E.'s place,[264] back among the hills—curious awkwardness of Mazie. A mist blowing, the hills beautiful. Mazie reminds of my sister Stella.

In the evening to play cards with Funk and when I came out the car covered with heavy sleet, turning to snow. Very lonely for E.

Sat., Dec. 19
Marion

Heavy snow and slush—breaking out on the same date as last year. The roads getting icy at night. Took a walk, to Lincoln Hill, in deep slush. The hill, south of town, very lovely. Had been all day in a very gloomy state of mind and unable to get cheered up. Aunt May went to get her upper teeth pulled. Mazie's baby ill. All the people in the streets seemed sad and hurt.

Sun., Dec. 20
Marion

Snow fell again in the night and the roads more icy. Mother ill with a headache. Took dinner with Funk and we had goose. Myself in a low gloomy mood.

In the late afternoon Ferd, Jap, and Mims arrived and we all dined at the hotel and later sat talking until midnight.[265] I got quite cheered up. Want E.

Mon., Dec. 21
Marion

Jap, Ferd, and Mims all day and no work—or attempt at work. We drove to Ripshin, in deep snow. John gone to W.Va. Just could get through from Troutdale. Aunt May gave high tea.

We went—the 3 and I—to dine at Wyatts[266] . . . and then to the hotel room to talk, until midnight of the problems of the theatre.

Tues., Dec. 22
Marion

The day again with Jap, Ferd, Mims. There was a bright sun, the ice melting on the roads. We went to Abingdon—the tobacco market, and then on to Bristol. The three much interested in the big market, the buyers, auctioneer, the pinhookers, the farmers standing and waiting.

The huge warehouse with the long rows of yellow tobacco in baskets.

We went on to Bristol and had beer, in a horribly ugly restaurant. Home by old road. Country lovely under the snow. Steak at Wyatts. Bob and Dave, Bob's terrible selfconsciousness, leading to monologue.

Wed., Dec. 23
Marion

Spent the morning getting Jap, Mims, and Ferd off. The visit did me a world of good . . . their problem so much my own. Got out of my worst gloom. Went with Dr. Graybeal to call on sick girl. Left him there and took long walk by the river—the road muddy but town beautiful.

Got into bed early and slept.

Thurs., Dec. 24
Marion

The house full of excitement, mostly feminine, over Christmas, although agreed no presents. Little E[2] having her possessive instinct built up to gigantic proportions.[267]

The whole Christmas thing, birth of the Christ, etc., absurdly corrupted everywhere.

When will understanding come? How can love come without understanding?

The women chatter, chatter, chatter. Thought dies.

Fri., Dec. 25
Marion

The usual Christmas disorder. One child, Mazie's, and all the elders showering gifts. Big turkey dinner with cocktails and wine—from Mary Emmett—and Wyse, the road man and wife in.

Afterwards to the top of Walker Mountain—the roads very greasy. The view strange and misty—the world of hills like a woman's skirt, thrown on the floor.[268]

Something out there very far away from all we were feeling to each other. E very lovely all day.

Eleanor Copenhaver Anderson.
(Trustees of the Sherwood Anderson Literary
Estate.)

Sat., Dec. 26
Marion

Worked, went to the mountains, with Mazie and Channing, for leaves—
played cards. A dull and stupid day inside me. There is a brotherhood
that seemingly can't exist. Everyone seems to live on a false basis, including myself, with myself. People both help and hurt too much, and yet I
cannot draw away from people.

I hate it when E and I go to bed in comparative silence, each drawn
away from the other.

She remains the best one, of all living people I have known.

Sun., Dec. 27
Marion

Worked and avoided big Sunday dinner and John Cronk.[269] Nick Carter
called. Went to call on Funk. Guests going in and out of house all day.
Mazie, Channing and baby left in the evening and I sat playing cards with
Mary until midnight.

Mon., Dec. 28
Marion

Mary at work, listing old manuscripts. Worked at Green Grass. It begins
to take form. Had long talk with Funk about Methodists and Bob's in-
ability to laugh. Eleanor busy with filing letters. A grey rather wet day,
ending in rain.

In the evening again at cards. Rereading Madame Bovary.

Tues., Dec. 29
Marion

Extraordinarily warm with splashes of rain. Work on Green Grass. E and
I drove to Rural Retreat.[270] We walked in the Black Lick Road. The big
man who did not know the name of the creek that ran through his own
farm.

The two toothless women with sagging breasts, sawing wood.

In the evening to Funk's. Burt [Dickinson] drunk. The constant irritation of the phrase—"I don't want to bore you."

Wed., Dec. 30
Marion

Cloudy and too warm. Mother and May gave a party for Mary—cards.
Mary and I had a talk, by the windows, in her room. It was about money,
to let me go on working and she was fine.

I drove out, beyond Chilhowie,[271] on the White Top road, parked the car and walked until dark. The hills lovely, like sleeping women, drawing blue and purple robes over them as night came. Dined alone in the room.

E getting, more and more, a nice laughing quality I want for her.

Thurs., Dec. 31
Marion

Worked and wrote to Van Eck about Holland edition "Kit."[272] Walked with E along White Top Road. Grey misty day. Noted Chilhowie slums. Someone should write of small town slums.

In the evening to Bob's—Bascom, Laura Lou, May, Mary, E and myself. Good dinner with wine. Finished rereading Bovary. Could not sleep. We all sat up to see the end of the year. Clear, star-lit night, with a moon.

1 9 3 7

Up early, after a night without sleep, and at work. Left Marion at 2 p.m. with E and Mary [Emmett] and drove to Asheville, N.C. by Mountain City, Blowing Rock, Linville and Burnsville. Dinner at Burnsville—the last 75 miles in heavy rain . . . the 1st 3 hours lovely—soft grey afternoon light. Mary bought whiskey and we sat in the room drinking and talking of a winter to be spent in South America.

Tired and slept well.

E having a conference with the leaders among the industrial girls. It has rained continually since we arrived here last night—all the streams in flood.

Worked at Green Grass[1] and then took Mary for a drive 1st through the section of the wealthy estates and later into workingman's and Negro section. It kept on raining and we went to the hotel room to play cards. Mary very nice all day. She consistently beat me at cards. E came in, wet and tired at 10, and we drank wine.

Got up late. A bright sun, after several days rain. Worked. Took a walk about the town.

At 4 E came with 3 of her industrial girls. Drove about town and to Grove Park Inn . . . very huge and ugly but girls impressed.

Went to call on Fielding Burke and sat several hours with her.[2] A fine woman but older than I expected.

Mon., Jan. 4
Marion

No work. We left Asheville at ten—came by way of Lenoir, then across to Kingsport and by Gate City, to stop at ABC store. Bought rum.

The day very clear and beautiful—stopped at tobacco market. Mary very excited finding the Chesterfield man. Played Mary's new game Bingo.

Tues., Jan. 5
Marion

Ill—in bed—a sort of half-flu—a let-down. Mary went out and had big adventure with poor ragged mountain girl of 15—taking her to stores and buying shoes, stockings, coat, hat, dress, etc. etc. She—Mary—came back much excited and very proud and happy.

I read Hugo—Hunchback of Notre Dame—very silly, florid writing and silly florid imagination.

In a slump—no effort to work—the day warm, cloudy and windy outside. Will be glad to get off South.

Wed., Jan. 6
Marion

Both Mother and myself in bed with flu. Played cards with Mary. She went to speak at college in the evening—told me she would allow me $150 per month to live and work on. Gave me 1st payment. We sat and talked—E, Mary and I—until 12.

Thurs., Jan. 7
Marion

Mary left, in the early morning, her visit a great success for all of us. Suddenly we all had a great tenderness for this woman. She is such a force, so wrong-headed at times, so warm and generous.

Mother still ill, with flu. Thought I had it licked but, when I went downtown was very weak. E and I played cards on the porch, in the sun. Early to bed.

Fri., Jan. 8
Marion

Beginning to recover from the flu. Pretty well. Worked just a little—sat in the sun—very lovely day.

In the evening at home, playing cards—nothing important.

No thoughts.
No dreams.

Sat., Jan. 9
Marion

Evidently recovered from flu. Still extraordinarily warm. Took E and
Aunt May to Ripshin—mud very deep—everything in good order there.
Made plans for garden and ordered seed from Burpee.

Sun., Jan. 10
Marion

The day at home, packing, etc. Very little work.

Wrote letters and took Mother, E and B. E. for a ride to the top of
Slemp Mountain. Went to see Bob and Mary.

Dreamed of Theodore Roosevelt, became a gentle retiring man with
whom I walked and talked.

Mon., Jan. 11
Marion

Packing, to leave for the South. Worked for an hour or two. Wrote letters.
Went to ride with Marvin Anderson who was much interested in Jack
Reed.[3] Played cards. Nervous and needing the out of doors.

Tues., Jan. 12
Southern Pines,
N.C.

Mr. Copenhaver all night with his brother Gord, said to be dying.[4] Hard
to get E off. Managed it, so that we left Marion at 11 . . . grey, cold, misty
day. Went to Jim Boyd's by Winston Salem over Bridal Gap. Boyd and
wife charming. We spent the evening in talk . . . the house very charming
and in wonderfully good taste.

Wed., Jan. 13
Southern Pines,
N.C.

The day in James Boyd's house—the best I've ever seen the life of a rich
man done but wouldn't want it.

A place of horses and dogs—everything in the house very elegant. Took
a walk with Jim and talked writing; then with E about the town. Talked
to callers. The day grey and damp. Did no work.

Thurs., Jan. 14
Southern Pines,
N.C.

The day at Jim Boyd's house. Katherine Boyd—the wife—an invalid, very fine. They do the rich thing very well, unlike most rich people, not always pretending they are poor. Mr. Boyd took E and I to Pinehurst, where I saw some beautiful trotters and pacers.

Fri., Jan. 15
Baxley, Ga.

We got in here at 5:30—having left the Boyds at 9—350 miles, all the way, except the last hour, in rain. Felt better than I have felt for days.

Sat., Jan. 16
Mobile, Ala.

A long day of driving—some 500 miles—clouds and occasional showers. We got to Mobile very tired, dined and at once to bed.

Sun., Jan. 17
New Orleans

Leisurely drive—only 150 miles. It had got warm . . . with a few showers. Spent the evening with Dorothy, Jimmy, Julius, Marc and Lucille.[5] Home to bed at 12 after a long discussion of communism, in which I talked too much but did not say what I felt.

Mon., Jan. 18
New Orleans

Staying at 2029 Marengo Street . . . very noisy with the house being rebuilt. Worked.

Went to visit Doris Stone and to see her digging from Honduras.[6] Went to dine at Elma's. A long evening with much talk, mostly without point.

Tues., Jan. 19
New Orleans

Heavy rain, all day a flood. Sat on the front porch of house on Marengo Street and wrote. Elma came to talk. Still the rain. E got me 2 new shirts. Went to Jimmy and Dorothy at 5:30. Dined there with some 8 or 10 others.

Wed., Jan. 20
Orange, Texas

Left New Orleans at 10:00 by new bridge over the Mississippi—very warm. Wore my new shirt E got me. She sad all day.

Grey skies. We laid in supply of New Orleans coffee. Wet fields everywhere and streams high. In one place we drove through water, on the highway, up to running board.

Thurs., Jan. 21
Corpus Christi

Arrived at Corpus at 5:20—616 miles from New Orleans. We came by lower road, Port Arthur, Galveston, Port Lavaca, Aransas Pass . . . delightful day.

We got into the same camp we were in 2 years ago—better place, right by the sea—$16 a week. We can cook our own meals. Should be good place to work and fish.[7]

Fri., Jan. 22
Corpus Christi

Day very dark and cold. Unable to work. E and I walked some 3 or 4 miles through the streets of the town in the rain. Sat at home and read.

Sat., Jan. 23
Corpus Christi

Still dark and cold—a heavy mist driven over the sea by a north wind. Ships keep coming and going. The city has grown since we were here. Wrote a long time. Tried to fish but got chilled.

Sun., Jan. 24
Corpus Christi

A little warmer but with a drizzle and the north wind still blowing. Felt rotten but tried to work. Went fishing but with no luck. In the late afternoon began to shake with a chill, followed by a fever. It passed about ten.

Mon., Jan. 25
Corpus Christi

Quite ill all day. Have caught a terrific cold. The weather remains quite cold and rainy. My fever, however, went and didn't come back. But I was weak and shaky all day and didn't venture out of the house. Read Brothers Karamazov.

Tues., Jan. 26
Corpus Christi

Felt a good deal better but the cold has left me with a painful neuralgia in the hips. The weather, however, cleared.

I could not, however, work. E caught the 1st fish, a flounder—and we ate it.

Wed., Jan. 27
Corpus Christi

Still dark and rainy and my cough no better, weakening me so I can't work. Sitting all day by the fire and reading Karamazov.

Thurs., Jan. 28
Corpus Christi

A bad day after a bad night. Again I could not work because of illness. Went to a doctor. No good. I had slept badly, a night of coughing and of absurd dreams. E and I fished and I caught a trout. I kept reading Karamazov. We got the car cleaned and polished.

Fri., Jan. 29
Corpus

Still no sunshine and prediction that the dark gloomy weather may go on for another month. My cough still racks me. Have been gloomy and unable to make progress in work.

Sat., Jan. 30
Corpus

A little better and able to go out for a walk. Did a little work. We took a walk on the jetty . . . the sky and the sea still grey. Vast floods in the Middlewest.

Sun., Jan. 31
Corpus

Indoors all day. A heavy fog so that the sea was lost in it—the fog turning to rain. My cold some better—a little work.

Mon., Feb. 1
Corpus Christi

Money came from Mary, also a long letter, with medicine from Henry[8] which I began taking and which at once relieved me.

It again turned cold, again what they call "a Norther" down here, bitter cold wind from the North. Was compelled to stay in the house most of the day.

Tues., Feb. 2
Corpus

The bad weather persists, and E is now half-ill, with cold and a sore throat. The day was overcast and biting cold, warming toward evening into a drizzle of rain. Went to walk—the tourist town like a county fairground at the end of the fair, people running shivering along—all gaiety gone.

Stayed at home, tried to work, read Brooks' Emerson[9] and played cards with E. Dined at Mexican restaurant.

Wed., Feb. 3
Corpus

The persistent cold and grey goes on. Went to the inner basin where some hardy fishermen stood in the water catching trout. The gulls and pelicans fought with the fishers for the catches and I saw a trout, dragged by the strong arm of a fisherman out of the very stomach of a pelican. It seems the pelican swallows a fish whole.

E half ill—the flu raging through this town. The work going very slowly and painfully.

Thurs., Feb. 4
Corpus Christi

[no entry][10]

Fri., Feb. 5
Corpus

I had a night of distress—much as before my other bad illness at home . . . cramps and misery all night. It is still dark and overcast. I had, yesterday, an attack of something like flu but tried to down it by eating and drinking.

Sat., Feb. 6
Corpus

Quite miserable all day. Marc, Lucille and Elma were to arrive. A wire said they were to be delayed a day. I laid about groaning all day and always hoping it would pass. Now that I am ill, glorious sunshiny weather has come here.

Sun., Feb. 7
Corpus

Awoke in the most terrible pain I was ever in. Thought I would die. Cramps doubled me. E much alarmed and ran to Oldfield. We decided to call a Dr. [Jerome] Nast. I was convinced this time I had appendicitis sure. The Dr. came and fortunately said "No." He gave me something to ease the pain a little and E gave me enema. Had to use dish pan. A horrible day.

Mon., Feb. 8
Corpus

Marc, Lucille, and Elma arrived last night, myself ill in bed, attended by Dr. Nast, a Jew and surgeon. He has a reputation of operating everyone and why not me, don't know. He had a sudden impulse to be honest. Eleanor, Marc, Lucille, and Elma all hate him. He keeps saying, "Could he be operated?" He says it is but a bad case intestinal flu, of which there is much here. I was all day in great misery and with fever. The day beautiful. E much upset and alarmed about me.

Tues., Feb. 9
Corpus

The crowd from New Orleans went all day out into the bay on a boat "the Ann" to fish. Marc a dyspeptic and full of ideas about me. E has the idea of having Henry come down. The day beautiful. I could eat nothing. The doctor came twice. E wanted a consultation of doctors but I would not have it. The day passed in great misery.

Wed., Feb. 10
Corpus

Suddenly decided, on advice of doctor, to go to hospital. Marc drove me there. Catholic hospital, run by "Sisters." E still suspicious of doctor that he plans, suddenly, to operate me. She much distracted.

The doctor, Lucille, and Elma, all Jews and all suspicious of each other. In room, at hospital with oil well driller, Rush Weatherby, recovering from operation. Vomiting all day but much interested in man. We talked all day.

Thurs., Feb. 11
Corpus

Still very ill. The hospital well run. After all the doctor not so bad, just self-conscious and blustery. E went to librarian to find out about doctors and it came out that I am a famous man, etc. Doctor impressed.

All day I kept getting tales of the oil field from my fellow in the room. Still with fever and vomiting.

Fri., Feb. 12
Corpus

Could not keep anything on stomach and began taking glucose through the veins directly into blood channel, feedings of 3 gallons of the stuff a day. More tales of the oil field. Weatherby very intelligent and fine, keeps reading wild west stories, but little later he tells of himself wonderfully well and intelligently told. Fellow workers kept coming to see him. At night the nurses made us quit talking. Fair weather outside, the 1st since we have been here. E looking very tired and worn.

Sat., Feb. 13
Corpus

More feeding, through the blood channels. Still vomiting. One nurse, Thelma Landig, particulary fine. She is a large fine figure. These nurses wonderful, except night nurse who when tired, got mad at me because I got vomit on her uniform. This night got special night nurse I didn't like.

Growing more and more fond of worker in room. Very handsome, really gentle man. He talks wonderfully.

Sun., Feb. 14
Corpus

Weatherby, oil man, went home. He's poor, lives in auto trailer he built himself. The story of the oil fields and men a great one. Better. Marc, Lucille, and Elma left yesterday. Fever down. Got rid of night nurse I didn't like. The big, powerful Thelma a treasure.

Begin to get interested in hospital life, listening to sounds, people brought in, later out. Moved bed to watch entrance. Begin to be hopeful of quick recovery, but still occasional vomiting.

Mon., Feb. 15
Corpus

Was able to dictate a few letters to E. There has been an air smash, two men brought in who both died, within the hour. Dr. Goode, the intern, comes in to sit and talk. I still vomit occasionally and cannot eat. Dr.

Goode feeds me through the veins. Miss Landig has wonderful hands. All day I look forward to the rubbing she gives me at 5. I had a dream, a short story of the lumber camps I call "Bluebird." Have had my bed moved to see the street and people passing.

Tues., Feb. 16
Corpus

Although this is a Catholic institution, many of the nurses are not Catholic. There is a sister, a nurse, a kind of manager on each floor. There are 3 floors. The operating is on the 3rd. I am on the 2nd. Also up there babies are delivered.

I have got Dr. Goode in the mood of telling me of each case as it comes in. He is the intern. Often at night the sound of hammering. They build forms and racks for people with broken bones. There is a flip, pretty little woman helper named Florence. We have jokes about the urinal pan. It is shaped like a duck.

Wed., Feb. 17
Corpus

I found I could hold a little tea. Good. I was put in a wheeled chair and wheeled down the hall to see the sea. Was very weak and easily wearied. Miss Landig, of the hands, has her father in here. He was struck down in the street by a car and his hip broken. He must stay for months. Got a new nurse, for night, Miss Conrad, of Amarillo, Texas, a tall, silent and mouse-like woman. She does everything with infinite care and slowness. It makes the night pass to watch her.

Thurs., Feb. 18
Corpus

I sit up in bed and have tea, two or three times at night. I can eat oatmeal. I vomit no more but there is a great running off of the bowels. I walked a little today. At night, as I drink my tea I get Miss Conrad to talk of her home, on a big wheat farm in the Texas panhandle. She came from Norwalk, Ohio, as a child, to Texas. She tells me of the way of farming with great fields, use of the combine, plowing at night, the dust storms, etc.

Fri., Feb. 19
Corpus

I eat more, walk more, go to toilet. The doctor says I may perhaps leave tomorrow. I do not need Miss Conrad but she comes and I learn more of the wheat farms. E comes, always at dawn. She looks tired. Roger Sergel sent me $100 to help pay for the illness. I can hold a book and read. E reads aloud Boswell's "Journey to the Hebrides."[11]

Sat., Feb. 20
Corpus

I am permitted to leave at 1 p.m. I give Miss Landig a copy my "Kit." Her hands on my body have been marvelously curative. There is a woman at the point of death with pneumonia.

We drive to beach and I sit out in the warm sun. Mrs. Oldfield makes me eggnogs. It is a beautiful day. It is strange to be out.

I awoke at midnight in pain. E said, "Eat." I did and it cured me of the pain at once.

Sun., Feb. 21
Corpus

Eating, sleeping, walking about, a little, getting well fast.

I sleep a lot. We play cards.

There are two women here who are real fishermen. They put in every possible moment. One is young, red-haired and handsome, the other old and heavy. They have met here, founded their friendship on the fishing passion.

Wrote a long letter to Jim Boyd.

Mon., Feb. 22
Corpus

Stronger. The day started fair but ended with a strong cold wind. Fished but no luck.

Went for a drive to the oil fields, a wild, strange and terrible place. Men working in mud—the roar and scream of gas, escaping from earth's bowels, the heavy smells. There is the feeling of a vast disorder down below, men profiting by it at terrible risk. Everywhere grey mud and filthy sick smells. They light the escaping gas after conducting it high up in pipes. The dancing flames roar, night and day.

Tues., Feb. 23
Corpus

There is an old man who fishes from a boat and always catches great strings of fish. People follow him about the bay, anchor near him. They catch nothing.

The doctor talks of two things—surgery and getting rich via an oil well. I go to take shots, arsenic and iron. The town is in a great boom of cheap housing and oil.

Yesterday was fair and warm, with big drifting white clouds. Fished but caught nothing. Am in the dragged out stage of the disease. Wrote some letters. Finished reading Brooks' Emerson. In some way it never comes to a flesh and blood man.

Wed., Feb. 24
Corpus

There is a boy here—about 14—with hair like dry grass. He is always running in, declaring that a great fish has torn the line out of his hands.

I get better daily.

The town here has become a boom town, people crowding in, no rooms to be had. All are to get rich in oil. There are many houses going up, a crazy patchwork, no plan. It is a chance to see, in the raw, how American towns and cities have grown.

Thurs., Feb. 25
Corpus

A very cold raw day, with sun in the afternoon. To the doctor, for a shot. I dictated to E, telling the story of my brother Earl. Strength comes back slowly. In this cold the long pier before our little house, usually filled with fishermen, is quite empty. The town here is on the boom, many ships in the harbor, new oil wells opened every few days. Went for a walk with E but found myself still weak. The ships lying close together in the rather small harbor make a lovely sight.

Fri., Feb. 26
Corpus

Have been unable to find Weatherby, the oil driller, who is recuperating in the cafes. A blustering cold southwest wind came up, spoiling a lovely day. I go daily to Dr. Nast to get shots, arsenic and iron.

Had a steno in and tried to work but she was no good. Hoped to get at the Winesburg introduction. She was a raw and rather ignorant Jewish girl.

Read Peattie on the great naturalists—book called "Green Laurels."[12]

Sat., Feb. 27
Corpus

All day yesterday a heavy rain. I took a walk but could only go a few blocks, finding myself still weak. Had a steno in to catch up mail but she proved ignorant, vocabulary of 50 words, a rather brazen, really pitiful Jewish girl.

Doctor here also a Jew and very self-conscious and uncertain of himself. Had to practically rewrite all her letters.

I began an attempt to dictate the introduction to the book of plays, dictating to E, who takes it in long hand faster than most stenographers.[13] Did get my mail cleaned up and a few hundred words of the introduction down. Played cards with E (rummy) and was amused at myself. I found I became irritable and even ugly when I lost a game.

Sun., Feb. 28
Corpus

Dictated—the introduction to book of plays to E. Went for the longest walk yet, 1-1/2 miles, weak and weary when I got home. Bright sun, but cold.

Mon., March 1
Corpus

Feeling much stronger and worked. Took Dr. Nast a signed copy of Kit. He was pleased. Fished for a time but no luck. Walked and found myself not tiring so much. Got books at the library and read of Andrew Jackson, as soldier and pioneer: "Border Captain."[14] Day fair and growing warmer.

Tues., March 2
Corpus

Went to a place called "Flour Bluff"—from some white, flour-like hills, to a little fishing village. Got a boat there. E, a boy named Billy and Weatherby, the oil well driller. We got a boat and went out. Caught many fish but most of them the poisonous sea catfish. Stayed all afternoon and dined at home on sand trout and whiting. Drank an eggnog and had a severe headache but finally slept. Worked, in the morning, dictating to E.

Wed., March 3
Corpus Christi

I had written to Dr. Nast about his bill, which I thought too high. Went to him and he promised to reduce it.

Went to see Weatherby, the oil well driller who was ill again. He, with wife and child living in a trailer without wheels. Bought his wife thermometer and hot water bag.

Went fishing in the bay, in the boat "Ann" and hooked two huge drums. Lost one but, after 45 minutes landed the other on an 18 pound proof silk line. He weighed 55 pounds.

Thurs., March 4
Corpus

In the morning to work and then on the boat "Ann" in the rain. Several big western farmers, with their families. One, an Illinois man, kidding the others about Hoover. Hooked another huge drum that fought me for 45 minutes but I wore him out. Worked again, with E, dictating for the introduction.

Fri., March 5
Corpus

A high wind with rain. Dictated—writer stuff—and settled with doctor. Got him down from $125.00 to $75.00. We got packed to leave in the morning. Read Andrew Jackson and Madam Countess du Barry's Memoirs.

Sat., March 6
Galveston, Texas

The day spent driving from Corpus. Paid the doctor $75.00. We left Corpus at 10:30 and got to Galveston—250 miles—at 5 p.m. Drove most of the way and was much stronger, standing the drive well. No work.

Sun., March 7
Franklin, La.

Up early, at Galveston but had to wait nearly an hour for ferry. Came coast road to Orange, a beautiful day and fine drive—275 miles Galveston to here. Stayed at a very clean little frame hotel. Made tea with leaves in the room. The open air and driving are building me up.

Mon., March 8
New Orleans

Drove leisurely from Franklin to New Orleans—the country all different, after entering Louisiana. More Negro life, big sugar farms. Houses unpainted but with a kind of decayed loveliness. It was a warm soft spring day and most of the way we drove beside bayous.

We stayed for the night at Elma's and I took something to make me sleep, which I did heavily.

Tues., March 9
New Orleans

Lunch with Jimmy and Julius—dinner at Julius's house. Left Elma's and went to Buena Vista Hotel. Roger and Ruth arrived in evening.[15]

Stayed too long, talking at Julius's. Excited and couldn't sleep. Roger and Ruth came in apartment and we talked until 1 a.m. Finally asleep at 3 a.m.

Pursued by Pat O'Donnell.[16] He is interested in nothing on earth but Pat. Many of these young writers are simply impossible as human beings. Will have to be rude to be rid of him and after rudeness will suffer from remorse.

Wed., March 10
New Orleans

Too seedy to work, after the sleepless night. To lunch with Roger, Jimmy and Julius and then to walk, with Roger, through the French Quarter and by the river. The riverbank full.

To bed and dined with Roger and Ruth and to see the puppets. Thought them rather too childish and went home and to bed at nine.

Thurs., March 11
New Orleans

To lunch with Jimmy and Julius after working on the Burt Emmett.[17] We went to Jimmy's house, where we lit into him about his attitude, expecting a publisher to risk on their books. He was really pleased.

Went to dine with Marc and Lucille, after calling on Doris Stone, the anthropologist, and looking at her Aztec stuff.[18]

To Group Theatre to see "Love on the Dole," with Dorothy Feibleman. Very good. Some of the minor parts well done.[19]

Fri., March 12
New Orleans

Roger very sad and subdued. I dictated 1st draft of article on Burton Emmett. Took Roger for a drive, going uptown and crossing river at Jackson Avenue. River very high.

Down river and recrossed at Canal. Lunch at Arnaud's. Drove for 2 hours. Went to Lucille and then Jimmy for dinner. Roark Bradford, become big financier. Stribling a gentle small town preacher.[20] No sleep.

Sat., March 13
Brewton, Ala.

Breakfasted at Marc's. Roger and Ruth present and left at 9. Had not slept and was rocky. The out of doors and being away from so many people and impressions rested me.

The day was beautiful. In Mobile at 1:30 where we lunched. Drove on to this place, arriving at 4. Rather grimy hotel. Put car in garage where the man (not connected with hotel) would take no pay. Amazing man.

Sun., March 14
Atlanta, Ga.
Winecoff [Hotel]

Home of the "Gone with the Wind" lady. Alternate sunshine and showers. Road treacherous. I drove most of the way. Pretty tired, as Sunday driving annoying. We lunched at Auburn, Alabama—college town. My legs still rubbery, from flu.

The whole day spent in the cotton country—small and miserable shacks, often without windows and all unpainted. A great many Negroes, in cheap but gaily-colored clothes, in the road.

Mon., March 15
Atlanta

Bitter cold—the coldest day I've seen this winter and with a howling wind. I feel like a spoiled cheese.

Tried to walk but was too much buffeted by the wind. Dictated to E and read a life of Heine.[21] On these days, confined to my room, I smoke too much.

Tues., March 16
Atlanta

Dictated to a stenographer, got in, but quite miserable all day. Went, in the afternoon to the public library where I read the diary of Fanny Kemble.[22] Had E and Mildred Esgar[23] to dinner with wine and then to bed to read Alexander the Great's life.

Wed., March 17
Atlanta

A dull rainy day but I had a stenographer in and dictated well. The sky had cleared and it had grown warmer.

I went to an osteopath, a curious talkative fellow, who as he rubbed told me of a marvelous new electrical machine for diagnosing diseases and of his own life and deeds.

Thurs., March 18
Atlanta

To the doctor for a rub. He got to talking of himself and gave me a 2 hour treatment. Went with McGee, of Constitution to see the government housing project here—a very beautiful place—really new modern homes for some 1800 people at very low rent. We went through one of the apartments and found it most inviting. Had a talk on the phone with Margaret Mitchell, the $1,000,000 book woman.

Fri., March 19
Knoxville

To Chattanooga—from Atlanta—where I saw Julian Harris. Went with him to his house. Understand he is getting $25,000 a year as editor of the Chattanooga Times, belonging to Adolf Ochs.[24] He is still good fun but his whole attitude seems to me to have changed . . . much more conservative—anti newspapermen's Guild—rather platitudinous. Two grand young newspaper men present. Clements and another, Melvin.

Sat., March 20
Marion

A delightful drive, from Knoxville. At Knoxville we spent the evening at the house of John Moutoux, a reporter for the News-Sentinel and he told of the possibilities of a Guild strike there.

It was a beautiful sunny spring day and we drove via the mountain town, Gate City, where, in the State Store, I renewed my liquor supply.

Sun., March 21
Marion

Another lovely day. I spent Saturday evening in Funk's workroom. He has bought himself an elaborate woodworking outfit.

On Sunday John came over and he, Bob and I took a long walk, Bob very self-conscious. He talked continually of his triumphs and of his plans and ambitions in politics. He and I again went to Funk's workshop in the evening.

Mon., March 22
Marion

Made the 1st draft of the radio play, on textiles.[25] Bob came wanting me to do a piece on the small town. It was again a very beautiful day and I drove to the farm.

John had done a lot of work and among other things a painting of a little mountain girl I thought very beautiful. Talked over farm plans with John Sullivan.

Tues., March 23
Marion

E left for Nashville at 4—to be gone until Saturday. It was again a beautiful sunshiny spring day. I wrote a thing for Bob's paper and caught up with correspondence. The house seemed empty and dead with E gone and I was restless. After E left I drove, visiting several of the surrounding hills. There is a lovely view from Cemetery Hill.

In the evening went to Funk's workshop and helped him build a cabinet.

Wed., March 24
Marion

Dictated another draft—the radio play. Went to Ripshin but got caught there in a spring rain, the road from Ripshin to Troutdale very cheesy. In the evening to Funk's where we made the 1st drawing off of our wine. I should have about 25 gallons.

We were through at 9. Bob Williams came and we went up into his shop and talked until 11.

Thurs., March 25
Marion

Rather low. Miss E. Do not feel so good—result of working in Funk's damp cellar and tramping about in the rain, at Ripshin.

There was a dust storm. I worked in the morning—on the book of plays and then went, with Funk, to see a farm in Cleghorn Valley. He was to loan the man money. Still felt seedy so to bed right after dinner. Read a book of spies, of all countries.

Fri., March 26
Marion

To Johnson City, to get my eyes remeasured. The new glasses cost me $19, besides the doctor bill.

Went with Funk, to Gordon's furniture plant and was much upset. He is making rather cheap imitations of old hand furniture. It made me ill to see so many men at work, making second rate stuff.[26]

The whole experience gave me a queer physical setback.

Sat., March 27
Marion

It turned very cold. E arrived at 4 from Nashville, by train. We got into an argument about John Cronk, myself too annoyed by his big talk. I exploded. Think it was because it brought back all my days in an advertising office and so many absurd big talkers heard spouting there.

Sun., March 28
Marion

To Bob's, to dine, where I found him much nicer and less about himself. He is better when with Mary. The baby very fat and lovely.

E and I to walk in the park. Very cold. A stray cat followed us, coming out of an empty farm house. We brought it home.

Spent the evening discussing God and the Church with Mother.

Mon., March 29
Marion

Finished off the radio play. E and I drove to Ripshin and then on to Grant, to Mrs. Hoffman, to see about getting in on the government allowance of lime and then to order lime. I had the road design, by John, framed—a beautiful painting. Went to Funk in the evening but could not sleep later so got up and drank beer and ate cheese. Turned E a potato masher.

Tues., March 30
On Train

On train, bound for New York. E left for Louisville, Chicago and Des Moines at 4 and I at 9:44. John came from Ripshin. Mr. Copenhaver was planning his garden. At 4:30 I took Mrs. Copenhaver to the hospital where she engaged in a grand buying spree. She bought great quantities of clothes.

Got manuscript of the plays off to Scribner's.[27]

Wed., March 31
New York—54

Arrived in New York at 12 and went direct to 54.[28] Brought with me a painting by John. Lunched in a nearby bar.

Mary came in and we talked. She has made big strides in getting command of herself. Worked in late afternoon. Dined with the Millers and sat talking until 11.

Thurs., April 1
New York—54

Had a new woman stenographer in and succeeded in dictating a good deal to her. Took John's painting up to Stieglitz. He said fine things of it. Walked with Paul.

Dined with Elmer Adler, Eddie and Alice [Wolf], and Mary. A good time. Came home to hear discussions on the radio.

Fri., April 2
New York

Had a good morning of dictating. The day began with rain but presently cleared. Went in the p.m. to Max [Perkins] and we drank in the Waldorf bar.

Drunken army officer who wanted to talk.

Irish playmaker, looking for Tom Wolfe.

In the evening, with Mary, to see the Eastman film—Tsar to Lenin.[29]

Went to dine at the Red Barn. Home at 10:30 and to bed.

Sat., April 3
New York—54

Worked with stenographer. Went for a drive, with Mary. Triborough Bridge, very wonderful work.[30] It has a grand sweep. Saw the grounds for the New York World's Fair.[31]

Got back just in time to meet Dreiser—and his secretary. We dined at a small Italian place. Had good talk. Dreiser evidently not so rich. Fine, as usual.

Sun., April 4
New York

Stayed in the house all day. Cold and grey. Mary and I played cards. In the evening went to dine with Max Perkins and Tom Wolfe, at Cherio's—in 53rd St. We had good dinner and good drinks. Wolfe a huge man 6 ft 4— very alive and sensitive—too easily hurt. He is one of the few real ones.

Mon., April 5
New York

Intended to leave early tomorrow but Jap and Rose Schulman came. I had worked in the morning and gone to Miss Charles about the radio play.[32]

Jap, Rose, Mary and I sat talking and drinking. I took them, and the

Millers to dinner. We went to see the WPA play—Living Newspaper—Power.[33]

Very stirring—a great educational stunt—fine.

Tues., April 6
New York

No work—the day with Jap and Rose Schulman—to see Barrett Clark and Rockefeller Foundation. To see Marching Song[34]—with Joe Taulane and then to the 65th story of the Rockefeller Center to drink. Caught a cold.

Wed., April 7
Hedgerow

Caught a nasty cold at Jack Lawson play "Marching Song." All the Broadway and Hollywood tricks applied to a labor play.

With Jap and Rose to Hedgerow, by train, my nose running messily. To bed early.

Thurs., April 8
On train
to Marion

Bad head cold. Fasted yesterday. Jap and I talked of a play we might do together. Adrian took me to train. Spent most of the day talking with the Hedgerow players. Lived on citrus fruit. Everyone at Hedgerow excited by the Hershey riots.[35]

Fri., April 9
Marion

Cold about cured. Randolph home, bringing me a grand new winter overcoat, very swank. He looks fine and is fine—one of the most real sincere and honest people I know.[36] Bob up for dinner—as usual self-conscious. . . .[37] Elenore looking very lovely.

Sat., April 10
Marion

A cold windy day, with the town full of children, come in for the annual school contests.

Got back at the radio play. Took Mother and E into the country. In the evening played cards. Miss Fry came to work for me.[38]

Sun., April 11
Marion

Cold, with flurries of snow. John came over to dine. He will have to be operated for piles. Stayed in nearly all day. After several hours of work my nose flared up badly. Went to see Funk. Randolph talked of Japan and China.

Mon., April 12
Marion

A bright beautiful day and I went through the radio play again. Randolph, E, myself and the dog went to Ripshin. Everything lovely there. We planted fruit trees. The yard was filled with jonquils. In the evening we played cards.

Tues., April 13
Marion

Warm, with occasional spring showers. John came over. Is to be operated, for piles Friday, at Abingdon. Finished off the radio play. Bob came and talked of buying papers at Wytheville. In the evening went to Funk's workshop. Spring showers.

Wed., April 14
Marion

Worked and dictated all morning, back at the adventures. Mazie came. E drove with me in the rain to Ripshin. The rain grew worse and we found John in the ditch at Gordy Pierce's old place. Picked him up and got back into highway. It rained all evening.

Thurs., April 15
Marion

A beautiful spring day. Randolph and I took John to the hospital, at Abingdon and drove to Bristol for lunch. We went to the Tom Buchanan farm to see the champion sheep shearer at work. He used a system, brought into our west by shearers from South Africa. It was a thing very beautiful to see.

Fri., April 16
Marion

In the morning I went to Ripshin, to plant a weeping willow tree and then got E and we went to Abingdon. Met John coming out of the operating room. He seemed pretty cheerful. He had 4 hemorrhoids taken out. Bob and Bob Williams to dine on a big steak I had got. We played cards and I won all games.

Sat., April 17
Marion

The day bright and wonderful. John stood his operation O.K. Within a few hours the blossoms suddenly broke forth on the cherries. John will have to stay in hospital about 10 days.

Sun., April 18
Marion

Another lovely warm day. Took E, Bob and Bob Williams to see John. On the way back was given a ticket for bad driving. Passed a car too close to a hill and just then a road cop appeared. In the evening, Randolph and I to Funk's workshop. Much talk of bird dogs.

Mon., April 19
Marion

Worked in the morning. The day again lovely. Went with Randolph to see John at hospital and to see a man who had trained the dog Boy.

In the evening again to Funk's to turn a handle for chest and to take a walk before sleeping.

Tues., April 20
Marion

Again a fair day—occasional light showers. Dictated to E. Took a walk and talked to Margaret Fry about working for me this summer. Henry on the way but did not arrive until I had gone to bed. Went to Funk's and turned knobs for chest of drawers. Randolph had two army men guests for the night.

Wed., April 21
Marion

Dr. Henry[39] and I went to see John in hospital.

In the evening there was a family picnic, in a pavilion at the park. I was much shocked, as Mr. Copenhaver had brought his man, a gardener, who did not eat with us but sat off, like a dog alone. It brought back certain moments of my own life and spoiled the picnic.

Thurs., April 22
Washington

The day on the road, E, Randolph, Mr. Copenhaver and myself—a beautiful day with fruit trees everywhere blooming.

In Washington we went to a sea food place and then E, Mr. Copenhaver and myself to see the Good Earth—a picture technically almost perfect but the acting, I had heard much praised, pretty shallow and dead.[40]

Fri., April 23
Washington

Worked in the hotel room. Maverick, Feis, of the State Department, Herb Little and Marquis Childs. To lunch with Randolph and a brother army man.

Went with Childs and Little to drink. Dined with Little. Went to Pat Jackson. Saw a lot of people there. Slept in Marquis Childs' house.[41]

Sat., April 24
Media, Pa.

Drove from Washington to Media, stopping at Baltimore. Saw the most beautiful production of 12th Night I had ever seen. Harry and Katy were superb and Henry Jones did a fine Sir Andrew. Again I got the desire to write plays.

Sun., April 25
New York

We sat up, Mims, Jap, Ferd, E and I until 3 a.m., talking and drinking.

At noon we went to Esherick's where we dined, driving on to New York by the back way—the road very crowded. The Eshericks as usual, Wharton making some beautiful stuff for C. Bok.[42] E with Alice and Eddie, to see Richard 2nd[43] while I went with Mary to see some wonderful song books of the Civil War.

Mon., April 26
New York—54

A cold raw day. I slept late and then wrote a lot. I ran about doing small errands. E had not slept and, after dinner, at the house, I made her go to bed while I played cards with Mary. Nothing very vital happened. The spring is badly delayed here.

Tues., April 27
New York

A cold day with a drizzle of rain. I wrote fairly well, then went out, to walk about and to the circus.[44] It was in Madison Square Garden and very gaudy, with a lot of remarkable feats . . . the most remarkable, a man shot from a cannon.

There is a nice little dancer in the performers. Mary was ill with cold when I got home.

Wed., April 28
New York

Had a new stenographer, very handsome, named Miss Bay. Dictated until 12:30. Mary ill. I went to see the Giants play Brooklyn, Mungo pitching. It was 3 to 2 Mungo.[45]

In the evening E and I dined at Ticino's and saw Frank Blum, looking very nervous and self-conscious.[46]

Played cards with Mary until bedtime.

Thurs., April 29
New York

Again working with Miss Bay and then to see the Giants whip Brooklyn. A bright warm day. Mary still ill, with a sore throat.

In the evening with Joe and Ann [Girsdansky] to dine at a Swedish restaurant. We went later to a cabaret, very dull, tall dull women throwing their fannies about. E was particularly lovely. Joe and Ann suspicious of each other.

Fri., April 30
New York

Dictated in the morning. It was a clear fine day. Went to 2nd-hand book stores.

Went to see Catherine Cornell in Candida.[47] It was a good performance. Stayed at home in the evening and to bed early.

Sat., May 1
Hedgerow

Got up at 9:30 and at 11 set out for Hedgerow. Got there at 3. Sat drinking with Jap and Joe Taulane. Saw the play, Noah—Jap leading.[48] Fine job. Sat talking with Ferd, Jap and Joe, until 1 a.m.

Sun., May 2
Hedgerow

Slept until noon. My nose was bad. Sat all afternoon, watching rehearsal of the play "Round Table."[49] They did dress rehearsal in the evening. Very charming play. Katy had a hard struggle with her part.

Mon., May 3
New York

Left the inn, at Media, after an uncomfortable night of coughing. Took Harry Sheppard and wife to Philadelphia. Drove to New York in a half daze. It was very warm, a clear bright day of blossoms. Walked about with E and to bed early. Mary in grand form, preparing for her big party.

Tues., May 4
New York

Spent the day, after a morning of dictation, in small errands. Mary preparing for a big party. It was a hot, almost midsummer day. Went with E to Knox factory store, where I got shirts, ties, and socks.[50] As usual got much more than E, who got a hat. Got new shoes. Went with E to Cafe Royal where we had a conversation with a Yiddish poet.

Wed., May 5
New York

I did not work. Karl came in and we went to see the Giants defeated by the Cincinnati team. In the evening Mary had her big stowaway party, some 50 or 60 people and a great flood of food and drink. I found them a very mellow fine crowd. I drank too much.

Thurs., May 6
New York

The house a wreck from the party. Went down into Nassau Street to Chase Bank and got money from Russia.[51] Went to see Moe, for John.[52] Had lunch with E in sidewalk cafe. It rained. Went to talk with a German man, about Winesburg.

Went to see Maurice Evans in Richard II, very absorbing—beautifully staged.

Fri., May 7
New York

Dictated on the big book. I went to lunch with Tom Smith and saw Jim Rorty and Ernest Boyd. Saw Posselt—the German about a production of Winesburg.[53] Went to have a drink with Max Perkins.

Sat., May 8
Aurora, N.Y.

Spent the day driving to Aurora, New York, through the Catskills. Beautiful day. Saw a lovely production of Oedipus Rex, by the students. Saw Lankes and Galantière. Sat up late drinking and talking.[54]

Sun., May 9
New York

Had a big breakfast party with a professor of the Economics dept. and his wife. Whitaker, the architect, there.[55] Grand talk. Left at 12 and drove 300 miles to New York, through heavy traffic. A big day. Very tired.

Mon., May 10
New York

I worked until 1 and then went to Brooklyn, to see Brooklyn play St. Louis—Van Mungo pitching. He pitched a beautiful game.

In the evening went with Paul and E to dine and then to Paul's house, where I attacked New England.

Tues., May 11
New York—54

Dictated—not too well I thought. Went to lunch with Jim Rorty—a clever man but I feel not rich. Went from him to get my hair done and then home, to play cards with Mary.

Went for cocktails to Elmer Adler and in the evening to see the play "Tobias and the Angel," by James Bridie, at the Provincetown.

Wed., May 12
New York—54

Working all morning on the long book. I went to see Brooklyn play the Pirates—a good game, Brooklyn winning.[56]

In the evening a big party at the house and I had to make a short speech. It was a party given for young artists.

Thurs., May 13
New York—54

A dark cloudy day. Miss Bay came and I dictated until noon. I took Elma [Godchaux] to lunch and she told me her marriage experience.

Went to see Carl Hubbell of the Giants win his 21st straight victory, against Pittsburgh.[57] In the evening went to dine alone at Cafe Royal and home, in the rain, to bed. Mary gone to the farm.

Fri., May 14
New York

Worked all morning and then to lunch with Ernest Boyd—talking until 4. Home to play cards with Mary until 6. Went to dinner with Posselt and Drake to talk of possible plays and sat until 10.

It rained all day and evening.

Sat., May 15
New York—54

Good work on book. Went to double header, Giants and Phillys. Had Elma Godchaux, Joe and Ann to dinner. Got into a fight about going to town—ugly with E—determined, silly. Eddie had to go to hospital and Mary spent the night with Alice.

Sun., May 16
New York—54

Mary busy all day about Alice and Eddie. Worked all morning and until 3. Went with E to walk on the east side.

Went to the Morosco, walking up, to see a show called Penny Wise— very silly and second-rate show.[58]

Mon., May 17
New York—54

It was a bad foggy day and no work done. I felt heavy and no good . . . tried to work but failed. I loafed about, went into bars. Mary came and we played cards. I was stupid.

We went to dine at Ann Morgans and Mary bought champagne. It did no good. I went to bed and slept heavily.

Tues., May 18
New York—54

Stupid day . . . work no good. I finally went off to watch the Yanks play Chicago and saw a young Georgian—named [Spurgeon] Chandler shut out the Sox—Ted Lyons pitching.

Came home, played cards with Mary, took E to dine at a little Italian place on Houston Street and to bed. Very dull day.

Wed., May 19
New York—54

Destroyed a lot I had done and felt better. Worked a little. It rained. Went uptown and to a theatre to see the coronation pictures. In the evening John Cournos and wife, Carl Randau, Leane Zugsmith and Lewis Galantière to dine. Good talk until after midnight.

Thurs., May 20
New York—54

Worked but uncertain. Went to Dr. Treves—wife old friend of Maurice.[59] Went first to lunch with Leane and Mary Vorse—Mary telling of life among the sit-downers. Rather low in spirit. The day cloudy and rather cold.

Fri., May 21
New York—54

The cloud over my mind seems to have lifted again. Lankes came, a rather silent [man], awkward but fine mind. I had dropped the book temporarily and was trying to do the story of the delegation. Lankes and I went off to see a fine ball game, St. Louis Browns and Yanks and Yanks won tight game 11 innings.

Evening in the house.

Sat., May 22
New York—54

Lankes in town. I worked well, on the thing called "The Delegation,"[60] letting the book go for the time. Am in a jam on it. It was very hot.

Went to Tom Smith for cocktails and then to Cafe Royal to dine—Mary, Lankes, and E. Pretty girl came to table—also old man who had written book on Mars.

Sun., May 23
New York—54

Slept quite late and didn't work. Went with Lankes, Mary Vorse, Mary and E to Nyack and to call on Jean Mouquin. Saw her rock garden. Sat on porch during a rain and drank fine wine. Mary went off to dine and Paul, Lankes and I to see the play Tovarich, with Marta Abba and John Halliday, great fun.[61] It was a benefit performance.

Mon., May 24
New York—54

Worked in the morning and then to the stadium, to see the Yanks and Cleveland, a bad defeat for Cleveland. Sat in the bleachers. In the evening Lankes brought a sculptor, whose name I didn't get and we dined. Went to bed early.

Tues., May 25
New York—54

Worked and in the afternoon went to see Yanks and Detroit Tigers. Good game but Mickey Cochrane badly hurt by pitched ball.[62] Sat in a box. It was a beautiful day. Lankes had left.

In the evening Paris newspaper man, Edmonds, came to dine. Went with Sol Greear to see the dancer [Helen] Tamiris. Very beautiful. Did not sleep well.

Wed., May 26
New York—54

Feeling rotten. Worked a little. Got my new white trousers from tailor. Got box cigars for Eddie. In the late afternoon, with Mary and E to Throckmorton's . . . then to restaurant where we met Mary Vorse and Charles and Adelaide Walker . . . Adelaide very lovely.[63] Got news from Bob and had to put up four hundred to save paper for Russell and Mimi.[64]

Thurs., May 27
New York—54

Beginning to pack to get off. Went to lunch with E and the Cournos—Longchamps.[65] Did small errands.

Very hot and damp. In the evening, Farrell and Miss Alden, Max [Eastman] and Eliena, Paul [Rosenfeld] and Mildred [Esgar] to dinner—a really beautiful dinner party. There was a lot of talk of the artists and of Trotsky, etc. but the evening really fun.[66]

Fri., May 28
New York—54

A wet gloomy day. Wanted to see Phillys play Yanks but no game. Played cards with Mary.

In the evening dined Ashley and Ethel [Miller], E, Mary and I. Played cards again. I came out ahead.

Sat., May 29
Media, Pa.

Bad time getting away from New York. Battery dead. Roads very hot and crowded. Got to Hedgerow at 6:30. Saw St. Joan—not so good. Sat drinking with the players until 1.

Sun., May 30
Salem, Va.

Got up at 9:30 and took E to a breakfast at Bryn Mawr.[67] Went for my own breakfast. Left for home at 11:30. Roads again crowded. Dined at Lexington and drove on to Salem for the night. Very tired.

Mon., May 31
Marion

Drove from Salem, arriving at Marion at 12:30. All OK there. Went to see Bob about Mimi check. Nothing certain yet. Prepared to get at cleaning and opening Ripshin in the morning.

Tues., June 1
Ripshin

Took colored man and wife to Ripshin and spent the day cleaning. John has decided to stay for the summer. The house in terrific disorder. Went to Marion at 5:30 and played cards in the evening.

Wed., June 2
Ripshin

Red Book turned down Brother Death, saying it was very beautiful but too sad.[68] There was a sprinkle of rain. We spent most of the day in house cleaning. John is to have a woman for the summer. Ripshin is beautiful. Dictated speech for Colorado State College.[69]

Thurs., June 3
Ripshin

N. B. Fagin came, unexpectedly, from Baltimore. He is going to teach in the Bryn Mawr summer school.

E and I drove to a place called Milton, in North Carolina to try to get a cook but her father and mother were ill. We got caught in a heavy rain. John Sullivan and I set a bed of zinnias, I got from Joe Wyse.

Fri., June 4
Ripshin

Got word Mimi will not need the $400 now so the summer is safe. We are going to try to get through with Ruby.[70] Fagin left, right after breakfast. He is a rather pathetic little Jewish man. I did a piece for Canadian Forum.[71] E went off to town. John cut hay. It kept threatening rain but the rain didn't come. [Margaret] Fry worked on the 3 stories.

Sat., June 5
Ripshin

I got the Colorado speech ready. Copped a lot of it out of Notebook. No one has read it. Got the cabin in fine shape and tacked the new blue oil cloth on the kitchen shelf. Am full of work but there are, just now, too many facets. Will have to hold myself down. Fry satisfactory. Rain threatened but didn't come.

Sun., June 6
Ripshin

Slept late. Bob was disappointed that we did not come to his bathing beauty show. E went to Marion. Fry copied stories for Red Book.

I finished speech for State College, Colorado, and worked on the writer's conference stuff.[72] In the evening, Fry, John, E and I played cards. It was a day of constant threats but no rain.

Mon., June 7
Ripshin

Dictated part of the 1st of the Colorado speeches. Went to town and did a lot of shopping. I had caught a slight cold. Came home to find a heavy rain had fallen. Got proofs to a part of the book of plays. To bed early . . . a good deal of coughing.

Tues., June 8
Ripshin

Great clouds coming and going, all day. I worked on one of the Colorado speeches. I felt pretty seedy from the cold. In the afternoon, E having gone off to town, I spent the time tying up my grapes. In the evening it rained. I beat John 4 games before the rain came.

Wed., June 9
Ripshin

Ferdinand Schevill and Mary Emmett arrived. Mary had an accident, her car loose on the mountain. Ferdinand in fine form. Read proof and worked on speeches.

Rain.

Thurs., June 10
Ripshin

E went off early to Marion. Mary worked in garden. I spent the morning in the cabin at work. Got off a lot of letters. John is fixing up the green house for his love.[73] Had a good round of croquet. A night of rain.

Fri., June 11
Ripshin

Morning at work, bright and clear. Everything is growing riotously. The calf got into a hornet's nest. Ferdinand and I went off to town. I was tired and played a bum game of croquet. The day went off beautifully.

Sat., June 12
Ripshin

A fine sunny day so that we got our hay cured and in. I worked in the morning and Ferdinand and I went to walk along the creek, finding a fine pool where we bathed. The oats look fine. Mary got coal oil all over the house in trying to fill the heater. Bob and Mary came to dine and we had ham in milk. We sat telling tales of my family until 11.

Sun., June 13
Ripshin

It was the day of the big June at St. Clair Bottom and Ruby and Rose went off to it. We all drove to Marion, to dine with Mother. A young boy showed movies of the college girls at Ripshin.[74] We came home to find 3 Washington friends of John, who stayed to supper. A beautiful day.

Sherwood Anderson with his wife's family in 1937. Left to right:
Mary Emmett, Eleanor Anderson, Katharine Van Meier, Eleanor
Wilson, May Scherer, Sherwood Anderson, Randolph
Copenhaver, Laura Lu Copenhaver, Mazie Wilson, B. E.
Copenhaver, and Channing Wilson.
(Trustees of the Sherwood Anderson Literary Estate.)

Mon., June 14
Ripshin

Bright warm day. I went to sawmill and ordered material to make over the tent houses.[75] Got back to the novel.[76] It was fun to work on it. Mary, Ferdinand and I went for a walk, also to the sawmill, to see the men at work. They are working up half-grown trees—shameful.

We had a fine evening of croquet and cards but later my head got full of ideas and I didn't sleep.

Tues., June 15
Ripshin

A day of rain. We were to have a picnic, on Flat Ridge but the rain stopped it. The man, with the bloody head, on the top of Iron Mountain had been fighting with his brother. E took Ruby and Charlotte [Sullivan] to a movie, in Marion. The road was so slick that I went to Troutdale and sat in the garage to drive them home.

Wed., June 16
Ripshin

A long day of rain, after a sunshiny early morning. John brought his woman friend, a Mrs. Jubell. She seems intelligent and charming. She has a little daughter of eight, not very healthy.

Ferdinand's nephew, the son of the sculptor Karl Bitter, came.[77] E had gone to Marion with Ferdinand. Mother has not been well. It was a downpour and I had to go into Troutdale to drive them out. Bob and Mary came for the evening. Bob entertained us with tales of mountain crime.

Thurs., June 17
Ripshin

The dark rainy days continue. Mary Emmett is making a great play with the flower beds, reconstructing them, getting peat moss from the woods, sand, manure, earth. Ferdinand and his nephew left in the rain. I worked on the novel.

Fri., June 18
Ripshin

Showers and sunshine. . . .[78] The wild strawberries are huge. I went to town for my teeth and a haircut. Had to get new battery for my car.

Cornelia is coming, to visit Bob and Mary.[79] Mother and Aunt May
have both been ill but they are both better. Mary is making flower beds.

Sat., June 19
Ripshin

Herbert Little, and his wife, Ruby Black came from Washington for the
weekend.[80] There was much talk of Washington and the Roosevelts. It
was a bright clear warm day. Mary suddenly made up her mind to drive
off to the Wolfs.[81] Cornelia was in Marion and John went off with Mrs.
Jubell. Worked on Green Grass.

Sun., June 20
Ripshin

A warm pleasant day. I did no work. In the morning we were all lying in
the sun, in the garden, listening to Herb Little and Ruby Black talk of
Washington political life. Dave Greear and Bob Williams came.

At 3 we drove off to Marion, to see the park and have tea at Mother's,
Aunt May getting it up. We drove home later in the early evening by the
old road, in the moonlight. E very lovely, all day.

Mon., June 21
Ripshin

E preparing to get off to her conference of industrial girls.[82] She went to
Marion. She got the car tuned up. I had to buy new batteries for the car
and a tire for the truck. I won my 1st bout with Viking.[83] Herb and Ruby
left for Washington.

Tues., June 22
Ripshin

Sent story—Moonlight Walk—to agent. Finished story—Two Lovers.[84]

John Sullivan and I took the bull calf, in the truck to Mr. C. Got 100
lbs. sugar. Had tea and, later dinner with Eleanore Jubell. Good. Miss Fry
came and Ruby served. John and I drove to Troutdale to hear the Louis-
Braddock fight.[85] Mary Emmett didn't get back.

Wed., June 23
Ripshin

Advanced the novel. Finished the story, "The Two Lovers." Mary [Em-
mett] came. I hauled stones and hay with John. Mary tired and very nice

and quiet. Played with Eleanore Jubell and John. It was a fine clear, cloudless day.

Thurs., June 24
Ripshin

Big day of work, on the novel. Mary, Margaret Fry and I went off to town at 3. I had fixed it with Ruby to move Mary, upstairs, while we were gone. We did a lot of shopping, Mary and I each spending $5. We went to Wytheville to dine and get liquor, coming back to sit with Mother and B. E. until 9. Mary drove home, in the moonlight. She has brought us a new Aladdin lamp.

Fri., June 25
Ripshin

The house, with a queer empty feeling, with E away. Got $25 for use of fragment, in college textbook. The days still warm and clear. We had John, Eleanore and Ann to dine and help eat a thick steak I had got. I cooked it outdoors.

Mary keeps working in the garden. I think she a little worries the plants.

Sat., June 26
Ripshin

Hot dry clear day. Worked—Green Grass. Mary and I went to Marion, taking Worth Price and wife. They have a son Sherwood and a daughter Eleanor.

Got fertilizer. Went to Chilhowie for plants. No good. Mary arranged for Francis to come over and go over plumbing. The Fry went off afoot, with the Sullivan girls, to meeting, in Troutdale.

Sun., June 27
Ripshin

Got quite a long way with Green Grass. I am of an age when a man wakes up in the morning with a weight on his shoulders.

A good deal of thinking of Bob and his persistent pushing of himself. He may have got it from me.

Mary worked all day in the flowers. John [Sullivan] picked great quantities of cherries, which Ruby canned. The Jersey cow went on the rip for the bull.

Mon., June 28
Ripshin

Worked O.K. It was a big day of cherry picking and canning, John and Major in the trees with fat Rosy sitting on the ground eating falling cherries. I ran the pitting machine.

Mary worked all day at the hollyhocks. I went on with Green Grass. It seems to be coming O.K.

Tues., June 29
Ripshin

Still the cherry harvest. A dull cloudy day. Worked O.K. Went to town and got the gas stove. Missing E terribly. Orlie came out to fix the stove, Mary supervising.[86]

In the evening Dave came with his brother John and two young foresters.[87] They had been drinking and were very gay. They got John, the Fry and Jubell and went off to a country dance hall.

Wed., June 30
Ripshin

A day of showers. E is coming tomorrow. Mary keeps watering the flowers. She gave us a new gasoline stove and had a great time teaching Ruby how to run it. John Sullivan brought us two big pails of his big cherries. Bob has a new scheme to change form of his debt to John.[88] E will be here tomorrow evening and the house will be alive again.

Thurs., July 1
Ripshin

E arrived late at night, bringing Jean Brown. Mary left for Wisconsin. It was a beautiful day. I drove to Marion in the truck, in the p.m.

Fri., July 2
Ripshin

Cool—almost cold. I worked—Green Grass. Mowed lawn, worked in garden. Little Ann Jubell came and told me tales of life at home. We had new potatoes, out of the garden.

A friend of E's, Jean Brown, came. We played croquet and cards, in the evening. We are working out the corn, for the last time, before laying by.

Sat., July 3
Ripshin

A day busy with people. I worked, but ineffectually. The lane of rhododendrons is in full bloom. E went to town. Jerry Gordon came and also Russell and Mimi but without the kids. Jean Brown is here. Talk of the New World that has already begun to bore me unbearably.

Sun., July 4
Ripshin

A house filled with people. Jerry Gordon wanted to read his play to me but I got him sidetracked.[89] We all went for a swim, in the Fox pool. It was a very grey low-toned day. People just sat about and talked quietly. Went for the Sullivans to church and found Major, very drunk and leaning on his mother's arm. Ruby was crying.

Mon., July 5
Ripshin

Worked in the morning. The house got cleared out, Russell, Mimi and Jerry leaving. After working went to Marion, in a heavy rain and spent the night there. Had long talk with Funk and was relieved to talk again of human, rather than economic problems.

Tues., July 6
Ripshin

Very exciting day. E and mine's anniversary. Chambrun wrote that he had sent the check to Viking and had sold Moonlight Walk to Red Book for $750.

We are rebuilding the tenthouses and they are going to be fine. It was a day of showers and sunshine.

Wed., July 7
Ripshin

It was difficult to keep working on the novel with the building going on. Jean Brown left in the evening and Mary came back, bringing her car filled with flowering plants.

New Yorker turned down the story "The Lovers" and I sent it to Chambrun.

Thurs., July 8
Ripshin

Got the little tent house pretty much done. Mary had brought a lot of flowers to set out. It was the hottest day of the summer. I wrote for 2 hours but did not dictate. Went off in the truck, with Mary to Marion for lumber. Miss Fry off for the afternoon.

Fri., July 9
Ripshin

Mary half sick from lack of sleep. She however worked, all day, in the garden. Rain threatened all day but didn't come. We got in the bark for the houses. Wyse and his wife came to have dinner and John and Eleanore also came.

Sat., July 10
Ripshin

Rain all about but none on us. I did not work well. We just about finished up the 1st guest house. I drove the truck to town and brought home lumber and a new desk for E. In the evening Burt Dickinson came pretty drunk but infinitely amusing. John brought the portrait of Tressy [Sullivan]—which I want to buy.

Sun., July 11
Ripshin

Unable to work. Bob and Andy brought the new heifer. We all went to Marion to a tea party at Mother's. Bob, Andy and John got pretty high on moon. It threatened rain but none came. The house in disorder, for the plumbers.

Mon., July 12
Ripshin

The house in disorder, with the 3 plumbers getting a new and bigger main to the house. Mary doing it, as a present. Rain threatened all day but didn't come. I had a bad letdown and did nothing.

Tues., July 13
Ripshin

Lucille [Antony] and Elma Godchaux came. We got water back into the house in the evening. John and Major cut clover, in the upper field. Felt a bit better. Took the wine bottles to Marion, to be washed.

Wed., July 14
Ripshin

Got the hay cut. The plumbers finished at noon. Went again to Marion, to take the wine bottles to Funk. Marc [Antony] came. We sat in the evening and drank.

We began putting the bark on the 1st of the little guest houses.

Thurs., July 15
Ripshin

Too much talk of my success with women. It sickened me.

We about finished the 1st of the guest houses.

I did no real work. The novel is at a stop. Elma's talk of writing gets my goat.

We went on a big picnic and then to the Barter Theatre. I got upset about Porterfield[90] and jumped on Elenore.

Fri., July 16
Ripshin

No work. Took Marc into town, to shop—and we lunched at Mother's. The plumber's bill was $122.00. We all went to the Swan farm, where the Sullivan boys were cradling oats—very lovely. We had a swim in the pool. The night was lovely, with bright moonlight. We played croquet in the moonlight and sat up talking until midnight.

Sat., July 17
Ripshin

Preparing for trip, cleaning and packing. This was the day for bottling off the wine and I got 200 bottles. We had a big family picnic at the lake and I drove home in the truck with Elma, being nasty to her.

Sun., July 18
Ripshin

Mary left. We finished packing and preparing the house for Herb Little. We all went to Marion to spend the night. We went to dine at Bob Anderson's.

Mon., July 19
[Louisville]

Spent the night at Mother's—Marc and Lucille leaving for New York—Elma, E and I for Chicago. Drove, this day, to Louisville—the last

100 miles in a hill country and in a hard, driving rain. I drove all but 50 miles.

Tues., July 20
Chicago—at
Sergels

Drove from Louisville, by Bloomington, Lafayette, Crawfordsville, etc. A warm sunshiny day—the whole country looking prosperous. We had many detours. In the evening we talked until 10, largely of philosophy.

Wed., July 21
Chicago—Sergels

Went downtown—to get tickets west. Went to the old Critchfield office. Saw Smith. Got Daugherty to lunch with Sergel.[91] Went with both to Sox-Senators ball game. Party at Sergels—Ferdinand, [Frank] Knight, Percy [Wood] and wives. E down with bad case of diarrhea.

Thurs., July 22
Hays, Kansas

Eleanor had bad night and couldn't leave with me. Me pretty sick of Elma's pawing over, mentally and physically. Went alone, by day train to Kansas City. Phoned E. Better. The air conditioned trains have made traveling much easier. In funny subdued mood all day.

Fri., July 23
Hays, Kansas

Spoke at Kansas State College.[92] This is a Russian-German, Catholic community. Larry Freeman, editor The Review at Ellis,[93] and his wife—a knockout—took me for a long ride over the plains and to neighboring towns. I went and spent the evening at their house and talked until 12. A yearning female author waiting when I got back to hotel.

Sat., July 24
Denver—Brown
Palace

The day spent on a slow Union Pacific train, Hays to Denver. Got to Denver at 3:15—tired. Spent the day reading of Tibetan mysticism. Very lonely for E.

Went to see an Emerson-Loos show—"Saranac."[94] Pretty cheap in its whole outlook. To bed early. Very hot.

Sun., July 25
Denver—Brown
Palace

Heavy and sleepy. E was to arrive at 11:45 a.m. but train did not get in until 1:25 p.m. Sat in station. We went in the afternoon to watch amateur ball games at a big amusement park and dined there. Very hot. E looks pretty well. Life is unlivable without her.

Mon., July 26
Boulder, Colorado

The morning at Denver. Went to Greeley, Colorado, by bus at 1:30—arriving 3:15. Went to the house of a Doctor Cross. Spoke at 4—the state teachers' college—a big crowd.[95] Spoke on Realism. Crowd attentive, apparently interested. A student drove us to Boulder, through a beautiful irrigated country.[96] Went in the evening to Davenport's house.[97] They read a foolish manuscript—evidently thinking it funny.

Tues., July 27
Boulder

Nothing is, at bottom, more silly than this idea that writers may be made in a school. Have been reading manuscripts. They are universally without the spark. It is exhausting. In the evening Burnett spoke—very badly. Davison is drinking himself to death.

Wed., July 28
Boulder

Am already sick of this writers' conference. Burnett, Bishop and I had a short story conference. It was terrible.

The people here seem nice enough but this eternal talk of writing has sickened me.

Thurs., July 29
Boulder

Was half dead all day—the result of the round table. Sat and walked about. Rode up a long canyon with young Thom Thompson of Amarillo, Texas.

In the evening delivered my 1st long talk to a big crowd.[98]

I was pretty good.

Fri., July 30
Boulder

With John Peale Bishop tried to conduct a class. Didn't make much out of it.

The day was warm and cloudy.

In the evening went to hear Howard Mumford Jones—tired man who resorts to wisecracking.

Sat., July 31
Boulder

In the afternoon, after a morning of manuscript reading, went with Davison and others to Central City. Was excited by the aspects of the old mining town but much disappointed by the attempt at theatre there. It was Ibsen's Ghosts, revised by Thornton Wilder. Home at 2:30 a.m.— glorious drive over the high mountains.

Sun., August 1
Boulder, Colo.

Went into Denver at 11 to see the ball games—the country lovely. The wheat, very heavy, is just being cut.

The Refiner's team, headed by Rogers Hornsby,[99] beat the team from Springfield, Illinois and the Negro all stars—a grand team, beat the one from Seminole, Oklahoma.

The crowd surprisingly fair to the Negroes.

Mon., August 2
Boulder

The writers' conference grinds on but, for the most part, they let me alone. Last night was the big dinner at the Country Club and we all made brief speeches. I had a class on the short story and spent the time talking of racehorses.

Tues., August 3
Boulder

Spent the morning doing nothing. Went to hear the drama woman in the p.m. Went with Bishop and Tommy Thompson to drive in the mountains.[100]

Went to a cocktail party.

Pretty useless day.

Wed., August 4
Boulder

To hear Ford, on Greek and Chinese literature. After lunch went for a drive, Lovett, E, myself and lady.[101] Went through strange and lovely mountain canyons.

Went to dine with one of the trustees of the university where I tried to put in some good words for Davison.[102]

Thurs., August 5
Boulder

Long conference on regional literature—very dull. The place was full of aged literary ladies. The Chamber of Commerce gave a steak fry on Flagstaff—a marvelous view of wide plains.

We went to Ford's and sat until midnight.

Fri., August 6
Boulder

The only event was a very stupid round table conference, on regionalism in literature. Bishop, Ransom, myself and a Colorado poet, named [T.H.] Ferril. It was stupid enough.

Sat., August 7
Boulder

Went with Davison and others on a long and magnificent ride over the great divide and to the west slope, and back by another pass. We started at 9 and got home, very weary, at midnight.

Sun., August 8
Boulder

Up early and to the mountains again, this time with a Dr. Fisher and wife. We went to Mount Evans, again—taking lunch. Again it was magnificent but I was weary of mountains.

Mon., August 9
Boulder

Had to conduct a prose class but made Ring Lardner carry me through. Read his story "Nora."

In the evening Ted Davison made a fine lecture on the poetry of force.

Tues., August 10
Boulder

Went to have my voice recorded—at the University. Read "The Story Teller" and "Book of the Grotesque."

In the evening I lectured, on "The Obligations of the Writer."

Wed., August 11
On train

Natalie Davison, Mrs. [Ford Madox] Ford and Cohen[103] drove us to Denver where we took the Zephyr on the Burlington at 4. It is a very marvelous and smooth running train that slips along at 90 miles per hour. We got into our berths early.

Thurs., August 12
Chicago

We got into Chicago at 8:30 and waited for Roger to get us at the station. The philosopher Perry, University Oklahoma, was at Sergel's.[104]

Spent the day talking. In the evening Percy Wood, of the Tribune and the professional footballer who has become a social philosopher.

Fri., August 13
Chicago

With Roger Sergel to the north side to see the Cubs play Cincinnati. Won 16-20, a miserable game. Roger cooked a delicious dish—sweet breads. We sat about all evening and talked of philosophy.

Sat., August 14
Richmond, Ky.

We got up early but didn't get away until 9. Went by Indianapolis and Madison, Ohio [i.e., Indiana] on the river. Got to this little southern town at 7 p.m.

Very hot all day. We had a beautiful drive along the Ohio.

Sun., August 15
Marion

Another hot day of driving. We came by Harlan, Ky.—famous toothpick town—a terribly depressing place.[105] Got onto 58 and arrived at Marion at 4:30. Channing and Mazie waiting to see us. We were both tired from the 2 days drive in the heat.

Mon., August 16
Ripshin

Got over to the farm at 10. Everything in good shape. John hauling lime. Old man Sullivan dead.[106] Bought a new small piece of land. The crops look fine.

Spent most of the day getting unpacked and settled. John gone off to Mimi. Big lot of mail to take care of.

Tues., August 17
Ripshin

Got back into the novel but did not feel much like work. Went into town in the afternoon with E.

I bought a new car—a Dodge. There was a terrific rainstorm and I drove the old car home. There was however no rain at Ripshin and the spring had gone dry.

Wed., August 18
Ripshin

Still in a queer depression, brought on by Boulder. The whole position, out there, in some way false. Drove to Marion, to bring home the new car. The new house, Mother is building, seems an ugly, box-like affair.

Thurs., August 19
Ripshin

Still low in spirits. Got E to go with me for a drive, to Marion, via Konnarock. Very hot. Ran about town, doing errands. Saw Funk and went with him to drive. Got up on local politics. Bob involved. We are still hauling lime to the upper field, the Swan place.

Fri., August 20
Ripshin

Still not working, although I did an article on the movies.[107] It was a very beautiful day, with a soft rain in the afternoon and later beautiful moonlight. I was much in love with E all day. It is good to be alone with her.

Sat., August 21
Ripshin

Think I may have got back into the book. Worked on it and then drove off to town. Aunt May was having a party. A Mr. [Frederick] Springer, a painter from Cincinnati, was in town. Lunch with him, and wife. He is doing art for the treasury dept. Sent them to Ripshin. Dave and a young forester came. The evening was rather dull. E delightful.

Sun., August 22
Ripshin

A half torrential rain that began about 11 and lasted most of the day. Russell, Mimi and kids arrived in the midst of the downpour. There was some jockeying, trying to get the kids stowed away, in the green house and out from underfoot. I worked on Green Grass.

Mon., August 23
Ripshin

A grey day, ending in rain. John announced his intention of marrying Mary Eleanore. We went for a walk and talk of marriage. It seems to depend upon Mary Eleanore's holding her job. In the evening I drank too much, being bored and annoyed by Mimi's children, always underfoot.

Tues., August 24
Ripshin

It was a solid day of rain with no let up and it rained all night.

I worked a little but my nerves are upset by the constant noisy crying and general bad behavior of the ill trained children.

Wed., August 25
Ripshin

An annoying day, with rain. Went to town, taking Mimi and [daughter] Karlin. When we got home the sun was out. We had left in the rain.

The water became exhausted in the tank. Too many using it, the children constantly. Now we will all have to carry pails of water for ordinary toilet uses.

I seem to have none of the common male anxiety that my line be carried on. These children are simply a pest to me. Loaned Mother $700.00.

Thurs., August 26
Ripshin

Worked rather well, chapter man dancing. The day started grey but turned out clear. John Sullivan and I went to Young and tramped the hills trying to find property line. Word that Hilda Smith and Letty are coming.[108]

Fri., August 27
Ripshin

Got the story Playthings ready to send Chambrun. Went to town to meet Hilda Smith but she didn't come. Bought Mother a watch, for her birthday. In the evening Dave Greear and the forester Biggs came, bringing Mary Sue Carter.[109] Dave was in grand talking form and was very amusing. It was a beautiful day. We got a lot of mushrooms.

Sat., August 28
Ripshin

I have been reading a lot of Gorki. Turgenev is the greater master. Started a short story. John and I went off in the truck, to the top of Pine Mountain and got caught in a downpour. The road is rough.

For the 1st time in weeks E and I had an evening alone together in the house. It was nice.

Sun., August 29
Ripshin

Another long day of rain, but I have been feeling tops and yesterday finished the long short story "We Little Children of the Arts."

Have been in good spirits and after working yesterday, spent the afternoon outdoors in the rain. We went to Sullivan's, to hear the Louis-Farr fight[110] and came home to find Letty Esherick out in front of the locked house, waiting in the dark and rain to get in.

Mon., August 30
Ripshin

Again rain steadily, until noon, when the clouds began to clear . . . at last.

E is busy with the men's party. We are spending too much money.

Letty Esherick is here but is hard to talk to. It may be my fault. E off to town and I took Letty to the woods, for mushrooms. Dave came for the evening.

Tues., August 31
Ripshin

John and Major—labor bill $56. May have to put new roof on house. Sent John Cournos $100—a loan. He's broke.

Went to town with E to get food, for the men's feast—10 men coming to dinner Thursday. Got word agent can't sell the story "Playthings"—too grim.

Wed., Sept. 1
Ripshin

Eleanor went off to town early and stayed all day. After working I took Letty into the woods to gather mushrooms. She would like to leave her man but wants someone to definitely tell her to do it.

Thurs., Sept. 2
Ripshin

Letty left in the early afternoon. Worked. The house in a great bustle of preparation. For dinner—Lynn Copenhaver,[111] Funk, Burt Dickinson, Bob Williams, B. E., Bob, John, Marvin Anderson.

All seemed to be having a good time.

Eleanor is doing too much and is too much tired.

Fri., Sept. 3
Ripshin

"How Green the Grass." After work E and I went off to town. Letty had left and we were alone. It was the day when Bob was elected head of the young democrats in the district. There was a barbecue and a dance. We went to look on. It was held in the park.

Sat., Sept. 4
Ripshin

Because of the eruption on E's face we had to stay late in town, while she took a treatment. We came home, at noon and I worked a little. Cary Ross came with a friend, a young TVA lawyer,[112] from Knoxville. He left for Roanoke, after dining with us. Dave Greear and John Greear arrived with a friend and took John off to a dance.

Sun., Sept. 5
Ripshin

A bright sunshiny day. Did not work. Tried but no good. Went off to Marion, after lunch, with E and Cary Ross. He is a charming but ineffective little man. Paul Rosenfeld came at 4 and we drove home by Flat Ridge, the country very beautiful. Paul, apparently, in grand form.

Mon., Sept. 6
Ripshin

A big morning of work, 2000 words. It rained all day. John has started to plow the upper field at the Swan Place. Mr. Ross's friend Fowler came at

4. Paul has brought some beautiful records. Fowler and Ross left at 5—
after drinks. Grand dinner. We played cards in the evening. It rained all
night.

Tues., Sept. 7
Ripshin

Again a long day of rain. E had prepared a big feast for Tom Wolfe which
[sic] did not come. Got offer $150.00 for Dutch edition Kit Brandon.
Mary sent $150.

I worked, fairly well. Paul, John Anderson and I went for a drive to
Konnarock. We hung the Dove[113] in the bedroom. Paul, E and I played
cards. I did not sleep well.

Wed., Sept. 8
Ripshin

Tom Wolfe came, with Mary and Bob. It had been a grey day. John, Paul,
E and I had gone for a swim—in the Swan house pond. We climbed the
hill to where John Sullivan and Major were plowing and on the way down
Paul fell and hurt his leg. Tom Wolfe took command in the evening with
the tale of his troubles.

Thurs., Sept. 9
Ripshin

I laid off and gave the day to Tom Wolfe. He is 6 ft. 6 inches, and gigantic
in every way. He is like his writing. We drove, the back way to Wytheville
and then lunched with Mother. He is generous and big, in every way, but
a good deal the great child.

Fri., Sept. 10
Ripshin

Again a grey day and cold. Worked, fairly well. Paul is evidently in the
stock market and stocks are down. He is blue.

Mother came, with E from town. Paul and I went to get mushrooms
and found an abundance. We played cards in the evening and I won,
irritating Paul.

Sat., Sept. 11
Ripshin

In an odd mood all day. I did not want others. I tried to keep a laughing
outside. I went along as though I was part of others but was not.

I worked. I went with Paul for a walk. I dug up some roots of butterfly weed. I played cards with the others in the evening. All of my association with others was on the surface only.

Sun., Sept. 12
Ripshin

Cold, sunshiny day. B. E. came in the early afternoon. We played croquet. My work hadn't gone well. B. E. had a good day. After B. E. and Mother left we went for a drive, along Flat Ridge to Grant. Corn cutting had begun. My work went flat.

Mon., Sept. 13
Ripshin

Work went better. It was my birthday. E gave me a beautiful bag and, from Mother, I got a coffee table and some pewter. We went to dine at Mother's and I got angry at Paul for his attack on labor. He seems to have a dread and fear of all workers. An unpleasant evening.

Tues., Sept. 14
Ripshin

The days extraordinarily cold, for this time of the year, but a bright sun shining. Bruner[114] is at work on the 2nd guest house. Paul left, feeling, I'm sure a bit hurt because we do not go with him in his attitude toward labor. We went to town in the afternoon, had tea with Mother and dined at Bob's. Paul left at 8:49—and we drove home. I got some pewter, a morning coffee table—these from Mother—and a beautiful bag, for my birthday.

Wed., Sept. 15
Ripshin

A beautiful clear day, without a cloud, the sky, all day, a curiously luminous pale blue. It was very still. I worked in the morning, having moved, from the cabin by the creek to the finished bark house, the second one being constructed, and, in the afternoon, took E with me, to White Top to get roots of bee balm, for Mother.

Thurs., Sept. 16
Ripshin

John and Major finished plowing the big hillside field, at Swan Place. Bruner got the 2nd guest cabin boxed in. Bruner's wife sick. It is getting too cold to work here.

It was another clear bright cold day and, in the afternoon we made cider. The work did not go well. It is too cold to sit at a desk writing.

Fri., Sept. 17
Ripshin

A rather dead day. E went off early to Marion. It was too cold to sit at a desk without a fire. Bruner's wife ill and a nurse came from the charity run by woman's college fraternity. She had fever 104 but the family seemed indifferent.

Sat., Sept. 18
Ripshin

There was heavy mail and I wrote letters. Again no impulse to work. John Sullivan and wife, with sister, went off to a church meeting, at Saltville. We decided that we had better go to sleep in town, so that I could work there in the morning. We went at noon. I went to a ball game in the late afternoon.

Sun., Sept. 19
Marion

Staying nights, in Mother's house. The day was beautiful. Didn't work. Went to a ball game. Went to sit, in the evening with Funk, in his shop.

Bob called me out to announce that he was on the road to political power.

His attitude kept me awake all night.

Mon., Sept. 20
Marion

Spent the morning composing a letter to Bob, on the subject of his entering politics. Was upset about it. It was a lovely day. Drove to Ripshin and spent the afternoon painting one of the cabin guest houses. There was a heavy mist on Iron Mountain. John was cutting corn. We drove home in a beautiful evening light and went right to bed.

Tues., Sept. 21
Ripshin

The people of Green Grass, having gone, temporarily perhaps, away, I plunged into an attempt at a new kind of broken naive song, in prose.

Clear day. Went with E, to Ripshin and painted on one of the cabins. The day lovely. Went to Funk in the evening.

Wed., Sept. 22
Marion

Very little sleep. Again plunged in the new thing, without name. The day again very lovely. John Sullivan got through cutting corn. Bruner on last side of bark house. Spent the afternoon painting. Very conscious of the beauty all around me all day. Read Bishop's "Act of Darkness."[115]

Thurs., Sept. 23
Ripshin

Another gorgeous day. John Sullivan was seeding the upper field, on the Swan place, sowing by hand. I went up there to watch and help burn trash. The view from the field magnificent.

Worked in the morning.

Two young intellectuals came—uncertain purpose—some idea of escape from intellectuality—Boston and Connecticut—Jew and Gentile. Very self-conscious. Went to Funk's shop to play cards in the evening.

Fri., Sept. 24
Ripshin

The day in town. Went to Johnson City, to see [Dr. U. G.] Jones—re the pension matter. Took E, Mother and B. E. Glorious day.

In the evening I got a severe diarrhea lasting all night. I worked on the queer book. Don't know how it will come out.

Sat., Sept. 25
Marion

Wine making day. We made it in Funk's cellar—4 men engaged. I got 30 gallons—of the best [gravity?] wine. John came over and E came. We all dined at Funk's.

I had spent the night with a bad diarrhea and could do little. The day, again was very beautiful.

Sun., Sept. 26
Marion

Stayed in Marion all day. It was a dark gloomy day. I went to see Dr. [George A.] Wright, to be examined, for pension—the Spanish War.[116]

There was a ball game, Fries and Marion, and I went to that. E went with me. I went to Funk and we played cards. I always beat him.

I did some work on the book of the boy.

Mon., Sept. 27
Marion

A very cold day, with a heavy mist, so that, in the evening, coming home from Ripshin, the fog, on the mountains was very thick. We had to creep over.

I wrote and, at the farm worked around the bark house. The day stayed heavy and disagreeable.

Tues., Sept. 28
Marion

A clear fine day, after the cold cloudy time. Worked and then went to Ripshin. Expected the re-roofing of the house would have been started but John Sullivan could get no help.

I was rather dull and heavy. Sat a long time in the sun while John Sullivan picked apples. He climbed like a squirrel. Went to Min Price's to see the men thresh rye and oats.[117]

Wed., Sept. 29
Marion

Did not try to work, although I wrote a new introductory chapter for Book of Days. Drove E to Roanoke—to see a doctor there and she went on to New York. Went to Funk's wine making and we played cards later.

Thurs., Sept. 30
Marion

Worked pretty well. Got a bad case of hives. At the farm finished up the last of the guest houses. Pretty lonely without E. Her presence makes everything sweeter. Beautiful day. In the evening Dave, Mother and I played cards. Didn't sleep well.

Fri., Oct. 1
Marion

A grey cold day. I didn't sleep much but did work. Went to Ripshin and measured field for fence. I sat, for a long time outdoors, just looking at the hills—very strange and alive under grey skies.

Sat., Oct. 2
Marion

Worked well enough. The day warm, with huge white clouds. Went to Ripshin at noon. Dave, John and I took a long drive, in Dave's open car,

Speedwell, Elk Creek, Comer's Rock, Ivanhoe, Fries, Independence.[118] I came home with a violent headache but doped it away. Slept well.

Sun., Oct. 3
Marion

A misty day—with low hanging dark clouds. I worked in the early afternoon and went then to a ball game. In the morning Jean Brown came with her husband, mother and father. Husband nice—the others old and stuffy.

In the evening sat with Mother while we talked.

Mon., Oct. 4
Marion

Rain all day. I decided not to go to Ripshin. I worked and had the car gone over and heater put in. In the evening went, with the Funks, to see the movie of "You Can't Take It With You."[119] It was pretty dull.

Went afterwards to Funk and he talked until midnight, telling me an amazing personal story.

Tues., Oct. 5
Marion

Pretty steady rain. Worked badly. Went to Ripshin and John came over with me. He is to see about having frames made.

The continual wet weather makes me disagreeable. We played cards in the evening. My short radio play is to be in a book.[120]

Wed., Oct. 6
Marion

We got at the roof. A beautiful day, with big white wind clouds. Got one-half of one side on and will have 4 men on it tomorrow. Got check—Richmond Times-Dispatch.[121] Worked on short story—Great Man.

In the evening took Funk for a ride and sat beside road while he poured out the story of his insides.

Thurs., Oct. 7
Marion

A dark gloomy day. I got up early and rushed through work. Hurried over to Ripshin. Was afraid it would rain and the roof uncovered. The rain blew over. We had six men to dinner.

Fri., Oct. 8
Marion

Cold and clear. I ran off into a short story. I was up early and at work at 6:30. Went early to the farm. We got the big part of the house covered, all but a few strips.

In the evening I went to Frank Copenhaver.

Sat., Oct. 9
Marion

Did not try to work. Very cold and cloudy. Hurried over to Ripshin. Got the big part of house covered. Got roof off the wings. It started to rain. Wings of house leaked badly. Came to Marion.

Played cards with Funk in evening.

Sun., Oct. 10
Marion

Clear and cool. Worked on a short story. Went, in the afternoon, to Funk's workshop and sat, with other men to hear, on the radio, the last game of the World Series. Went to see Mr. Copenhaver's steers and walked over his farm. In the evening played cards with Funk.

Mon., Oct. 11
Marion

A clear beautiful day with heavy frost, but warm all day. The upper wing of the house roofed. Worked on the new short story.

Went to Ripshin and in the evening to Frank Copenhaver. John D. there and very uncomfortable. His tale of Mrs. Swift.[122]

Tues., Oct. 12
Marion

Eleanor arrived, from New York, on 41 at 9:20. Got up at six to work.

We went to Ripshin in the early afternoon, taking Mother. It was a clear lovely day, with the hills a mass of reds and yellows. Played cards in the evening.

To bed early.

Wed., Oct. 13
Chapel Hill

Drove to Roanoke, where E saw the x-ray doctor for her face poisoning. Went on to Paul Green's. Wilbur Daniel Steele there.[123] A big crowd of college men in the evening. Left for hotel at 11. A very pleasant evening. No work.

Thurs., Oct. 14
Chapel Hill,
N.C.

Worked at the hotel in the morning—short story—"Story of Story." Paul Green and wife came at 12. To their house, in the country, to lunch. Took a long walk and talk with Wilbur Daniel Steele. He talks of his detective stories. Spent the evening at the Greens—the North Carolina poet, James Larkin Pearson coming.[124] We dined there. E came from Durham at 10:30—tired. Grey cold day.

Fri., Oct. 15
Chapel Hill

The morning spent, at work in my room. Went to luncheon, the North Carolina State Library Association. Went to sit with Green and Steele in the p.m. In the evening I had to make a speech. Talked of the charge regarding so-called "immoral books." Sat very late, drinking and talking with Steele and Green.

Sat., Oct. 16
Marion

Started for Marion, at 9. Came by Greensboro, Winston, and Wytheville—190 miles. Got home by 2, pretty tired, heavy and sleepy. It was a beautifully clear fine day.

Loafed about all day and in bed early. Slept hard.

Sun., Oct. 17
Marion

The day, starting cold and sunshiny, became cold and threatening. Took last trip to Ripshin before leaving for East. Got a lot of chickens for Mother. Funk went with me. He talked of his ambition to someday be a writer. Went to him, in the evening, to play cards.

Mon., Oct. 18
Washington, D. C.

Left Marion at 9 and drove to Washington, by New Market and Luray . . . cloudy day—cold at Marion but hot in Washington. Went to Cullen's apartment.[125] Young professor from George Washington College came.

We all dined, at a seafood place. Professor and wife both desperate bores.
They kept us until after midnight.

Tues., Oct. 19
Washington

Rained hard, all day. Went to Cullen, at the Veteran's Bureau. Went to
Government hospital to be examined, for pension, Spanish American
War. Saw several doctors. Went home to Cullen's place and worked.

Wed., Oct. 20
Media, Pa.

The moment we left Washington the rain stopped and the day became
very beautiful. E was very lovely. We got to Hedgerow at 3, E going on to
New York at 7. Saw Misalliance—Shaw—a beautifully done job of acting. Sat up late talking to the people of the company.

Thurs., Oct. 21
New York
54 Washington Mews

A confused day. Stayed up—until so late and drank so much, I was in a
daze. Drove to New York in a bath of fall colors. A very still day. It was
nice to get back into the room upstairs at 54. Dined with the Millers.

Fri., Oct. 22
New York
54 Washington Mews

A grey dull day. Something very heavy and grey in me. I realized that the
themes, on which I have been at work are not, for me, true themes. Wrote
letters. Did not try to work. Walked about, very unhappy. Dull with E.
Wrote a lot of letters. The beginning of a theme, it may be a true one, in
me.

Horrid feeling of incompetence, all day.

Sat., Oct. 23
New York
54 Washington Mews

After several days of gloominess got to work on a new story that may
develop into a real theme. E came home at 3 and I quit work. In the
evening we went to Carl [Randau] and Leane Zugsmith and with them to
dine at Cafe Royal. Had a good many drinks and good talk.

Sun., Oct. 24
New York
54 Washington Mews

The day cold and clear. Tried to work on new story—not too successfully.
E and I took a walk and dined in German place. Took the car to get anti-
freeze. Played cards. I read Voltaire.

Mon., Oct. 25
New York
54 Washington Mews

Went back to the Book of Days and did one on Maurice.[126] It was a good
long day of work.

Went to see Chambrun. Went to sit with E and Georgia O'Keeffe.
Dined with the Millers and Eddy Wolf.

Tues., Oct. 26
New York
54 Washington Mews

Got up and worked a little. Went with Chambrun, to see Herbert Kelly, at
Crowell Publishing Company. He talked a great deal of his youth and
what Winesburg had done to him.

Went out to Karl's, to see the big mural he has done for the new government building, at Bedford, Ohio. Saw also Ray—same or worse.[127]

Karl's thing the most striking and beautiful of any thing of his I have
ever seen.

Wed., Oct. 27
New York
54 Washington Mews

Grey day. Worked on the Day book. Went to lunch alone and then later
went to Max Perkins. We sat in a cafe and he told me the story of the
fight, between Hemingway and [Max] Eastman . . . a very silly affair.
From Max's story it was pretty much Hemingway's childishness.[128] Max
gave me Mary Colum's book on criticism.[129]

Thurs., Oct. 28
New York
54 Washington Mews

Got up late and worked at "Day" book. Had a good day of work. Went to
see the bookbinders. Karl came in at 5—going to Cleveland to hang his

mural. We dined and, when he went to train E and I went to Madison Square Garden—to big rally of American Labor Party. Heard many speeches—the best by Dewey and La Guardia.[130]

Fri., Oct. 29
New York
54 Washington Mews

Worked on the Days. Went to walk on 14th Street and the east side. E came and we dined. She went to a labor meeting and I to the Garden. Saw the flyweight Henry Armstrong fight the Syrian Sarron. It was a fast interesting bout. Armstrong won, by KO in the 6th.[131]

Sat., Oct. 30
New York
54 Washington Mews

A clear bright day—heavy wind and dust. After work went with E over to Knox hat factory Brooklyn to get a new hat. First new one in 3 years. We dined over there.

In the evening stayed in and read the testimony, regarding Harlan, Ky., before the La Follette Committee . . . a very strange and revealing document.[132] It excited me so that I had a bad time getting to sleep.

Sun., Oct. 31
New York
54 Washington Mews

Cold clear day. Up late. Breakfast with Millers. Seemed to have a cold—not so good.

Got the car out and took E to see a friend in hospital. Went in the evening to call on Whit Burnett. Dull day. Very little work done.

Mon., Nov. 1
New York
54 Washington Mews

Was fighting a cold and did not work. Have been reading the report of the investigation of industries by the La Follette Committee. Pretty rank.

E gave a cocktail party, mostly her radical friends. Several speeches were made. It turned into a sort of meeting.

Tues., Nov. 2
New York
54 Washington Mews

Election day. Wrote about Days—of the Cuban War. In the afternoon went to Brooklyn and strolled about. A bright warm day. Went into Ebbets Field and saw a football game.

In the evening we took Millers to dine and went to see Garbo in Camille. Good acting, by Garbo, but bum script and poor support.

Wed., Nov. 3
New York
54 Washington Mews

Worked pretty well—the Days.

In the evening we went up to Columbia to see some English realistic films of English life—one of mail train—depressing picture of mill town in depression, etc. Went with Whit Burnett, Potter, Walter Pack and others to have beer.[133] Rode home, in Whit's car with woman playwriter.

Thurs., Nov. 4
New York
54 Washington Mews

A clear fine day. I wrote a short story called "Not Sixteen."[134] I keep working on the Day book. Don't know whether or not the story will fit in.

We had dinner with the Millers and sat and talked until ten.

Fri., Nov. 5
New York
54 Washington Mews

Not such a good day. Worked in the morning and then went to lunch with Max Perkins. He told me a lot of stories about Tom Wolfe, Hemingway, etc. Was rather done in all day. Dined with E at Ticino's and to bed early.

Sat., Nov. 6
New York
54 Washington Mews

Pretty good morning's work. Tom Wolfe came at 1:30 and we went to the Brevoort. Sat talking and drinking until after six. E came to join us at about 3:30. Tom, much quieter and in grand form. It was a story telling bout. Dined with Millers and sat until 10.

Sun., Nov. 7
New York
54 Washington Mews

Lazy day. Beautiful weather. We slept late and went to walk. Got a room in which I will work when I return here after Charleston trip. Broadway Central Hotel, lower Broadway. Went to see Bill Faulkner, Algonquin Hotel. He had fallen against a hot radiator and burned himself. Went to Newspaper Guild Cocktail party. Broun[135] got $5 out of E, $10 out of me. Went to dine with Burton and Hazel Rascoe. Burton's tragedy has aged him terribly.[136]

Mon., Nov. 8
New York
54 Washington Mews

Felt seedy because I didn't sleep. The work didn't go. I was dopey all day.

Took Paul and E to dinner and later we went to a picture—Elephant Boy—Kipling. Elephants wonderful—the rest sour.

Paul has rather recovered from the shock of losing the New Yorker job.

Tues., Nov. 9
New York
54 Washington Mews

Mary to arrive Thursday. Worked well—Days. Went to see dealers about John. Went to McDonald's to have academy picture shot. Saw Hendrick Van Loon.[137] Dined with the Millers and party.

Wed., Nov. 10
New York
54 Washington Mews

Worked O.K. Bill Faulkner on a big drunk, at Algonquin hotel. He had backed against a radiator and burned himself badly. Got the doctor and a nurse in for him.[138]

Had a cocktail party. Dreiser, Maud Fangel, Dr. Joe and Ann, Joe Taulane, Mayorga.[139]

Afterward went, with Mayorga, to the play "Susan and God."[140] Very superficial. No good. Bored.

Thurs., Nov. 11
Philadelphia

Mary to arrive on Washington at 2 p.m.

However, I left New York, with Joe Taulane, at 1. Drove to Hedgerow.

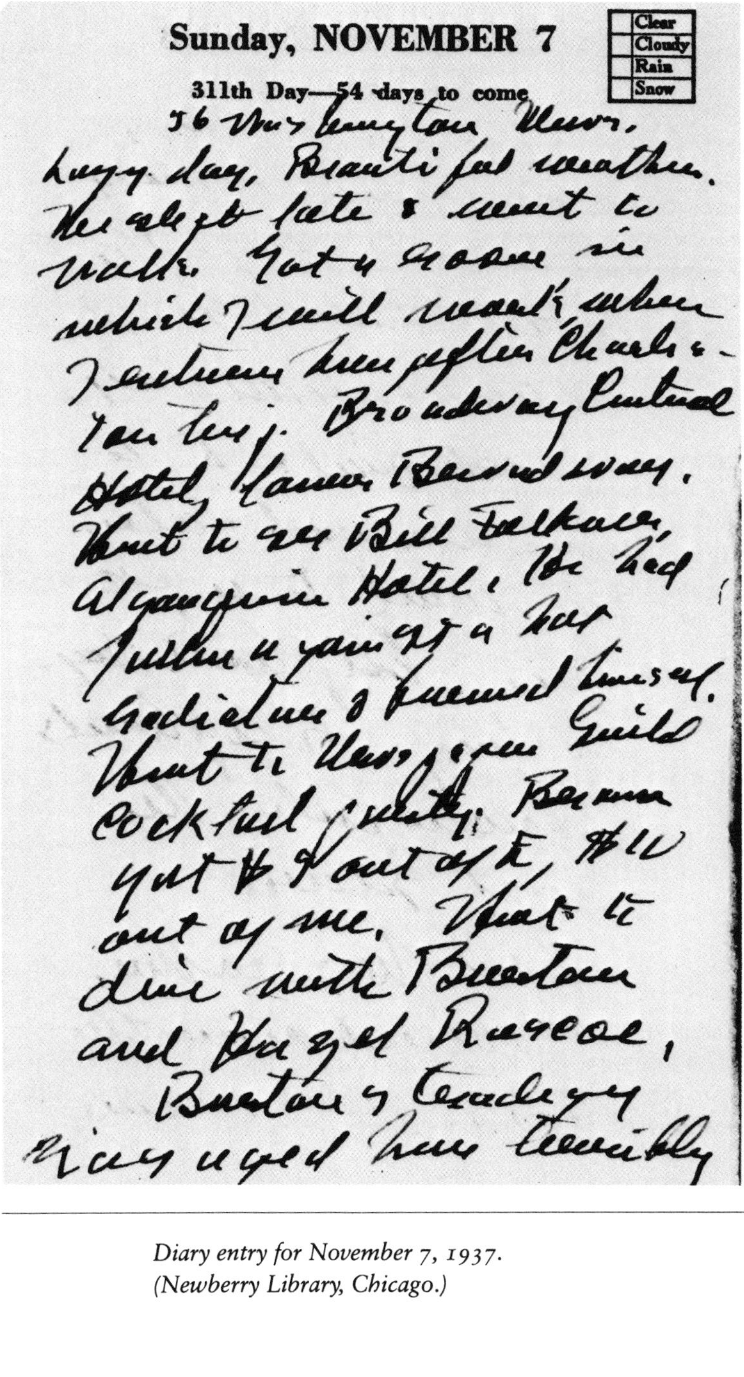

Sunday, NOVEMBER 7

311th Day—54 days to come

Clear
Cloudy
Rain
Snow

Diary entry for November 7, 1937.
(Newberry Library, Chicago.)

Saw Paul Green's three one acters.[141] White Dresses very beautiful. We all went to Inn and talked and drank until 2 a.m. Read for a time and slept well.

Fri., Nov. 12
Philadelphia

Went over to Hedgerow. Drove to Philadelphia. Grey day. Rain at night. Went to see a fine exhibition—Daumier—at Philadelphia Art Museum. Saw newspapermen. E came at 7.

   Spoke Academy Music—Obligations of the Writer. Small audience. Good speech.

Sat., Nov. 13
Baltimore

After being interviewed, by reporter, E and I left Philadelphia at 10. There had been hard rains and the roads were badly flooded. We got to Mazie's at 1 p.m. Channing came and we had lunch. Dr. [Matthew Page] Andrews came in and we talked until time to go to train, at 5. E took 5:30—to Chicago and I took 5:40 to Charleston. Reading Ralston's Ring—book about Nevada and San Francisco gold mines.[142]

Sun., Nov. 14
Charleston, S.C.
Hotel Charleston

Arrived at 8:30—a bright warm day. Went to the hotel and to work on my lecture on Realism, with which I am dissatisfied. Called Miss Pinckney but she had gone to the country. Walked a long time in very beautiful streets. This may well be America's most beautiful town.

Mon., Nov. 15
Charleston, S.C.
Hotel Charleston

Spent the morning on my speech, to be delivered here. Went, at 2:30 to lunch with Josephine Pinckney. She took me to drive out through the low country to the seashore where we walked and talked. We went to call on DuBose Heyward.[143] We dined together.

Tues., Nov. 16
Charleston, S.C.

Worked on my speech. Went to lunch with Mr. and Mrs. Tobias.[144] Back to the hotel, to work again. I dined tête-à-tête with Josephine. DuBose

Heyward and wife came. My lecture went well—big crowd—well held. Went later with several to talk and drink. Drove until one with excited architect.

Wed., Nov. 17
Fayetteville, N.C.

Left Charleston—Atlantic Coast Line, at 1:30 and came to Fayetteville— arrived at 6. Went in the evening to see a movie and vaudeville show, both very vulgar and dull. Slept well. The train ran, all the way down through lowlands and swamps. Many negroes . . . a good many cypress swamps. Did no work.

Thurs., Nov. 18
Southern Pines,
N.C.

Spent the night at the Prince Charles—in Fayetteville and worked there in the morning. Jim Boyd's man came for me at 2—arrived at Boyd's at 4. Kate much better. We looked at horses, dined and talked before the fire until midnight. I started to read a mystery story and it set my mind off so that I did not sleep well.

Fri., Nov. 19
Southern Pines

A drizzle of rain, all day. I did not work. In the afternoon Jim and I drove to see Doc Pashel's string of trotters. Saw some beauties. Jim and Jack were up early to hunt—went to Struthers Burt for tea.[145] Paul Green and Elizabeth came in the evening. Had a fine evening.

Sat., Nov. 20
Southern Pines

Colder. Walked about with Jim. Looked at horses. Did a little work. Wire from E—not to meet me on Sunday, at Baltimore. Went to Struthers Burt for cocktails.

Paul and Elizabeth Green came. We had a grand evening of fun. Jim drove me to Fayetteville where I took sleeper for Baltimore.

Sun., Nov. 21
Baltimore
Mazie's

Got in at 8:45. Channing met me. We went to the faculty club and played pool. In the afternoon Dr. Johnson came, also Gerald Johnson and wife.[146] Thought Johnson looked peculiarly like Henry Mencken. Took Dr. Johnson to dine. Got lost coming back. Fagin and wife came. Fagin strutted. E to come in the morning.

Mon., Nov. 22
Baltimore
Mazie's

A cold cloudy day. No work. Got car tuned up. Went to lunch at 14 Club with Gerald Johnson, Woollcott and others. Met E—from Chicago and Washington at 3:45. Henry's mess. In the evening Engeman and wife came.[147] We sat talking until 12.

Tues., Nov. 23
New York
54 Washington Mews

Eleanor and I came up from Baltimore—a clear sunshiny day. We came by Newark, Del. and Camden—ferrying across the Delaware. Got to New York at 4:30. E went off to a meeting and didn't return until 11:30. Very tired. I went with Mary to dine at Anne Miller's and we played cards.[148]

Wed., Nov. 24
New York

I had my first day in the room I've got, at the old Broadway Central Hotel, in Lower Broadway. It should be a grand place to work. Spent most of the day at letters. Sneaked off to the Old Glory horse sale at 94 and Madison.[149] Very sad that I could not bid for some of the beautiful yearlings. In the evening Mary, E and I to eat lobster at the Grotto.

Thurs., Nov. 25
New York
Thanksgiving

Went to my room at Broadway Central—to work. Went with Mary, to Old Glory sale. In the evening Mary, in a grand spending mood, took us to Jack Dempsey's restaurant.[150] We had Thanksgiving dinner with a quart of champagne. We went to the Garden to see the Rangers ice hockey team play the Leafs—of Toronto. Leafs won—3 to 1.

Fri., Nov. 26
New York
Broadway Central

Did a new thing—I hope for the book—I called "The Writer and a Woman." Went to second-hand book stores and got some Borrow, for Josephine Pinckney.[151]

Went to Pirie McDonald—an old fraud—to see photo for the academy. E got sentimental and wasted $40. Dined with Millers—pretty dull. Played cards with Mary Emmett and continued to beat her.

Sat., Nov. 27
New York

Worked and completed the revision of the story—"Not Sixteen." Sent it off to Mother to be copied. It was raining when I went out. Went to the bookstores, on 4th and got a fine copy Lavengro for 75 cents. It began to rain hard and we stayed in, E ill with a cold. Mary made dinner. We played cards.

Sun., Nov. 28
New York

Rain all day. I did not work well—revising "Pick Your War."[152] Played cards with Mary. We all went to Charles Studin's and then to Evelyn Scott.[153] Mary got rather high. We went to dine, taking Evelyn.

Kiss on the stairs.

Mon., Nov. 29
New York

Work on "Pick Your War." Poor progress. Not up to much. Went home at 2 and slept until 4. Played cards with Mary. She, E and I dined, at Keen's, on 36[154] and went to see the new version of Julius Caesar on 41st St.—Caesar in modern clothes and extraordinarily vivid and alive. The best show I have seen for years.[155]

Tues., Nov. 30
New York

Find I am no good at revision . . . so began to rewrite . . . "Pick Your War" and worked better. Saw Dr. Joe and had lunch with him and later went to the hospital. Doctor there from Havana. Experiments in curing hernias without operation. Dined with E and Mary. Saw [Cleon] Throckmorton and wife. Slept long and hard.

Wed., Dec. 1
New York

Work on "Pick Your War." Got my bound books. Got my new Irish tweed suit. Went with Max Perkins for cocktails.

At dinner—Tom Wolfe, Ella Winter,[156] Max Eastman and wife, Mary, Ethel, Ashley, Eleanor. Eleanor lovely in new dress. Tom Wolfe late and, in many ways, ruined the dinner—too much drinking.[157]

Thurs., Dec. 2
New York

No good after the dinner. Drank too much. Was pretty flat so went off to the 6 day bicycle race. Went to dine, taking Mary and E, to Mrs. Leonard—in 59th Street. Pleasant evening, in pleasant company.

Fri., Dec. 3
New York

Got a little work done. At 1 went to the New Yorker where Dorothy Parker spoke on Spain.[158] She was very effective. Went with Mary to see Eddie Wolf, just home from the hospital.

In the evening with E to Galantière and then with E. E. Cummings and wife to dine. It was the best company we have had here and we sat until after midnight.

Sat., Dec. 4
New York

I am in one of my stale periods. I write and tear up. Nothing I do has any meaning. Such times are insane times. I went to see the play, Father Malachy's Miracle.[159] Fine acting. Went to Tommy Smith and saw several people. Drank too much. Took a pill to make me sleep.

Sun., Dec. 5
New York

A quiet day and a long sleep—to quiet my rather jangled nerves. Wrote a little but tore up. Took E for a long walk, almost down to the Battery and then with Mary to a tea at an art gallery to meet the Irish players, who didn't come.

Early to bed and to sleep. Borrow.

Mon., Dec. 6
New York

A rainy day . . . myself, as regards work—still no good.

John Cournos came and we lunched. He is in a bad financial fix—having to do hack work to live. E and I had an evening alone together, dining at the Bamboo Forest.[160] I am still in a fallow state.

Tues., Dec. 7
New York

Bitterly cold, with flurries of snow, the first winter day we have had here.

At last I had a day of at least some work. I wrote of Maurice [Long].

In the evening to Bill and Helen Woodward's and there was a good company of people and mighty good talk.[161] I was foolish enough to drink coffee and so did not sleep.

Wed., Dec. 8
New York

A bitter cold day. I had not slept so, when I got to my work room, at the hotel, fell on the bed there and slept. Tried later to work but no go. Went to walk in the cold. In the evening, with Mary and E to dine at Dr. Treves.[162] Another doctor, from Kentucky, now successful here, was at dinner. It was nice to see the real friendship between the two men.

Thurs., Dec. 9
New York

Cloudy and very cold. I went to Wanamaker's and sent Mr. Copenhaver some wool socks. Went to lunch, at Edward Dahlberg and we had a long talk of writing.[163] Later went to dine at Maud Fangel's . . . met some charming people.

Went to an actor's benefit—The Fireman's Ball.[164] Stayed until after one. Pretty stupid.

Fri., Dec. 10
New York

Very cold. Day of failure in work. Gave it up and went to walk. In the late afternoon, went to Stieglitz and saw some of the earliest American things—also French moderns—the 1st.

Went to cocktail party at Max Perkins' house and saw many people I knew.

Sat., Dec. 11
New York

Very cold. I worked well enough and, in the afternoon went, with E to see the play, "Of Mice and Men."[165] It is very dramatic but, I thought, built to play on the nerves . . . a thing I didn't like.

In the evening went with some old friends of Mary's, to Barney Gallant,[166] where we had dinner, with wine and sat talking until midnight.

Sun., Dec. 12
New York

Very cold. An insane day of people. Charles Studin gave a party for Karl and me. Big crowd. We went off to Cafe Royal. Jap, Mims, Saxe and wife,[167] me and E. All went well til Joe [Taulane] came. He very self-conscious and ugly. He made a strange play, trying to give E a $100 bill. Went back to house and got Mary. Sent E to bed and myself went at 1. The rest stayed and talked until 3 a.m.

Mon., Dec. 13
New York

Still very cold. Went with Miriam Phillips and E to Dr. Joe's[168] where we dined. A lawyer and wife came. Got Joe's $100 back to him.[169] The whole incident very silly. I told him frankly what I thought of it.

Tues., Dec. 14
New York

Worked, at revision of all scripts. Went to see Barney Gallant and then home to bathe. Talked to Mims. Went to Jack's—West 43rd[170]—to dine with E, Robert Lovett, and a woman writer Miss Bishop. Had fine dinner, with wine and drinks. Mary went to farm and got her heater. Still very cold.

Wed., Dec. 15
New York

Somewhat warmer. I worked better. Took Miriam Phillips to the play "Having Wonderful Time."[171] Found it very charming. Stayed with her until she left for Philadelphia at 6. We dined at home. E very tired. Got present for Mary.

Thurs., Dec. 16
New York

Some work done. The day much warmer. Went to buy E a new bag. Went to play cards with Mary. Went to Studin's—to party for Boardman Robinson.[172] Took Mary and E to lunch and then to a silly movie. Karl was in for the night. He went to dinner at Maud Fangel's.

Fri., Dec. 17
New York

Warm and rainy. Got some work done, in the morning. At noon went to meet French newspaperwoman Miss Chaney—got Mrs. Arthur Ficke instead.[173] Tom Wolfe came in drunk and insulting.[174] Took Miss Chaney home and Millen Brand came—bring[ing] 1st copy edition—his book.[175] Went to Stieglitz. Saw O'Keeffe, Marianne Moore, Marin and wife.[176] Drove home in the rain.

Sat., Dec. 18
New York

Very warm. I did some work and took the actor Joe Taulane to lunch. In the evening Gilbert Wilson came, from Terre Haute.[177] He was very arrogant but finally, goaded to it, I went after him and shook it out of him.

Sun., Dec. 19
New York

Pretty good day of work. The day grey and cloudy. In the evening went to see The Golden Boy—well acted—basically sentimental.[178]

In the night Mary had an unpleasant incident—a man calling her—at 2 a.m.—to talk vile words—very strange. It made the very house seem unpleasant.

Mon., Dec. 20
New York

Cold and cloudy. Mary tearing the house to pieces for her party.

Went to lunch with [Edward] Dahlberg and discussed literature. Then to call on Ben Huebsch about possible new edition Winesburg. In the evening to Saxe Commins—and all evening his wife played the piano.

The cook turned out to be a great reader of my books.

Tues., Dec. 21
New York

Did a short piece, for the book. Drove far downtown with Alice Wolf to get some furniture for Mary. Mary had her big party for the Spanish—the house jammed.[179] I introduced Dorothy Parker.

Wed., Dec. 22
New York

A day of running about, preparing to leave New York. Packed. Went to a meeting of the Council—the Author's League. Spent the evening still packing.

Thurs., Dec. 23
Roanoke, Va.

Up early and on the road, to Marion—Mary and E with me, at 8. A grey day with sunlight in the late afternoon and then a light sprinkle of rain. We came by Lancaster, York, Gettysburg, and Hagerstown and got down to Roanoke at 10—after dining at Lexington.

Fri., Dec. 24
Marion

Got to Mother's at 12:30, Henry and Katharine there. Everything in great disorder—myself much put out by it. Tried to stay away from the house with Henry as much as I could. Finally got through the day without an explosion.

Sat., Dec. 25
Marion

Christmas, at Mother's—a grey day—no rain or snow. It was very hard for me to get past the Christmas morning, with the attempt to push back into childhood. We had a fine Christmas dinner. Went to Andy in the p.m. and was happy to sit alone, talking with a man friend. Depressed, all day.

Sun., Dec. 26
Marion

Began with dazzling sunlight but soon grey. Tried to draw up my feelings about Mary's money in a letter. Depressed again. We had a big dinner with a thick steak I cooked.

Went to Bob's. Found the baby walking about. Bob getting over a binge. Went to Funk's and sat with him two hours, talking and card playing. Took Channing to railroad station. Mary in bed sick, with cold. To bed.

Mon., Dec. 27
Marion

A grey rainy day. I worked again at the war piece. Went out, in the rain with Henry, while he took pictures. Trying all day to think my way through the Mary problem. Henry in bad with Mother. In the evening I went to call on Frank Copenhaver and, later, on Funk. Sat two hours with Funk.

Tues., Dec. 28
Marion

An amazingly bright sunny day and I was less gloomy. I worked.

In the afternoon we all went to the park and climbed up the path, built by the CCC boys to Molly's Knob. I did not go all the way up.

The evening at cards and talk at home.

Wed., Dec. 29
Marion

Another bright warm day. I drove Mary to Chilhowie where she got apples—and then to the lake. We met Henry and got watercress.

In the evening went to Bob, where I saw Cornelia, looking very well and very grey. It seems impossible that I ever lived with her.

Thurs., Dec. 30
Marion

Bright sunny day. Worked in the morning and went to Ripshin—through deep mud from Troutdale. Everything OK there. Mother and Mary both suddenly ill, also baby. We went to Bob's to dine. Mary got better and left for New York at 8:50.

Fri., Dec. 31
Knoxville, Tenn.

Coming down with flu but drove E to Knoxville for her conference with industrial girls, regarding camp. We got into Knoxville at 5—4 hours on way—166 miles.

Feeling rotten. Went early to bed. The street below filled with noises, fireworks and shots but I slept. E not looking so well. Henry and Katharine left for Stillwater.

1 9 3 8

I have to begin the new year with illness, attack of intestinal flu—in the Hotel Farragut at Knoxville, where I have come to escort Eleanor. It is a bright clear day but I cannot go out or do any work. I am reading the Growth of the American Republic by Samuel Morison—Harvard—and Henry Commager—New York University.

All day in my room—at the Farragut Hotel here—spent the day reading and running to the toilet. Went without food until night.

Much better. Felt well enough to get in the car and come here, driving most of the way. Came by 11 East, through Jonesboro and Johnson City—a bright warm winter day. Got to Marion at 3 p.m.

Another beautiful day with the sun shining, myself still somewhat weak, from the flu. I went back to the novel, took a walk, wrote letters, read, and in the evening played cards with E and Mother.

A bright clear day and after going over some chapters of the unfinished novel I went with E to Ripshin. We got back at 3:30 and, in the evening I went to Funk. I got into an absurd wrangle with him about old Andrew Jackson.

Thurs., Jan. 6
Marion

I caught a cold at Andy's so went off to Johnson City, to see Dr. Jones—taking E and Mother, Mother to get her eyes measured. My own glasses were also broke. In the evening Mary and Bob to dine—big steak.

May Scherer very ill of pneumonia.

Fri., Jan. 7
Marion

Most of the day in bed. It was a grey cold day. I had got a cold and did not eat. Read American history. Aunt May still quite ill. In the evening a C. I. O. man came who is organizing the Mathieson Company.[1] He seemed a very alive fine fellow.

Sat., Jan. 8
Marion

Cloudy—much colder. Went with Jay [Scherer] and B. E. to Copenhaver dinner at Arthur Copenhaver's.[2] In the afternoon talked with Jay and went for a goodbye visit to Funk. Spent the evening packing to leave.

Sun., Jan. 9
Louisville

We left Marion at 8:30. Stopped at Abingdon to get brakes adjusted and drove on to Louisville, getting in at six. Cold but beautifully clear and sunshiny day. No snow or ice. We went for supper and for evening to Mark Ethridge—Louisville Courier Journal.

Mon., Jan. 10
Chicago—Sergels

We left Louisville at 8:30. During the night it had rained and the rain had frozen. There was a light snow on this. We saw one wreck with 3 people killed. One man passed us and suddenly skidded and went head-on into a tree. We gave up at Lebanon, Indiana, the same town in which we got stuck in a blizzard two years ago, and came in by train, leaving the car in a garage.

Tues., Jan. 11
Chicago—Sergels

The day damp and cloudy and the streets slushy underfoot. I tried to launch a short story. After some hours work went to walk in the South-side streets. The city seemed very grey, ugly and gloomy. We went in the evening to see the play *Tovarich*.[3]

Wed., Jan. 12
Chicago—Sergels

I went ahead, trying for the feel of the new short story. Very much colder—streets icy. Went into the Loop and sat with advertising men. In the evening a group of young Trotskyists came and there was much revolutionary talk until midnight.

Thurs., Jan. 13
Chicago—Sergels

Cold and icy but high wind gone. John came, from Michigan City in the morning and we went to town with Roger.

Roger had got idea for selling a painting by mail, via colored movies. We went to Eastman's. Then John and I to the American painters exhibit.[4] Karl badly skied. John didn't get in.

Spent the evening at Roger's—Roger and John on their gadgets—Ruth and I at cards. E in late. She fell and tore her stockings.

Fri., Jan. 14
Chicago—Sergels

Warm and slushy. Did some work on the novel. I went, with Chris Sergel,[5] to his fraternity house to lunch and listened to the talk of the young student intellectuals.

John came, with his new wife—E not here. They stayed to dine and E came in the evening. She seemed O. K. It is a difficult relationship to establish.

Sat., Jan. 15
Chicago—Sergels

Again at the novel. Sergel stayed at home and, in the afternoon, we went for a walk. We went with the Sergels to dine at the University Faculty Club and then to the Perrys for talk and drinks.[6] E went home to work and the rest of us back to the club to dance until 1 a. m.

Sun., Jan. 16
Chicago—Sergels

Warm and bright. We slept late and dined at 2 p.m. In the evening there was a big party—for the most part men from the University and their wives. Saw Percy Wood. The man who most impressed me was Frank Knight—a man with a clear, if terribly pessimistic mind.[7]

Roger made his special sweet bread and it was delicious. Up until 1 and awake until 4.

Mon., Jan. 17
Chicago—Sergels

The day spent in gloom. Tried to work but couldn't. It may be the climate or the atmosphere of the house. There seems much unhappiness. . . .[8] I have perhaps made a mistake to stay here. I cannot, in this atmosphere, manage to feel my way into my work. I smoke too much.

Went down into the city to have tea with E, at the Palmer House. Am afraid the time here may be wasted.

Tues., Jan. 18
Chicago—Sergels

Cold and grey—myself again no good. Tried to work but it would not go . . . so stayed in my room and read.

In the evening went, with E to dine at the apartment of Robert Lovett's daughter. A wasted day.

Wed., Jan. 19
Chicago—Sergels

Still grey and cold and I continue not to sleep. I did not work but walked and read. In the evening went with Roger Sergel to dine at a small French restaurant and then to the International House[9] to see a French feature of a motor trip through eastern Europe and Asia. A very remarkable picture.

Thurs., Jan. 20
Chicago—Sergels

I did not try to work. Went into town and had lunch with E. Then went to see George [Daugherty] and Charlie Byrne and talked of old times.[10] Went to the office of Esquire but found my man out of town.[11] Went with Janet Chryst to John and his wife at Michigan City. Dined there and spent the evening and came home on the train.

Fri., Jan. 21
Chicago—Sergels

Still depressed and no satisfactory work. I waited all day to hear from Paul Cullen and got him, and his new bride in the evening. We went to dine at [?] on Lake . . . a fish dinner. E and Mildred [Esgar] came. I drank a good deal and slept.

Sat., Jan. 22
Chicago—Sergels

I did not try to work. I went down to have a look at the organization of a new non-partisan league—by labor. Went to the auditorium to see some Indian dancers. In the evening Morrow, Daugherty and Lovett came to dine.

Sun., Jan. 23
Chicago—Sergels

No work. Went with Ruth to drive, over the new North–South driveway, through old Streeterville. E stayed for the night. Ruth and I went to Morrison—to get Morrow.[12] We all went to a party at Percy Wood's apartment. Very fine party—fun. We did not get home until 2 a.m.

Mon., Jan. 24
Chicago—Sergels

I got to work. Grey and cloudy. I was up late, wrote many letters. I started again on the novel. It was warm but, in the afternoon grew cold.

An archeologist, of the University, named Ewing, came with his wife to dine. They were dull. I lunched with several professors. Eleanor stayed for the night. There was a howling wind. It snowed.

Tues., Jan. 25
Stillwater, Minn.

It turned suddenly bitter cold, with snow. I began working again. I went to lunch with E and a Chicago woman, head Industrial Dept., Y.W.C.A.[13]

I took the train for St. Paul and arrived at 10—very cold and drove to Katharine and Henry through drifts. I found their house very beautiful.

Wed., Jan. 26
Stillwater, Minn.

Very cold—10 below. The place lovely. Two Associated Press men arrived, to take snow pictures and got Henry, on snowshoes, going to see a mythical patient.[14]

Got my typewriter fixed.

Went to a German woman finger painter, Mrs. Kaiser, who served wine. Got into a row with my hostess about the poor, who, to her are all unworthy rascals. As she talked, kept thinking of my own mother.

Thurs., Jan. 27
Stillwater, Minn.

A few degrees warmer but still 10 below. I did some work in the morning and then went off to town with Doctor Henry, sitting in a small room, back of his office and listening in on his conversation with patients. Came home and played cards and to bed. Cough bad.

Fri., Jan. 28
Stillwater, Minn.

Somewhat warmer. I went with Henry to help deliver a baby, acting as anesthetist and holding pan for afterbirth. Henry passed me off as a New York doctor. It was tremendously exciting.

Then went to Mrs. Kaiser to see her finger painting.

Sat., Jan. 29
Stillwater

Did a good story. Went off to town, over icy roads, in Henry's Packard. Sat while he talked to patients. Made a call with him on an old lumberman. In the evening the doc, drunk of [whiskey], explained the story "I Want to Know Why."

Sun., Jan. 30
Stillwater

5 to 10 below all day. Drifts in the road. Went to town and E had eyes measured. Katharine had big party beginning at 4 p.m. and going on until 1 a.m. I got comfortably drunk. Had a good time and slept well. Probably made a fool of myself.

Mon., Jan. 31
Chicago—Sergels

Woke up—Stillwater, tired from the dissipation of the night before. Henry kept taking pictures and that irritated. We drove to St. Paul and took the train called the "400," for Chicago, at 3. Arrived at 9:30. Drove to Sergels and listened to Chris and Roger, in a deep argument, on socialism, until 12:30.

Tues., Feb. 1
Indianapolis

Spent the morning writing and doing letters. Went with E, to Lebanon, Indiana, to get car. Arrived there at 5 p.m. and drove on to Indianapolis. To bed early—Hotel Severin.

Wed., Feb. 2
Memphis, Tenn.

Drove all day, starting at 7—459 miles via Vincennes, Evansville, Henderson, Ky., and west Tennessee. It was a grey warm day. We got to Memphis at 6:20 and again pretty tired, to bed early.

Thurs., Feb. 3
Memphis-Hotel
Gayoso

Did a story of the woman on the stairs—3,000 words reeled off. We got the car out and rode—the river front very lovely. Went into the negro district. In the evening walked in the famous Beal Street.

Fri., Feb. 4
Natchez, Miss.

We met Mother in the early morning and drove south.[15] As they were road building, we crossed the Mississippi at Greenville and drove, through Arkansas to Natchez—a beautiful day—very warm. Arrived Natchez at 7:30. Saw old boatman Prince, running ferry.

Sat., Feb. 5
New Orleans
Monteleone

We had a beautiful drive down the Natchez trace—Natchez to New Orleans. Dined at Delmonico's—on St. Charles. Had a big party, lasting til 1 a.m., with the entire New Orleans crowd—at Marc's house.

Sun., Feb. 6
New Orleans

A fine fair day but done up by too much drinking last night. Went to dine at Julius's mother's. In the morning wrote of Tom Mooney.[16] Had to go to bed in the afternoon. Got up and went to a party, at Elma's.

Mon., Feb. 7
Beaumont, Texas
La Salle

We got started, at 9:30, after breakfast with Lucille and Elma, interrupted by newspaper photographer. Went over the new bridge, across the Mississippi and got a magnificent view of the river and city. Very hot all day. Got to Beaumont at 7.

Tues., Feb. 8
San Antonio

I was tired and very disagreeable all day. I spat out to Mother my anger with Katharine and her high flown talk. Then I grew silent and stayed so all day.

When we got near San Antonio, at the edge of town, had a flat. The man did a bum job fixing it. It was evident there were too many at Randolph's.

Wed., Feb. 9
San Antonio

I went downtown and got a room in a hotel called "The Prudential." Went to the hospital and about with Randolph to see some of his soldier patients. In the evening a brother medical officer came in and we drank and talked. I wrote.

Thurs., Feb. 10
San Antonio

Stayed in the room at the hotel, until 1—writing of Burton Rascoe and Ben Hecht.[17] It was a very hot day. E and Mother were at work on a dinner for Randolph's Colonel [Ballantine] and his wife. He turned out to be a peppery, generous, amusing one—a good drinker, eater, and talker. Charming evening.

Fri., Feb. 11
San Antonio

A good day of writing—the memoirs. In the afternoon to drive, with Mother, Randolph and E. We went to dinner with one of Randolph's brother doctors, who brought his mother. The dinner a failure, and infinitely dull.

Sat., Feb. 12
San Antonio

Worked well, on the memoirs. Very hot and damp, all day. In the evening all the others went off, to dine with some army man while I spent all the late afternoon and evening wandering in crowded Saturday night streets in the Mexican quarter.

Sun., Feb. 13
San Antonio

Pretty good day of work. Up at 7 to go see Randolph get off. No go. Ceiling too low. Back to hotel to write. We all dined at hotel and Randolph flew off at 3:30. Mary arrived, bringing Winona, at 4.[18] Mother took train for home, at 8:40.

Mon., Feb. 14
San Antonio

Winona's tale of Mary gone wild. I stayed in town to write. Took Mary to lunch. Saw his [i.e., Randolph's] squadron flight. Took Mary's car and realized how near a wreck it was. Went to Alamo. Dined at Randolph's quarters and the army crowd came in.

Tues., Feb. 15
San Antonio

Tried to get at Weeks Hall, in the memoirs.[19] Had pretty good morning of work. Went to trial of pecan shellers—now working $3 to $5 a week— big shot Seligman—a millionaire. This is a story.[20] Went to get Mary's car. We dined at Randolph's quarters. Home early, to pack.

Wed., Feb. 16
Monterrey, Mexico

Left San Antonio at 10. Went to Laredo and lost Mary at the customs. Drove through a flat wild country but very beautiful as we got down toward Monterrey. Stayed at Hotel Continental, on a little square—the air heavy with the perfume of orange blossoms.

Thurs., Feb. 17
[Mexico]

A long day's drive, mostly through a wild country, to this spot.[21] Mary ran low on gas in the wildest part but finally got some at a small village. This a rather violent town—hatred of foreigners in the air—many soldiers about. E got quite sick and after she got better I had an attack. Did not sleep. Continued crowing of cocks and ringing of bells. Winona highly nervous. The little old Indian in blanket in the court. Men and trucks passing.

Fri., Feb. 18
Mexico City

The day and drive were both magnificent but, at the very start Mary's car started to kick up. She was to ride with me but got into it and drove on. It just would run but got better. We lunched on a high mountain and were joined by a small underfed and very dirty boy with magnificent eyes, who ate like a little wolf.

In the city went to several hotels, but finally landed at the Geneve, very bourgeois, very comfortable—bedroom and parlor for 10 pesos.

Sat., Feb. 19
Mexico City

Do not too much mind being in this hotel, filled with rich Americans but cannot go, with the women to the restaurants where the same Americans gather.

Went to Sanborn's—hated it—to big cocktail bar—bad.

However dined in a Mexican restaurant where the crazy woman Rita came. Went then to drink beer in a little Mexican dive. Much nicer. Got bull fight and lottery tickets.

Sun., Feb. 20
Mexico City

The outstanding thing of the day, after a morning when my work would not go, was the visit to the bull fight . . . 8 bulls to be killed by 8 of the great Mexican champions. The whole thing a very curious experience, the absorption in the technique, that presently comes, this with awareness of danger, your nerves played on, the intense excitement of the crowd, the strutting of the fighters, the bull's confusion . . . at bottom the feeling that our own games, football and particularly baseball were at bottom healthier.

Mon., Feb. 21
Mexico City

It rained and I woke feeling rotten but, presently, got to work and the work went well. I drove with the others, out to a hotel, near the house of

Rivera[22] and then to a German osteopath where he talked a great deal of the world war as he gave me a treatment.

In the evening went to see some native dances, very beautifully done.

Tues., Feb. 22
Mexico City

Rewrote the scene with sister—in the kitchen at night.[23] Was pretty seedy. Going to a German osteopath. We went to another German place to dine. It has been unusually cold. My head has been bad. Mary and her friend went off, to dine with the Noel girls. Got what is practically an invitation to go to Hollywood—from John Emerson—will not go.

Wed., Feb. 23
Mexico City

After a good morning of work I went off in the car, with the usual crowd of women with whom I have been thrown here, to certain small Mexican towns . . . a delightful drive. We went to one very old and very poor town and then to one where there is a great church with a miraculous saint. In the evening we were called on by the wife of an exiled German professor and later met him but he had no English.

Thurs., Feb. 24
Mexico City

Bright clear day and I worked well—on the memoirs. In the afternoon went off alone with Mary to the park and country. The doctor here is a fraud. I shall drop him. In the evening tired and so just dined and to bed. Altitude here perhaps too much. Again I did not sleep.

Fri., Feb. 25
Mexico City

A bright fine day and after a night of no sleep, and a morning of work—doing Faulkner and Hemingway[24]—went with E to the market.

Mary went off to the country to get the Noels. E and I went to the Ritz, to cocktails with a Texas girl,[25] friend of Mrs. Perry of Chicago University. Early to bed, to try to sleep. No good.

Sat., Feb. 26
Mexico City

To break the sleeplessness tried not working at all. Loafed in the car and went with E to walk in the markets.

In the evening to a party of American newspapermen—the party got up by two Texas girls.[26] E got sick. I drank a great deal and at last, had a real night's sleep.

Sun., Feb. 27
Mexico City

Did not try to work but went off with E, Emily Barksdale and a very charming Spanish couple[27] to the country. Dined outdoors, under banana trees, saw grotesque dances in a village,[28] drove back through snow. It was an extraordinarily delightful day with delightful people.

Mon., Feb. 28
Mexico City

Had to tell Mary Emmett that the climate here keeps me too high strung and nervous, unable to sleep, etc. Worked well.

In the p.m. went to visit the Maximilian Palace—a very beautiful location—the palace and grounds, not state property, very beautiful.

Dined with a party, including K. Noel, at a good restaurant.

Tues., March 1
Mexico City

Worked well, although still no sleep. Went to lunch at the Embassy—Ambassador Josephus Daniels.[29] Good story teller. In the evening went to Lady Baltimore with Strackbein and Kirk. Sat late talking to woman of [B. Pul. ?] Association and New York Times.[30]

Wed., March 2
Mexico City

A cloudy, rainy day. The work went fairly well. I went on a long shopping expedition with E and in the evening to the Noels. Ineffective man—attractive wife and daughters.[31] E had bad luck and smashed her finger in the car door.

Thurs., March 3
Mexico City

A clear bright day. E and Mary Emmett went off to visit some Mexican town, staying for the day. I worked and then went to walk in the big market and do errands. Decided I would go to Acapulco, leaving here Monday. In the evening Emily Barksdale came and we all went off to a big restaurant where we had a big dinner with wine. E's smashed finger better.

Fri., March 4
Mexico City

A long feverish day of work that left me exhausted. We all went in the late afternoon to the home of a German philosopher,[32] driven out of Germany because he had a German [i.e., Jewish] wife.

Manuel Negrete came to show his painting.

Was knocked out by a letter from a lawyer about the Barton mess and could not sleep.[33]

Sat., March 5
Mexico City

The morning pretty much devoted to writing a letter to try to clear up the Arthur Barton matter. It is one of the most unpleasant affairs I was ever in.

Then went, with the others, escorted by Emily Barksdale, to see a big hacienda, to which I had been invited. Eleanor having an attack of diarrhea.

Sun., March 6
Mexico City

A bright clear day. Worked well. Rode about in the p.m. and went to Noel's for tea. In the evening [Sam] Marshall—Detroit Daily News—came and Bill Lander—United Press—came and we all dined together. Marshall going to Acapulco with us.

Mon., March 7
Iguala, Mexico
[Hotel Madrid]

We got off from Mexico City at 11—had lunch at Cuernavaca. On the road Mary's car got overheated near Taxco and she and I had a row—over her giving orders. The country very magnificent. Sam Marshall, Detroit News—with us. We spent the night at Iguala. Sam fine chap.

Tues., March 8
[Acapulco—Hotel
Mirador]

The drive down, from Iguala to Acapulco was, I believe, the worst I ever went through—blinding dust, many detours, bands of Indians with wheelbarrows, Mary's car going wrong, my quarrel with her, etc.

And then the cool beauty and wonder of the sea, at the end.

Wed., March 9
Acapulco

We fall more and more in love with this place. Mary and Sam will leave us on Friday and we will have a time alone together here. Wonderful quarters, above the Pacific and the finest bathing I have ever known. I am working well.

Thurs., March 10
Acapulco

Mary and Eleanor went off, with some Kansas people on an inland lagoon trip and came home hot and disappointed. It turns out that Sam Marshall—Detroit News, who is with us, is a tightwad.

We saw old Gilda Gray,[34] living in a trailer on the beach. I worked O.K.

Fri., March 11
Acapulco

Mary and Sam Marshall up early and off to Mexico City in Mary's car. Sam driving—a fear that he will bully Mary. The days all the same here, sun, the sea, a soft breeze. Work and then to eat and then sleep. Awake, bathe, eat again and sleep.

The American world seems a million miles off.

Sat., March 12
Acapulco

Bright clear day. Here we get up at 9—eat breakfast. I go to work. Quit at 1. We lie about and read until 3—go to the beach—stay until 7—dine at 9 and to bed.

Sun., March 13
Acapulco

The town very quiet. It is filled with sailors, from 4 Canadian warships. We drove off, along a sea road to the lagoon. Came back to swim, went to the town for the evening.

Mon., March 14
Acapulco

An advertising man I formerly knew, when he was at Firestone appeared. I wrote a short story called "His Chest of Drawers."[35] Again the beach and in the evening an hour or two sitting in the plaza of the town.

Tues., March 15
Acapulco

It is almost impossible to keep up notes in this place. All days seem the same. I wrote a beautiful short story. As usual work, siesta, the sea.

Wed., March 16
Acapulco

Bill Spratling came from Taxco and, all day we sailed in his boat.[36] Stopping to swim at a lovely beach. In the evening a big party for some New York people.

Thurs., March 17
Chilpancingo

We left Acapulco at 2:30—after trying to phone Mary and drove to above town. Very hot and dusty but in the town suddenly cold. There was a dance in the park and we danced, paying 10 cents Mexican. The little boys sat with us, trading Mexican words for English ones.

Fri., March 18
Iguala

We got an early start, over a mountain road, terribly torn up, so that, for 60 miles, we could make but 15 miles an hour. It was terribly hot and dusty. We stayed again in the above town, walking in the market, and sitting in the little park. It was good to be in a Mexican town, off the route of tourists.

Sat., March 19
Mexico City

The government has taken over the oil companies and there may be a shortage of gasoline, to get out of the country. Up early and we breakfasted at Taxco—looked at the town and went on to Cuernavaca. We stayed about there for 2 hours and came on, into the city, arriving at 4:30. Again I felt the tenseness that seems, inevitably, to come with the high altitude.

Sun., March 20
Mexico City

Half ill from being unable to sleep. Unable to work. The decision made to go north Tuesday. The town full of rumors because of confiscation of oil companies. Went in the afternoon, to Lena, to where came a newspaperman from Ambassador Daniels. Evidently the oil men overreached themselves and got good too late.

Dined at the German place.

Mon., March 21
Mexico City

Again no sleep. Was in desperation. Sent off story to Chambrun—"His Chest of Drawers." Drove about with Mary and then we went with Noels, Sam Marshall and Mrs. Reuhle to the Hotel Ontario, where we had a big dinner with wine. Mrs. Reuhle wanted to talk of writing. Drove her home and got lost.

Tues., March 22
Villa Juarez

Up at 6, to leave at 7. Mary up to see us off—very sad. 3 nights without sleep. I drove over the mountains to Tamazunchale—very tired. Drank a bottle of tequila and passed out, E getting me, in some way, into the hotel at Juarez. Woke up feeling fine. There was a circus in town and we went. Met a Lee County boy.

Wed., March 23
Monterrey

There was a big country-wide labor demonstration, in favor of Cárdenas—and his taking over the oil companies.[37] We saw people marching in the towns but got to Monterrey too late for the big parade.

We walked about the town, much changed and Americanized, E said, since she was here, and to bed early.

Thurs., March 24
Brownsville, Texas

We drove from Monterrey, by a dirt and gravel road to Reynosa, on the border, where we passed the customs. The road was through a wild looking uninhabited country. It was very hot. We drove down through orange groves, on the American side and at the little Miller Hotel, got room— better quarters than we had here before.

Fri., March 25
Brownsville

A windy, gusty day. Worked on a story, to be called "Mexican Night." E and I went to the new ship channel to fish. Caught 2 crokers. The day continued windy and the fish not biting. Very warm.

Sat., March 26
Brownsville

Heavy wind, but, after a morning of work rewriting again Mexican Night, went to the new ship channel, with E and succeeded in getting a red fish. Had it cooked for dinner and went to a crazy movie, starring Hepburn.[38] The movies still seem empty to me.

Sun., March 27
Brownsville

Finished and sent off the story. Mexican Night.[39] We went to Boco Chica—at the mouth of the Rio Grande—to fish but had no success. Caught only sea cat. A strong wind blowing. We gave up and came home early.

Mon., March 28
Brownsville

Very windy. I did two pieces for the book [*Memoirs*]. The window of the room here looks straight up the Rio Grande—the Mexican town Matamoros to be seen on the left.

We went to the ship channel to fish but had no luck. The wind was very strong. There were few fish caught.

Tues., March 29
Brownsville

Very dark and windy. I finished up the Mexican Night story. We went to the channel but didn't get a bite.

Wed., March 30
Brownsville

I did a new thing called "Mexican Impressions."[40] We went to Matamoros—very hot—got liquor and glass. Had lunch over there—the hottest day we have had here.

Thurs., March 31
Brownsville

Cloudy and hot. Tried to work but had no success. We went to the ship channel but the little flies ate us up. I got badly burned. The city is filled with Texas schoolteachers. Got wire from Mary who is to meet us at San Antonio. Wrote letters.

Sherwood Anderson fishing at Brownsville, Texas, in 1938.
(Trustees of the Sherwood Anderson Literary Estate.)

Fri., April 1
Brownsville

Went, in the afternoon to the channel to fish and, sitting naked to the waist, in the wind, got a heavy chest cold. Felt very miserable.

Sat., April 2
Brownsville

Sick and miserable all day. Spent the day reading Prescott's Conquest of Mexico.

Sun., April 3
Brownsville

Still sick. All day in room. Finished Conquest of Mexico.

Mon., April 4
Brownsville

A little better. Got out of the room in the evening to dine. Mary arrived, from Mexico, at 10 p.m.

Tues., April 5
Brownsville

Still better. Did not try to work. Finished reading Conquest and Bob Coates' Natchez Trace.[41] We took Paul Roush and wife and all went off to Matamoros to dine, on quail and venison.

Wed., April 6
Corpus Christi

We got away from Brownsville at 9—the car packed, to capacity. Got to Corpus at 3. Hot beautiful day. Got our old quarters by the water. Went fishing and the trout were striking. The cough greatly improved.

Thurs., April 7
Corpus Christi

One of the coldest April northers in 50 years—with a terrific wind and snow, as far south as San Antonio. Nothing to do but stay in the house and read.

Fri., April 8
Corpus Christi

Still bitter cold and with a cold high wind blowing. E decided to go on ahead to San Antonio while Mary and I stay here until Monday morning. She got off at 1.

Sat., April 9
Corpus Christi

E in San Antonio, in Mary's car. It began to grow warmer. Mary and I went to fish on the lake. I wrote. We played keno.

Sun., April 10
Corpus Christi

Warm—at last, after this amazing April norther—crops spoiled everywhere. We went on the Ann—to the gulf in the a.m.—inner basin in the p.m. No fish. E returned from San Antonio.

Mon., April 11
Opelousas, La.

We left Corpus at 9—Mary very boyishly sad at our going. It is hard to leave her. It was a clear warm day and we drove pretty hard, going the southern way, by the gulf, but turning north to Houston at Lake Charles, we drove until dark. It was good to be alone with E but we missed Mary.

Tues., April 12
Tuscaloosa

We were up at six and drove through a heavy fog, to Baton Rouge. It was a day of hard driving, to get to above town, where we met Randolph, who is here, as a doctor, getting students to become flyers.
It was a warm overcast day.

Wed., April 13
Knoxville, Tenn.

Had breakfast, with Randolph, at Tuscaloosa, Alabama, and off at 8:30. A fine day to drive, all the woods along the way blossoming—dogwood and redbud. I drove most of the day. E's voice about gone, with a cold. Saw no one at Knoxville and to bed early.

Thurs., April 14
Marion

Up at 5:30 and off at 6:30. Again a very beautiful warm day. We came by 11 West—E planning to see the doctor for x-ray at Abingdon. Couldn't see him. Got home at 12. Spent the afternoon unpacking and clearing decks.

Fri., April 15
Marion

Very beautiful warm Spring day. I spent it answering a big batch of mail.
Bob moving to new quarters. E not at all well. We had Bob and Mary,
John and Mary Eleanore to dine.

Sat., April 16
Marion

A warm Spring day, with everything breaking out into bloom. I still worked to catch up with correspondence and then went to take a lot of stuff to
Ripshin and take my spring look. Everything fine and in good order over
there.

Sun., April 17
Bluefield, W. Va.

I began to work, a little, again. In the late afternoon I drove Eleanor over
the mountains to Bluefield, in the evening light, dogwood and apple
blossoms—vivid green fields and hills. We strolled about until she left at
10:20.[42]

Mon., April 18
Marion

Lewis Galantière married.
    Woke up late at Bluefield—heavy rain and fog. I got the stuff for cock-
tails at Wytheville. I got the old broken teeth pulled. It stayed damp and
cloudy all day.

Tues., April 19
Marion

Recovering from tooth pulling. OK until noon, and worked but then flat.
Tried to go fishing but had to give it up. Bright warm day. John came in
the evening and we drove out to his house—a rather large bare white
farmhouse, beautifully situated. Had impression he was not so happy.

Wed., April 20
Marion

Feeling rotten from the tooth pulling of Monday but went and had the
others out. Not painful but myself weak and sick later. Tried to work a
little but no good. May and Mother came to play cards. Trout fishing
began today and half the town went.

Thurs., April 21
Marion

A dreary rainy day and myself laid low from the tooth pulling. It is like recovering from a long illness. Got the car fixed. Read all day and played cards in the evening—a wasted day of illness.

Fri., April 22
Marion

Another wet rainy day and I had to stay in, doing nothing. Funk got home from his trip. Joe Wyse and wife came in evening and he tells me he will, this year, stone the road from Troutdale to Ripshin.

Sat., April 23
Marion

Bright, clear but somewhat cold day—a light frost. My face still swollen, and enough knocked out so that I can't work. Spent the afternoon in Funk's shop—watching him work and to bed early. Uncomfortable night.

Sun., April 24
Marion

Much better. Spent the afternoon out of doors, seeing a ball game, and the evening with Funk. A letter, about the unemployed, from Dr. Henry upset me and I blew off to Mother. It was a glorious Spring day.

Mon., April 25
Marion

My face much better. Had been unable to sleep and didn't arise until 10. Went to the farm—the creeks along the way lined with fishermen. Everything at the farm is flourishing.

In the evening to see Snow White, the 1st entirely satisfactory movie I've seen. It is gorgeous fantasy.

Tues., April 26
Marion

A very beautiful day and, after working all morning I drove to the Rye Valley and spent the afternoon fishing. Got trout and red eyes. The whole country very beautiful. Reading Prescott's Peru.

Wed., April 27
Marion

Worked hard at my desk all morning and then went trout fishing, getting some nice trout. It was very beautiful out—a good many other fishermen on the streams. Sat all evening on the back porch looking at the stars and talking to Mother.

Thurs., April 28
Bluefield, W.Va.

Another bright beautiful day. Bob is moving the print shop. Worked and then, in the late afternoon, drove to Bluefield, to stay over night and meet E's early train. Went in the evening to amateur boxing at Bluefield, Va.

Fri., April 29
Marion

Got Eleanor off the train at 7:20 and had a delightful ride home with her. Home at 10. Worked and went to the farm in the afternoon—back at 4. Very windy. Dogwood in full bloom. John came in the evening. Had not slept the night before. Face almost well.

Sat., April 30
Marion

Rain—nearly all day. Worked so long at my desk that I was done up. Took a walk and got wild flowers—with E. Stayed at home and to bed early. Headache.

Sun., May 1
Marion

Bright sunshiny day. Worked. Bob Williams and John Anderson to dinner. Went with John and E to a ball game. The college girls in the yard all day rehearsing for their Mayday. We went twice to Mr. Copenhaver's farm to take care of his stock—he being sick.

Mon., May 2
Marion

Another clear fine day—planting going on everywhere. E and I went fishing. Got none but bought some to make a show. I had worked all morning. E left for New York on the 8:50 p.m. train. Bum sleep.

Tues., May 3
Marion

Again a bright hot day—the leaves popping. Worked and went to farm—
planted willow by the creek and 100 petunias. Had not slept well. Went
with Mother to get plants at Chilhowie. Housecleaning.

Wed., May 4
Marion

The morning bright and clear and a fine shower in the p.m. Worked and
went fishing, below the red bridge and got caught in the rain. No fish. In
the evening took a long ride with Funk who was full of his problems.

Thurs., May 5
Marion

A cloudy day. Worked and went, taking May, to Ripshin. It did not rain.
In the evening I sat with B.E. and Mother, and May came to play cards. I
slept pretty well.

Fri., May 6
Marion

Worked and then went to the river in the p.m. Very beautiful although I
caught no fish. In the evening several of us went out to John's and drank
beer and played cards.

Sat., May 7
Marion

A bright clear day but rain much wanted. Worked and in the p.m. to a
ball game. All in with a headache and to bed early, forgetting the possible
coming of Mimi. Reread Free for All.[43] Disturbing letter from Eleanor.

Sun., May 8
Marion

A long morning of work. It rained after we had feared a long dry time.
Bad for college girls at Ripshin. Went to Funk and we sat talking of marriage and then played cards. Took a walk to the station and then over
Lincoln Hill. Got home before another big rain. E has been offered a big
job.[44]

Mon., May 9
Marion

Like a fool I sat too long absorbed at my desk in a cold house and caught a cold. Took Mother and Jones [Gross] to the woods to get flowers. Am knocked again.

Tues., May 10
Marion

I am laid up with a cold. As John Sullivan predicted it has turned very cold. Had to lay up all day but did get down in the afternoon to court. No work.

Wed., May 11
Marion

Cold and raw as John Sullivan predicted. I went down to the courthouse to see a trial. Feeling floppy and ill but sat up in the evening and played cards with Aunt May.

Thurs., May 12
Marion

In bed—ill all day and outside a cold rain. I just stayed in bed and read.

Fri., May 13
Marion

Alone here in the house but the cold [not] better so I can't work. Rainy. John has taken Mother and B.E. to Warrenton.[45] I hope for the sun. Have been able to do nothing but read.

Sat., May 14
Marion

Very cold, with occasional downpours. The trip of Mother, John and B.E. to Warrenton a fiasco. They got home at 8:30. Mary is called to New York—inheritance tax. Sat all afternoon and talked to Funk while he did up his meat.

Sun., May 15
Marion

Still very cold and with a high wind, occasional showers, patches of sunlight and more winds. Worked both morning and afternoon and in the evening went for a long talk with Funk who is still in a state.

Mon., May 16
Marion

Cold and clear and I managed to get back to creative work—a big day.

In the evening took a long slow drive with Funk who was in one of the moods in which a man talks for hours of past adventures with women. Alas, I joined in it.

Tues., May 17
Marion

Warmer and clear and after a rather bad night worked and then went to farm.

Everything beautiful there, song birds everywhere. Bought bacon for the summer. Read life of Lafayette.

Wed., May 18
Marion

A grey rainy day and after work I went to call on the new head of insane asylum, Mr. Blalock.[46] Liked him. In the evening went, with several others to Funk's, to play cards.

Thurs., May 19
Marion

Very hot day but slept so little rather knocked out.

In the afternoon simply ran small errands, got lumber to build screens for bark houses and then went to bed. Headache all day.

Fri., May 20
Marion

After work to Ripshin, in the rain, to take supplies for the cleaning. Went to an absurd trial of a faker who had taken a lot of money from citizens.[47] In the evening found Funk in a horrible depressed mood and tried to get him out of it.

Sat., May 21
Marion

Dull all day for lack of sleep. I however worked and in the afternoon went to Funk's to build new screen doors for the bark houses at the farm. To bed early and slept.

Sun., May 22
Marion

A soft beautiful day and slept—so I felt grand. Took Bob, Mary and baby beyond Wytheville to see a saddle horse—cold . . . worked . . . painted screens—went with Funk for a long walk at night.

Mon., May 23
Marion

My sleeplessness continues. I am having to dope myself almost nightly. We are having a long rainy time. Tried to take it easier and stay more out of doors. The evening with Funk. Hot and rainy.

Tues., May 24
Marion

Another rainy day—after a night of rain and hail. Worked and in the afternoon got at it and finished the screens. Spent 2 hours at dentist.

Wed., May 25
Marion

Rain all day—with work and sitting and talking with men in the evening. Sam [Dillard] the sheriff telling stories of his experiences.

Thurs., May 26
Marion

Still rain. After working I went to the dentist and then drove to Wytheville to get liquor. It was Mr. Copenhaver's birthday and Mother had a men's party. I took a long walk over Lincoln hill in the evening.

Fri., May 27
Marion

Grey and cloudy all day and the ball game with Abingdon couldn't come off. After work went to the farm. We have more bird's nests than usual about the house and the delphiniums have begun to bloom. Also have big yellow lillies. Went to the Negro high school graduation.[48]

Sat., May 28
Marion

Bright clear day. Worked. Got new tires for car. In the evening went to Bob's young democrats and noticed no working people. Got into making indiscreet remarks to the politicians so I came away. Did not like attitude.

Sun., May 29
Marion

Dark, cold—rainy, all day and night. Some work done. Bob and Andy both deep in gloom, so that I had to spend part of the day with each.

Mon., May 30
Marion

Very cold and rainy. Mother in bed from her fall. After work I went to the farm where I found all in good shape but needing care. To Funk's to sit in talk.

Tues., May 31
Marion

At last the sun. Was floored from lack of sleep but worked. John came with his wife. Drove about and the country more green and beautiful than ever. In the evening listened to the Ross-Armstrong fight.[49]

Wed., June 1
Marion

Eleanor arrived unexpectedly. Had gone to train and there she was looking very beautiful. The whole tone of the house changed at once. She and Funk went with me to address graduating class at Ivanhoe.[50]

Thurs., June 2
Marion

A long day of rain so that we couldn't go to the farm. Went to call on John and wife. Backed into a car on Main Street and jammed it badly. No hurt to my car.

Fri., June 3
Marion

At last a clear warm day—spent getting settled at Ripshin. We drove back here for the night. Things got pretty well settled. Great flurry because our silver is gone.

Sat., June 4
Marion

Got in a few hours work at my cabin at Ripshin. We spent the day unpacking and putting the house in order and in the evening to see the college girls' play. E very lovely all day.

Sun., June 5
Ripshin

We got permanently in the house and pretty well settled. Took a walk over to the Swan Farm and picked wild berries. Funk and wife came for the evening—bright moonlight and very lovely.

Mon., June 6
Ripshin

We started to cut a door off porch into north log wing of the house and started work on it. It will make a grand new guest room.[51] Ruby and Charlotte [Sullivan] are moved into the upper bark house.

Tues., June 7
Ripshin

E is more lovely and charming than ever. We made progress on the new room. Started a new story I call—A Late Spring.[52]

Wed., June 8
Ripshin

Off to town to get framing for doors, hardware, etc. for new room. Funk and wife, Wyse and wife to dinner.[53] We had some of the fine liquor brought from Mexico. E and I took a walk in the moonlight, a very beautiful night and we in love with our home.

Thurs., June 9
Ripshin

A big day of work, on the new story, "A Late Spring," and an outline made. Between times of writing—painting in the cabin. In the afternoon E and I went off to town, taking the Sullivan girls and returned at 10 p.m.

Fri., June 10
Ripshin

Much writing and painting and the new room in the house finished. Clouds all day and at 6 p.m. a terrific storm. E went off to Wytheville to pick Mimi and daughter off a bus. . . .[54]

Sat., June 11
Ripshin

Mimi here with child. Writing and painting, all day and in the evening Bob and wife, John and wife to dine. Dave [Greear] came with his girl. It was a very beautiful day and evening but got into awkward political discussion with Bob.

Sun., June 12
Ripshin

Work on A Late Spring. Then painted for a time and went off with E, Mimi, Karlin, Ruby, and Charlotte to Marion, where we went to a ballgame. The sky overcast and the wind strong. It was the day of the Big June at St. Clair Bottom.

Mon., June 13
Ripshin

Cool bright day and I worked away at Late Spring. Then I put in the day painting in the new room—E having gone off to town.
   Evening at home, playing cards.

Tues., June 14
Ripshin

A bright day, all day and we were cutting hay. I was on the story all morning, then some house painting. In the evening Mr. Copenhaver's [Sunday school] class—some 30 strong, all big men, mostly farmers, came for an outing—from Marion.

Wed., June 15
Ripshin

Yesterday was E's birthday,[55] so we went to town in the p.m., taking Ruby and Charlotte. Had the new head of the asylum to dine. He has a pretty wife. It rained. Went to a hearing of the N.L.R. Board on Mathieson.[56] The girls kept us waiting and we drove home at ten in a heavy rain. Worked in the morning on A Late Spring.

Thurs., June 16
Ripshin

The day spent at work—painting the woodwork and writing in my cabin. It was dark, rainy and cold all day. I began reading Maugham's Of Human Bondage.

Fri., June 17
Ripshin

Another rainy day, spent at the story and at painting. We got the new room settled and it is nice. We got new pot hangers for the fireplaces. We went early to bed and slept hard.

Sat., June 18
Ripshin

Rainy, cold and wet but worked well. Went off to Marion, in the p.m. and the sun came out a little. Went to a rather dull ballgame. In the evening went to a banquet, given for Joe Wyse, road engineer, by his men. He is being transferred.

Sun., June 19
Ripshin

At home, all day. It kept raining. I worked on the long story and E came in the afternoon while I painted. The Sullivans had gone off with the truck. We read Gorky's "Hermit" aloud. It was a happy day and E very lovely.

Mon., June 20
Ripshin

More rain. Worked all right. We began to break up the old hill, above the garden, for grass and buckwheat. E in town all day dictating. I painted at the cabin.

Tues., June 21
Ripshin

Grey day, with more rain in the morning. Had bad night for sleep, and in no shape to work. E went to town in car and I followed in truck. After dinner we drove to Bluefield, W.Va. to meet Miss Dieckmann from Chicago[57]—drive very beautiful.

Wed., June 22
Ripshin

E and I woke up at Bluefield at 7 and met Miss Dieckmann at 7:30—no breakfast. We drove to Marion and had breakfast at 9:30. E and Miss Dieckmann got off in the car at 10—for camp.[58] Got home at 11 a.m. and worked and painted all day, going to the garage to hear the Louis-Schmeling fight.[59]

Thurs., June 23
Ripshin

Very lonely here with E gone to her camp. We managed to get up our orchard hay. Went to Marion in the truck, dined there at Mother's and came home to go to the poor little tent theatre at Troutdale.

Fri., June 24
Ripshin

A bright clear day and I worked on revision and on the cabin. In the evening Mary Eleanore, John and Ann came to dine. We sat until 9. I was very lonely for E all day.

Sat., June 25
Ripshin

Spent the morning on revision. Did some painting, in cabin. Drove to town—Mother ill. Sat in Funk's kitchen. Drove home in the evening—a black night, very lonely—without E.

Sun., June 26
Ripshin

The day no good for work. I found it wasn't going well and spent the time painting. Went to Marion but came right back. Was afraid I would have to invite Jack Scherer—who bores me.[60] It was a lovely day.

Mon., June 27
Ripshin

Threat of rain all day. Worked fairly well. In the evening Funk came, for the night, on the whole a pleasant visit—except we got rather irritating toward each other at croquet.

Tues., June 28
Ripshin

Day of sun and clouds. Very cold. After a bad start wrote well. Finished the painting of the cabin and made a hurried trip to town. The loneliness for the return of E grows at night.

Wed., June 29
Ripshin

It has come a cold time but the rainy time is over. We cut more hay. E will be home tomorrow. The nights are most lonely.

I finished the painting of my cabin. I went trout fishing, down to where the Fox comes into Laurel,[61] climbing over many rocks—the water beautiful but no strikes. The trout, if any, were not feeding.

Thurs., June 30
Ripshin

The day for E to return and I was as excited over the prospect as a young lover. Could not sit—so, after working spent the day, at work on the lawn and flower gardens. John Sullivan had gone off to a funeral with the truck. The day was fine—sunshiny and warm. I worked well.

Fri., July 1
Ripshin

Miss Dieckmann of Chicago, at the house. A good morning of work. Went to Marion, to do last minute shopping before our long trip, to Chicago and Iowa. Am in a good working mood—on Late Spring. I hate to drop it.

Sat., July 2
Ripshin

A warm clear day and we got the cutting of hay done—in orchard and vineyard. Went to Marion and brought May, Mazy, Channing and child for dinner. Dave Greear also dropped in. In the evening a concert of Mexican music.[62]

Sun., July 3
Cincinnati, Ohio
Hotel Gibson

We left Ripshin shortly after six and drove to Marion to unload the Wilsons and May. Got away at 7 and got to Cincinnati at 7. The town crowded. Had to [pay] $6.00 for room. All day the roads, over mountains, crowded, the day grey, with rain after Lexington. Left Miss Dieckmann at Cincinnati.

Mon., July 4
Michigan City,
Indiana
Duneland Beach

An easy drive from Cincinnati and we arrived at Ferdinand Schevill's house at 3. Had a swim and in the evening sat on the beach a long time watching the people along the beach celebrate with fireworks.

Tues., July 5
Lake Okoboji,
Iowa

This day, after Ferdinand got us up at 5:30 and we had to make a complete circle of Chicago, we made 557 miles and arrived at this place at 8 . . . very tired and sleepy. It was terrifically hot all day. We took turns driving. We came for a conference, working and business girls E had to attend. We got a very comfortable cottage by the lake.[63]

Wed., July 6
Lake Okoboji,
Iowa

A warm sunshiny day. Worked and went to the town of Milford to shop. Swam and loafed all afternoon. This looks a very rich and is a very beautiful country. The farms look big and prosperous. We are in a little house by a beautiful lake.

Thurs., July 7
Okoboji Lake

Worked all morning on the introductory essay for Late Spring. In the afternoon went fishing but no luck. Drove to Spirit Lake in the evening and saw a bad movie, made half ill by the vulgarity of Rudy Vallée.[64]

Fri., July 8
Okoboji Lake

A very beautiful day and I had a long morning on the introductory essay to Late Spring.

In the afternoon took E on a fishing trip down the lake. The day continued lovely but we got no fish.

Sat., July 9
Okoboji Lake

The days very beautiful and the nights cool. As I have worked well am loving this little cabin by the lake.

After work had Nelson—Wisconsin professor[65] and two women for drinks. Went to hear the stenographers discuss advisability of throwing married women out of jobs so single women could get them. Very naive and human. Got bad headache from too many drinks with Nelson.

Sun., July 10
Okoboji Lake

Beautiful hot day and the resort here crowded with week-enders—big Iowa farmers with families. Went bathing with Rose—Italian factory girl. Dined at the women's camp. In the evening went to Gull's Point to picnic and fish.

Mon., July 11
Lake Okoboji

Good day of work. Awoke with headache but it went away. Driving old Chevrolet while garage man works on Dodge. The garage man and mountain girl. Man with trained dogs. E brought 3 of her women for drinks. Hot all day but with gorgeous breeze.

Tues., July 12
Lake Okoboji

Day of extreme heat and mosquitoes—the corn fields very beautiful here. Got my car back from tuning up. Went to ballgame in town after working well all morning. Talked to insurance man from Omaha. Fished at night off wharf at Gull's Point.

Wed., July 13
Okoboji Lake

A long morning of work in which I finished the essay to go in front of Late Spring. Made a short speech at E's Conference on Mexico. Listened to a dull discussion of international affairs. Bright day and hot in evening. Mosquitoes bad.

Thurs., July 14
Waterloo, Iowa

After work and a finish to the introduction of Late Spring, we left Okoboji at 3:30, driving 200 miles that evening to Waterloo—the country very lovely in the evening light. Dined at the place with the soupy fish.

Fri., July 15
Evansville, Ind.

We arrived at this place at 7:30 p.m., having driven over 500 miles. We had intended staying for the night at New Harmony, Indiana, the Robert Owen town but as it was all commercialized and made a tourist sightseeing place, we hurried through.

Sat., July 16
Louisville, Ky.

Stopped to see Mr. Steele, at Owensboro Ditcher, an old advertising client.[66] Got to Louisville—the Henry Waterson—at 2:30 p.m. In the evening got into touch with Mark Ethridge and wife, of Courier Journal and went with them to the estate of a big whiskey man—a crowd of millionaires. Had a good time shocking them—got half drunk.

Sun., July 17
Marion

Up early and drove to Marion—from Louisville, through Bardstown to Corbin and Cumberland Gap—then by 58 to Bristol. A terrific rain and wind storm struck us at Abingdon and lasted to Marion. Most cars driven off the road but we pushed on, arriving at 6 p.m.—very tired.

Mon., July 18
Ripshin

Back home to a rainy day, the grass everywhere rank, the streams full. John had got the rye cut but not the oats or the clover. The buckwheat in the new field is showing, the bee balm and holly hocks riotous.

Spent the day getting settled and hoping to work again.

Tues., July 19
[Marion]

Rain again, all day. E left in the evening, for a short visit to New York. She is to accept the headship of her department. Myself very sad, wanting her not to work but knowing I could not support her.[67] Stayed the night in Marion.

Wed., July 20
Ripshin

To Ripshin after trading at 10. Suddenly decided I had to change the form of the story.[68] The idea of telling it in letters too cumbersome. After a morning of experiment started new, in a new form. It rained all day until I quit work at 5—then the sun came out. Spent the evening bagging grapes.

Thurs., July 21
Ripshin

Rain all day long and I began to get the story underway in the new and more comfortable form. Began in the rain to bag grapes. Read Jonathan Daniels' book on the South.[69] The creek is a roaring torrent.

Fri., July 22
Ripshin

Rain all night and all day again—the creeks higher and higher. The water getting low in our tank. Helen Dinsmoor came and spent the afternoon . . . an intelligent and fascinating woman. She seemed much at sea. She is doing a thesis on me for her M.A.[70] I let her take home 8 or 10 of my books.

Sat., July 23
Ripshin

Terrific rain all morning and steady rain all afternoon and the creek up to the bridge floor so that we thought it might go. Took Ruby and Charlotte to town. Sat with Funk. Home before dark. A wet world.

Sun., July 24
Ripshin

The tank empty but at last we got the rain going. There was a little sun and the creek cleared. I went off to Marion after an early lunch—and E came, with Bill and Bern Stewart at 5.[71] Bill had got him a big second-hand Rolls Royce—as big and heavy as a truck. He is proud of it. In the morning I worked again on A Late Spring.

Mon., July 25
Ripshin

Wrote until I was exhausted. The sun kept trying to come out. E went off to town. Bill, Bern and I walked. The men got into the oats in the p.m. and they may be saved.

Tues., July 26
Ripshin

The sun out, nearly all day. We got the oats cut. The Solves, from the University of Arizona came.[72] I took them, E, and the Stewarts for a long ride, over White Top Mountain. I worked rapidly, at my desk, all morning.

Wed., July 27
Ripshin

Bright warm day and we finished off the oats. Took Bill off to town to lunch with Bob, John and Dave. He told me the story of his marriage. We sat outside until 10—the 1st time this summer. Solves, of Arizona here but no feeling of closeness to them. . . .[73]

Thurs., July 28
Ripshin

Very hot. E off to town with the Solves. They ended their visit. He did a painting of this house—very commonplace. Took Bill and Bern up over Flat Ridge and to Hungry Mother. They have started the last stretch of our highway. In the morning worked well.

Fri., July 29
Ripshin

Another rainy day, but before the rain we got the oats in the barn. I worked and then bagged grain. Bill and Bern Stewart left. Very satisfactory guests. John, Major and I built a new bed for the new room. The vet came to inoculate all of the neighborhood dogs—for rabies. The creek high again.

Sat., July 30
Ripshin

Again rain all day, and an attack of indigestion in the night. Nevertheless, I worked and after working E and I took the two girls, Ruby and Charlotte to Marion, driving in a heavy rain. It rained harder over there. We came home in the early evening and I painted the bed in the new room. I felt rotten.

Sun., July 31
Ripshin

A bright clear day and we alone in the house—a fine rest.

We drove over to Healing Springs, at Crumpler, North Carolina, where we ate a big country dinner, then around by the long way home, all the country very beautiful.

Mon., August 1
Ripshin

Worked well but am a little afraid the chapter is becoming a bit garrulous. Painted the porch chair and the well head for my [pink?] pump. We succeeded in getting the hay into stacks and have two fine stacks in the barn lot.

Tues., August 2
Ripshin

Sunshine and rain. Worked well and went off to town where I did small errands in the rain. Coming home I ran the car into the ditch and had to have a truck haul me out.

Wed., August 3
Ripshin

Worked a long time in the morning and just as I finished Henry came and I went off to Marion, angry at myself for going. We started to clear the new field behind the barn. I made E come home with me at 3 and in the evening we had a big row. Neither of us slept.

Thurs., August 4
Ripshin

Could not work so did letters. E and I, at peace again, drove to Wytheville, via Independence to get liquor. It rained terrifically. In the evening B.E., Mother, Henry and Katharine to dine. Dave came also. The night was very beautiful.

Fri., August 5
Ripshin

Wrote a short story—"The Writer"[74]—and advanced the novel. Intended to go to town but slept. Went to watch the workers at the rock crusher. The day exquisite.

Sat., August 6
Ripshin

A fair morning's work. Sunshine and then heavy rain. Went to town, taking the girls, and then [with] E's mother and father, Dr. Henry and Katharine to Washington Springs to dine. The landlady read us a poem denouncing Roosevelt. Home at 10, just in time to escape another rain.

Sun., August 7
Ripshin

Did not succeed in working. Lewis and Nancy Galantière arrived at 10:30 and the day was spent in walking about and talking. Nancy has hurt her back and must lie down most of the night.

My nerves rather on edge and in the night a sharp attack of indigestion. No good.

Mon., August 8
Ripshin

Quite ill in the night, cramps in the stomach. Could not go to work and compelled to stay in bed all day. In the evening the director of a theatre from New Orleans came. There was a big dinner I couldn't sit at. Wharton and Mary Esherick arrived at 11:30 p.m.

Tues., August 9
Ripshin

Still ill. Dr. Henry, Katharine and Mother came. John and wife came to dinner. John's wife pregnant. Mary Emmett arrived. I sat at table but couldn't eat. Wharton brought me a beautiful chair. Mary lovely. Feeling stronger.

Wed., August 10
Ripshin

Still weak and unable to work. Wharton and Mary left. E off to town for supplies. I could not work. In the evening Katharine, Dr. Henry and Mother came. We dined outdoors, on the terrace . . . a beautiful night and Lewis very wonderful.

Thurs., August 11
Ripshin

Beautiful day ending with thunder shower but 2/3 of hay got into stacks. Got a little back into story after my illness. Had to spend most of the day loafing and walking about. Lewis Galantière and Nancy extraordinarily fine guests.

Fri., August 12
Ripshin

In form again. The day bright and clear. Much to do in town. Made a speech, for the Shriners, at the Park. Lewis and Henry to White Top. In the evening they were both vulgar—Lewis for the 1st time in my experience with him. He made too much point of being an exquisite one.

Sat., August 13
Ripshin

After a long morning of work, at my desk, off to town where Mother was giving a big party. Raced about all afternoon to hot stores, doing errands and by the time the party was on did not give a damn for it. Lewis was, however, brilliant and Henry did not strut too much. Home late, lovely moonlit night. Settled weather at last.

Sun., August 14
Ripshin

A bright warm day. Worked and then loafed in the sun. Bob, Bab Finley, her husband Dr. Hahn, Marvin Copenhaver and wife Fanny, and Mr. B.E. all came for a plate supper on the terrace.[75] Got into a jam with Bob about politics.

Mon., August 15
Ripshin

Pretty good day's work. The morning bright—but a heavy rain fell in the early afternoon. Lewis and I went for a walk by Mrs. Anderson's[76]— Hack Privett's and over the hill by the old cabin site. He is marvelously fine company.

Tues., August 16
Ripshin

A hot day with some work done on the book. Took Lewis for a long walk, by the Swan place and down by the old road to ford of Fox [Creek]. E in town until late. A great rain storm at 6 p.m.

Wed., August 17
Ripshin

The book advanced. The plumbers came to put the shower in the new room and stayed all day. Big Jim much afraid of John Sullivan on account of Charlotte.[77]

Thurs., August 18
Ripshin

Spent the entire work time over a long letter to a young Ohio writer.[78] Mary and I went to Independence, Wytheville, and Marion. May sick in bed at Marion. Hot, clear day.

Fri., August 19
Ripshin

A bright clear cool day but a day of utter gloom and misery for me—the novel at which I was at work seeming suddenly to fall all to pieces under my hand. My son John came with some new paintings in the evening but I could see nothing.

Sherwood Anderson in his writing cabin at Ripshin Farm.
(Greear Studio, Marion, Virginia.)

Sat., August 20
Ripshin

I have had to set the novel aside for the moment. It gave me a blue day. It is not rich enough. I will have to begin again at the beginning.

The girls went off to town in the truck and we picnicked in the field beyond the barn. We had a bonfire. The night was lovely.

Sun., August 21
Ripshin

Fair cool day. I could not go on with the novel. I did a piece for the young writers book.[79] We took Lewis and Nancy to town. Nancy became ill. It is very pitiful to see such a beautiful woman with an injured back. They left on the evening train for New York. They have been among the most delightful guests we have ever had.

Mon., August 22
Ripshin

The house seems very empty without Lewis and Nancy. E went off to town. After 350 pages of manuscript of the novel I began again, at the beginning. I went to the field to burn brush.

Tues., August 23
Ripshin

A bright clear fine day. E off to town early. Mary in overalls in the flowers. I got the new version of my story under way and then painted the truck. It is a bright scarlet.

Wed., August 24
Ripshin

Grey and cloudy. Went to town with E after working. In town had a long talk with Funk about his problems. Came home in Bob's car—he taking mine to go to Richmond for his candidacy. Mary's nephew Ed Emmett came with his blond wife—Mary's problem.

Thurs., August 25
Ripshin

Mary's nephew Ed Emmett, with blond wife, at house. He wants Mary to back him in the hardware business. They off to town. John clearing the brush in the new field beyond the barn. Flanagan and wife came to dinner. He is the new road supervisor.[80]

Fri., August 26
Ripshin

Mary Emmett has got all the Sullivans busy making flower beds. Eleanor went to town. Ed Copenhaver came with three Copenhaver women.[81] I spent the afternoon with John, making new ground, clearing the upper field.

Sat., August 27
Ripshin

E off to town again. I had a good morning of work. The day very beautiful. Andy Funk came in the late p.m. and later Dave Greear who stayed the night. We spent the evening at cards. A professor—Horton from North Carolina University[82] came with wife, son and sister. The sister an old friend of Y. K. Smith.

Sun., August 28
Ripshin

Work went pretty well. We went to Marion. Bob is elected president of the state young democrats. Dave came and took pictures. His car, with Mary in it, broke down. We dined at the park, a very bad dinner.

Mon., August 29
Ripshin

Worked. E to town. Bob had my car to go to Richmond for the election. There is some mystery.

Mary has built a place to plant young delphiniums. She has had Major and Bruner working for two days. I found a new form for the book— returning to the Winesburg form.

Tues., August 30
Ripshin

Dead. No sleep at all, so I didn't try to work. Bob has burned out the differential of my car. It will cost him $50. Millen Brand came.[83] There was a circus in Troutdale and all went. I was so dead for sleep I had to go home.

Wed., August 31
Ripshin

Mary, Millen Brand, Jean and Ed Brown, from Washington, and good looking woman from Philadelphia all in the house. John cut the big dead

chestnut by the barn and it fell just right across the creek to make a foot
bridge. We put on floor and railing. Bright warm sun and periods of grey
cloudiness. Worked in the morning O.K.

Thurs., Sept. 1
Ripshin

Day of sun and showers. Worked O.K. as I have got a theme I love. Millen
Brand—lacking in vitality, somewhat soft, earnest and honest—has tal-
ent.

Both E and Mary went off to town. I got my own car back. We are
getting ready for threshers and clearing the old garden, to throw it into
pasture and start a new one.

Fri., Sept. 2
Ripshin

Fine clear cool day. Took E to town in the truck. Brought back lime.
Mother with problem, and conference with Bob Williams. Bob came to
dine. The evening getting dull. Thinness of Brand.

Sat., Sept. 3
Ripshin

Gloomy, rainy day. E got a letter from Mother, ill and discouraged and
she went to Marion by bus. Worked O.K. in the morning. In the evening
Mary, Millen and I went to Healing Springs to dine. Got cuts from Fox
grapes.

Sun., Sept. 4
Ripshin

I find Millen Brand a little dull. He lacks vitality. He is curiously vain.
There is however a real sweetness but some spark, you want from a man
burns very small.

Took him and Mary for a ride in the hills. Mary has been very fine. We
dined at home. Played cards but Brand's terrible slowness got my nerves. I
hope he doesn't know how he bores me.

Mon., Sept. 5
Ripshin

E off early to Marion. A very beautiful day. Worked in the morning. John,
Major, and Mary came to clear out the underbrush before my cabin,

planted rhododendrons. Took Millen with me to Sugar Grove for truck load of lime. Mary took Brand to town. He is returning to New York by bus.

Tues., Sept. 6
Ripshin

A very quiet day in which I finished the 2nd of the new series of tales—for Men and Their Women.[84] It is an inexhaustible theme. Mother very much upset by the new state scheme for adult education, etc.—is afraid it will take her woman workers.[85]

Wed., Sept. 7
Ripshin

Got into the 3rd of the new story series. Went to Mrs. Charlie Greer's funeral where the doctor who had killed her sang over her body—a ghoulish affair.[86] Mr. Bill Wright and wife with boy Sherwood to dine. He looks like a wise little Chinaman.

Thurs., Sept. 8
Ripshin

The day warm and pleasant with occasional threats of rain that did not come. The tall young Nick Carter here.[87] Mary working on the hedge. We tore out the fence about the old upper garden and will plant to grass.

In the evening John and Mary Eleanore came and it was so warm we sat out in the moonlight all evening.

Fri., Sept. 9
Ripshin

A cold misty day. E off early to town. Worked O.K., although cabin cold. Was worried about money but got it from Mary.

Mary and I to Wytheville for liquor. Then to Marion. E stayed the night there, to pick up Schevill and Lovett in the morning.

Sat., Sept. 10
Ripshin

Dark foggy day. Finished the Sidney Bollinger story in the new series.[88] Ferdinand Schevill and Robert Lovett arrived for a week's visit. We sat by the fire and talked, walked, played croquet. It was a good day of good company.

Sun., Sept. 11
Ripshin

The sky cleared and it was a beautiful day but I could not work. I was too high, too intense.

Lovett, Schevill, Mary, E and I drove to see the mill village at Fries, Va.[89] We went by back roads to Marion and dined there. Had B.E. and Mother to dinner.

Mon., Sept. 12
Ripshin

A very fine clear day. I had not slept and thought I would be unable to work but did work, starting a new tale.

In the p.m., took Lovett and Schevill to White Top, returning through North Carolina. May came from Marion, with E, to help prepare for my birthday party tomorrow.

Tues., Sept. 13
Ripshin

My birthday. Misty rain early. E was giving a woman's card party for Mary so Ferdinand and Robert Lovett and I lit out. I made a mistake trying to find a short cut and we landed in the deep mud on a side road. Some lumbermen got us out. Mother gave me a big birthday party. We all came home in heavy rain.

Wed., Sept. 14
Ripshin

For once E stayed at home all day. I tried to do the Tom Flanagan story and got started. Had a fine day with Schevill and Lovett.

Thurs., Sept. 15
Ripshin

Worked on the Tom Flanagan story but felt myself coming down with a cold. Played croquet with Ferdinand and Robert. Mother came. The two men guests spent the evening reciting and reading poetry.

Fri., Sept. 16
[Knoxville]

Up early and drove Mother to Marion. We went on to Knoxville but I had to spend the p.m. in bed while the rest went to Norris dam with [John]

Moutoux. He gave a party for us in the evening—TVA men—but I could only stay an hour.

Sat., Sept. 17
Ripshin

Stayed in bed all morning at Knoxville, then got up and drove home. Ferdinand left for Chicago. He gave me the cloth for a new suit.

We came by Gate City and got home at 10:30 after dining at restaurant in Marion.

Sun., Sept. 18
Ripshin

Very blue all day, hating the coming of the summer's end.[90] We went in the p.m. to Marion to get Lovett off. I had a stiff headache. Life seemed closing in on me and, for the day, I was no good.

Mon., Sept. 19
Ripshin

At home, at work. We began cutting corn. It has turned cold, with a high cold wind. I have been depressed and unhappy about work.

Tues., Sept. 20
Ripshin

Still very cold and the high wind still blowing. Mary has made the hedge very beautiful. She went off to Marion. Dave Greear came in the evening with his brother Sol and a young Mr. Hurt. Did not like Sol.

Wed., Sept. 21
Ripshin

Still cold and raw. Work a little better. In the evening went with E and Mary to Independence—beauty contest, very vulgar. Mary was one of the judges.

Thurs., Sept. 22
Ripshin

Sunk deeply into the blues—the black dog constantly on my back, hating the summer's end, feeling my own inefficiency. It seems to me that I have done nothing.

Still cold but the skies clear. Why do I always feel I must be accomplishing?

Fri., Sept. 23
Ripshin

Very beautiful clear day. The blues broke a little. E, Mary and I went to Marion and dined at Funk's. Went in the p.m. to see a high school football game. Hope the blues have broken a little.

Sat., Sept. 24
Ripshin

A very beautiful warm day. Worked well and went to Marion to take my bottles for the wine. Dave came. In the evening we all went to burn brush in the new cleared land beyond the barn.

Sun., Sept. 25
Ripshin

A very warm beautiful day. I worked, did the Henry Bollinger soliloquy. Dave stayed for the day. In the afternoon I went to the new field to burn brush. The blues seem to have gone away.

Mon., Sept. 26
Ripshin

The day started, clear and warm. The grain threshing machine was coming down Ripshin road. I worked, not too well. I went up the road to meet the machine and got caught in a heavy rain. Later there was a great storm with a high wind and hail.

Tues., Sept. 27
Ripshin

A bright warm day but I did not succeed in my morning's work. The threshers came at 3 p.m. and we had good results, getting over 100 bushels of oats, rye, and buckwheat.

I got a case of beer for the men.

E to town.

Wed., Sept. 28
Ripshin

Work O.K. Another bright day—the skies clear, fall colors coming on the mountain sides. Went to Sugar Grove with Mary Emmett to get a truck load of lime. John and his wife came. He has a commission to paint pictures for the new schoolhouse at Marion. E to town.

Thurs., Sept 29
Ripshin

Dark rainy day. Worked a long time, too long in the cold wet cabin. Stayed outdoors too long in the rain. Felt myself catching cold.

Fri., Sept. 30
Ripshin

In bed sick with cold. Still cold and wet.

Sat., Oct. 1
Ripshin

Still sick, in bed. Went to Marion to stay until well.

Sun., Oct. 2
Marion

Sick in bed. At night E left for New York.

Mon., Oct. 3
Marion

Still in bed, weak and sick.

Tues., Oct. 4
Marion

Beautiful day. Got up. Quite weak.

Wed., Oct. 5
Marion

Beautiful day. Got up and drove to Ripshin to pack. Mary busy with wall that tumbled in on her garden. Took my belongings to Marion, ready to leave.

Thurs., Oct. 6
Marion

Another lovely day, the road to Ripshin so lovely it hurt. Got a chance to get Winesburg produced in New York but the Barton matter in the way.[91]

Fri., Oct. 7
Marion

Another beautiful day. They started to hard surface the road to Troutdale. I caught more cold but went to see Funk in the evening.

A rotten day for me.

Sat., Oct. 8
Marion

A setback in my illness, with fever. I had to stay in bed all day. The weather is very beautiful. I have given up the Ohio trip.

Sun., Oct. 9
Marion

Still weak from illness. Went to Funk's to hear the World Series. Mary went off to the farm at 4.

Mon., Oct. 10
Marion

Mary got through at Ripshin. I drove to see Dr. Jones but he had gone off to medical meeting. The days still fine. Mary prepared to go at dawn.

Tues., Oct. 11
Marion

Did not try to work although stronger. Drove to Ripshin for last visit. Everything ship-shape there. The road over will all be hard surfaced by this next weekend. The fine fall weather still held.

Wed., Oct. 12
Marion

No work. Day cold and grey, then warm and fine. Knocked out a tire. Dined at John's and went to say goodbye to Funk.

Thurs., Oct. 13
Winchester, Va.

In the car driving, at first through fog and then the day cleared. My head also cleared. Drove from 8:30 until 4 and stopped at hotel at Winchester, on my way to Hedgerow.

Fri., Oct. 14
Media, Pa.

Got to Hedgerow at 3 and put up at the Inn. Found Hedgerow quite changed, with many new faces. In the evening E came from New York. We saw Twelfth Night and sat up until 1:30.

Sat., Oct. 15
Media

Up late. We saw the Second Mrs. Fraser[92] and three of Paul Green's short plays done by Philadelphia Negroes. Sat talking again until 2:30.

Sun., Oct. 16
[New York]

Jap to breakfast with us at the Inn and then to see rehearsal of the play The Nuremberg Egg.[93] Watched until 3:30 and then drove to New York. Roads packed. We got in worn out.

Mon., Oct. 17
New York

Tried to get into work but with poor success. The house here too confusing, too many things. Things impinge. They assert. In the evening went with E and Mary to a $10 dinner for Spain—an English Lady M.P. speaking. Gave $10.

Tues., Oct. 18
New York

A terribly depressing day—sunk in deep gloom—unable to work. The sun was shining but I was all black inside. No work done. I met E and we walked home together.

Wed., Oct 19
New York

I began a new treatment for my sinus. Tried to work but it did not go well. Met E at her office and, after dining, we went to see Orson Welles' presentation of an old play—"The Death of Danton."[94]

Thurs., Oct. 20
New York

Sun shining. Any real work still eludes me. Karl came and we walked about. Went to see Max Perkins and met Tom Wolfe's mother. She explains much of poor Tom.[95]

Fri., Oct. 21
New York

Again no good work. Went to a luncheon where I saw and talked to Heywood Broun. Went later to cocktails, with Lewis and Nancy and then to dine at Paul's. A good evening there.

Sat., Oct. 22
New York

The Millers moving out of the house. Mary Emmett went off to the Eastern Shore of Virginia to plant flowers in the Wolfs' garden. I began a little to work. E came home and I went shopping with her. We went to call on Joe and Ann and then went early to bed.

Sun., Oct. 23
New York

No work. E at home. We dined in 59th Street and went to the Rascoes. I had carried off the key to the Millers' car, leaving them waiting for hours at home.

Mon., Oct. 24
New York

Began to work a little again. We went to dine with the Galantières—a delightful evening.

Tues., Oct. 25
New York

Worked. The sun out and the day delightful. We had the Millers for a farewell dinner.

Wed., Oct. 26
New York

Worked steadily a long time. It rained. We went to dine at the Italian's on Sullivan. Felt well and strong all day.

Thurs., Oct. 27
New York

Rain but again worked O.K. Took my car to be fixed. We went to dine at Paul's. Miss Marshall the critic was there.[96]

Fri., Oct. 28
New York

Rain all day. Felt down but worked. Got only $75 for the story—"A Chest of Drawers." Mary cooked a steak and we dined at home.

Sat., Oct. 29
New York

I have begun to come out of my bad time, one of the worst I was ever in. I worked and then E and I drove over the bridge to Brooklyn, to the Knox factory store. We got hats and shoes.

Sun., Oct. 30
New York

Up late but worked. A beautiful clear day. E and I walked on Fifth Avenue and then went to see the game of Jai Alai at the Hippodrome. It was very beautiful. Mary came in late and we played cards.

Mon., Oct. 31
New York

Worked O.K. and had, at lunch time, a long conversation with the Japanese cook. Went for a long walk to look at people. Mary gone all day. E and I dined in 52nd and went to see the play Oscar Wilde.[97] The play didn't convince me, as intended, that he was a great man.

Tues., Nov. 1
New York

Worked on the new long story. It was a pleasant day and I walked. E came at five and packed to take the train for Niagara Falls. Sat playing cards with Mary until 11.

Wed., Nov. 2
Niagara Falls

Up at 6—after a bad night of little sleep. Half ill. Intended to stop with Ralph Church[98] at Ithaca but pushed on, feeling better. Drove hard, through Catskills and Genesee Valley and got to the Falls at 7—very tired.

Thurs., Nov. 3
Niagara Falls

Slept hard—tired from long drive. Worked a little. Stayed in old Hotel Cataract . . . very pleasant with pleasant weather. Spent the p.m. out of doors. The rapids right under the window here.

Fri., Nov. 4
Niagara Falls

Another remarkable fine warm day and many people sitting out in the park by the falls. Worked late and went to be a long time looking at the falls. In the evening played Bingo and lost my money.

Sat., Nov. 5
Niagara Falls

Fine day. Worked and E came shortly after noon. We drove to Canada and along the river shore to Hamilton, Ontario and back by an inland

road. Grapes, peaches and other fruit along the shore, and the inland like
Western Iowa—the whole like a piece of America—houses and people.

Sun., Nov. 6
Niagara Falls

Worked until exhausted. Another warm beautiful day. E gone about her
work all day. Drove along the gorge toward Lake Ontario on the American side. Road packed with cars so I came home early and read.

Mon., Nov. 7
Niagara Falls

The fine weather held on. I managed to finish the 1st section of a story. E
at her job all day. I took a long ride and walk. Have been sitting in my
room and working until my eyes ache.

Tues., Nov. 8
Niagara Falls

Bad cold rainy weather all day and I was confined to my room. It was
election day. All day I was blue and discouraged about my work.

Wed., Nov. 9
New York

Did not sleep so up at 4 a.m. E awoke and we dressed and started off for
New York in the bitter cold but the skies had cleared. I felt rotten. We
however drove on, going by Albany and down the river and got to New
York at 4:30. I had some fever. To bed.

Thurs., Nov. 10
New York

Rather done up from lack of sleep, the trip from Niagara Falls and a sharp
attack of indigestion, but better during the day. There was a heavy mail, I
got answered. Made unsuccessful effort to renew work. Millen Brand
came, very naive and nice about himself and his work. Went to dine at
Ticino's and saw several people I knew.

Fri., Nov. 11
New York

Feeling better. E and I hoped to have a long weekend but she had to go off
to Richmond at five. I worked until one and then played about with her.
In the evening dined with Dr. Joe at Lüchow's and then to see "Kiss the

Boys Goodbye," a very smart claptrap play by the wife of the owner of Time.[99] It was, at least, the last word in the rather tiresome wise-cracking art.

Sat., Nov. 12
New York

E off to Richmond last night. Work rather ineffectual. Mary had a card party so I escaped with Joe Taulane. We went to Hy Li game. Sat with Mary in the evening and early to bed.

Sun., Nov. 13
New York

Work still ineffectual. Mary went to the country. I slipped off to professional football game to be outdoors—Polo Grounds. In the evening took Mary to see Hi Li—very exciting.

Mon., Nov. 14
New York

E came home from Richmond at noon. I went to take my car and forgot a lunch engagement with a critic. Paul came and we went for a long walk.

Tues., Nov. 15
New York

Too many ideas in my head. A long letter from John Emerson, telling me I am passing through masculine change of life. I worked a long time but felt it ineffectual.

Wed., Nov. 16
New York

Still ineffectual as regards work although I keep at it. Went to lunch with Orson Welles whom I liked much. He may really survive in our theatre. E and I went to a French movie—The Story of A Cheat—very clever and nice.[100]

Thurs., Nov. 17
New York

Began a new tale—chucking the one on which I was at work. It is a tale of two brothers. Mary out so we had a grand quiet evening—E and I together.

Fri., Nov. 18
New York

The work went better. E, Mary and I gave a big cocktail party—a great success and later went with Dreiser and O'Keeffe to dine.[101] It was an evening of good fun.

Sat., Nov. 19
New York

Rain—all day. Miriam Phillips staying in the house. After working I went with her to lunch and then took her to Hi Li. We all dined at Ticino's.

Sun., Nov. 20
New York

A clear beautiful day. Work and then in afternoon with company—Paul Green and wife, Joe, Mims. The talk was good. E, Mims and Mary went to the theatre and I alone to Hi Li—a very fast fine game. Had a bad time trying to sleep. Had finally to dope.

Mon., Nov. 21
New York

Some work done but Mims here and too much night life. I went with her to see the long Hamlet—Maurice Evans—and liked the production but thought he terribly violated the speech to the players. Home very late.

Tues., Nov. 22
New York

Damp day. Tried to work. Pretty ineffectual. Went with Mary to see Lucile Swan's sculpturings. Dahlberg and Olson came bringing books. Mary, E and I dined at Margarita's on 59th.[102]

Wed., Nov. 23
New York

Worked better. Went to see old Stieglitz and a new lot of John Marin's oils, very alive and lovely. Went to dine with MacKinlay Kantor, whose novel Long Remember I liked. Found him very childish and disappointing.[103]

Thurs., Nov. 24
New York

Thanksgiving. E stayed at home while Mary went off to the country. Worked and took E to old Glory horse sale, where we saw many beautiful horses.[104] Very thrilling. Snow and sleet when we came out. We dined with Mildred Esgar.[105]

Fri., Nov. 25
New York

Winter here with a vengeance. Very cold with deep snow and the streets blocked. Had to have my car hauled out of the Mews. Stayed pretty much at home and worked.

Sat., Nov. 26
[Westport]

Worked a little bit, pretty good. Tried to start the car but it wouldn't go. Had to send it to the garage. We all went to Karl's by train and the life there made me ill. I couldn't take it. Got indigestion.

Sun., Nov. 27
New York

Sick as hell all day but we got away from Karl's at 3 p.m. More and more snow. When we got home the lock to the door wouldn't work and we had to break a window to get in. I was mighty sick.

Mon., Nov. 28
New York

Still weak and ill from the trip to Karl's. . . .[106] Had to spend the whole day in bed.
    No good.

Tues., Nov. 29
New York

In the evening to a place in the fifties to dine with [Marco] Morrow. Morrow the same as in Chicago 25 years ago—still with same boyishness. His talk very rambling. He embarrassed by trying to pretend people knew me when they didn't. He is an old patron of the place and the whole Italian family came and sat with us. They were fascists.

Wed., Nov. 30
Media, Pa.

Got up early and worked—then drove to Media, through deep slush. E in Philadelphia but came to Media late at night. Had a long real visit with Jap who was in a fine mood. Very much in love with E.

Thurs., Dec. 1
Media, Pa.

[No entry.]

Fri., Dec. 2
Media
Hedgerow

Worked beautifully—the Great Man theme—W. F.[107] Wharton
[Esherick] buried his mother—87. Mary came at 6:30. She, Wharton and
I dined. We saw the play [The] Frodi—very stirring and fine.[108] I was full
of my new theme and very alive all day.

Sat., Dec. 3
Baltimore

On Friday evening we saw a fine production of Dreiser's American Tragedy. We made the mistake of staying to hear Jap read an uncut version
Shaw's Man and Superman. It was a ghastly bore.
    Nice drive to Baltimore—arriving for lunch.[109]

Sun., Dec. 4
Media, Pa.

Left Baltimore at noon and ran into a heavy fog—very dangerous—so
that we stopped at the Inn, Media. It cleared and Mary and E decided to
go on. It was a mistake. A rough trip in the fog.

Mon., Dec. 5
New York

Got home—after a drive from Media in rain and fog to find painters at
work in my rooms. Could not work. It rained all day. I went to see the
painting of Rifka Angel.[110] Stayed at home in the evening. Many ideas in
my head about the new book.

Tues., Dec. 6
New York

Pretty good morning of work. In the afternoon went to American
Place[111]—to see the Marin oils and Stieglitz. Went to try on my new suit.
Spent the evening at home, after dining at Margarita's.

Wed., Dec. 7
New York

Work, as usual. Clear cold day. In the evening went to dine at Margaret Marshall's—Cruch—dramatic critic[112]—and a scientist who talked of deep sea photography.

Thurs., Dec. 8
New York

Work—not sure of it. To Knox [in] Brooklyn, to get new shoes. With E and Mary to Stieglitz and O'Keeffe to dine. Stieglitz irritable—Georgia charming.

Fri., Dec. 9
New York

Dark gloomy day. Did a good morning's work and went with E to get watch for Mary.

Dined at Galantière's and saw the Sherwood Lincoln.[113] It was a fine thing while it remained in the personal relations field, but later fell to pieces.

Sat., Dec. 10
[New Milford, Ct.]

Grey day. Good day of work. In the afternoon E and I went, by train, to New Milford, Conn., to spend a day with George and Betty Anderson.[114]

Sun., Dec. 11
New York

Another grey day and no work. We sat in the Anderson house all day and talked. Anderson seemed unhappy and puzzled. He was formerly big business man.

We got back to the city at 8:10.

Mon., Dec. 12
New York

Pretty good day of work. Got my typewriter overhauled. It rained in the morning. E and I went to dine at Ticino's. Played cards with Mary. Got some money.

Tues., Dec. 13
New York

Cloudy and cold. Good day's work. To Stieglitz to get his photograph.[115] Leane Zugsmith to dine. Got into a nasty quarrel with a very egotistical young man who tried to take me down. I hated his hate.

Wed., Dec. 14
New York

Cold and clear. A good day of work. Went to tea with O'Keeffe and then with E on a shopping spree. Home early and to bed.

Thurs., Dec. 15
New York

Very cold. Did good stint of work. In the evening went for cocktails to Charles Studin and then to dine with Bruce Bliven[116] and wife and others. Mary having party—Pete, Dolly and sister and husband. Had to get up. Caught a cold.

Fri., Dec. 16
New York

Worked and packed to leave. In the afternoon [Robert] Lovett came in. Got a watch for Mary.

Sat., Dec. 17
Roanoke, Va.

Up and off for Virginia, E and I at 5. Went by 29 to Paoli, then 30 to Hagerstown, Maryland, where we got onto 11. Arrived at Roanoke at 6 p.m.—about 480 miles.

Sun., Dec. 18
Marion

Drove over from Roanoke and arrived at noon. Saw Fallon who gave E an orchid.[117] Spent most of the afternoon unpacking. Went to see Funk.

Mon., Dec. 19
Marion

Went to Ripshin. Bright cold day. The road is all paved and there is a new stone road out to the farm. John Sullivan not there. Got sore at Funk and Bob about the birds.

Tues., Dec. 20
Marion

Clear and cold. Worked and then flew about doing last minute Christmas chores.

The evening spent with Funk helping him in his shop.

Wed., Dec. 21
Marion

Work. In the p.m. to Ripshin—cold and clear. Funk came bringing 12 birds. Then came Bob bringing 10. Played cards. Went to see Frank Copenhaver—still in bed with his long illness.[118]

Thurs., Dec. 22
Marion

Good day of work. Ran about town doing errands. In the evening went to call on Bob and Mary. Later John and wife and Dave [Greear] came to call.

Fri., Dec. 23
Marion

Mist and rain all day. I had a long morning of work. In the p.m. I did errands and in the evening went to Dave's with Andy and John to play pool.

Sat., Dec. 24
Marion

Misty and rainy in the morning—clear in the p.m. Mary [Emmett] arrived at 3. E and I went for a walk and found John painting. The house a hubbub in the evening.

Sun., Dec. 25
Marion

Christmas. E and I gave Mary a wristwatch. It was a beautiful cold clear day—much Xmas fuss in the house but I stayed in my room at work.

We had birds and wine. We all went to Bob's. Mary got the whole house stirred up about a lost pocketbook that wasn't lost at all.

Mon., Dec. 26
Marion

Work—not very effectual—off wrong. Work to be chucked.

Went to Funk who told the story of the night in the cold in his underwear. Went with Mary Emmett and Mazie to dine at John's.

Tues., Dec. 27
Marion

Worked but no good. Mother had a big supper—Andy and wife, John and Eleanore, Bob and Mary, Dave. Much Civil War talk.

Wed., Dec. 28
Marion

Cold and clear—I got started on a new section of the book. We drove to the farm and found snow and ice at Ripshin. In the evening went to cocktail party—Dr. Willis' house.[119] The furnace went out of order so to bed to keep warm.

Thurs., Dec. 29
Marion

The day at home—pretty good work. Stayed about all day entertaining Mary and others. Cold and clear. In the evening the house got on fire. It was soon put out. Light snow in evening.

Fri., Dec. 30
Greensboro, N.C.

No sleep. Started early to drive to Greensboro—where E having conference industrial girls. Mary going to take John with her to New York. Came by Roaring Gap and Jonesville.

Sat., Dec. 31
Greensboro, N.C.

Worked in room and saw two young reporters, both nice. Then down to Chapel Hill, to Paul Green—Helen Stallings came with D. Cohn[120] — also [Phillips] Russell and his beautiful wife. We sat up talking until 1:30. A very charming evening. E couldn't go there with me.

1 9 3 9

Returned from Chapel Hill at 5 and E and I spent the night at the O'Henry Hotel. At Chapel Hill, after breakfast at 10 went with Paul Green to a big reception at some rich woman's house, Green saying that all his writing for movies had affected and hurt his work. It was hard he said to shake off the effects of it.

A very bright beautiful day and we left Greensboro at 7 and got to Marion at 11. We came by Fancy Gap, the road all clear of ice and snow. Channing was at the house, for the weekend. Went to sit in Funk's shop where we had supper and listened to the Rose Bowl football game, over the radio. Got later irritated with Mother over a game of cards.

Unable to sleep because of the row with Mother. Tried to work but made no progress. It was a very beautiful day and I took E and Mother for a ride, getting back into her good graces. Spent the early part of the evening with Funk and the later part with the women.

Started on the trip to Olivet, going by the above to talk with Kenneth Douty about a newspaper to be started at Front Royal.[1] 300 miles—fog and wet roads a part of the way. Evening spent talking with Douty, and E left for New York at 10:30.

Thurs., Jan. 5
Athens, Ohio

Got onto the wrong road and went nearly back to Marietta. I had tried to work and started late. The day was very beautiful. I dined with Helen Dinsmoor and her father and mother—in their house. We had a very good wine. It was a beautiful moonlight night. Had much talk of writing with Helen Dinsmoor. Went to call on Trillena White at City Hospital, Springfield, she condemned to death of cancer. She was very fine.[2]

Fri., Jan. 6
Fremont, Ohio

Intended to stay at Clyde, which I reached at 5 p.m. but there is no hotel so after seeing Herman Hurd drove to Fremont—returning to spend the evening with Herman and wife.[3] Asked many questions about people remembered—many dead. The evening was very pleasant but I was full of thoughts of Trillena White. Eleanor seemed present with me all day.

Sat., Jan. 7
Battle Creek,
Mich.

Had car washed and greased. Left Fremont at 10—clear cool day—road dry and good. Picked up working man, auto builder out of work. Got his curious slant. He says Carnegie's "How to Win and Keep Friends" has done him more good than any other book.[4]

Sun., Jan. 8
Olivet, Mich.

Arrived here at 4—staying at President's house.[5] There was a faculty reception. I caught cold. It seemed a pretty good crowd. The town pleasant and weather still wonderful.

Mon., Jan. 9
Olivet, Mich.

Got arrangements made for a room in the college library to spend my morning. We eat in the big girl's dormitory. I got my program for work here laid out for me. In the p.m. went to Charlotte to get measured for the blue suit Mother gave me. It rained but still not cold and no snow.

Tues., Jan. 10
Olivet

Got into the work quarters. In the afternoon a student, a young poet John Verber, came to talk. We rode over to Charlotte and sat over beer. Spent the evening with Ramsay, Gosling and Parkinson—took them some Scotch. I like them.[6]

Wed., Jan. 11
Olivet

The weather still cold and clear and roads clear. I drove over to Charlotte. In the evening I had to talk on contemporary literature and did not do well. I had no prepared talk. I'll prepare next time. In the evening went with the same men to drink at Charlotte.

Thurs., Jan. 12
Olivet

Snow flourishes all day but not too cold. I was much depressed, feeling I did not handle my talk well and so worked writing out the next one. I had interviews with two students, drove for a time and in the evening sat with the painter Rickey[7] and the professor Gosling, talking until one in the morning.

Fri., Jan. 13
Olivet

Snow nearly all day. I had to stay on the work to be done here. There was a faculty tea at 5—students and faculty. In the evening to Baker's apartment where we sat until 12.[8] There is good talk and good company here.

Sat., Jan. 14
Olivet

The roads clearing. Went after work to Charlotte to send flowers to E. In the evening Baker and wife, Gosling, and Ramsay came to the house and Ramsay cooked a delicious dinner.

Sun., Jan. 15
Olivet

Got into library after some trouble and worked on lectures. Found broken water pipe. Went to faculty tea at 5—bored. Sat with Gosling and Parkinson until 11, then to Bellevue to eat. Bed at 12.

Mon., Jan. 16
Olivet

Still working on the speeches I must make here. Went to Charlotte to get stuff for feast. Sat a long time smoking and talking in faculty club room. Went to spend the evening at boys' fraternity house. Young Whitehead boy got me out of bed to talk.

Tues., Jan. 17
Olivet

Steady snow all day but not very cold. The scene from the window of my workroom very lovely.

Saw people—held a class and worked on my lectures. Gave steak dinner for Ramsay, Parkinson and Gosling, with baked potatoes and wine. Went to a college basketball game.

Wed., Jan. 18
Olivet

Occasional snow all day but not too cold. The scene in Olivet very beautiful. In the evening I spoke on Personalities to a big crowd of students and they seemed to enjoy it.

After I spoke several men came to the house bringing a bottle and we talked and drank until 12.

Thurs., Jan. 19
Olivet

Clear day with some sun and the roads clear. I had 6 boys for my conference. In the evening, with Ramsay and the dean of women[9] and 3 girl students, went to Ann Arbor to hear the Italian Benjimino Gigli sing.

We got home at 1 a.m. Dined in Ann Arbor with Ramsay and [his] mother.

Fri., Jan. 20
Olivet

Put last touches on speech. Snow flurries. Went to Charlotte to send E flowers and to sit drinking beer with some of the students. It was the night of my big public speech here and there was a crowded house. It seemed a success.[10] Later some of the men sat drinking with me until 1 a.m.

Sat., Jan. 21
Olivet

Snow melt—roads clear. Felt a little seedy and didn't go to dinner. Went to bed early and slept. Light touch of flu. Dean Ramsay down with it. Queer woman reporter Miss [Ethelyn] Sexton came.

Sun., Jan. 22
Olivet

Much colder. I felt a bit weak and shaky. Carrow DeVries came at 12 and stayed until 5. Dined at Virginia's and Alice's house.[11]

Mon., Jan. 23
Olivet

Quite cold—6 or 8 above in morning. Felt better. Went over speeches. In the later part of the day snowed more. To bed early. Read Life of Moliere, having finished Moby Dick. Hoped to get out of Battle Creek speech but see little chance.

Tues., Jan. 24
Olivet

Quite recovered from cold. Two of the boys came in for a talk and, later, I went to sit in on Glenn Gosling's class where there was more good talk. Some snow—pretty cold. Spent the evening at Joe's Boys.[12]

Wed., Jan. 25
Olivet

Quite busy day. Colder but no snow until night. Went with Brewer to address combined men's clubs at Battle Creek. Made anti-Fascist talk. At night talked about little magazines at the college. We all went to Dave Baker's house.

Thurs., Jan. 26
Olivet

More snow, on top of what we have had. It was a grey day with snow flurries. Worked in the morning and saw boys in the p.m.

In the evening to Lansing where I spoke, with the governor, at a state meeting of newspaper men. I talked to them of experiences running papers at Marion. Pretty good. The governor seemed an ass.[13]

Fri., Jan. 27
Olivet

The last day here.[14] It is a great deal warmer. The sun shone all day. Went to Charlotte to get my new homespun grey suit, a very fine job of tailoring. In the evening we all went to the house of Joe's Boys and ate and drank until one.

Sat., Jan. 28
Springfield, Ohio

Left Olivet [at] 10 and got here at 5. Snow drifting in Southern Michigan, deep slush about Toledo and then dry fast roads. I just ate and fell into bed for a long sleep.

Sun., Jan. 29
Yellow Springs,
Ohio

Work in my room. Went to call again on Trillena White, who is dying of cancer. Went to see Snyder—English Dept.—Wittenberg College. Found him stodgy. Drove to Antioch in rain and fog. Spent the evening at Vernet's house,[15] with members [of] faculty Antioch.

Mon., Jan. 30
Yellow Springs,
Ohio

At Antioch College. A talk with President [Algo D.] Henderson and with [Walter B.] Alexander, the dean. Went with a women writers group to lunch. Worked on my speech. In the evening went to a dinner with faculty and business men of the town. Went then to the house of an Indian professor.[16] Rain that in the evening turned to an icy sleet.

Tues., Jan. 31
Yellow Springs,
Ohio

A pretty busy day, working on my speech, going to a luncheon, and in the evening making a long speech in Kelly Hall here.

The speech went well and afterward many people came to the Vernet house where I am staying.

Warmer—clear skies.

Wed., Feb. 1
Yellow Springs,
Ohio

Busy day. The weather cleared. I went to lunch with the theater crowd and to a so-called "Bull" session with about 20 boys—talking of education.

The evening a seminar on the short story—very dull.

Thurs., Feb. 2
Hancock, Md.

Gilbert Wilson[17] decided to come east with us. We left Antioch at 7:30 and had good weather through Ohio and into the mountains but in the late afternoon, in the high mountains, a dense fog came up. We had to creep along but made Hancock on the east side of the higher ranges.

Fri., Feb. 3
Philadelphia

Drove from Hancock, Maryland all day in a driving rain that never let up, in many places the road flooded. Got to Philadelphia at 3. Wilson went by bus to Baltimore. E arrived from New York at 6:30. We stopped at Sylvania.

Sat., Feb. 4
Philadelphia

Slept until noon and then wrote letters. We drove to Hedgerow, dined there and saw [A. A.] Milne's The Romantic Age—a very silly play.

Sun., Feb. 5
New York

Wilson came from Baltimore at 1:30 and we started for New York at 2—arriving 5:30. Took Wilson to Cafe Royal. Trip over in beautiful winter day. Spent the evening unpacking.

Mon., Feb. 6
New York

A cloudy rather warm day with many children playing in Washington Park. I spent a large part of the day catching up with my correspondence. Mary to the theater, with [Andy?], and E and I to dine late at Ticino's. I have come to a determination to get away from my present situation as soon as possible.

Tues., Feb. 7
New York

Light snow on the ground in the morning but it soon melted away. High wind. I began to write on running small town newspaper. Enjoyed it. Karl came and also the man Mary is backing at Baltimore—Clint Woods. Mary has new negro maid. Went uptown to walk down with E. We called on Ann Girsdansky.

Wed., Feb. 8
New York

Sun shining but cold. Worked on newspaper thing. Went to walk on 6th Avenue watching the workmen tearing down the old elevated. Went to see Pins and Needles[18] and then to E to walk home with her.

Thurs., Feb. 9
New York

Sun shining. High wind. Worked in the morning. Went to see neighborhood dancers in 46th Street—quite lovely dancing. Met E there and went to Elmer Adler's for drinks and then E and I dined in 52nd. Mary up very late with Clint Woods.

Fri., Feb. 10
New York

Rain steadily all day. To lunch with John Cournos who told me the story of editing the Belmont book.[19]

In the evening to Lewis and Nancy Galantière—where I met Elmer Rice and wife at dinner.[20] There was a great deal of talk of painting. Mrs. Rice has a very bad voice. I could not sleep later and had a bad night.

Sat., Feb. 11
New York

Cold windy day. Worked in the morning. E came home early. Took her and Mary to the Red Barn. Mary became ill, evidently from something she ate there. I was ill in the night.

Sun., Feb. 12
New York

Did not go out. Ill with a sick headache all day. Could not eat and spent most of the day in bed. E went out to cocktails at Wolfs.

Mon., Feb. 13
New York

Lincoln's birthday and all the newspapers, theatres and churches full of him. Got over my illness but weak. Had to stay in most of the day—day warm and beautiful. Went to Margarita's on 59th with E, Mary and Chinese girl to dine. Made up vegetable order Burpee.

Tues., Feb. 14
New York

Grey warm day. I worked pretty well and in the late afternoon went to sit drinking with Max Perkins. Picked up E and we walked down, dining on the way. We went to Doctor Joe's and found a big poker game on. Mary came home with a big crowd and we dressed and went down. Sat talking until 12.

Wed., Feb. 15
New York

Finished the story of the newspapers, I hope to be able to sell. Heavy rain with high wind in the p.m. It blew in a big plate glass window at 8th Street and Broadway as I sat in a nearby barber shop. Went with Mary and E to dine at the Ashley Millers.

Thurs., Feb. 16
New York

Rainy. Tried a new tack in approaching a theme. Went out with Joe and Ann. They quarreled all evening. Ate and drank too much. Kept trying to change the atmosphere. No good. They seem to like it. Their kids rather grand.

Fri., Feb. 17
New York

Still working away at the effort to get a theme that takes hold. Writing letters. Dined with Cournos, wife, son and daughter-in-law. They full of flu. Think I'm getting it.

Sat., Feb. 18
New York

In bed with flu—aching, feel rotten.

Sun., Feb. 19
New York

Flu. In bed all day. Picked up Kipling's Kim. Thought it too damn British.

Mon., Feb. 20
New York

In bed—flu. Think E getting it. Am better. Read life Zola by Matthew Josephson. E came home also with flu.

Tues., Feb. 21
New York

Better but E down with flu and with a lot more fever than I had. I felt weak but got up and dressed and got about. No work. A few letters.

Wed., Feb. 22
New York

Washington's birthday. Got in doctor for E. Mary off to the country. Offered John $25 for watercolor landscape. Read a detective story.

Thurs., Feb. 23
New York

Relapse—in bed again ill.

Fri., Feb. 24
New York

Ill with flu and fever. Had to give up Washington trip.

Sat., Feb. 25
New York

In bed with flu.

Sun., Feb. 26
New York

In bed with flu.

Mon., Feb. 27
New York

In bed with flu, fever hanging on.

Tues., Feb. 28
New York

In bed with flu.

Wed., March 1
New York

In bed with flu, but fever down.

Thurs., March 2
New York

Up and dressed for the 1st time but very weak. Caught this book up to date. Went through mail.

Fri., March 3
New York

Up and about but very weak. Thought I had passage on a boat to New Orleans but at the last found the boat full. Tried to work a little. Walked out. Went out to dine.

Sat., March 4
New York

Weak but got down 1000 words. Sent the newspaper article off to agent. Feel weak and poisoned. Went out to walk in spite of rain.

Sun., March 5
New York

Got some work done. A warm rainy day. Walked out but pretty weak. We stayed in house most of the day.

Mon., March 6
New York

Very blue. Stayed at home and tried to work a little but with no success. The flu had left me weak and despondent.

Tues., March 7
Washington

Set out to go south feeling no good. Planned to stop at Hedgerow but didn't. In Washington went to the Powhatan but found it picketed by strikers. Went to the Raleigh.

Wed., March 8
Sanford, N.C.

Drove to above place—near Southern Pines. Very weak and sick all day but kept going. Fortunately had fine weather.

Thurs., March 9
Macon, Ga.

Felt better. Up at 6:30 and drove fairly hard all day—a clear warm one, feeling stronger all the time. Slept well. Think I have the flu licked.

Fri., March 10
Mobile, Ala.

Up early 6 a.m. Gained an hour by change of time. Very hot. Feeling about all right. Got to Mobile at 5 and found town crowded but got room at Cawthon.

Sat., March 11
Mobile

Took the day off—to work a little. Then drove over to Fairhope to see the place where I once spent a winter.[21] Man who fell from plane. Man who lost his sight.

Sun., March 12
New Orleans

Up fairly well and worked. At 10 started for New Orleans, getting there at 4. Dined with Marc and Lucille and went to their house to get books to read.

Mon., March 13
New Orleans
[Hotel Monteleone]

A very beautiful day and I worked at top speed until 1 p.m.—then to lunch with Julius.

In the afternoon to Marc's shop and then later, with Elma [Godchaux] to his house to dine. People—the Fields—young writer and wife, came in. Got back to hotel at 12.

Tues., March 14
New Orleans

A very bright lovely day. Worked O.K. Expected Olivet crowd but they didn't come. Went with Marc to see paintings of Doctor Souschon—very striking—was much excited by them.[22]

Stayed in and to bed early.

Wed., March 15
New Orleans

Day began cloudy and damp, but no rain. Uncomfortably hot. Didn't do much work but escorted the crowd from Olivet College about the town. We all dined at Gentilly's on Rampart. They are a fine crowd—Glenn Gosling, Phoebe Sours, Fred Witkop, Laura Marshall.[23]

Thurs., March 16
New Orleans

Worked pretty well. Mark Ethridge in town. Saw him but for a moment. Lunch with Glenn, Jimmy and Julius [at] Broussard's. Dined at Jimmy's in his new house. Marc's work fine but the whole thing too expensive and badly planned. It seemed no place to work and live. Up late, a good deal of drinking.

Fri., March 17
New Orleans

Cool but bright sunlight. I have been coughing a good deal in the mornings.

I took the Olivet 4 down the river and we walked on the levee. Went to Elma Godchaux to dine. Several people came but at 10:30 I slid out and to bed. Worked O.K. in morning.

Sat., March 18
New Orleans

Worked in the morning and drove, in the p.m. with Olivet crowd, Lucille and Elma, to Reserve. Beautiful day. Dined with Olivet crowd.

Sun., March 19
New Orleans

Olivet crowd left. My cough bad. Dined at S. Fields, a Nazi. Went later to Jimmy Feibleman's.

Mon., March 20
New Orleans

Ill all day, with bad cold. Stayed in my room, unable to work. Severe cough.

Tues., March 21
New Orleans

Stayed in room all day, unable to work—bad cough. In the evening went to Mother Godchaux with Elma, Lucille and Marc. Glad to be leaving New Orleans. The conversation ridiculous at Mother Godchaux's.

Wed., March 22
Vicksburg, Miss.

Did not want to but went to breakfast at Elma's. Then to Marc's shop where Lucille gave me a fine present for E. Decided to go north by new river road. Drove to Vicksburg—very tired.

Thurs., March 23
Gadsden, Ala.

Turned east from Vicksburg on No. 80 and got by night to Gadsden, Ala. As my smoking was cut I felt better. Excessive smoking may be 1/2 my trouble. Hard to quit after so many years of it.

Fri., March 24
Knoxville, Tenn.

Took wrong road out of Gadsden and had to return. Made long drive, partly over dirt road in bad shape to Knoxville. Feeling stronger and much better.

Sat., March 25
Marion

Got off at Knoxville at 9 and into Marion at 3:30. Word I had sold the editorial [to] American Magazine for $400.[24] Having good going in cutting the smoking. Feeling much better. Folks well.

Sun., March 26
Marion

Went through mail. Went to farm, taking Andy Funk. Brought flowers to John's wife, in hospital. Went to see Bob and Mary's new babe. Took Mother for drive. John was building wall at farm.

Mon., March 27
Marion

Work didn't go so well. I felt the morning a failure. I bought a new Dodge car, trading in the old one. Went to Wytheville for liquor. In the evening took Mother for a ride in the new car and then to Funk's. It rained hard.

Tues., March 28
Marion

Work no good. Went to the farm and brought back chickens and flowers. In the evening sat for a time with John and Dave and then drove about until I got some ideas and went home to try to do a little work before night.

Wed., March 29
Marion

Grey day, turning colder and with rain in the evening. Worked in the morning and in the p.m. drove to Bristol to get typewriter fixed, taking B.E. The town dead—early to bed.

Thurs., March 30
Marion

The day began cloudy but came off very beautiful. Went to Ripshin after I got through work and spent the p.m. going about the farm with John Sullivan.

In the evening sat until nearly midnight with Funk who was in one of his bad times.

Fri., March 31
Marion

Worked in the morning and ran errands in the p.m. Funk in bad shape and stayed with him talking of his problems until midnight.

Sat., April 1
Marion

E came and so no work. It rained and hailed most of the day. Got the car tuned up for our trip. No work. In the evening went to Bob's to dine.

Sun., April 2
Marion

Alternate clouds, light showers and sunshine. I took all of E's family to Ripshin. Later I took B.E. to Will Copenhaver's house at Chilhowie. Will's dead body was laid out there.[25]

Mon., April 3
Greensboro, N.C.

Up early and drove E from Marion to Greensboro, N.C. Sprinkle of rain when starting but the day cleared. Left at 7:30, arriving 12:30—O'Henry [Hotel].

The hotel filled with minor league ball players—Cincinnati farm men. Had a headache all day. Went out to look at ball players. In the evening went with E and another to look at meeting Workers Alliance—very pathetic.

Tues., April 4
Greensboro, N.C.

Up fairly early at the hotel and worked well.

Then drove to Madison to see Russell, Mimi and babies. Found Mimi more cheerful and Russell better. He has been made a magistrate. They have better house and car. Went later to see Cincinnati farm ball players at the big park at Greensboro. Stayed in the hotel with E in the evening.

Wed., April 5
Salisbury, N.C.

Drove over from Greensboro in the morning—bright sunlight. Worked in hotel at Salisbury. A splash of writing. Tired. Drove to Davidson, N.C. in the p.m. to see a ball game. All in from the writing. Fell into bed at Salisbury and slept stupidly.

Thurs., April 6
Charlotte, N.C.
[Hotel Charlotte]

A cloudy rainy day. I began a really dangerous story that I have always wanted to do. Had the p.m. free and went to see the Marx Brothers— really funny and in a clean way. Then in the evening to see an old show of Will Rogers and [?]—as music critic.[26]

Fri., April 7
Marion

Really worked. Was in the room at hotel at Charlotte—at it until 1:30.

E came with some newspapermen. We got off at 2 and home by 4—a beautiful drive, through beautiful country on a beautiful day.

Got sore because of a mood in the house and was angry all evening and slept badly. Badly down on Christians.

Sat., April 8
Marion

Spent most of the working day over correspondence and trying to work out something that might be a help to Steve Coombs.

Heard also the sad story of J. Collins.[27] Funk has gone to psychoanalyst. Went to bed early pretty tired and puzzled by people.

Sun., April 9
Marion

Beautifully sunny day—Easter—the family at church. E and I to Ripshin with a young willow tree from Gord B's—to set it by the creek.

Mon., April 10
Marion

Up early and to work. The work went well. In the p.m. loafing about town.

Went, in the evening for a long ride with Funk and to let him get relief by telling of the complications of his life and loves.

Tues., April 11
Knoxville, Tenn.

Drove E over here, where she had work to do. Grey and cloudy out of Marion and then—the last 75 miles—a downpour. Got right back to work and then walked about the town. To bed early.

Wed., April 12
Chattanooga, Tenn.

No work—a few notes taken. We drove to the above town, from Knoxville by a new way—No. 20. Picked up a destitute family— attractive children. Went to see the St. Louis Cardinals play an exhibition game, very cold. Half insane man who thinks himself a great ball player.

Thurs., April 13
Erwin, Tennessee

We left Chattanooga in the late morning and drove to Knoxville where I went to see a ball game, New York Giants against Cleveland Indians while E went to interview a man at Norris. Met her after game and we drove to Johnson City where she got wire and then to Erwin where she had another interview.

Fri., April 14
Marion

Drove to Marion, arriving at 11. Did some work. My nerves got on edge
from the roaring voices of the radio and I exploded. I got very ugly and
after explosion tramped off to bed. Put myself to sleep with dope.

Sat., April 15
Marion

Worked O.K. Grey day. Worked editing Phyllis Steele manuscript.[28] Had
word American Magazine had bought editorial—300.

Got offer 1500 for story—The Letter Writer.[29] Took E for stroll in
Saturday night crowds.

Sun., April 16
Marion

Worked passionately from 9 to 2 p.m. and got down draft of story. E left
at 4 for Nashville. Very high but stayed out until quiet.

Mon., April 17
Marion

After the big splashy day yesterday I didn't try to work. Went with Funk
to drive and see farms on which he was making loans.

Went to Frank Copenhaver's at 4. There was a man from the head
office, an admirer. We had drinks. Dined with the man and Glenn[30] at
Lincoln [Hotel]. Went to sit for 2 hours with Funk.

Tues., April 18
Marion

Worked on story of doctor—Letter Writer. A clear beautiful day. Drove to
Wytheville, returning by Independence and Ripshin. Got whiskey and
rum.

In the evening a long drive, with Funk—following 58 from Red Bridge
to where it comes out on No. 11.

Wed., April 19
Marion

Day not good. Was at my desk all morning but what I wrote no good. Got
in the car and drove. Went over Walker Mountain and drove a long way in
the Rich Valley. The day grey and somber, land lovely. Was very lonely for
E. Saw places we used to go together. Stayed in the evening with Mother.
Day wasted.

Thurs., April 20
Marion

Fair day at new story for Readers Digest. Went to Troutdale to trout fish on Fox Creek but although everyone else got trout I got none. Tired and early to bed.

Fri., April 21
Marion

Got the Letter Writer story down. Am sure it is fine. Met Eleanor's train from Nashville at 3:30 p.m. She was never more lovely and charming. I was deeply in love with her.

Sat., April 22
Marion

Put the final touches on the story for Readers Digest. In the evening went to see Funk and then packed to leave for the east.

Sun., April 23
Baltimore

Driving all day, in Sunday crowds—very warm. We decided to go to Baltimore and spent the night there with the Wilsons.

Mon., April 24
On Road

In the morning drove to Washington where E went to Labor and I went to State Dept. Lunched with Herbert Feis. He took me to head of Dept. Justice to see whether or not I had to register because of connection with international peace organizations.[31] They didn't seem to know.

Tues., April 25
New York

We drove to a small town near New Castle Ferry and spent the night at country hotel. Very hot and noisy. We drove into New York, arriving at 12:30. Wrote letters in the p.m. In the evening went to a birthday party— The New School.[32] Very dull.

Wed., April 26
New York

Spent most of the day taking care of accumulated mail. Robert Ramsay came to town. We lunched at the Brevoort and had a long talk. It rained in the p.m. We went to dine at Ticino's. Mary arrived home late at night.

Thurs., April 27
New York

Spent the morning in last going over of Letter Writer story. Wandered about. Warm but cloudy. Robert Ramsay came. We had drink, dinner and then wine. Mary got piqued. We went to see Tobacco Road—5th time for me. I still liked the show.[33]

Fri., April 28
New York

Very cold and cloudy. Had a fine day of work. Had intended going to a ball game but it was called off. In the evening went with 2 of E's friends to dine, a rather gay nice party. Had lunch with Volkening, Tom Wolfe's close friend.[34]

Sat., April 29
New York

Saturday—grand day of work. Cloudy and cold. All in after work. Went to a ball game—Brooklyn and Philadelphia. Home early and to bed.

Sun., April 30
New York

Lazy day. Didn't try to work. The World's Fair opened. E and I loafed the whole day away.

Mon., May 1
New York

Bright sunlight. Another full rich day of work, after which I was all in. Took a walk and looked at labor parade. Loafed the evening away.

Nothing in my mind but work.

Tues., May 2
New York

Good day of work. Went off with Luise Sillcox to see Jules Romains. Lunched with Luise. Went later to see and drink with Max Perkins. Went to Downtown Gallery for dinner honor E. E. Cummings—William Carlos Williams Society.[35]

Whole idea no good. Cummings sensible enough to stay away. Sat with Bessie Breuer[36] and went away to drink with her. Drank too much.

Wed., May 3
New York

Excited about the new story—Black Night, on night life. It is keeping me high. Mary gone to the farm and I lunched at home. Talk with Anna about the book.[37] In the evening with 3 refugee professors from Germany and Horace Kallen to dine at Gene's.[38] My mind too full of my story to get much from them.

Thurs., May 4
New York

Work O.K. Did also a lot of letters. Went with literary editor [i.e., agent] to see [Edwin] Balmer of Redbook. Walked home with Chambrun.

In the evening went to big dinner, Mary, Karl, Eleanor—for Spanish Secretary of State before Franco victory.[39]

Dinner for refugees to raise money. Gave some. Mary wanting to go 2nd party but I wouldn't.

Fri., May 5
New York

Worked O.K. A bright warm day. I went off in the p.m. to see Brooklyn beat Chicago at Ebbets Field. Good game.

Stayed home and went to bed early.

Sat., May 6
New York

Worked O.K. Very hot. We drove to Knox [in] Brooklyn and bought winter overcoat for next year, suit, shoes etc. Went to dine with little Rose and husband.[40] Man no good.

Sun., May 7
New York

Did little work. E at home all day. We loafed together. Very hot. In the evening with Mary to Bankhead in Little Red Foxes.[41] Fine acting.

Mon., May 8
New York

Worked. Went to see the Giants play Chicago Cubs. They [i.e., Giants] lost. E and I dined at Ticino's.

Tues., May 9
[Ithaca], New York

Up early and left at eight, to drive to Wells College at Aurora, N.Y. Fog and rain—but later clear. Went only to Ithaca. Kiwanis, dressed as cowboys, shooting guns in the hotel lobby.

Wed., May 10
Aurora, New York

Spent the day largely with Lankes who was much upset over wife troubles. Ridgeway's wife having baby.[42] Turned out to be twins. Spoke very badly. A nice party later and the people kindly after my bust.

Thurs., May 11
New York

Up at six—bright clear morning. Had breakfast at Endicott. A very beautiful spring day. Came by road 17 and into New York by 2:30.
  Big party at night. Was tired and drank a lot to keep going.

Fri., May 12
New York

Stupid day—the effect of the drink and the driving all day. To bed at 1. Was no good all day so went off to ball game with Doctor Joe. Mr. B.E. arrived at 7.[43]

Sat., May 13
New York

It rained all day. B.E. came to see the fair. I wrote a story—"He Built the Boat." I went to the fair, rain, rain. We took B.E. to the Red Barn.

Sun., May 14
New York

Long drive in morning with B.E. Copenhaver. No work. To ball game—[Carl] Hubbel's first. Grand game. Hubbel won 2–1. Evening at World's Fair. Dined there E and B.E. Home late—cool beautiful day.

Mon., May 15
New York

More and more in love with E. Her father didn't go as expected. Worked. Still clear but cold. E sent [her] father to movies and then to fair in p.m.

We dined at Young China. Mary came home late from Alice and Eddy's place.[44] She seemed in good form.

> *Tues., May 16*
> *New York*

Clear. Went to the Warwick for cocktails with Edna [Shafner?] and daughter. Heard Eddie story. Went to Paul's. It was hot and got warm walking, then sat in bad draft in restaurant—result heavy chest cold.
  Had worked O.K.

> *Wed., May 17*
> *New York*

In bed all day with heavy chest cold reading book of adventures in treasure seeking in American Southwest. No work.

> *Thurs., May 18*
> *New York*

Still in bed. Read life of Cervantes. Somewhat better. No work. Day clear and warmer.

> *Fri., May 19*
> *New York*

At home and at work on the novel—the weather very hot. E came in late with Margaret [Forsyth] and we went to dine at a Chinese place. I cleaned up a lot of letters.

> *Sat., May 20*
> *New York*

Worked in the morning and in the p.m. took E to ball game—Yanks and White Sox. We went to Cafe Royal to dine.

> *Sun., May 21*
> *New York*

Rather flat all day. Had bad cough after cold. No work. Went in the late afternoon to Galantière's. Half sick all day.

> *Mon., May 22*
> *New York*

Still flat and no good, cough that shakes me to the toes. Stayed in bed most of the day. Went with E to dine at Ticino's and we got caught in heavy spring rain. Photographer from P.I.C. here taking many photographs.

Tues., May 23
New York

Still no good—cough bad but somewhat better. Unable to work. Managed to get up to Ettie Stettheimer's party.[45] Weak afterwards. Wasted day.

Wed., May 24
New York

Still pretty much under tone with the cold and unable to work effectively. A newspaper woman came from the Argentine with a newspaper man from Puerto Rico.[46]

Myself still no good.

Thurs., May 25
New York

Began to work again. In the p.m. went off to ball game—Detroit–New York. Yanks won again.

In the evening to dine with Dr. and Mrs. Treves.[47] Big time lawyer there. His stories of administration stupidity too shallow.

Fri., May 26
New York

Worked O.K. The days have at last become really warm. Mary went off in the early evening to Virginia. E and I went to Stoltz,[48] then to dine later at Rowe's. Jewish lawyers speaking of methods at nearby table. Day warm and fine. Cold better.

Sat., May 27
New York

House empty. Day warm. Anna left early—going to fair. Mary gone—Miss Keener gone.[49] Wrote piece for Fair Almanac. Tore it up. In the p.m. E and I went for a long drive and dined at Armenian Restaurant in 28th.

Sun., May 28
New York

Did new piece for Village Fair.[50] Got some more down on book. Spent afternoon with Enrique Amorim and wife—Uruguay[51]—and Maria Bombal—Chile.[52] Dined with E at Cafe Royal. Very hot.

Mon., May 29
New York

At home. Worked. E went to office—talk with Anna. In the evening to Lewis [Galantière]—with Maria Bombal—a very fine evening—the conversation of the best.

Tues., May 30
New York

Decoration Day. Worked O.K. E went in the morning to office. Met her at theatre. Saw Bill Robinson in Hot Mikado.[53] Wonderful dancing. Dined with Margaret and the Bishop's daughter.[54] Hot night. Took a long drive. Later could not sleep.

Wed., May 31
New York

Very hot. Worked pretty well. Went off to Polo Grounds to see Brooklyn beat Giants. In the evening E and I to the brass shop—Allen street, where we bought things for Ripshin.[55]

Thurs., June 1
New York

Cooler. Off early to go [to] country—Carlos Davila[56]—at Mrs. Migel's house.[57] Beautiful place but too much wealth. All South American people except Swiss playwright. The company fine. To Charley Studin and then to Cafe Royal to dine. Mary came home at 8 p.m.

Fri., June 2
New York

Clear and cooler. I had a bad depression all day. I stayed at home and, in the evening to the Blue Bowl.[58] Have about decided to confine myself, for the present to short things.

Sat., June 3
New York

Worked on "Fast Woman."[59] Man from California, a movie man came and stayed 3 hours.[60] Could not get rid of him. In the evening with E to see Juarez—a rotten picture to my mind. Very bad acting.[61]

Sun., June 4
New York

Very little real work. Day with E—Mary away. In the evening with Cleon Throckmorton, wife and party for a big bust at Minerva Tavern.

Mon., June 5
New York

Rather a wreck from the bust with Throckmorton last night. Bad head-ache. It cleared and I had a good long time of work but by night was dead and couldn't sleep. Stayed home and played cards with Mary.

Tues., June 6
New York

Bright warm windy day. Work in the a.m., and at 2 left the house with Paul Rosenfeld to go to the Polo Grounds. Cincinnati and Giants. Giants on big hitting spree. 17 to 3—7 home runs. Dined with E at Ticino's. The man Safford came in again.

Very dead for sleep but sat up until 12.

Wed., June 7
New York

Worked in the morning. Mary had company coming. I rather stayed about in the p.m. Wrote letters. In the evening to cocktail party at Charley Studin's. Came home with Max Eastman and Eliena. We dressed and went to dine at 7 × 11—on 55. E joined us. Richard Bennett bought us champagne. We went up to Negro artists' show at 125.[62] There were many beautiful fashionable negro women.

Thurs., June 8
New York

Stomach out of order but worked on the short story. Hung about, took a snooze and went to the Algonquin to bid Maria Bombal good night. E and I walked home. We dined at 9th and 6 . . . nice Italian girl. We sat with Mary and played cards until 11 o'clock.

Fri., June 9
New York

Hot—knocked out with indigestion and no work. Stayed in bed and read.

Sat., June 10
New York

Better—but still no work. Went for E in car—packed to get off. Feeling better but weak.

Sun., June 11
Paoli, Pa.

Left New York at 2. Went to Hedgerow. Dined there. Saw part of rehearsal. Drove to Wharton's. Had rain, then beautiful sky. Slept there.

Mon., June 12
Marion

Made an extraordinarily fine drive down, after putting E on train at Paoli. Came by York, Lancaster, Gettysburg and then across to No. 11. Made average of better than 40 all the way. Found everyone well at Mother's.

Tues., June 13
Marion

Up and off to Ripshin with a big load, after errands in town. Walls all back, garden fine, plumbing out of order. Ruby and two girls at work. Big rain coming home. Spent evening with Andy Funk.

Wed., June 14
Marion

Didn't work—too much to do at the farm. Went over there. Settled cabin. Ran two errands. Settled things in cabin. Came back to town at 4. Spent the evening at home after a walk.

Thurs., June 15
Marion

Very hot day. Worked on new story—Father and Son[63]—dropping "A Fast Girl" for the time. In the evening with Funk driving about to get cool.

Went to Ripshin in the p.m.

Fri., June 16
Marion

Worked on new story and again to Ripshin. Again a very hot day. The new story went well. Spent the evening at home, reading Paul Green's plays.[64]

Sat., June 17
Marion

Worked on new story. Stayed in town and went to ball game, Richlands-Marion. Richlands quit after 4 innings. Walk with Saturday night crowds.

Sun., June 18
Marion

Showers. Went early to Ripshin on errands for E. In afternoon took Funk and wife to ball game at Damascus.

Mon., June 19
Marion

A rainy day. Got up early and went to Ripshin in a heavy rain. Got books for E's camp.[65]

Home and to work on story until 1 p.m. Got story of crazy man from sheriff. Mary came in her station wagon from New York at 7 p.m. Stayed home.

Tues., June 20
Marion

E's train did not arrive until noon and I got little work done. In the p.m. took Mary Emmett to Ripshin. Home at 4 and doing errands for E.

The evening at home. E looking well.

Wed., June 21
Sapphire, N.C.

Got off from home at 7:30 and went to Ripshin. Mary Emmett joined us there. We drove to E's camp by Boone, Asheville and Sylva. Stayed at road-side camp for the night. Day very hot, drive all mountains.

Thurs., June 22
Sapphire, N.C.

A very warm beautiful day. E's camp getting underway. Spent most of the day doing errands for her. Mary uncertain of her plans. The place back in the mountains by the lake very beautiful. I did not try to do any work.

Fri., June 23
Sapphire, N.C.

Worked in the morning. The night quite cold. Made several trips to bring people and baggage. Played cards with Mary Emmett. Went early to bed.

Sat., June 24
Sapphire, N.C.

Heavy rain at night—but the day clear. Colston Warne here lecturing to working girls and doing a grand job.[66] In the evening the girls danced. In the p.m. I cut out and went to a ball game at Asheville.

Sun., June 25
Sapphire Camp

Up early to take Mexican girl, suspected of having small pox to the doctor at Waynesville, N.C. It turned out to be a harmless rash. Mary left for Hot Springs, Ga.

Mon., June 26
Sapphire

Bright warm day. Worked on speech for Olivet. Took 5 girls from camp to Highlands, N.C. and got stung as they hung about until late afternoon and I had to wait for them. The stay here has made me sick of females in the mass.

Tues., June 27
Sapphire

Dropped story writing for the day and worked on a speech for Olivet. It was bright warm day. To get away from the camp and too much femininity I got in the car and went to West's. Spent the afternoon secluded in my cabin reading. The place here is very beautiful and I went with the others to a picnic in a beautiful spot by a river.

Wed., June 28
Sapphire, N.C.

Did some work in my cabin. Warm fair day. In the afternoon went up to Mrs. Clay's house to read in the sun and escape too many women. To a place called West's in the evening to listen to the account of the Louis-Galento fight. Louis in 4.[67]

Thurs., June 29
Marion

Up and away from the camp by 9. Many bags to carry. Took 2 women to Asheville, one of them, Ella Ketchin,[68] coming home with us. Came by Blowing Rock to Ripshin to unload baggage. Rain. We went on to Marion to spend the night there.

Fri., June 30
Ripshin

Rainy day. Much shopping to be done to get the house furnished. Came to Ripshin, heavily loaded in the late afternoon. Ella Ketchin staying.
    Mary Emmett showed up at 7—all in, having been in a wreck.

Sat., July 1
Ripshin

First full day at Ripshin. We put up hay. I caught up correspondence. Mary Emmett went off to town. Lewis and Nancy Galantière settled— they came at 9:20 Marion and I met them. Bought mower and hay rake $128.00. Most of the day spent getting settled.

Sun., July 2
Ripshin

Finished story Unforgotten. Funk, wife and children and Bob Williams came. We played croquet and Funk insisted on pushing. I was rude to him. The children at dinner was very tough.

Mon., July 3
Ripshin

At home. Eleanor went to town with Mary. Mary to get her wrecked car repaired. It stayed warm and cloudy. Ella Ketchin, of Washington, a government official, and Nancy lying out in the yard.

Conversations with Lewis. He is unsure of himself. Nice man but over-sells himself as sophisticate.

Tues., July 4
Ripshin

Not much celebration of the fourth. No fireworks. Men and boys standing idly about the garage in Troutdale and at road crossing. Got a beautiful big glass cylinder from Orlie. In the evening took Ella to Marion to get train to Washington. All in bed when we got home. Fine rain all day and at night.

Wed., July 5
Ripshin

Eleanor off to town to dictate and shop in the early morning. It rained nearly all day. In the p.m. the man came with the new mower and rake. John [Sullivan] and I about equally proud.

I started a new story, about Ida and boy.

Thurs., July 6
Ripshin

After the morning's work went off in the car with Mary Emmett at 11. We went to Wytheville for liquor and then to Marion. We had a pretty honest

Sherwood Anderson with Mary Emmett at Ripshin Farm in
1939.
(Trustees of the Sherwood Anderson Literary Estate.)

talk on the way. I have decided to take no more financial help from her.

It rained in Marion. Took Aunt May for minnows, and then to fish. Did a lot of shopping. As Mary's car was fixed, she drove it home. She told me the real story of the wreck in N.C.

Fri., July 7
Ripshin

Woke up ill with a bad diarrhea—and Eleanor slaughtered with a headache. The diarrhea made me weak so I could not work. E got better later in the day.

Took Lewis for a drive in the p.m. Mary went off to town for the shopping. Rain at night.

Sat., July 8
Ripshin

Rainy day. Went to town for medicine for the diarrhea. Pretty weak. E all right. We got a fine big piece of luggage, all arranged for picnics from Lewis and Nancy. Nancy had been ill but got downstairs.

Sun., July 9
Ripshin

Had a sharp return of the diarrhea that put me to bed in the evening. In the afternoon took Mary and E for a drive to Mouth of Wilson to see Dave [Greear] and [his] mother.

Mon., July 10
Ripshin

Ill and weak all day. I stayed in bed, the diarrhea quite bad. Mary went off to town as did E. E went to consult doctor and get me medicine.

Tues., July 11
Ripshin

Mary in town. A certain tension taken out of the place. I have had to decide I can no longer keep the bargain with her. The money involved gets on my nerves as she does. Good but vulgar.

Still with a touch of diarrhea and weak. It is however better.

Wed., July 12
Ripshin

The disease still holding on a bit but better. Worked early and then went off to town with E. Saw doctor and got medicine. Did a lot of shopping and home at 4 p.m. The weather has cleared. Hay made and oats cutting begun.

Thurs., July 13
Ripshin

Beautiful clear day. Worked on material for Olivet and did part of my packing. E to Marion. John, Eleanore and baby came for dinner—the baby very beautiful.

Hard thunderstorm at night.

Fri., July 14
Marion

Mary got up and left before daylight. I worked on speeches for Olivet. We all drove to Marion and Lewis and Nancy Galantière left for California. We stayed the night at E's people's house in Marion.

Sat., July 15
Portsmouth, Ohio

We left Marion at 8—going north the long way, via Ashland, Kentucky and Portsmouth, Ohio—all day in the mountains. The night at Portsmouth, very tired.

Sun., July 16
Sandusky, Ohio

Went to Antioch, Ohio to see Gilbert Wilson's murals. Went to Springfield to see Trillena White. Went to Clyde and drove about through old scenes. E took train for New York at 5:40.

Mon., July 17
Olivet, Mich.

Left Sandusky, Ohio at 7. Drove slowly. Stopped at Adrian for a visit with Will Burnham and wife.[69] Will much nicer than wife. He has aged well. Got Olivet at 1:30. At 5 went to Joe Brewer's. We spent the evening on Ford.[70] Padraic Colum, John Bishop, Katherine Porter.

Tues., July 18
Olivet, Mich.

I have taken a great fancy to Padraic Colum. He has a delicious sense of humor. I took part in what was called a "parliament."[71] The tone here is pretty literary. In the evening I lectured and it went off with a bang. Later drinks and conversation at Joe Brewer's house.

Wed., July 19
Olivet

Uneventful day. Very beautiful here. Went to hear Padraic Colum on poetry. It gave me an insight into the transplanted European. Attracted to Beulah [Charmely?]. Word that I got $1500 for the piece in Literary Digest.[72]

Thurs., July 20
Olivet

Man in love with a cat. The [?]. The trembling man. I did a short story hour at 11 a.m. In the p.m. went to the doctor for a return of the diarrhea. He fixed me up. Had to tell a man named Hutton how bad his stuff was. Went with John Bishop to Charlotte for whiskey. John Bishop talked well in the evening.

Fri., July 21
Olivet

I took Mary Colum's place—delivering a lecture used at Olivet during the winter. Drove two women students about the country. In the evening we all read—Colum, Bishop, Porter and self.[73] We all went to Marshall later for a party.

Sat., July 22
Michigan City,
Ind.

George Rickey and I drove to Michigan City, Indiana, to see Ferdinand Schevill. Stopped at some people named Ramsey. Very beautiful blond French woman. At Sergels—Wilson and wife,[74] Roger and Ruth, a historian from University of Chicago and wife—historian of art.

Sun., July 23
Olivet

Left Ferdinand's at 2:30. Went back to Ramsey where I had left my hat. Went to Gull Lake Country Club at Kalamazoo. Entertained by Mrs. McCall. I was in a wild gay mood. We got to Olivet at 11 p.m.

Mon., July 24
Olivet

I spoke on sources of the writer's material, using "Untold Lie," "Death in the Woods," and "Man of Ideas."

I took Padraic and Mary Colum for a long drive. In the evening I talked to Miss Clift of Medina, Ohio.

Tues., July 25
Olivet

John Bishop made a fine speech on style. I took Miss [Charmely?] for a ride to talk with her of her work. Parky came from Chicago and went with me to Charlotte where I got the Ferdinand suit.[75]

In the evening the waiters, from the dining room gave a party for us.

Wed., July 26
Olivet

Very fine talk by John Bishop. I took the mail order Hungarian woman, Kratovil, for a ride and talk. Karl Detzer eating his own dung made me half ill.[76] Had a long walk and talk with Bishop.

Thurs., July 27
Olivet

Fuss all day about Sandburg's coming. He didn't come. I worked for him. Did two stories to fair sized audience. Notable thing of the day a speech by John Bishop. My car caught on fire—not badly damaged.

Fri., July 28
Sandusky, Ohio

Left Olivet in the late morning and drove to Sandusky to meet E, arriving in a heavy rainstorm. I went there to a wine company and bought 3 cases of wine. It still rained. I went off to bed early.

Sat., July 29
Huntington, W. Va.

E arrived from New York at 7:50 a.m. We breakfasted and went to Springfield to see Trillena White. Went by Clyde, Tiffin and Washington Court House. Miss White lovely. It rained frequently all day. We drove on to Huntington to spend the night.

Sun., July 30
Ripshin

Went to Bluefield via Logan, W.Va.—rain and clouds all morning—after Bluefield sun and very warm. Got to Marion at 2:30. Drove on to Ripshin in the evening.

Mon., July 31
Ripshin

Pretty tired from the long drive. Tried to work. No good. Am on short stories.[77] Went to town. John and Major bringing in oats and rye. When we were gone there was a 1/2 cloud burst that took away the footbridge by the barn. It is nice to be for a time alone with E who is very lovely.

Tues., August 1
Ripshin

The work did not go. We got the oats down to the barnyard and have 6 stacks, hay and oats. The corn looks good. We spent the p.m. in town. We are looking forward to the men's dinner on Friday evening. Mother has been ill, bleeding of the tongue, result of high blood pressure. She looks very beautiful these days.

Wed., August 2
Ripshin

Began a new and quite terrible story I call the Primitives. It is tense. Worked in the a.m. and, in the p.m. went off to town with E. We played croquet and dined there, having a wonderful dinner. We came home in the moonlight.

Thurs., August 3
Ripshin

The story went along. The morning fair but rain in the p.m. E and [I] drove to Marion, lunching there. We came home in the rain. May came. Much preparation for the feast—the court house crowd. A heavy rain here while we were gone, the heaviest of the year so that water came down the hill into the kitchen.

Fri., August 4
Ripshin

After the rain the day came off clear and beautiful. Worked on the story and then hurried off to town for supplies.

   In the evening we had a big feast, for all the county officials of Smyth County. Fifteen men sat down, all great eaters. They did eat.

Sat., August 5
Ripshin

The story went along. We went quite early to town. Mother alarmed by again bleeding at the tongue. Mazie came, with Channing, Mrs. Wilson and the children. John Anderson is to return with them for a going over at Johns Hopkins. We got home just ahead of a rain at 9 p.m.

Sun., August 6
Ripshin

Mother quite ill. I took it in my hands to get Dr. Smith over. Paul [Rosenfeld] came at 4 p.m. and we went to dine at the park where we met the French woman interested in Lincoln.

Mon., August 7
Ripshin

Mother reported better. I began the 1st rewriting of the Primitives. We built fence and planned the new barn. E went off to town. The little dog I brought from Marion had a fit and ran away. We searched and could not find him. Major says it is worms and can be cured.

Tues., August 8
Ripshin

I worked on the new story a long time and when I finished work was nervously exhausted. I was listless and picked flowers and blackberries for the house. We laid out the foundation for the new barn. I got $1350 for a story from Readers Digest.[78] E came from town at 4 and we played croquet. I lost my temper and made a scene. Glenn Gosling came at 8 p.m.

Wed., August 9
Ripshin

Because of my senseless anger with E in the evening I did not sleep and was in bad shape so that I wrote little. Went off to Marion with E to shop and see Mother who is quite ill and has been bleeding at the tongue. We had a fine evening with music on the phonograph.

Thurs., August 10
Ripshin

Putting down the foundation of the barn. Cloudy in the morning but clear later. The dog Rip seems O.K. Took Glenn Gosling for a ride in the hills. He, Paul and I went to swim in the big hole.

In the evening Dave Greear, Miss Thomas,[79] Jim Birchfield and wife to dine and spend the evening.

Fri., August 11
Ripshin

All the days now begin with heavy clouds but before noon they are all gone. The afternoons and evenings are fine.

Paul and Glenn went off to the Folk Musical at White Top, returning for dinner. E went off to Marion. We worked on the foundation for the new barn. Worked O.K. In the evening we played cards.

Sat., August 12
Ripshin

Davis and Penny Baker came with their dog, arriving in the evening.[80] In the p.m. I took Paul and Eleanor for a drive over Flat Ridge mountain. We had a buffet supper and in the evening Dave and Sol Greear came. Worked O.K.

Sun., August 13
Ripshin

We all set off to Marion after lunch—rain. We went to call on Mother— she some better. We went to see John's paintings. Went swimming in the lake. Paul had us to dinner. Came home in the rain. Worked O.K. in the a.m.

Mon., August 14
Ripshin

We have now six guests—the house and green house quite full. It rained all day—a slow soft rain but we mowed weeds on the upper field of the Swan Farm. Wharton Esherick and Rose Schulman arrived at 5. Four of us went swimming down to the big hole and came back in a pouring rain.

Tues., August 15
Ripshin

A drizzle of rain all day. I worked well in my cabin but we could do little or no work on the farm. Everyone sat about all day. The Bakers' dog a great nuisance. In the evening we played poker, penny ante, and to his delight Paul won 52 cents.

Wed., August 16
Ripshin

The rain kept up all day. It has gone on steadily now for three days.

In the evening E and Aunt May gave a big party for E's two little cousins from Richmond, Mary Grace and Betty.[81] There were about 20 to a buffet supper. They had a good time.

Thurs., August 17
Ripshin
Still steady and persistent rain although we had a little sun in the a.m. John and Major clearing old field above cabin. Drove to Independence, Wytheville, and Marion to get liquor and see Mother. Had flat. Got good supply of liquor. Mother some better. Struck more rain. We all played poker in the p.m. It was a day of not much work done.

Fri., August 18
Ripshin
Rain all morning again but a little sun in the p.m. Pauline Pasley—now Mrs. [Carl] Neel, who used to be my secretary came to dine—a cripple but nice. Pauline very fine. We finished clearing the old field by my cabin and worked on new field by the barn. Worked on Primitives. Wharton and Rose Schulman left for Pennsylvania.

Sat., August 19
Ripshin
At last the sun—really shining . . . a beautiful cool day. E went off to the hairdresser in Marion. Mother better. E brought Mazie home with her. We all went into North Carolina to the Bromide-arsenic springs to dine. [?] not running the place. We played poker and I won. Worked O.K. in the a.m.

Sun., August 20
Ripshin
Clear beautiful day. Little work. Felt flat. We all went to town and Paul left for New York at 3. Mother better. We took Betty, now quite the little lady, to the park to dine with us. There is a new moon. We came home and sat on the terrace in the moonlight.

Mon., August 21
Ripshin
Making a new effort to cut down on my cigarette smoking. I tried to work but no success. Went to Marion with E and left car to be worked on. Home at 3:30. Two local newspapermen, Fries and Hillsville,[82] called. C.I.O. organizer Lancaster and wife called and stayed for dinner.[83] They tried to get me to come there and speak.

Tues., August 22
Ripshin

A clear cool beautiful day but I was nervous and high and couldn't get into work.

So I went up to help on the foundation of the new barn.

We are making apple butter.

E went off to town. I have the car in Marion, waiting to have the burned seat fixed.

Wed., August 23
Ripshin

Bright clear day. Worked at my desk in the a.m. We finished pouring the cement for the foundation of the new barn. Cut my cigarette smoking to a pack a day. A new moon. We played cards in the evening.

Thurs., August 24
Ripshin

Sunshine and showers. Got temporarily off the Primitives to do a dream story. Went up to the barn and worked. Rain stopped the work. Virginia and Guy Denit came to dinner. We found them delightful people, Guy one of the most charming men I ever met.[84]

Fri., August 25
Ripshin

A cloudy day. Up early to finish the dream story. Glenn, E, and I to Roanoke to hear Bob speak. We went the back way via Hillsville and Floyd. Bob too decent for the crowd. Byrd's foxiness.[85] Home to Marion at 7 for Mother Copenhaver and Father Copenhaver's anniversary dinner.

Sat., August 26
Ripshin

Girls off. Corrected Griffith story for copyist.[86] We went to Marion. Went to Frank Copenhaver's. Dined at Frank Lemmon's. Jack Cronk showed up. I got into a nasty and unnecessary fuss with E about relatives.[87]

Sun., August 27
Ripshin

Worked pretty steadily on the long story Primitives. We went off to town and called on Bob. We had a pick-up supper at home. Clear fine day.

Mon., August 28
Ripshin

Work on the long story. E and I went off to town and to Bristol to get the burned back seat of the car properly done. Alice Armfield came from Concord, N.C.—a delightful woman.[88] We got home for dinner.

Tues., August 29
Ripshin

Worked on long story. We got the new barn started. Guy Denit and wife came to dine. The long story will pretty much have to be all rewritten. It will be an absorbing job. Did some work on a speech for Princeton.

Wed., August 30
Ripshin

Alice and I had a long talk about Glenn. Do not want, as I hoped, to work on textbook with him.[89] Worked about the barn in the p.m. after a morning with the long story. Weather fine with a full moon.

Thurs., August 31
Ripshin

After morning's work on long story we all drove, through heavy rain to the county fair at Galax.[90] No rain there. Horse races tame. The fair filled with little but fake stuff. The old fashion county fair about gone. We dined at little hotel at Independence. Pretty bored with Glenn.

Fri., Sept. 1
Ripshin

War is in the air. It will now invade everything. There will be nothing else thought of or talked of. It will be a great sickness in everyone.[91]

Glenn and Alice left in the morning. We went to Marion. We worked on the new barn. Day clear and fine.

Sat., Sept. 2
Ripshin

To Marion early. War talk everywhere. Everyone pretending to an opinion on international affairs. Karl [Anderson] and Stanley Young came with Mrs. Young.[92]

Sun., Sept. 3
Ripshin

Peaceful happy fine day with guests until evening, when E came from Troutdale full of war news. Reports actual war begun. I had to flee the house to be in darkness.

Mon., Sept. 4
Ripshin

Put story aside to work on speech for Salem and Cornell.[93] The threshers are in the neighborhood and we stopped work on the barn.

The war in Europe is on again. I was sick thinking of it.

Bob, Mary, John with his Eleanore and Anne came to dine. There was a heavy thunder shower. The war in everyone's mind.

Tues., Sept. 5
Ripshin

I had to drop everything else to work on the speech for Princeton. It was a beautiful fall day. We spent most of the afternoon in talk. In the evening we drove Stanley and Margaret to a Holiness meeting at Sugar Grove and went on to Marion for the night. Karl not well. We were to meet Augusto Centeno in the morning.[94]

Wed., Sept. 6
Ripshin

No work. We had to drive Mazie with her babies to Dublin. We got Augusto Centeno, of Princeton off the train at Wytheville. Drove to Dublin and then back to Marion and home. Had flat. The whole afternoon and evening spent in talk.

Thurs., Sept. 7
Ripshin

The day, a very beautiful one, spent largely in talk with the man Augusto Centeno, of the Spanish dept. of Cornell [i.e., Princeton], for a lecture there.

We all went to town and to John's to see his painting. We dined on the porch at Mother's. Centeno left at 8:40. John Anderson came home with us for the night.

John Anderson came over to spend the day and to talk with Karl. I paid John for the Baltimore trip. All day we walked about, all of us and talked. Started the corn cutting. In the evening Stanley Young recited poetry. John and Eleanore Anderson left at 10. I worked in the a.m.

Karl, Stanley Young and wife left for Connecticut after breakfast. I worked in my cabin until noon. It was the hottest day of the year. We drove to Marion. Funk was making wine. We had an argument about unions. We all dined at the park. Home at 9.

Worked on a story about 2 brothers, letting the long story wait. Went to dine at Mother's in town and to call on Bob and Mary. Got home early for a quiet evening with E.

Work on the barn. I tried a short story that didn't come off. To relieve my disappointment went up and worked all afternoon on the barn. The work put me in a better mood. Was happy at last alone for a night in the house with E.

We worked more on the barn. Again I tried the short story and again failed and again worked about the barn to relieve my feelings. The road man Flanagan, with his wife and child came to dine. A pleasant evening. Thought I heard someone stealing our chickens and looked for gun to fire and scare them—a false alarm.

A bright warm day and I returned again to the long story. It was my birthday but I had forgotten. Mother came from Marion with E. John and Major cut corn. Mother gave me a beautiful table and E a tie. She also got me a heater for the car.

Thurs., Sept. 14
Ripshin

Mother over to spend the day. Cloudy but it cleared. I did a piece on trotters and pacers.[95] We got the framework for the roof of the barn up. It is going to be quite splendid. Gilbert Wilson came, annoying, set on saving civilization. His presence annoyed me. I went off to Tolstoy's War and Peace.

Fri., Sept. 15
Ripshin

Working on barn. Spent the day polishing story on harness horses and entertaining Wilson who could talk of nothing but Art Young.[96] We got the barn roof rafters up. E took Mother and Wilson off to town. The evening dull. E brought Elsie [Groseclose] home to clean up my letters.

Sat., Sept. 16
Ripshin

Got Wilson off—a great bore. It continues hot and dry. Dictated to Elsie all morning. We are beginning to close up the house for the season.

Sun., Sept. 17
Ripshin

Did no work. We went to Marion to dine at Mother's. Spent the p.m. with them and with Funk.

Mon., Sept. 18
Ripshin

Growing cold. This is the last day of life on the farm for this year. Started a new story. Went to work on the barn in the p.m. E spent the day in town. It was very cold in the house at night.

Tues., Sept. 19
[Marion]

Worked for a time in the a.m. It was a grey cold day and we were closing the house. We left at 11 a.m. for Marion and, after dinner drove to Roanoke. E took the midnight train for New York—looking very tired but infinitely sweet. I did not sleep for a long time. I loved her much.

Wed., Sept. 20
Marion

I drove to Roanoke College where I was to speak at 11 a.m. I liked Doctor [Charles J.] Smith the president. There was a procession with robes but I wore none. My speech went well. There was a luncheon—English Dept. I liked the men.⁹⁷ I drove to Marion. Saw Funk in the p.m. I listened to the Louis-Pastor fight on the radio.⁹⁸

Thurs., Sept. 21
Marion

Worked at my desk in the morning, revising the trotting horse piece.

Then went to Ripshin and cleaned out my work cabin there. It was a very beautiful fall day but I was still tired by the effort at Roanoke College. The meeting of new people, as at Roanoke, always takes too much out of me.

Fri., Sept. 22
Marion

Had to work on the Princeton speech while ideas, got when delivering the speech at Salem were fresh in my mind.

Went to Ripshin. In the evening went to football game at Emory and Henry. A clear fine day but cold at night.

Sat., Sept. 23
Marion

Reworked Princeton speech and went to the farm to take material for the new barn. The roof was going on. It will be a fine barn.

My stomach a bit wrong and I have cut out drinking. I still smoke too much. Walked about in the Saturday night crowds. It was a joy.

Sun., Sept. 24
Harrodsburg, Ky.

Drove over here, from Marion, staying at Hotel Harrod, where I used to come 20 years ago, when an advertising writer. Here for Lexington trots. Will stay here—comfortable room cheap. The drive hot but interesting.

Mon., Sept. 25
Harrodsburg, Ky.

Fixed up an article called "So You Want to be a Writer."⁹⁹

The drive over to Lexington from here very beautiful. You go through the old Shaker town where I once stayed.[100] The Bohons, for whom I worked here, as advertising writer, went broke later. They are both dead.[101]

The trots tracks very beautiful. Peter Astra won the Futurity easily, not pressed, a wonderful colt.

Tues., Sept. 26
Harrodsburg, Ky.

A big day at the tracks. Up early to get my work done and over then to see the workouts. I was called to the stand to help present the cup for the Futurity.

Had my picture taken with champion 2 year old pacer and dined with horsemen in the evening.

Then went to Walnut Hill farm to see the new yearlings sold at auction. A big day. Warm and clear.

Wed., Sept. 27
Harrodsburg, Ky.

A fine day at the races. I took a vacation and went early. It's nice in the morning, seeing the horses work. I sat in the betting shed. The races in the p.m. were all close and exciting. I bet a little and then quit.

Came back here early. There was a fight, two young drunken country boys in the street under my window.

Thurs., Sept. 28
Harrodsburg, Ky.

Another bright hot day and all the grass country burned up. Racing good again. Saw Greyhound—very beautiful. Peter Astra was to go for new record but wind too strong. Got a batch of mail from home. A man named Alex Bower did a fine piece in the Lexington paper.[102]

Dined in town and drove home slowly in the moonlight.

Fri., Sept. 29
Pineville, Ky.

Took the day off to spend it all at the tracks but, at noon rain came and spoiled the tracks so the races were called off.

Started home—in a heavy rain and drove to Pineville, Ky. It cleared and I went to see a high school football game. I have written a good piece on the harness horse.

Sat., Sept. 30
Marion

Got in from Pineville at 1:30. In the afternoon more rain. I spent the p.m. and evening with Mother who was particularly lovely. She can be at times strikingly beautiful.

Sun., October 1
Marion

Caught up with part of correspondence. Drove to Ripshin with John in heavy cold foggy weather. Felt knocked out by the cold and dampness. Sore throat.

Mon., October 2
Marion

Felt myself taking cold but did do one essay for This Week.[103] It may do. Sent off two things to Chambrun.[104] It was cold, cloudy and wet all day but I went to Ripshin to take John's money. In the evening I felt the cold clamping down on me.

Tues., October 3
Marion

Had to stay in bed all day—a horrid head cold, so did nothing but blow off snot.

However the day brightened and I read a silly meaningless book. Dull books are best when you are sick.

Wed., October 4
Marion

Doing more letters. The cold going away but has left me weak. I didn't try to work. Went to Funk's and turned out new pegs for our croquet ground on his lathe.

Thurs., October 5
Marion

Wrote essay for This Week—needs more work. Went to farm and brought grapes, apples, peppers and butter. Did a mass of letters. Brought pictures for Funk's new house. Got, as a present a fine painting by a woman painter (Day).[105]

Fri., October 6
Marion

Worked on an editorial for This Week that may bring in money.[106] The day fair and warm. Went on a last visit of the season to Ripshin. In the evening to Funk where we played cards and barked at each other.

Sat., October 7
Marion

Worked at my desk until noon. Went to hear the World Series on the radio—Funk's. Went to John's. Dined at Bob's—3 weekly Virginia newspaper publishers, all middlewesterners—much talk of newspapers and old days in Chicago.

Sun., October 8
Harrisonburg, Va.

Early morning packing. Went to John's to dine, and then started east. Very hot. Slow going in Sunday traffic. Got to Harrisonburg at 7 and stopped at Hotel Warren. Pretty sick and tired and with a headache.

Mon., October 9
New York—54

Slept late and felt badly starting but got new life as I drove so that, at seven, arrived in New York O.K. Went out to dine with E. It was as hot as a July night. E very lovely and I happy to be with her again. Mary Emmett away at her new doctor's in the north.[107]

Tues., October 10
New York—54

Worked on stories of men. It was very hot. Word came that Mary could not come down from Canada because of bad eyes. J. J. Lankes showed up with pert little gal for whom he has chucked his family. He was in a sad mood. We took him to dine with his girl who kept trying to talk art.

It was all pretty sad.

Wed., October 11
New York

Did little work—tried but was ineffectual. Went to meet Eleanor about getting a fur coat. Got word that a piece I wrote had sold for $800.00.[108] We went to dine at the Brevoort. We were both tired and E with a fresh cold. Millen Brand came at 10 but I pushed him out.

Thurs., October 12
New York

Cooler—a grey day. Work doesn't go well here. I shall work on speeches. In the p.m. after the effort to work went to see "Pins and Needles."[109] It seemed still very fresh and alive. Kept wondering what would happen to these girls when they must go back to their shops.

Went to see Lewis and Nancy Galantière—they in fine form. E has caught my cold. She looked done in.

Fri., October 13
New York

Mary still at Dr. Locke's in Canada so will not see her. She has trouble with her eyes. Cooler. Grey day and then sun. Got the car repaired $18. E got me a grand new bag. After working went and loafed in the old book stores 4th Avenue. We went to dine with Paul Rosenfeld and then to call on Lewis Mumford and wife.[110]

Sat., October 14
New York

Worked in the morning, then for a walk. It was a cold cloudy day. E came home quite early in the afternoon and we did what we could of the packing for our trip. In the evening went to Ticino's. Forgot and left the key sticking in the door.

Sun., October 15
New York

Saw Eleanor off for her conference at West Point, N.Y. Went to professional football game—Philadelphia-Giants, at Polo Gounds with Dr. Joe. His tale of abortionists. Went to dine and met Throckmorton and wife. Throck drunk. We had a time getting him home.

Mon., October 16
New York

Work in the morning. In the p.m. went to dine with Lewis and Nancy Galantière. Jean Untermeyer was there.[111] Lewis was in fine form, talking with keen insight about the Germans; facism, communism, etc. He is doing a book on the subject and is widely read, having the benefit of knowing the languages. Head filled with thoughts, night of faces. Little sleep.

Tues., October 17
New York

At home most of the day working. Went again to Galantières' and after dinner to Maurice Werner's, where we saw Cummings and wife.[112] Others came in and we talked and drank until 1 a.m. Then we went to Tony's on 52nd and sat there talking until 2:30.[113] Lewis was particularly brilliant.

Wed., October 18
New York

Worked in the morning. Bright warm day. E got in at about 5. We had to run her girls about. Dined at Stewart's,[114] packed.

Thurs., October 19
Princeton

Drove over to Princeton, arriving at 11. Went to lunch at Nassau Inn. Aspiring writers. Went to Allen Tate for tea. Dined at Centeno's. The Dean and wife there. Spoke in large hall, good success.[115] Went to drink beer at faculty club. Tate and others came to Centeno's house. Bed at 1:30 a.m.

Fri., October 20
Paoli, Pa.

In the morning after breakfast drove to Hedgerow and spent the day with Jap and others. Listened to rehearsal and reading. Wharton came and he, Jap and I dined at the Inn. Met E at 8:40. We slept at Wharton's house.

Sat., October 21
Wheeling, W.Va.

We left Paoli at 9 and got here at 6:30. The mountains all along very beautiful in their fall colors. Stayed at Hotel Windsor here.

Sun., October 22
Terre Haute, Ind.

Drove from Wheeling today. Clear, warm and very windy—the roads pretty much jammed with people. We had a nice hour's visit with Trillena White. Because of sun in our eyes we stopped driving at five.

Mon., October 23
Topeka, Kansas

This day we drove from Terre Haute to Topeka—491 miles. We went around St. Louis but through Kansas City. We went on to Topeka to see Marco Morrow. Roger Baldwin[116] was speaking and as Morrow thought he ought to go so we went. Afterwards we all went to Morrow's house. Saw Baldwin's rich wife. His speech heavy.

Marco's son an interesting case—evidently mother fixation.

Tues., October 24
Goodland, Kansas

We had a flat and ran on it too long. Had to buy new tire. Did not get away from Topeka until after nine. The road wonderful. We went through Kansas on No. 24. Monday was extraordinarily hot 92—today cooler. We found the country very dry and desolate—a wheat country—the farmers afraid the wheat, already planted would not germinate.

Wed., October 25
Denver
Brown Palace

Up early and finished the 200 mile drive to Denver by 11 a.m. Another fine day—cooler and with a bright sun, but E and I both feeling the altitude which made me stupid and dull. Slept a little and walked a little. Wire from [Ted] Davison about speaking at the University at Boulder $75. Agreed. Davison came in with a friend and we had drinks. To bed early but bad time sleeping.

Thurs., October 26
Denver
Brown Palace

Dictated letters all morning, pretty largely about people's personal problems—and to men who were doing theses on my own work. It rained a little. I went for a walk. E working so dined alone. Went to see the picture, "All Quiet on the Western Front"—very fine anti-war propaganda. E's new fur coat came. Very beautiful.

Fri., October 27
Denver

Bright clear day—somewhat cooler. Worked on speeches. Went for a walk about the town. My stomach somewhat disturbed. I shall have to give up drinking. Dined alone. Read most of the afternoon. Am not yet acclimated—the altitude flattening me. Sent many letters.

Sat., October 28
Denver

Worked morning. Stomach kicking up trouble. Went to football game—Denver-Utah—7 to 7—with Ted and Natalie Davison, D'Armes and wife. We dined at University Club—E joining us. I was ill all night later.

Sun., October 29
Denver

As I was ill all night was weak and shaky today. When we got up a heavy snow was falling but it cleared during the day. E was out at work all day. I stayed in getting on my feet again.

Mon., October 30
Boulder, Colo.

Up quite late and packed. The snow gone from the road. Left E to finish in Denver and drove off to Boulder, to Ted Davison's house.

   Began at once to see people, going to a cocktail party and people in the evening. They stayed late but at 11 I left and went off to bed.

Tues., October 31
Boulder, Colo.

A busy day—many men calling at Ted Davison's house. I took the car to be greased and drove about the college. It died on me and I had to walk to Davison's and phone for repairman—dirt in carburetor. I spoke to journalist class at 4, went to cocktail party, dined with faculty at 6:30, spoke again at 8. E arrived at 11. There was a party at Davison's after speech.

Wed., Nov. 1
Las Vegas, N.M.

We decided to go the southern way to avoid snowstorms in the high mountains. Went straight south to Raton and over Raton Pass. Followed the old Santa Fe trail—the country more and more strange and beautiful as we went. The day was fine with streaks of white clouds. Towns far apart—many cattle ranches.

Thurs., Nov. 2
Williams, Ariz.

A very adventurous and strange day of driving. Miles of barren upland, Indian towns, the Painted Desert, then the uplands, between Holbrook and Williams, up about 7500 feet—beautiful pines. The day very soft and lovely and the road good so that, not realizing we had driven so far, we came 500 miles.

Fri., Nov. 3
Tonopah, Nevada

Left Williams, Ariz. early and drove up to Grand Canyon. Then back to Williams—120 miles. Left Williams [at] 10 and drove to Kingman, Arizona—then by wonderful new road to Boulder Dam. The road more impressive than Grand Canyon. We went then to Death Valley, Goldfield and Tonopah, Nevada where we spent the night. A remarkable day.

Sat., Nov. 4
Reno

Drove over to Reno, arriving at noon. Judge Bartlett insisted on our staying at his house. Monte and Dorothy both beautiful. We also saw Dr. Don Caples—an old friend[117] with a new charming wife. The whole visit was very charming and warming.

Sun., Nov. 5
San Francisco

We came to San Francisco—to Hotel Canterbury—a beautiful day, over the high Sierras. No snow—the drive very beautiful. We were tired. Dined at a French place. Saw Brownie and Helen[118] and then off to bed, after so much driving.

Mon., Nov. 6
San Francisco

The weather very beautiful, cool and sunshiny and the city all excited about a political campaign for heavy old age pensions, called Ham and Eggs. There was rather a heavy lot of mail to answer. Eleanor went off to Berkeley and I went to lunch with Leon Gelber[119] and then afterward to see the town.

Tues., Nov. 7
San Francisco

I find that Chambrun has sold a short editorial of mine to a magazine called This Week—for $400—so I feel quite rich.[120] This seems an old woman's hotel. I haven't got to work yet—so I went off for a long walk to see the town.

E didn't come in from Berkeley until nearly midnight. Still grand weather here.

Wed., Nov. 8
San Francisco

The days keep being very beautiful here. I went after morning's work with E to Oakland, over the new bridge, a beautiful ride. Got an expensive and beautiful new Italian hat. In the evening E and I went to dine with Brownie and Helen in a charming house overlooking the Pacific.

Thurs., Nov. 9
San Francisco

Worked in the a.m. and then lunch with Leon Gelber. It was again a beautiful warm day and in the p.m. I went to the house of Don Caples' son Robert. He has evidently married a rich girl, has a delightful house, has become a young painter. The head of the painters WPA project was there.[121] Much talk of young Segura.[122] Eleanor and I spent the evening together.

Fri., Nov. 10
San Francisco

Another lovely day. I finished a new short story and then to lunch with Mother's cousin, Jim Scherer, at [Joe DeMayo's?] place—on Fisherman's Wharf. Home to the hotel then and letters. In the evening to Robert Caples' house to dine. His wife one of the loveliest women I have met.

Sat., Nov. 11
San Francisco

No work—although I tried. Gave a very stupid interview to the [San Francisco] Chronicle and there was a very stupid picture.[123] Went to a football game and then dined alone. It was another amazingly beautiful day. Eleanor very lovely when she came in at 10:30.

Sun., Nov. 12
San Francisco

Did a short piece on Tom Mooney.[124] Then went off, with John Terrell[125] and his girl to lunch—Fisherman's Wharf. Then in the late p.m. with E to visit the western Scherers.[126] They are a story. We dined alone together.

Mon., Nov. 13
San Francisco

The 1st cloudy day we have had. I did no work. Went to the Bohemian Club with Joseph Jackson[127] and John Terrell. It is far far from a Bohemian club.[128]

In the evening went with E to dine—industrial girls. Then with Brownie to hear the Chinese writer—Lin Yutang.[129] Thought it pretty second rate.

Tues., Nov. 14
San Francisco

Went with Ted Lilienthal, by car to spend the day with John Steinbeck for whose Grapes of Wrath there is a great rage just now. He has a ranch in the mountains near Los Gatos, California. A big man physically with a big wife. I didn't like [her] as I did him. She may push him too much. There was a lot of talk of the danger he was in from money and popularity that has done such evil things to so many writers.

Wed., Nov. 15
San Francisco

Got started on a new story and worked on it rapidly all morning. All in after a long siege. Dined alone. Went to Ted to send a book to John Steinbeck. Liking him. Turned Ella Winter down for breakfast.[130] Saw a man about doing a book on the American small town. To dine with John [Terrell] and Caples and wife. Packing.

Thurs., Nov. 16
San Francisco

Stayed in all morning to work. Went to lunch alone. Went to see Ted Lilienthal who gave me several copies of my own "Modern Writer."

In the evening we went to dine with Robert Caples and wife at an expensive place—she apparently very rich. Packed. E and I both rather all in and little sleep.

Fri., Nov. 17
Fresno, California

We left San Francisco at 7 and going first to Monterey—where E wanted to see some old friends. We went by a poor winding road through high hills by the sea. There was some trouble with the car. We had to spend money on it. The trip in the p.m. was through beautiful grey hills. We got to Fresno at 4:30. Hotel Sequoia.

Sat., Nov. 18
Fresno

This is another big fruit and vegetable center. The climate wonderful. I wrote many letters. Did a piece for San Francisco Chronicle.[131] In the p.m. went out to a park to watch the Brooklyn baseball tryout. In the evening to see the movie Livingston and Stanley. The African scenes good—the acting rotten.

Sun., Nov. 19
Fresno

Amazingly beautiful weather. After work I again went to see boys work out for big league scouts. In the p.m. I took a load of factory girls to see some of the labor camps near here—horrible enough places.

Mon., Nov. 20
Fresno

Worked a long time on the new story and then went to drive through a flat country past miles of grape vineyards. This is a big wine center. In the evening with E and a Miss Church to dine at a Chinese place.[132] I caught a cold and felt miserable.

Tues., Nov. 21
Los Angeles
[Figueroa Hotel]

We drove to this place—first down through a long valley and then over mountains. My cold had taken a real grip of me and when we got here I couldn't go to dine with Anita Loos as I had hoped.[133] My old friend John Emerson ill and in a sanitarium. Talked to him on the phone but he seemed very depressed. Stayed in.

Wed., Nov. 22
Los Angeles

Laid up in the room all day with a grippy cold and reading Anna Karenina. Did a few letters but very sore and miserable.

Thurs., Nov. 23
Los Angeles

Ill all day. It is evidently flu. Fine warm weather—day in the sun in the sun room at the top of the hotel. Could do no work.

Fri., Nov. 24
Los Angeles

No better. Stayed all day in the hotel room reading Tolstoy's Anna Karenina. Could again do no work.

Sat., Nov. 25
Los Angeles

Too ill to go to John and Nita and so had to stay in my room. Too bad for E. Finished the Tolstoy. Managed to go out to dine with E, Monte Bartlett and Foster[134] from Roanoke.

Sun., Nov. 26
Los Angeles

Better but weak and unable to work. Sat on the roof in the sun and walked out. E at work.

Mon., Nov. 27
Los Angeles

Still unable to work although better. E went to meeting and I was compelled to stay in hotel all day.

Tues., Nov. 28
Los Angeles

As happens in so many towns I find here that the girl who makes up our room and the nicest people in the hotel are the waitresses. The place is filled with fussy upper middle-class old women, perhaps sent out here by their children to be rid of them. They are a deadpan lot.

Wed., Nov. 29
Los Angeles

My flu seems gone. In the evening I went to an old Spanish restaurant with a young Armenian scholar B. K. Melekian—who is doing a thesis on my work. Saw some very vigorous and charming Spanish dances and had a wonderful time. Got a new story "For What?" ready to send off.[135]

Thurs., Nov. 30
Los Angeles

Worked on the story—"There Are Such People." Eleanor not well but won't give up. In the evening went to the house of young Putnam—running horse man—rich—who married Gene Bartlett.[136] Monte continued to embarrass. We liked the young man and little hard-boiled Gene. The Bartletts have all known too many famous people in their least notable phases.

Monte is almost a psychopathic but has a real sweet way. There is a tremendous story in the three girls.

Fri., Dec. 1
Los Angeles

Eleanor with a fever but going it all day. I did not know she had a fever until we had gone off to dine with Teddy and Helen Dreiser. The old boy in fine form but intent on defending Stalinism. We saw the beautiful new Union Station here, one of the most beautiful buildings I have seen in America.

Sat., Dec. 2
Los Angeles

Worked on new story. Young Count [W.S.] DeWitte came and talked, telling tales of things that had happened to his family during and after the Russian revolution. Went for drinks with a young German who talked of the German people, Hitler, etc.

Sun., Dec. 3
Los Angeles

Day filled with the tragedy of my boyhood friend John Emerson—the end of all his scheming, charm, money getting—the day with him—the subject of a terrible novel to be called "American Money."[137]

Mon., Dec. 4
Los Angeles

The most remarkable thing here the Loos-Ross medical clinic where I found the best and most intelligent medical treatment and advice I have ever experienced.

A curiously nasty letter from Monte Bartlett that I quickly destroyed. I shall be glad to leave here—an unhealthy city in spite of the fine climate.

Tues., Dec. 5
Phoenix, Arizona

Day spent driving. Met E at her train—from Fresno at 8:30—in the really beautiful Los Angeles station. The drive was again through a desert country, with many strange fantastic hills. We got to Phoenix at six. I thought a rather dull town and as E had to be with her people I went to a dull movie. I am at work on an extension of the Princeton speech—for their book.[138]

Wed., Dec. 6
Tucson, Arizona

Drove down to Tucson arriving at noon and stayed at the expensive Pioneer Hotel. Went shortly after lunch to Paddy Walsh and stayed all afternoon. Dined there and went later to the Solves, where we sat talking until 11 p.m.[139]

Thurs., Dec. 7
Tucson

Felt pretty dead, I think from the John Emerson experience. Paddy and Mims Walsh as fine as ever. In the p.m. went with them to see the Dowdeys, young Virginia writer and wife.[140] We all went off to a Mexican restaurant where I gave a dinner party and we had much good talk.

Fri., Dec. 8
Tucson

Finished the "Letter to an English Writer."[141] Erskine Caldwell was in town. E, Paddy, Mims and I took him to a ranch—"The Boss Ranch." Miss Hart who taught for 45 years at Wellesley entertained us at dinner.[142] Fine old woman but a very dull party. We all went later to Paddy's and drank. Miss Hart a great enthusiast for "A Story Teller's Story."

Sat., Dec. 9
Alpine, Texas

Although we only got to bed at 12 we were up at 5 and drove 550 miles to this place, for the most part through beautiful desert country—Arizona, New Mexico and Texas. Although we lost 1 hour we got here at 6 p.m.

Sun., Dec. 10
San Antonio

A very hot day. We drove first to Del Rio and went into Mexico. Got 8 bottles liquor and glasses for house. Got to Cope's[143] at 4:30 and soon Channing came. He looked ill. They were planning a big hunt.

Mon., Dec. 11
San Antonio

While Randolph and Channing went off on their hunt E and I went to town. I went to Maury Maverick the mayor, who just escaped a sort of frame-up, and he, E and I, after lunch went to see what he is doing to improve the town. We saw where 70 acres of tenements had been cleared away for new houses and many other remarkable things. In the evening to a Mexican restaurant to eat.

Tues., Dec. 12
San Antonio

Channing and Randolph again off hunting while I wrote letters. Went to town with mail. In the evening we all to the house of the Colonel commanding Kelly Field where we had a game dinner, quail, wild duck and geese. Randolph had shot 2 deer but we didn't tackle venison. The dinner was fine but wanted wine not offered. A Norther came up with a high wind.

Wed., Dec. 13
Houston, Texas

We drove to Houston. 210 miles, arriving at noon. E with a cold. It was a dry windy Norther. We went to the Sam Houston Hotel . . . had one of the 2 big beds taken out. I got settled and did letters. E went off to work, feeling rotten.

Thurs., Dec. 14
Houston, Texas

Did a piece on Maury Maverick.[144] Wrote letters. Went out to search for my own books in second hand bookstore. Got copies Many Marriages and Horses and Men. The day grey but the Norther passed. As E was busy went to a movie but it was very bad and left after 30 minutes.

Fri., Dec. 15
Houston

This town growing fast—a start of early Chicago, pushing ahead—oil and shipping. Had a bad case of blues. Went to a movie. It got worse. The day grey and warm. Tried to work. No good.

Sat., Dec. 16
Houston

A wasted day. Work would not go. Warm and murky here and great crowds of Christmas shoppers in the streets. Like the town better. Walked about in the crowds. In the evening went to the Ice Carnival—Coliseum—Sonja Henie and her company. Very beautiful.

Sun., Dec. 17
Houston

Very dull Sunday, after an intense morning of work. Developed a boil on my neck. The town here jammed with people on Saturday night, like Broadway at 42nd.

Mon., Dec. 18
Houston

Pretty good morning's work although I did not sleep. In the p.m. went to a movie Geronimo but couldn't stand its falseness.[145] We went to dine with a manufacturer, fine man but with a silly wife trying to be literary.

Tues., Dec. 19
Lafayette, La.

In Houston had a good morning of work. Grey day. Picked E up at 3 p.m. and started east for New Orleans. We drove to LaFayette, La., getting there at 8:30. After dark all of our lights went out—this near Sulphur, La. We had to drive to Sulphur in darkness, everyone along the roads shouting to us to put on our lights.

Wed., Dec. 20
New Orleans

Arrived here at noon. We came by Algiers and the ferry. Spent the p.m. with Marc and Lucille. No work. Then to Jimmy Feibleman's for dinner. Some glum talk about [?] and his bungles in the world of feeling.

Thurs., Dec. 21
Chattanooga,
Tenn.

Both of us feeling seedy from too much party at Jimmy's but up at 6 to meet Channing. He loaded with baggage and game. All day driving and made 550 miles in 11 hours—another clear sunshiny day. Got to Chattanooga at 7:30 and fell into bed.

Fri., Dec. 22
Marion

After a big night's sleep felt better and we drove on to Marion, arriving at 3:30. Mazie there with 2 children. Mary [Emmett] coming. Mr. Copenhaver much upset because I playfully said Cope might marry Cooky.[146]

Sat., Dec. 23
Marion

Cold grey day. The house at Marion in the grip of babies and Christmas. Went to the farm to carry gifts to the Sullivans. In the p.m. a snow started. The house more or less a bedlam.

Sun., Dec. 24
Marion

Heavy snow on the ground. Worked on a mass of accumulated mail. Mary and Edward Dahlberg arrived by car in the evening. He conducted a literary monologue.

Mon., Dec. 25
Marion

A big day in the family. At dinner Bass, Laura Lu, Eleanor, Mazie, Edward Dahlberg, Aunt May, Mary Emmett, little Eleanor Wilson, Channing. In the late afternoon a cocktail party that went off well, Mother, B.E. and May hiding out because of strong drink. Dahlberg kept on literature, Channing on hunting. I did not get many gifts. Dahlberg left by bus for New Orleans, Channing by train for Baltimore.

Tues., Dec. 26
Marion

More snow—cold damp weather, very bad for me. In any northern climate too much of my energy must go into the fight to keep in shape to work. But for E I would at once go off south.[147]

However the country here is very beautiful under the snow.

Went with E to Funk's for a bird dinner. Sleet fell. Funk's new house very comfortable. I did not succeed in getting any work done.

Wed., Dec. 27
Marion

Soft ice and snow. Low in spirits so could not work. All day snow, half rain. Eleanor's father preparing to get off to San Antonio about his eyes. In the evening we all . . . [unfinished].

Thurs., Dec. 28
Marion

Went back over old script done in the past—"There Are Such People," only to find it bad writing. Threw away. Got in the car and went to Wytheville for liquor. Took Mary and E to the pottery at Old Glade.[148] Got mad at May and Mary. Excited and could not sleep.

Fri., Dec. 29
Marion

Still cold and the ground covered with snow. The work began to go better. I was busy and excited at my desk all day. Finished the open letter to An English Writer. Mother in bed with cold.

Sat., Dec. 30
Marion

Finished the piece on Maury Maverick. Mazie and children left for Baltimore. Still cold and snowy. Mother better.

Sun., Dec. 31
Marion

Mother still ill and in bed. Too much Christmas. She grows every year more lovely. Did the article called "The Finding."[149] Think it may be good. We went to Ripshin—cold and icy.

1 9 4 0

Cold with more snow. Worked well. John, wife and Ann with Dave came to dine. In the p.m. I drove with Mary to farm. Funk sick—piles—may have to be operated. Working on the series of portraits. Have definitely decided can't live at Mary Emmett's house this winter so wrote to engage space at Hotel Royalton—in 44 St.

Worked on the Italian poet portrait then drove to the farm to see John Sullivan but he gone off fox hunting. Charlotte with baby boy. Went in the evening to Funk to play cards. He better. Still very cold for this country. Mary left for New York.

Worked on the story "Italian Poet in America."[1] Composed a letter to Mary, saying I could not stay in her house this winter. Went to Andy Funk's to play cards in the evening. The weather somewhat warmer.

Knocked out and could do no work. John and Major came to make plans for the farm. Packed bags to leave. The evening at home.

Fri., January 5
Lynchburg

No work—the morning spent packing to leave and running errands.
Mother taken ill again and E alarmed. We got the doctor and, as she was
better, got off at noon, arriving here at 4:30. The country very beautiful,
hills with snow. Called Mother and she better—also good word about
Mr. Copenhaver's eyes.

Sat., January 6
Lynchburg

The day spent on letters and in reading a life of Heine. In the p.m. an old
woman reporter called from Carter Glass's paper.[2] She told me she had
been a reporter here for 25 years. Went in the evening to Robert Glass's
house. Bad word from Mother Copenhaver—by phone. Her kidneys are
bad and she plans to set off by train for San Antonio and Randolph
tomorrow morning. Aunt May to go as far as Chattanooga with her.

Sun., January 7
Lynchburg

Cold and grey in the a.m. Stayed in and polished the story Italian Poet.
Read Life of Heine. Heavy snow all afternoon and evening. Mother got
off for San Antonio. Took a walk in the snow and then stayed in the rest
of the day and evening. E in at 8:30 tired.

Mon., January 8
Washington, D.C.

We left Lynchburg at 11. 12 inches of snow. Had to buy chains. It snowed
hard the first 50 miles. Could only make 25 miles per hour. Later roads
got somewhat clearer so we got to Washington at 6 p.m. Tired and stayed
in.

Tues., January 9
Baltimore

The morning at Washington spent with Edwin Rosskam and Roy Stryker
in Washington. We went over pictures for the small town book they want
me to do.[3] Got through at 3:30 and at 4:15 we started to Mazie's in
Baltimore. They took us to a friend's house to dinner. Played games.
Pretty boring. I drank too much.

Wed., January 10
New York

A bad head. At 10 we started for New York. Felt better driving. We went to Hedgerow and saw Deeter, Mims, Katy, Rose, Mary, David and others. Went on to New York and got into our new quarters at Hotel Royalton 44 West 44. Big room and everything very comfortable. Very tired when we got unpacked.

Thurs., January 11
New York

At Royalton—44 West 44th. A big nice room to work in. Dull day. In the morning made notes on the small town book and then went up to Valley Cottage—to Mary's to leave car in her garage for the winter. It rained in the evening. Dined with E and we stayed in.

Fri., January 12
New York

Dark and rainy but very happy to be in the comfortable quarters in this hotel. The hotel full of actors. I resurrected a short story out of "A Story Teller's Story."⁴ Went downtown in the rain for coffee and whiskey. E and I dined at Japanese restaurant.

Sat., January 13
New York

Worked on book—"Other Men's Houses." Rainy day. In the evening went to drink and talk with George Nathan. Lewis Galantière came. We dined at Algonquin with Lewis. Went then to big party at home of man named Rogers in 11th St.⁵ Met many people. Talked and drank until nearly 4 a.m.

Sun., January 14
[New York]

Heavy rain all day. As we were out so late we stayed in bed until early afternoon—then went to dine at Mary Emmett's. She had the man Tate there—a pickup—quite a liar I thought . . . not impressive.
  Went to the show—"Margin for Error"—claptrap but amusing.⁶

Mon., January 15
New York

Got work on book pretty well underway but was interrupted by arrival of stenographer. Dictated for 2 hours. Took a walk and sat in small restaurant listening to conversation. Paul Rosenfeld came and we dined, Japanese place and spent the evening in conversation.

Tues., January 16
New York

Very cold. Got up late. Worked on the book. Took a walk up to the park and to see the skaters in Rockefeller Center. Then in the evening went off to a dinner of the Euthanasia Society. Mostly doctors. Made a short speech. They thought I was Maxwell Anderson so I let it go at that.

Wed., January 17
New York

Worked in morning. Very cold. Went to lunch with Stanley Young and Harcourt Brace crowd. They proposing children's book. Saw Paul on street and walked with him discussing his problem. Snowing. Went to Wendels[7] at Hotel St. Regis and saw Arthur Richman.[8] Liked him. Then went to Academy dinner but walked out on it. Seemed too dead a place among the pundits.[9]

Thurs., January 18
New York

Worked on book all morning. Karl came in and we lunched at the Algonquin. He seemed in good form. Went to drink with Stanley Young who made a fine offer of an advance on book. Met E and we went to dull cocktail party. Stayed in, in the evening.

Fri., January 19
New York

Work all morning. Went to lunch with Oscar Cargill—N.Y.U.[10]—Swede who told me tale of how Sinclair Lewis got Nobel Prize. Went to sit with Mary Emmett. E came home and we went over new stories.

Sat., January 20
New York

Finished one of the short sketches for the book. E at home in the p.m. We went to Arthur Richman, then to John Rogers, then to Joe Girsdanski's in the evening.

Sun., January 21
New York

Wrote a short but good piece on Ford Madox Ford.[11] E and I loafed. In the evening we went, with Mary Emmett to see the Moss Hart, [George

S.] Kaufman comedy—The Man Who Came To Dinner—pure carpentry and clever stage tricks.[12] No one human.

Mon., January 22
New York

Pretty rotten. A night of no sleep but did a section for the book.

Took Beth Wendel to lunch and we talked of John Emerson. In the evening dined with E and we went to Maurice Werner's where we stayed talking for 2 hours and then home to take sleeping powder Mildred [Esgar] sent me.

Tues., January 23
New York

Worked on American Money section of book.[13] Lunched with Bercovici. Saw Robert Nathan[14] and Morris Ernst. Had a call from Chris Sergel with his wife Hope—grand young couple. Went to dine with Paul Rosenfeld, E, and young pianist John Fitzpatrick.

Wed., January 24
New York

Good morning of work. Then to lunch with Bercovici, he talking of how editors have decayed. Saw Morris Ernst and Robert Nathan. Saw Arthur Ficke.[15] Went to play cards with Mary. Went to dine with Joe Girsdanski and Ann and then with Doctor Joe to see Armstrong fight at Garden.[16]

Thurs., January 25
New York

Pretty bum—no sleep but did work. Walked about, tired and distraught in the early p.m. Then John Dos Passos and a man named Henry Miller—just home after 10 years in Europe—came. We drank and talked together. Had late dinner alone with E. Took sleeping powder and had big sleep.

Fri., January 26
New York

Worked in the morning. Lunched with Chambrun. Secretary came and got off a lot of letters and an article, written in the a.m. Went to dine with Franco—La Guardia man—, Dorothy McConnell, Margaret Forsyth, and E.

Sat., January 27
New York

Good morning of work. Took Mims Phillips to lunch. E came. Saw Ben Hecht and sat with him. Went to cocktails at Charlie Studin's. Went to dull dinner at Ashley Millers. Couldn't take it. Fled at 10. Very cold.

Sun., January 28
New York

A long lazy day at home, with E—no work. We stayed in all day and, after dinner at Cafe Royal went back home and early to bed.

Mon., January 29
New York

Worked until 1 p.m.—then to lunch with Koppell.[17] Miss [Jean] Black came at 3 and dictated until 5. Mims Phillips came and we went to Marshall Bar.[18] E came. We went to Japanese dinner. George Nathan called but was too all in to go out with him.

Tues., January 30
New York

Wrote a new essay. Went to lunch alone—stomach bad and headache. Laid around all the p.m. Signed contract Alliance Book.[19] In the evening [with] Mildred Esgar and E to Rockefeller Center to dine and watch the skaters. Saw one woman, young, strong, beautiful whose skating was a poem. It was gorgeous.

Wed., January 31
New York

Flat all day—indigestion. Very little work. Went to lunch with Stanley Young and a man named Hamilton—rich—interested in doing the Winesburg play.[20] In the p.m. Karl came and we went to tea at Maud Fangel's. Then to a wonderful French movie, very simple and moving, called "The Harvest."[21]

Thurs., Feb. 1
New York

Still knocked out by an attack diarrhea—but did some work. Mary came early. I found her asleep, an eye in a bandage in hotel lobby. Drove her home. Very sorry for her but not sorry enough to go back there to live. Can do so much more work here.

Fri., Feb. 2
New York

Worked on the book—memoirs—in the a.m. Lunched alone. Miss Black came and I got off a lot of work. Chris Sergel came and talked of his proposed South Seas trip—place to set up a communistic community—very charming and naive. E and I went to get flowers for Mary Emmett's birthday. To bed early and slept.

Sat., Feb. 3
[Princeton, N.J.]

Worked in the morning and in the p.m. went, with E, to Princeton, to Augusto Centeno. Several members of the faculty came in and there was good talk until 1 a.m. Met the man at head of the book department.

Sun., Feb. 4
Washington

No work. We left Princeton at 12:30, E getting off at Baltimore while I went on to Washington to the Hotel Washington. E came in later and we dined together.

Mon., Feb. 5
Washington

Worked on the small town book until 3. Went to see [Edwin] Rosskam. Came back and wrote editorial. Went to dine at Rosskam's house—he, Mrs. Rosskam and Marion Post.[22] Had fine time. Came back to hotel and found Herb Little and Ella sitting with E. To bed at 12:30.

Tues., Feb. 6
New York

Worked but not very well. Didn't like Washington atmosphere. Lunched with Williams—N.Y.A.—Herb Little and Ella Ketchin. E there for a drink. Went to see and hear Mrs. Roosevelt. Liked her.[23] Fine dignity. We left Washington at 6—got here at 10—day coach—pretty tired.

Wed., Feb. 7
New York

Bad night without sleep and could do no work. Miss Black came in the p.m. and I did letters. Mother's letters indicate better. We took the Sergels to dinner and sat with them until bedtime.

Thurs., Feb. 8
New York

Did a section of the small town book. Went to see Stieglitz. Dorothy Norman took some shots of me, with her camera.[24] Went to sit drinking with Max Perkins. Went to Mary. E late. We dined in Chinatown at 9:30—home at 11 p.m. Slept.

Fri., Feb. 9
New York

Worked on small town book. Miss Black came for dictation. She says she wants to be a writer. At 5 went with George Nathan to Ritz bar to have picture taken for Life—then to 21 for another.[25] E and I dined with the Sergels. Saw [William] Saroyan's "Time of Your Life"—disappointed—thin and tricky. Fake whore.[26]

Sat., Feb. 10
New York

Rainy day. Worked and then to Lewis for liquor.[27] In the evening to 21 to a party given by Ben Hecht—George Grosz, German painter.[28] Henry [Varnum] Poor, American painter. Wyndham Lewis, English painter.[29] We drank mixture of ale and champagne called Black Velvet. Had a fine evening. Home at 12:30.

Sun., Feb. 11
New York

Lazy day—no work—loafing about with Eleanor all day. Stayed in until late afternoon, then took a walk and dined. Beautiful day. Went to bed early—a day of complete rest.

Mon., Feb. 12
New York

Wrote in the morning and lunched with E—then dictated to Miss Black in the p.m. Went to dine at Mary Emmett's—Denny Wortman[30] and wife, Roger and Chris Sergel with wives, E and I. Home at 11.

Tues., Feb. 13
On Train

Worked on American Town in the a.m.—dictated to Miss Black in the p.m. Dined with E. Took train for Oklahoma City via St. Louis at 8:35.

Wed., Feb. 14
On Train

Slept well on train. Heavy snow about Pittsburgh. The train late. Snow all through Ohio and Indiana. Clear in Illinois. Made the connection from Pennsylvania Railroad to Frisco all right. Thought we would miss it. Read Sholem Asch—The Nazarene.[31]

Thurs., Feb. 15
Oklahoma City,
Okla.

Arrived at 8 and was met by local school man. Found I had to make 2 speeches. Went to luncheon of school men. In the p.m. worked on evening speech to rural teachers. Got through that. High cold wind with rain at night.

Fri., Feb. 16
Oklahoma City

My big speech to the teachers of the English Dept. of the schools and colleges of the state seemed to go over in a fine way. I got many congratulations.

Sat., Feb. 17
On Train

Up early to catch a 6 a.m. train. A heavy snow storm that turned to rain. I had caught a cold and felt miserable. Got into Memphis and into the sleeper for Marion at 9 p.m.

Sun., Feb. 18
Marion

Got into Marion at noon. Mother not here and the house very lonely without her. John came and later I went out to see Robert and Mary. Soft snow on the ground here. Cold better.

Mon., Feb. 19
Marion

Laid up with a slaughtering cold but went about attending to income tax, etc. at home. Had to get into bed early . . . a chest cold with a racking cough.

Tues., Feb. 20
On Train

Ill all day with cold. Bob and John called. Left on 8:44 p.m. train for New York feeling rotten.

Wed., Feb. 21
New York

Got to New York at 11 a.m. Missed E at train. Coming down with flu.

Thurs., Feb. 22
New York

In bed with flu. Read life of Sun Yat Sen by Sharman. Good solid book.[32]

Fri., Feb. 23
New York

In bed with flu. Read life of Boss Tweed by Lynch.[33] Full of early New York corruption.

Sat., Feb. 24
New York

Still in bed with flu. Very weak. Mazie and Channing came to town, Mazie called with woman friend. Stayed in bed reading.

Sun., Feb. 25
New York

Flu somewhat better. Up most of the day. E went off to take the Wilsons and friends, Jack Scherer and wife to dine.

Mon., Feb. 26
New York

Up but now E down with flu. Fortunately we can get meals sent up to room. Up all day and strength coming back. Hope to get back to work tomorrow.

Tues., Feb. 27
New York

Pretty well over flu. E foolishly went off to work and in the p.m. was down again. Did a little work. In the late afternoon snow. Went out. The city suddenly beautiful.

Pretty blue and discouraged.

Wed., Feb. 28
New York

Felt better so to work and got the matter for Princeton book in shape. E in bed. Miss Black came and I got mail cleared up. Went to sit with Ben Hecht. Went to basketball in the Garden.

Thurs., Feb. 29
New York

Mistake to go to Faculty Club. Down again with flu—worse than 1st shot. Had to cancel date Maud Fangel—dinner. Rotten.

Fri., March 1
New York

Still weak from flu and unable to work. Stayed in all day.

Sat., March 2
New York

Still weak from flu but better. Wrote letters. No work. We have been dining in room.

Sun., March 3
New York

Much better but unable to work. Sat reading until evening. E and I dined at Japanese restaurant. No work.

Mon., March 4
New York

Feeling fine and got back to work. Heavy rain, turning to ice. Was at the small town book. Dined with E and we stayed in.

Tues., March 5
New York

Pretty floppy but did get back to the small town book, getting it in hand. Went to a big party—Mary Emmett's guest—sharecroppers—but didn't stay. Mrs. Roosevelt there, big crowd. Pretty far away from sharecroppers.

Wed., March 6
New York

Worked pretty steadily. At 4:30 went to sit and drink for 2 hours with Henry Miller. Dined alone—Japanese place. Walked for an hour. Restless and couldn't sleep. Good day.

Thurs., March 7
New York

Rotten day—no good. Tried to work. No go. Karl came and we talked until 5. To Ettie Stettheimer. Drinks. With E and Paul to dine. Nerves on edge. Went to see Italian primitives at Modern Gallery.

Fri., March 8
New York

Worked O.K.—on small town book. Then dictated to Miss Black. Went to drink and dine with E and got 1st real night of sleep.

Sat., March 9
New York

A busy day. Worked well. In the late afternoon went to "21" with Nathan, Rex Smith of "Newsweek" and others. Then to [John] Rogers, on 11th. Lunch with Augusto Centeno and wife. We all met at Rogers and went to Hotel Winthrop where Mother Copenhaver is staying for show. Henry and Katharine came.[34]

Sun., March 10
New York

Suddenly very cold with a cold high wind. After morning's work went to see Mother at Hotel Winthrop. Dined with her, E, Henry and Katharine. Henry in a suit for which he wove the cloth—very fine.

Went to Florine Stettheimer's to see her painting.[35] Crowd of young intellectuals. Home early and to bed.

Mon., March 11
New York

Very low in vitality all day—much depressed. Day very cold. Lunched with Luise Sillcox and Fleischer in regard to straightening out Barton Winesburg matter.[36] Went to flower show and dined with E. No work.

Tues., March 12
New York

In better shape. Worked O.K. In the p.m. went to the flower show and dined with Mother and E at Blue Bowl. Then home.

Wed., March 13
New York

After morning's work, went with Whit Burnett to Overseas Club—hearing talks by [H.V.] Kaltenborn and by man from League of Nations on possible international peace. To Paul Rosenfeld to dine, Margaret Marshall, Henry Miller and woman, and E. Fine evening. E very tired.

Thurs., March 14
New York

Worked (not too well). To lunch with Nick Carter and much talk of advertising. Went to Phil Moeller's where I saw several people and had good talk.[37] Came home to hotel in a heavy rain.

Fri., March 15
New York

All day in the room, working and dictating. In the late p.m. went to see Mother and dined with her. E home late. Lewis Galantière sent flowers for the room.

Sat., March 16
New York

Had Miss Black in and worked with her. A wet snow all day. In the evening took Mother to dinner and went to flower show.

Sun., March 17
New York

E went off to flower show and I worked in hotel room. It was a bright clear Easter day.[38] Walked with E on Fifth Avenue and went to Arthur Ficke's. In the evening went to Male Animal, a fine amusing show.[39]

Mon., March 18
New York

Caught cold at the play and had to cut many engagements and spend the day in bed. Missed dinner at Lewis Galantière's.

Tues., March 19
New York

Cold much better so that I got in a good day's work. Miss Black came in the p.m. and we got on with the book. Dined with E.

Wed., March 20
New York

Mother came up from her hotel to lunch. After morning work met her, E, Katharine and Henry for lunch. Took her to Modern Art Gallery. Brought her to hotel to dine. Put her on train at 7:30. E to dinner at YW. Went to Levy—58th St.—to meet Davisons—Boulder, Colo.

Thurs., March 21
New York

Good morning of work. In the p.m. had Miss Black in for dictation. Went to dine at Elmer Rice's—Hotel Ansonia,[40] Ted and Natalie Davison there. Saw a fine collection of painting. Had a charming evening.

Fri., March 22
New York

Cold again—snow in the a.m. and then sunshine. It was Good Friday and E spent most of the day shopping. Worked on the small town book and gave a party, E, Katharine and Henry Van Meier, Glenn Gosling of Olivet and a young librarian of Olivet. The young man pretty drunk.

Sat., March 23
New York

Very cold. Good morning of work. E came for lunch and then went to Mary Emmett's. Went there an hour later to see Palencia—Spanish Republican Ambassador to Sweden.[41] Stayed later to drink with small party and then home. Icy cold.

Sun., March 24
New York

A lazy day in the hotel room with E. Worked but 1 hour. In the late p.m. to Dr. Joe's and then to Cafe Royal with Katharine and Henry Van Meier to dine. Very cold all day.

Mon., March 25
New York

Very cold. Upset stomach from drinking at Dr. Joe's. Managed to work. Miss Black came to take dictation. In the evening went, as Elmer Rice's guest to see his "Two on an Island." A mild and amusing play, keenly observed.[42]

Tues., March 26
New York

Work on small town book and then went to Mary Emmett—who is in bad shape with her eyes. Went to cocktails at Charles Studin's. Dined at

Young China. Went back to Mary's to play cards. Suddenly very ill with headache. It went off after 2 hours.

Wed., March 27
New York

Feeling shaky but got in pretty good morning's work. Went to speak at noon at Overseas Club.[43] Miss Black came. Dined with Katharine and Henry Van Meier. Went to see Old Time Movies, early Chaplin and Rogers.

Thurs., March 28
New York

Good morning's work. Young Daniel Lerner—NYU—came for long talk. He is doing a Ph.D. theme on 1910 to 40. Went to PEN Club—dinner and spoke briefly. Saw many old friends.[44]

Fri., March 29
New York

Rainy. Work in the room all morning. Miss Black came at 3. Went with a Miss [Jane] Varick to talk of her work—a strange creature. Bill Stewart[45] came and he, E and I dined at the Algonquin. I went with Dr. Joe to see Louis knock out [Johnny] Paycheck, a calm beautiful quick job.

Sat., March 30
New York

A rainy day but springlike. Took Natalie Davison and E to the Algonquin to lunch after morning's work. It cost me $6 . . . too expensive. In the evening went to see the revival of Liliom, beautifully done with Burgess Meredith as Liliom.[46] Katharine and Henry left.

Sun., March 31
New York

The first real spring day. It was difficult to stay at the desk. Went to get E at 12:30 and we walked until 3. We went to Mary Emmett, in bed with bad eyes. She got up. [Cleon] Throckmorton and wife and Ingram—foreign newspaper correspondent—came. We all drank while he talked of the World War. We dined late.

Mon., April 1
New York

Coming to the winding up of 1st draft of Home Town book. Have enjoyed writing it. Went to see fine French movie, "The Baker's Wife."[47] Went, with E, to Lewis Galantière to dine—Bunny Wilson and wife and Burton Rascoe.

Tues., April 2
New York

Work in the morning. Another springlike day. In the p.m. a young Indiana man came to talk of his problem. Miss Black came to take dictation. Went to Mary Emmett's house and E joined me. We dined at nine and came home.

Wed., April 3
New York

Work in the a.m. Lunch with Jean Jolas, Edward Dahlberg, poet named Sweeney.[48] Fine talk. In the afternoon to Erskine Caldwell's to big cocktail party. Margaret Bourke-White just home from Europe.[49]

Thurs., April 4
New York

Work on the book in the morning. In the p.m. dictating to Miss Black. Went to join E at 6:30—drinks and then to dine. Home early—the 1st spring thunder shower.

Fri., April 5
New York

Worked in the a.m. Went to Mary's at Nyack to get car. Went to Arthur Ficke's—to party. Went to Mary Emmett where I met Bill Ingram and an English captain.

Sat., April 6
New York

Worked in the a.m. and then went up to Valley Cottage to get the car. Packed. We went to Arthur Ficke's and then to Mary's for the evening.

Sun., April 7
Atlantic City

We had a glorious drive down to Atlantic City and went to Hotel Madison. Walked on Boardwalk. E went to meeting. I walked and then to bed. No work.

Mon., April 8
[Marion]

Left Atlantic City early. Went by Cape Charles. Came on to Marion the next day. Have lost a day here somewhere.[50] Had an accident, forced into ditch. Just managed to escape bad accident.

Tues., April 9
[Marion]

Traded cars. It was a dull cold day. Went to Ripshin. The spring very late there. Things in good shape. Did many errands about town. John came in the p.m. Mother in bed but looking fine.

Wed., April 10
[Marion]

Got some work done on book and sent off an essay for *This Week*.[51] Went with Bob Williams to visit schools. In the evening went to Funk's shop. Funk and Bob Anderson spent most of the evening in arguments.

Thurs., April 11
Burlington, N.C.

Left Marion at nine, after making new arrangement to hold John's work. Rain. Drove on 58 to Martinsville and then to see Mimi. She doing a good job with the paper. She has nice children. . . .[52]

Fri., April 12
Burlington

Rainy. Here at work on book. Going to Paul Green tomorrow. Rainy and cold.

Sat., April 13
Chapel Hill

Bright, very cold morning with frost. Spent afternoon and evening with Greens. Hallie Flanagan and [Phillips] Russell came.

Sun., April 14
Southern Pines

Drove to Boyds at Southern Pines. Clear cold morning . . . the whole country in bloom. Got to Boyds at 12. In the p.m. walked about with Jim and went to call on a tubercular young man. Katherine Boyd quite recovered from her long illness. Jim and I sat up talking until midnight.

Mon., April 15
Southern Pines

In the morning with a Mrs. Smith to the trotting horse tracks at Pinehurst where I saw many lovely fast animals in training. Did no work. In the p.m. to see Struthers Burt.[53] Went off to bed early. Very beautiful day. E phoned from New York.

Tues., April 16
Southern Pines

Went to the tracks at Pinehurst and then to the country to sit in car and work. Man came to see Jim from Princeton. We all went off to bad movie—Rebecca.[54] Jim and I sat talking until 1 a.m. The day very clear and warm.

Wed., April 17
Southern Pines

Up early to meet Eleanor, who came by train from Atlantic City. A beautiful warm day. E with a cold. After breakfast we went to the tracks. In the p.m. walked about and went later to Struthers Burt. Phillips Russell and wife came from Chapel Hill for the evening.

Thurs., April 18
Orange, Va.

We set off for New York after breakfast, going north on road 25—through a beautiful country. It began to rain in the afternoon. We stayed at the James Madison at Orange. E and I had a quarrel but made up quickly.

Fri., April 19
Baltimore

Went to Baltimore and arrived in the rain. Went to the Maryland Club to talk of the Winesburg play with the producer Hambleton.[55] Stayed the night with the Wilsons.

Sat., April 20
New York

Left Wilsons at 10 and drove by Pennsville Ferry—No. 40. Heavy cold rain all the way and I arrived in New York with a cold.

Sun., April 21
New York

A dismal rainy day and I am all day confined to the hotel room with a cold. Miss Davis called about the new organization that wants to do Winesburg. Eleanor stayed in with me all day.

Mon., April 22
New York

Gone sour with a light attack of flu. An experimental crowd of actors out of work anxious to do Winesburg. Want to open on May 15, Irving Theatre. Lunched with them and went with E, in the evening to cold theatre to hear readings. Cannot let them have the play. Too bad. Not enough time for work.

Tues., April 23
New York

Still knocked out with cold and unable to work. Had to turn down the eager young players who wanted to get Winesburg right on the stage . . . the setup—time to work on it, etc., unsatisfactory. Dined with E and we stayed at home.

Wed., April 24
New York

Decided to buy 8 acres more at Ripshin. Sent money through Funk. Got word 2 pieces sold $600. Took car to Mary's farm and came back with her man Robert.[56] Grey day with occasional sun. Dined at 9th and 6th. Went to spend evening with Mary Emmett. Eleanor lovely.

Thurs., April 25
New York

In shape to work again. The sun came out. Miss Black came to clean up mail. Mary gave party (Spanish relief) at Commodore.[57] When speeches began I ran out on it to bed.

Fri., April 26
New York

Did 1st draft of church article for small town book. Went to ball game—Giants vs. Boston—Giants winning. Whit and Martha Burnett came and we had drinks and then dined at Margarita's. E and I went to newspapermen's party in 34th St. and got home at 11:30.

Sat., April 27
New York

Each Saturday I give Mauda, the woman who does the room $1 for doing it while I am at breakfast. Worked on church chapter of book. Went to lunch with E and a Birmingham, Ala. woman, to the Game Cock.[58] E and I walked. We went to dine at a Mexican restaurant. Both tired and sleepy. To bed.

Sun., April 28
New York

A real spring day. Work in the morning and then lunch and a walk with E. We had Mary to dine and took her with us to see some marvelous Negro dancing at Windsor Theatre.

Mon., April 29
New York

Work in the a.m. Lunch with Dahlberg—a bit tense. Miss Black came for letters. Mims and Mary Esherick came. Took E to dine. We stayed in.

Tues., April 30
New York

On the school portion of the book—drawing toward its end. In the p.m. went to Mary who told me a strange revealing story. Dined there and then E came and, after cards, Robert drove us home.

Wed., May 1
New York

Work in the morning. Grey day. Went in p.m. to Pins and Needles, pretty dull.[59] Dressed and went to Emily Clark to dine. Gogarty, Carl Van Doren and wife, [Henry S.] Canby and wife. Enjoyed Carl and wife best. Not impressed by Gogarty.[60]

Thurs., May 2
New York

Worked in the morning and with Miss Black in the p.m. It was a bleak rainy day. In the evening Jap came in and later we went to dine at Stettheimers. Phil Moeller and Paul there. Very strange evening.

Fri., May 3
New York

Morning of work. The sun came out in the p.m. and I went to the Stadium to see the Yanks and White Sox. Yanks won. Cold in the evening. We stayed at home.

Sat., May 4
New York

Suddenly slaughtered by another cold. Miserable all day.

Sun., May 5
New York

Ill all day. Did nothing but lie in bed.

Mon., May 6
[New York]

Still helpless in grip of cold. In room all day.

Tues., May 7
[New York]

This slow fever hangs on. No work. Can just lie about and read. Reading life of Alexander Hamilton.

Wed., May 8
[New York]

Fever still on me. Finished Hamilton. No work. Lewis Galantière brought Turner's "Frontiers of American History."[61]

Thurs., May 9
[New York]

Fever still with me and no work. Much bored. Turner is a relief.

Fri., May 10
[New York]

Fever still on me. I listen to baseball scores on the radio. . . . Read Turner
and Moby Dick. No work.

Sat., May 11
[New York]

Finally got a doctor in—woman—very charming—said I was too fat and
hurt my pride.[62] Making Turner last as long as possible.

Sun., May 12
[New York]

No fever but very weak. Eleanor at home. Mary has her captain back. It is
fine weather outside. No work.

Mon., May 13
[New York]

Floppy but did a few letters and read. For first time went out to eat. Rood,
the young sculptor, having a show here, came and stayed 2 1/2 hours.
Enjoyed him but it tired me too much.[63]

Tues., May 14
New York

Managed to work a little—finishing up small town book. Weak yet and
quite exhausted after 2 hours work. Lunched with Lewis Galantière and
Frenchman from the Critics. Fine talk.

Wed., May 15
New York

Got a start on the new book, "Mountain Boy."[64] Still weak and floppy.
Dined out with E. It may be that the whole illness is due to the thing
going on in Europe. It is in my mind all day and my dreams at night.

Thurs., May 16
New York

Again unable to work because of weakness. Went to the doctor and to
Mary. It was a dark rainy day. The whole city seems sick and depressed
over the war in Belgium. It is a world sickness.

Fri., May 17
New York

No work done—trying to pull out of weakness after flu. Wharton Esherick came and we lunched. The World War news all bad and everyone feeling it. Sickness in the air. Dined with E at Japanese place.

Sat., May 18
New York

Decided to give up and loaf until I get some strength back. Went to the doctor and then, in the rain, to Mary where we spoke of her helping John. E and I dined out and spent the evening in the hotel room. Reading Frank Swinnerton's autobiography.

Sun., May 19
New York

Beautiful day. Wrote a brief radio speech for Whit Burnett. E and I dined in French restaurant in 44th. We walked about in the sun and spent the evening playing cards.

Mon., May 20
New York

Got in a morning's work. A reporter came from World-Telegram to gather up my wisdom.[65] Miss Black came for letters. Channing Wilson came and we took him to dinner. He and E went off to World's Fair and I came home to read.

Tues., May 21
New York

Work in the a.m. Went to lunch with some delightful men of Lippincotts who wanted to sign me for an autobiography. Didn't do it. Went to Mary who is in a jam about her captain. In the evening to a radio studio—guest of honor on program for Story Magazine—very amusing.[66]

Wed., May 22
New York

Did a new article for This Week. Sent off small town book. Went to ball game—Cincinnati and Giants—Hubbell—[Paul] Derringer—Giants won 6–4. Went with E to silent movies—very amusing. War news a bit better.

Thurs., May 23
New York

Dark and rainy. Got wire from Reader's Digest wanting short anecdote. Sent one. Dictated article for This Week.[67] Felt another cold coming and got after it hard.

Fri., May 24
New York

Got new piece off to This Week. Did short thing for Reader's Digest. Went to lunch with the publisher Koppell. Dark and rainy so spent the evening in hotel room with E.

Sat., May 25
New York

Planned to go out to Madison, New Jersey, to see Bob and Mary at the horse show but it was another dark rainy day and didn't go. Did no work. Mary E came to dine and play cards in the evening.

Sun., May 26
New York

No work. Another cold wet day. At noon E and I went by train to Croton,[68] for the p.m. with the publisher Koppell and wife—charming people. Max Eastman—Eliena, Selden Rodman[69] and wife came. We got back to town, in the rain, at 8 p.m.

Mon., May 27
New York

Dark and rainy. Had E, Stanley Young, and [left blank] to lunch at Algonquin. Benjamin of Alliance came wanting me to do a book on small town newspapers. Paul Rosenfeld came to dine and was so persistently gloomy that I grew angry and spit at him, spoiling the dinner party.

Tues., May 28
New York

No work—the day spent in packing, lunching with Chambrun, seeing Myrtle Centeno,[70] who is in trouble, and in cleaning up. In the evening went to Galantières where we had a delightful dinner and evening. The first sunshine for 10 days here.

Wed., May 29
Baltimore

Finished packing. Went to see Mary Emmett. Eleanor did not come until
3:30 and we drove to Baltimore. Mother there and looking fine. She had
had a slight operation. We spent the night there.

Thurs., May 30
Roanoke

We did not get off until ten—a grey cloudy morning. Went by Harper's
Ferry. From Winchester on heavy rain so we stopped for the night at
Roanoke.

Fri., May 31
Marion

We were up early and got to Marion at 10 and in the p.m. went over to
Ripshin. Everything fine over there.

Sat., June 1
Marion

Spent the day getting settled, unpacking, renewing touch with the town.
In the p.m. went to a ball game. Bought material for the opening of
Ripshin. Fine day—with rain in the p.m.

Sun., June 2
Marion

It was graduating day at the college. In the p.m. E and I drove to Ripshin.
Later saw a ball game. E left for New York at 8:50.

Mon., June 3
Marion

A bright warm summer day but I had to spend it in fighting off a cold.
Stayed about town and went off to bed early.

Tues., June 4
Marion

Did letters and went to Ripshin. 4 women at work at the house cleaning.
It began to rain and I came back to town and to Frank Copenhaver's
where we played cards. In the evening to Funk's shop where we talked
until after 10.

Wed., June 5
Marion

Worked on new story—clear bright warm day. Mother came—O.K.—
from Baltimore. Went to Ripshin in the p.m. John painting blinds. The
house cleaning nearly finished. Came home at 4. Saw Funk. Played croquet with Mother.

Thurs., June 6
Marion

Another beautiful day. Work on a story "Who's Your Friend?" In the
p.m. took Miss May to Ripshin. Fay had gone off to have her tonsils out.
It rained.

Came back to town and played croquet. Ryan[71] and Miss May. Went
for a drive with Funk.

Fri., June 7
Marion

In writing you often start one thing and it turns into another. It is happen-
ing to me in the present story. Fine rain at Ripshin. Fay had her tonsils
out. Took Mr. and Mrs. Copenhaver over in late afternoon and dined
there at restaurant. The hedge at Green House very lovely now. Went in
the evening to look at the crowds and later rode with Funk.

Sat., June 8
Marion

Warm day with showers. After working in the a.m. went to Funk's to dine
and then with him to ball game at Wytheville. Then home to take Mr. and
Mrs. Copenhaver and May to park to dine.

Sun., June 9
Marion

After work to the farm. It rained all the p.m. so sat with Major while he
shot sparrows and starlings. Came home to hear that Italy had gone into
the war. It looks as though France is gone. Was very unhappy so got in the
car and rode around.

Mon., June 10
Marion

Work on the new story in the a.m. Went to Ripshin—soft rain all the p.m.
Settled my cabin. John and I put new oil cloth on the kitchen shelf. In the
evening joined the town in waiting for the count in the town election.

Tues., June 11
[Marion]

Rain and more rain. After working in the morning went to Ripshin and worked there the rest of the day.

Wed., June 12
[Marion]

More rain. Painted dining room table. Cut nearly a bushel of rhubarb to can. Looked for cook. Set out flowers. In the evening drove about with Funk.

Thurs., June 13
[Marion]

Work on book. Bright clear day—no rain. Got plants from Miss Bell.[72] Went to Ripshin to do work there. We started to paint barn. Worked on curtains for green house. Went to Funk's to make croquet pegs for Mother.

Fri., June 14
[Marion]

Work on book. To Ripshin where I worked all day.

Sat., June 15
Marion

Work at Marion at my desk and then to Ripshin. I had left the key inside my cabin and John had to break in. Engaged Eula McGrady to cook. Drove to Wytheville, via Independence, for liquor. Rain in Grayson. Warm and cloudy in Marion. Very hungry to see Eleanor. Spent evening with Mother.

Sun., June 16
Marion

Rain all day long. Did no work. The result of the war in France has left everyone stunned.[73] Went in the rain to Ripshin, taking Funk, and drove back by Flat Ridge and in the evening played cards.

Mon., June 17
Marion

Rain all day. Work and then to Ripshin to work on the green house and do other jobs. The rain continued through the afternoon and evening. Stayed at home.

Tues., June 18
Marion

Up early—thinking E would come. Did no work at desk but went to Ripshin. Sprayed grapes. Depressed all day about the war situation. Evening with Funk.

Wed., June 19
Marion

E arrived on morning train. It was a day of sunshine and rain. We went off to Ripshin at noon and worked there. Ted Roe, wife and student came in the evening.

Thurs., June 20
Marion

No work. Went early to Ripshin to get the house in shape for Centenos. They arrived at 4:30, bringing E with them. We all spent the night there.

Fri., June 21
[Lake Toxaway,
N.C.]

We left Ripshin at 9:30 and arrived at the camp Lake Toxaway at 5. Came by Boone, Asheville, Brevard. A bright warm day—all the way in mountains.

Sat., June 22
Toxaway, N.C.

Tried to work in a cold cabin here by the lake and caught cold so went off to Brevard. Sat in the sun and watched a ball game, then to the hotel to dope myself and to bed. It was the most delightful little hotel I was ever in. Wanted to stay there.

Sun., June 23
Toxaway, N.C.

Came back to E's camp and spent the day loafing and trying to shake off the cold. In the p.m. went to hear a pretty Negro girl talk of the problems of her race. She and the white working girls tried to sing spirituals, but it was all pretty sad.

Mon., June 24
Toxaway, N.C.

A warm day of sun and showers. Worked in my car . . . then drove to Highlands, Franklin, Sylva, N.C., beautiful mountain country. Too many women.

Tues., June 25
Toxaway, N.C.

I leave the camp of factory girls and women after breakfast, sit beside some mountain road and write until noon. The mountain roads are banked with laurel, now in full bloom. In the p.m. I took a load—5—of the women from the camp over the road to Franklin, N.C. and then to Sylva—a 3 hours drive.

Wed., June 26
Toxaway, N.C.

Worked in the a.m. beside the road that goes into South Carolina. Again in the p.m. took 5 factory girls, all from New Orleans, and a drive to Highlands, N.C., and then south to South Carolina. Wrote a short story in the a.m. It was a bright cool day with a high wind.

Thurs., June 27
Toxaway, N.C.

Went to sit on the road into South Carolina and work, sitting in the car beside the road. In the p.m. took a load of girls, Winston Salem and Houston, Texas, on a trip to South Carolina. Went to a town named Pickens. Very hot—the girls chattering and singing.

Fri., June 28
Toxaway, N.C.

Worked again in my car beside a mountain road. In the p.m. drove Ella Ketchin and another woman to Asheville. Drove back to the camp in a violent rain storm.

Sat., June 29
Ripshin

Up early, packed and off for home. Got word Lewis and Nancy Galantière not coming to Ripshin. Nancy has gone to the hospital. Drove the Chinese woman Miss Dung to Asheville. Got home at 5. Very tired. Ripshin very beautiful.

Sun., June 30
Ripshin

Letters. An offer has come to produce Winesburg play which I had to refuse because of Barton mixup. Took E to Marion where we dined. Home at 11:30. We had supper with Centenos.

Mon., July 1
Ripshin

Long morning of work. Did the story of my first attempt at love making with a woman—its ridiculous ending. E off to town. I was nasty and irritable in the early morning. There was a high wind. Augusto, Myrtle and I took a long walk over the farm. Rain in the p.m.

Tues., July 2
Ripshin

Dark and rainy all day. Major has ulcerated tooth. We have hay down that may spoil. People keep writing, filled with hopelessness about the war. In the p.m. we all went off to Marion, taking Major. The evening at home was dull. In the a.m. had worked on book.

Wed., July 3
Ripshin

Had a long work session. E went off to town, taking Major. It rained all day, a cold rain. In the evening John and wife came with the clay artist Scheier—and wife, to dine.[74] We found them very charming people.

Thurs., July 4
Ripshin

Worked in the house—well—because cabin too cold. At last the sun came out. Randolph suddenly arrived by plane from San Antonio and Mazie and Channing from Baltimore. Mimi here with 2 children—Mike and David. Much excitement, E hurriedly off to town. Mimi's husband Russell sad and silent all day.

Fri., July 5
Ripshin

I offered to keep one of Mimi's children for the summer. It was an impulse and may have been a mistake as I am not good with children. There was a big buffet supper and party in the evening. B.E., Laura Lu, Randolph, Bob and Mary, Channing and Mazie, Aunt May. It went off well. Had a silly quarrel with E. We made up. Got the hay up in the old cabin field.

Sat., July 6
[Ripshin]

The break came between Augusto and Myrtle Centeno. She found some letters from his sweetheart—a day of tears. We took them off to town and tried to keep them apart. I spent hours of talking to her. We all dined at Mother's.

Sun., July 7
Ripshin

A stormy day with the couple here—the breakup of a 12 year marriage, the man determined, in love with another woman, the woman in tears. I went off and worked and E brought Aunt May to help. I took them all off to dine, at Shatley Springs.[75]

Mon., July 8
Marion

Myrtle Centeno was out of bed at 6 a.m. and having it out with Augusto. She left, after much weeping, at 10:30, taking Aunt May. I was upset by it all. In the p.m. I took E to town and spent the night there. Myrtle had got off, after lunch. Augusto stayed at Ripshin. Mr. Copenhaver suddenly alarmed about Randolph and sending wires. It rained again all day.

Tues., July 9
Ripshin

John Peale Bishop arrived on the morning train from the East. Again showers all day. Could not work. Took John, Augusto and E to White Top—very beautiful drive through rain and clouds. Much good talk.

Wed., July 10
Ripshin

A fair day at last—only 2 or 3 light showers. E went to town but came home early. I took John and Augusto over the road to Flat Ridge and back. Dr. Ham Scherer and wife came for dinner.[76]

Thurs., July 11
Ripshin

A good day on the book. In the p.m. we took a long walk—along Fox Creek and up over the hills to the top field at the Swan place. John and Augusto just missed getting at each other's throat. A long evening of talk.

Fri., July 12
Marion

Did no work. Finished packing and helping Augusto to close the green house. We all went to Marion in the p.m. Took John Bishop and Augusto to the Park. We dined at Mother's and Augusto left on the evening train.

Sat., July 13
Washington Court
House, Ohio

We were off early for Olivet, Michigan, all day through the hills, E and I driving. We got to Harry Daugherty's town at 7:30.[77] Small town crowd dancing and having fiesta in the hotel dining room. We were all tired and went off to bed.

Sun., July 14
Olivet, Michigan

We were up fairly early, John Bishop very slow, and went to Clyde— where I left my overcoat with Johnny Becker. Lunched at Sandusky where E took train to New York. John and I pushed on, dined at Marshall, Michigan, and got to Olivet at 7:30.[78]

Mon., July 15
Olivet, Michigan

Sunshiny day. Did letters in my room. Went to Marshall for whiskey. Was rude to rude young Harvard kid. Went to hear Robert Penn Warren on poetry. Liked him, the cut of his jaw, his quality. Bishop talks too much of foods. Katherine Ann Porter cold woman. Too many middle aged women about.

Tues., July 16
Olivet, Michigan

Could not do any work. Wrote letters and in the p.m. went to Marshall. Margaret Widdemer spoke.[79] Very slick saying of nothing. It was, on the whole, rather vulgar.

Wed., July 17
Olivet

Had my first show here and devoted it to telling how several stories had come to me. The thing seemed to go O.K. Rode into the country and spent the p.m. under a tree, in the car, reading bad manuscripts. Pretty tiring. Katherine Ann Porter in the evening.

Thurs., July 18
Olivet, Mich.

I found a fairly good novel, by a Mrs. Judd.[80] It should be published. I performed in the evening—a good crowd to hear me and afterward walked and talked a long time with Robert Ramsay. Strange life of Carl Sandburg and family. It was a very beautiful night. I miss E terribly.

Fri., July 19
Olivet

Very hot. I had the satisfaction of making Mrs. Judd happy by liking her work.

Very hot. In the evening we all went to Marshall to drink. I didn't go to hear [Glenway] Wescott. Warren left.

Sat., July 20
Olivet

Another very hot day. I had a class in the late morning. Talked to Chicago woman about bad play. Allan Seager[81] came from Adrian, also poet from Saginaw.

We went to Charlotte to drink. Discussion of MacLeish on writers in the evening.[82]

Sun., July 21
Olivet

To Battle Creek—as guest of the Archie McCalls. Drove over taking Robert Ramsay, in blistering heat. Fired the cannon to start several yacht races. Much bored.

In the evening took part in an All Star session here. Read Triumph of the Egg. It went big.

Mon., July 22
Olivet

I had my last class. Was ill all day and went to a Dr. Engle here. My tummy—probably the heat. In the p.m. there was a cooling shower but the heat came back. Robert Ramsay cooked dinner. Took one of the women to ride in the evening.

Tues., July 23
Olivet, Mich.

Again very hot. Went again to the doctor, although the indigestion was better. Drove some of the students about. Read a bad novel by one of

Sherwood Anderson and Katherine Anne Porter at Olivet College in 1940.
(Trustees of the Sherwood Anderson Literary Estate.)

them. In the evening Padraic and Mary Colum performed. Rode again, to
cool off.

Wed., July 24
Olivet

Again very hot. It is impossible on account of constant interruptions to
work here. There was a late supper at Joe Brewer's house—with much
good talk.

Thurs., July 25
Olivet, Mich.

Last full day here. That Detroit woman keeps throwing notes over the
transom of my door. I cannot write here. It continues hot as hell. Drove
some people to a lake to swim—the best as chauffeur. Party at Joe's. Rain
at last, at night, and cooler.

Fri., July 26
Sandusky, Ohio

Left Olivet immediately after lunch, picking up Ferdinand Schevill at
Marshall, Michigan. We drove to Sandusky, dined and slept there. It was
a record day of heat. Ferdinand in fine form.

Sat., July 27
Lexington,
Kentucky

We got Eleanor off the train at 8. Went to Dorn Winery and got 4 cases of
wine. Went to Clyde and got my winter overcoat left there with John
Becker, tailor I knew in my boyhood. Coat had to be altered. Drove to
Springfield and saw Trillena White—near death—a very sad hour. Drove
on to Lexington, Ky., arriving at 7 p.m.

Sun., July 28
Marion

We got away from Lexington at 7 a.m. This was one of the hottest days we
had. I did the driving—through the mountains to Bean Station. Very
tired. Everyone delighted to see Ferdinand. When I had got to bed and to
sleep [Millen] Brand, the novelist, arrived. Made short shift of him.

Mon., July 29
Ripshin

Word that Randolph is going to be sent to Alaska. We got things going at
Ripshin, unpacking and getting settled. Word came that Stanley Young is

to arrive by plane on Wednesday. Crops on the farm looking fine. Glad to be home.

Tues., July 30
Ripshin

A long day of rain—the hardest and most determined of the year. Did little but clean up correspondence. In the evening the skies cleared. Must have 2 days sun to insure hay crop.

Wed., July 31
Ripshin

Wrote a piece for This Week. Very hot. E, Ferdinand and I went off to the Tri-City airplane field beyond Bristol to get Stanley Young.[83] Saw big plane off. Heavy rain on way to Marion. Got home for late dinner and sat talking until midnight.

Thurs., August 1
[Ripshin]

Worked on childhood scenes. Then a long talk with Stanley Young about the book. In the p.m. spent the time with Ferdinand and Stanley. John and family came for the evening.

Fri., August 2
Ripshin

Went to work but had caught a cold. We had to drive beyond Bristol to Tri-City Airport to put Young on plane. We all lunched at park and spent the evening with Ferdinand at home.

Sat., August 3
Ripshin

Sunk with cold but we drove to Marion to lunch at Bob's.

Ferdinand left at 4:18 and we came home and I went at once to bed . . . to try to shake off cold.

Sun., August 4
Ripshin

Got off review—Country Editor—for PM.[84] Went to Marion—then to Chilhowie to meet Randolph, who came, by plane, from San Antonio. Dined at Mother's—big family party. We had a beautiful drive home. Bob and Funk had been at the house.

Mon., August 5
Ripshin

I stayed at the farm while E went to town to be with Randolph. I worked, went up in the hayfield, picked berries. It rained. I was lonesome for E all day.

Tues., August 6
Ripshin

We wanted a fair day for all the family coming but in the afternoon it began to rain. They all came shortly after five—Mother, B.E., Henry and Katharine, Randolph, Aunt May, Mazie and Channing with the babies. We sat about, ate, sang and talked. They went at 9. Wrote a new short story.

Wed., August 7
Ripshin

Did another new short story—"Woman in Kansas City." We went for the p.m. to Marion. Mary came with Robert [Booth]. Randolph took us all for a big dinner in the park. We got home at 10 p.m. in heavy rain.

Thurs., August 8
Ripshin

At last the sun came out and we got our hay stacked. Wrote a new story for the book. Walked with Mary. Too much talk of [Dr.] Locke.

Went to Mother's for Henry's steak party on the croquet lawn. Fine evening but bored by too much picture taking.

Fri., August 9
Ripshin

Misty in the a.m. and then fair. E off again, with Mary. Worked on the book. In the p.m. was in the hayfield and at the place where Major and Bruner were making the new ford. E came home at 4:30, Mary after dinner.

Sat., August 10
Ripshin

Worked too long at my desk and was knocked out for the day, but went to Marion. The family too much for me so I ran off to a ball game. Bad game. Mary gave a dinner at the hotel and later I had a near row with her. I wouldn't let E ride in her car while she was driving.

Sun., August 11
Ripshin

Did another story for the book. It rained again. Took E and Mary off to town where we had supper at Mother's. Beautiful evening, followed by more rain.

Mon., August 12
Ripshin

More rain—all day. Had a good morning at my desk. E had arranged a card party for Mary so lit out, taking Henry. Spent the p.m. in town. Got back and the house was still full of women. It continued raining—a torrent, water and women.

Tues., August 13
Ripshin

Rain steadily all day. I worked in my cabin in the morning and in the evening we gave a wedding party for Dave Greear and his fiancée. John Anderson and wife, Bob Anderson and wife, Dave and Virginia Thomas. It rained steadily. They stayed talking until after 11. Dave brought in the beautiful head of Elizabeth Anderson.[85]

Wed., August 14
Ripshin

Rain heavy all night and then a flood. Our bridges both went out. Great logs came down Ripshin and the road is badly torn up so the mail man cannot go his route. There is enough left of the bridge so that we can go across on foot logs but the cars are marooned. We went to work at once on a new bridge.

Thurs., August 15
Ripshin

Again clouds and rain all day but had good morning of work and made new progress with the bridge. Went to the mountains for flooring. Rain and more rain. Major left to work in Loudoun County.

Fri., August 16
Ripshin

I found myself unable to work much. It was too exciting and interesting to take part in the bridge building. Again it rained, a soft steady rain nearly all day. We went into the woods to get logs. We found the storm had also wrecked our water system and we had to send to Marion for the plumber.

Sat., August 17
Ripshin

The plumbers came and fixed the water system. The bridge building went forward rapidly. Between showers the sun came out. We went to see Dave Greear married to Virginia Thomas. We went to dine at Independence. It rained again but later the bright sun came out.

Sun., August 18
Ripshin

Clear after a week but later occasional showers. I got a little work done and then we went off to Marion to spend the rest of the day. Mary took us all to dinner.

Mon., August 19
Ripshin

We finished the new bridge, high above the water. I was knocked out for the day by diarrhea.

We all went to Burt Dickinson's cabin for dinner. It is up in Walker's Mountain above the lake.

Tues., August 20
Ripshin

The bridge all finished and better than the old one. We had the family to dinner. One of the cows got choked with an apple and there was great excitement, neighbors coming to run lawn hose down her throat. They got it out.

Mary got soused and rather spoiled the evening for me.

Wed., August 21
Ripshin

Cold, like all the days of this summer. I worked but later went off to Wytheville to get liquor. Drove then to Marion and home from there. In the p.m. we worked on the ford to the new land. Mary went to town for the night. Alice Armfield came, as delightful as ever.

Thurs., August 22
Ripshin

Rain and sunshine. Alice Armfield is here—a very delightful person. In the p.m. we had a men's dinner. Burt and Nathan Dickinson,[86] Nick Carter, Bob Williams, John Anderson, Andy Funk, Frank Copenhaver, Bill Wright. It went off in fine style. Got contract from Harcourt Brace.

Fri., August 23
Ripshin

A long day, mostly clear. Mary getting ready to go. She is mending the stalks of flowers, broken by the long rain, with sticks and cord.

The afternoon with Alice, very delightful, walking and talking. She is nice—shy about herself, very lovely.

Sat., August 24
Ripshin

Sunshine all day. I had a good morning, doing the Grace piece for my book.[87] We expected Mimi but she didn't come. E, Alice Armfield and I went to Marion where we found Mother, Mazie and Mazie's babies all ill.

We went to Scheier the potter's and got some beautiful ware.[88]

Sun., August 25
Ripshin

The most beautiful day of the summer. As usual E went off to town. Alice and I walked and then played croquet. Eula did not come.

E came and, late in the p.m., we drove to Independence to dine. The hotel was closed. We came home and I made a rare dish of eggs and cream.

Mon., August 26
Ripshin

The finest day of the summer. E went off to Marion. I worked well and then played about with Alice. In the evening Bob and Mary to dinner. We sat on the terrace and there was a good deal of big talk about government, etc. However the night very beautiful.

Tues., August 27
Ripshin

Rain in the early morning but the sky cleared and it was a fine day. E at home. Played about with Alice. In the p.m. Scheier the potter and wife came, also the young newspaper man Greer Williams who is down here writing a novel,[89] with his wife, also Mazie. They dined with us and stayed late telling stories.

Wed., August 28
Ripshin

Sunshine and then rain, spoiling John's haymaking. I wrote a piece Ben Hecht had already written.[90] Alice Armfield had got up and left with E at 7 a.m. There was a flat tire. She just made her train.

I was dull and stodgy but managed to walk it off. E and I, alone together, had a bonfire in the field by the creek.

Thurs., August 29
Ripshin

I rewrote a story Ben Hecht once wrote—out of a common experience.

Went off to town to spend the afternoon in the street with men. It was Mother Copenhaver's birthday so we had a birthday dinner. Drove home in rain and fog at night.

Fri., August 30
Ripshin

I did a piece for the book. Again it rained in the a.m. but cleared later. E and Mimi went off to town but returned at 4, bringing Mother. Two mannish women came from Washington. In the evening a great crowd to be fed and Eula with a headache. They stayed until late at night.

Sat., August 31
Ripshin

Shower in the morning. I did a good piece for the book of memoirs. Mimi and E went off to town and in the evening two women arrived from Washington. They are in government. . . .[91] We all sat over the fire in the evening.

Sun., Sept. 1
Ripshin

Because Mimi was leaving in the early afternoon I did not stay long at my desk. Bob and Mary Anderson came to dine. We sat about talking and playing croquet. Mimi, Bob and Mary left at 4. The rest of us went for an evening drive. The weather beautiful all day.

Mon., Sept. 2
Ripshin

I caught cold during the ride to Mouth of Wilson last night and had to spend part of the day in bed. However went to Marion and bought a truck.

Tues., Sept. 3
Ripshin

Cold better but full of dope. Stayed in bed in the morning. In the p.m. Greer Williams came. Then Wharton Esherick and Mims Phillips came from Pennsylvania. They were tired and we all went to bed early.

Wed., Sept. 4
Ripshin

I brought the new truck home—a Dodge. We got the hay cut in the old cabin field. Went to Wytheville for liquor. Went off with the key and left E stuck in Marion. She came with Mr. and Mrs. Funk who dined with us. I wrote a short piece.

Thurs., Sept. 5
Ripshin

As the car was in Marion E went off with the new truck—and a load of wood for Mother. I worked all morning and in the p.m. John came, to talk of woods with Esherick. John brought a very lovely carving he had made. He stayed for dinner.

Fri., Sept. 6
Ripshin

Worked in the morning and then played with Wharton and Mims Phillips until late afternoon. We went to town to stay the night with Mother— dining at the restaurant in Hungry Mother Park.

Sat., Sept. 7
Ripshin

Wharton and Mims Phillips left early—at dawn. Max Perkins of Scribner's came on the early morning train. We spent the day walking about and discussing the new book.[92] He is very anxious to have it.

Sun., Sept. 8
Ripshin

No work—the whole day spent with Max. Other publishers being anxious to secure this book, I have been doubtful. Put off decision. Max left on the late afternoon train. I have a cold.

Mon., Sept. 9
Ripshin

We began getting the lime spread on the new field. It was a beautiful day. Went to town after work to get the truck. Came home early and burned stumps. It was a beautiful moonlit night but later rained with a storm of wind. Put off decision in the book matter.

Tues., Sept. 10
Ripshin

A cold rainy day but I worked well. E and I went off to Marion in the truck. I went to see John, who is getting ready for the trip to Florida. He has built a trailer for the truck.

Wed., Sept. 11
Ripshin

E and I alone in the house. It was very cold, and, working in my cabin, I got a chill. Will have to move work to the house. Work not so good. E went to town but I stayed and in the p.m. burned brush piles. Grapes are ripening fast.

Thurs., Sept. 12
Ripshin

Wrote a long piece I did not like so destroyed it and wrote another. Mother came to teach the neighbor women rug making. John was painting the barn. The grapes are ripening. The night was very cold. In the evening we took Mother back to town.

Fri., Sept. 13
Ripshin

I began the story of Old Mary for my book.[93] Had to work in the house by the fire. There was quite a heavy frost but a good deal escaped. Mother came again for her class in rug making, bringing Mrs. Russell and Elsie [Groseclose]. They stayed to dine and we drove them to Marion in the moonlight.

Sat., Sept. 14
Ripshin

Worked on Old Mary section of memoirs again and then in the p.m. went into town. Spent part of the p.m. with Funk and then dined at a restaurant with Mother and Father Copenhaver. A man from Rockingham County came and talked of turkey, poison ivy and the Dunkards.

Sun., Sept. 15
Ripshin

Most of the morning on correspondence. The Primitive Baptists were holding a big Assembly in Troutdale and we went to hear the preaching and dine outdoors with the Baptists. The preaching was a half wild song. There was a great crowd of mountain people.

Later we drove to Marion and then home early to enjoy the moonlight.

Mon., Sept. 16
Ripshin

Did a short piece on the American Spectator[94] and then worked with John in the grape arbor. We got out about 13 or 14 bushels of beautiful grapes and took them to Marion, to Funks, to be made into wine.

Tues., Sept. 17
Ripshin

Beautiful fall day. I did a piece on American Spectator for the book. Then I went by truck to Marion and in Funk's car to Wytheville for liquor. Got him 1 gallon—me one-half gallon for men's party. Got home early and Dave Greear and his new wife came to dine.

Wed., Sept. 18
Ripshin

A day of failure and let-down. Worked but the work was no good and I went into a state of depression. The day however fine. The depression is no doubt due to a reaction from several weeks of intense writing. Word came that E must leave on Sunday.

Thurs., Sept. 19
Ripshin

Still in a low state and unable to work at my desk so spent the day working outside. Men's dinner in the evening—Funk, Bob, John, Jack Flanagan, Dr. Thompson, Arthur Stager, Billy Vines, Judge [Will Birchfield] and Jim Birchfield.[95] They all seemed to have a grand time.

Fri., Sept. 20
Ripshin

A beautiful day but laid up all day with a cold. John Anderson came in the truck to pack his household goods preparing to go off South for the winter. Cattle buyers came but we did not sell.

Sat., Sept. 21
Ripshin

Fine day but still unable to work—effects of cold. We got through distributing lime. E went to Marion. Elma Godchaux came with Hope Fagin, a sea captain. Mother came with E for the night.

Sun., Sept. 22
Ripshin

Beautiful day. No work. We spent the morning packing and went to Mother's to dine. E leaving for New York. She left on the night train. My cold a good deal better.

Mon., Sept. 23
Marion

Rain threatened but didn't come. I worked O.K. At Ripshin two men were opening the ditch to drain the cellar. John was cutting corn. I got the truck from John and loaded with drain tile. Worked O.K. in the a.m. Spent the evening with Funk.

Tues., Sept. 24
Marion

Got through a good morning's work. Got the truck from John Anderson and took drain tile to Ripshin. Went to see Funk. There was a hard rain at 5. In the evening to Dave Greear's to a farewell party for John.

Wed., Sept. 25
Marion

Good morning's work. It turned very cold with a cold rain and fog. Went to Ripshin and arranged about Hugh Turner taking Tex—the pointer dog. John got off for Apalachicola with family looking very Okie.

Thurs., Sept. 26
Marion

Good morning's work. Cold but clear. Went to Ripshin and brought Mother 2 bushels of grapes. Bruner in bad trouble.[96] He is arrested as the father of an unborn child. . . .[97] Brought Mr. Sullivan and Charlotte in with Copenhavers' winter supply of canned fruit. Went to Funk's in the evening.

Fri., Sept. 27
Marion

Worked in the a.m. Went to Ripshin and took John on a cattle buying expedition. We got only one calf.

Chambrun sold Big Fish to This Week—$500.[98]

May came to play cards.

Sat., Sept. 28
Marion

Worked at desk all morning—then to Ripshin with Bob, in his truck to gather grapes for wine. Gave Bruner money to try to get out of his trouble. John, Bob and I went to a man named Woods, at Grant where I bought 3 calves. Walked about with the crowd on Main Street in the evening.

Sun., Sept. 29
Marion

Worked at my desk and then to Funk's to dine. The day beautiful. Found Funk in his most unpleasant and most argumentative mood.

The household in a bad jam because Leona is gone.[99] Tried to get Fay but the Pences are having threshers. Funk gave John Sullivan advice about his bastardy case. Went to bed early.

Mon., Sept. 30
Marion

Beautiful day. The house in disorder because of the absence of Leona. Jones in jail for non-support.

Went to Ripshin and loaned John $50 to clear up Bruner's mess. . . .[100] He is lucky to escape prison. Half the men over there seem to have been lying with [the girl involved].

Tues., Oct. 1
Marion

Another beautiful fall day. Bruner finally got all clear on the bastardy charge. Went to Ripshin and, in the p.m., we built fence in the new field. I got in an extra good morning's work and went to bed early.

Wed., Oct. 2
Marion

Did a short story on Treely Walls.[101] Went to Ripshin and found John cutting corn. Labor on the farm for the month cost me $44. Detroit beat Cincinnati in 1st World Series game. Dave came and played cards.

Thurs., Oct. 3
Marion

Feeling low so did no work. Went to Ripshin to pay off. John making cider. In the evening went with Andy Funk and K. Snyder to see Bady Gwinn in hospital at Abingdon.[102] He has the John Emerson disease. Had a bad diarrhea all night and morning but got it checked.

Fri., Oct. 4
Marion

Wrote a short piece for the book. Did not go to the farm but took a long drive in the hills and at night went with B.E. and Mother to dine at Edgar Copenhaver's.[103] Saw an old house built about the time of the American revolution.

Sat., Oct. 5
Marion

No work. Just when I was getting out of bed got word, from John Sullivan that a steer was very ill. He had got stomach pack from dry grass. Took Dr. Brown who treated him—steer very sick.[104] Heard Detroit-Cincinnati ball game—world series. Detroit won.

Sun., Oct. 6
Marion

Ed Rosskam here taking pictures, for publicity—the Home Town book. Book looks good. He arrived late so went to Bob's to dine and then with Rosskam to Ripshin.

Mon., Oct. 7
Marion

Spent the day with Edwin Rosskam of Alliance Books, who made a regular movie actor out of me. I liked him but was much annoyed by the picture taking which I never like. After he left went to the farm to bury the dead steer. It rained in the evening. The hills are very exciting now.

Tues., Oct. 8
Marion

Good morning's work on the book. Went to Ripshin to take shots for black leg in the calves. Stayed at Orlie's to hear the last game of the World Series, won by Cincinnati.

In the evening went to Wytheville to watch the cattle auction.

Wed., Oct. 9
Marion

Wrote on experience with publishers, for the book. Another grand day. Went to the farm and, later, took Mother for a drive into the hills. The whole mountain country a sea of color now.

In the evening played rummy with Funk.

Thurs., Oct. 10
Marion

Had good morning's work and then took a long drive over Walker Mountain and down through Rich Valley, to soak up the fall beauty of the country. Spent the evening playing cards with Funk. The country very lovely now.

Fri., Oct. 11
Marion

Eleanor came home unexpectedly for the weekend so did no work but spent the day with her. We went to the farm and then spent the evening at home.

Sat., Oct. 12
Marion

An upset stomach that prevented me working. Had to stay in bed most of the day. Eleanor was here and was never more lovely. She spent the day taking care of me.

Sun., Oct. 13
Marion

Somewhat better but weak. Did no work. Eleanor went off to church and I stayed in bed. In the p.m., took E, B.E. and Mother for a drive on country roads. Eleanor left for New York at 8:40.

Mon., Oct. 14
Marion

Weak from illness but drove to Ripshin. The most beautiful day yet but had to come home and go to bed. No work.

Tues., Oct. 15
Marion

Day started fair but turned cold and rainy. Could not work so loafed about with men. [In] p.m. had several pictures from the new book. In the evening went to Funks and played cards.

Wed., Oct. 16
Marion

Cold grey fall day and the street full of young men registering for the draft. It was like a return to World War days. They try to make a joke of it but do not succeed very well. Some 1300 registering from this town. Took a long ride, after work, to look at the lovely fall colors in the grey light.

Thurs., Oct. 17
Marion

Good morning's work. Went to farm. We have a fine array of calves there now. We dynamited some rocks in ditch on new land. The barn, with its white trimming looks fine. It was again a very beautiful day. In the evening I went to dine with Bob and Mary.

Fri., Oct. 18
Marion

A very beautiful day. Did a good morning's work and then went for a long drive, going by 58—from Abingdon to Adwolf. There was a heavy mail and I answered that. This has been the most beautiful fall I have ever known here but I have been terribly lonely for E.

Sat., Oct. 19
Marion

Grey day, turning fine in the p.m. Worked O.K. Went to Ripshin and in the evening to a football game, Emory and Henry. It was nice out under the lights.

Mr. B.E. pretty bad about the operation, constantly working on Mother, keeping her tense.[105] His naivete about the Bible, which he seems to take literally and his struggle to get his Sunday school lesson is very charming. He will however be hard on Mother from now on.

Sun., Oct. 20
Marion

Long morning's work. I went then taking Mr. Copenhaver—hoping to break his gloom, for a long ride, by old road to Ripshin and then by Konnarock and Chilhowie. He indulged in many flights of oratory about the hugeness of earth, havens of happiness, etc. but was charming. Spent the evening talking, first to Mother and then to Funk.

Mon., Oct. 21
Marion [?]

No work. Packing to leave. To Ripshin and then to my packing. Bob drove me to Bluefield for train. Before I left word came of Randolph's marriage. . . .[106]

Tues., Oct. 22
Detroit

Three long waits at railroad station, 2 hours at Bluefield, W. Va., 2 1/2 hours at Columbus, Ohio, 2 hours at Toledo, Ohio. Got to Detroit at 4:30 p.m. Dined with Ted Kuhlman, a jeweler here and wife Carol. We went to a German place and had good talk. She a student when I was at Olivet College. Staying here at the Book-Cadillac. Went to see the gaudy Fisher Building.

Wed., Oct. 23
Ann Arbor

Mrs. Ted Kuhlman drove me to Ann Arbor—beautiful day—flat uninteresting country. We drove by the big Ford place. Went to the Union and met Allan Seager. Lunch with him. Had lost checks [for] my baggage left at Detroit and spent an hour phoning. Went to Seager's class and spoke in a big hall at 4:15. We drove to Seager's farm,[107] his father, the farmer, a very colorful man, used to work for my friend Will Burnham.

Thurs., Oct. 24
Detroit

Spent most of the day at Seager's farm, inspecting farm and stock, seeing sheep being bred, inspecting huge hogs, talking of writers and books. We had two plump pheasants for lunch and then Seager and his wife drove me to Detroit, through heavy traffic and I was tired and went off to bed early.

Fri., Oct. 25
Olivet

Got up late and went over my speech. Spoke at luncheon—at 1 p.m. "Life of a Writer."[108] It went all right. Robert Ramsay and Glenn Gosling came and drove me over here. Went to a college show with them and then sat and talked with them, Brewer and others until 1 a.m.

Sat., Oct. 26
On train

Again up late—no attempt at work. Lunched at college. Spent an hour talking with students of story writing, went to a hockey game. Robert Ramsay (dean) drove me to Battle Creek where I took the train for New York.

Sun., Oct. 27
Royalton—New York

Arrived in town at 8:30, E at Station and looking lovely, and very happy to be with her again. We spent most of the day in the room, very happy, but in the evening went to dine with Mary Emmett. The Noels were there, from Mexico, and we went to Chinatown, E getting suddenly sick. We saw a crowd of 10 or 12 men arrested in a Chinese restaurant. E quite sick so we ate hurriedly to get her back to hotel room.

Mon., Oct. 28
New York

The whole town full of politics, women with buttons for voters on every corner, E going out to speak for Roosevelt, the newspapers against him, the President here. Nevertheless I stayed at my own work, only going with E in the evening to see the mass of people gathered about the Garden, where the President was to appear at 10:15. I did letters and then went back to work on my book. The bookstores filled with the new Home Town book.

Tues., Oct. 29
New York

Got well back to work on the book. In the evening E went to speak for Roosevelt, from Mary's car and I went with George Nathan to an opening—Langner's Suzanna and the Elders—very dull, too much brooding talk.[109] Had dined with George and we had a good talk. Saw Walter Winchell who wanted me to go to the Stork [Club] but I came home instead.

Wed., Oct. 30
New York

I seem to be in for bad shows. Went last night to a little Long Island town to see a try-out of Chris Morley's play Trojan Horse.[110] It seemed very amateurish to me—really a bore. Besides got caught and couldn't get away so did not get home until 2 a.m. Bad business.

Thurs., Oct. 31
New York

To lunch with E and Sidney Fleisher—lawyer. The Barton matter in regard to the play not yet straightened out. Went to see Madam [Isabel de] Palencia who gave me a copy of her new book[111]—a very delightful woman. Went in the evening to Lewis Galantière where E and I dined with Lewis and Max Schuster and wife.[112] Mrs. Schuster a very charming woman, small and amusingly alive.

Fri., Nov. 1
New York

No work. It did not go. Went to lunch with the friend of E's from Olivet. Discussed the school, she not too sympathetic. Jim Boyd showed up and we dined and went to a negro show, Ethel Waters and [Katherine] Dunham—not so good. Jim lovely. Dunham has made a mistake, not to stick to her own line.[113] Jim has been working in Washington for Department of Justice, trying to get some short plays on radio.

Sat., Nov. 2
New York

Intense day in the presidential campaign here. Roosevelt apparently in real danger. E out campaigning for Roosevelt. I stayed in my room and did a big morning's work, then to the Ritz with Max Perkins. Then to Mary Emmett where there was a South Carolinian horseman. Listened to horse talk, then rode through the city with a political cavalcade.

Sun., Nov. 3
New York

Up late and worked for a time. E and I went to Stettheimers and then to Edwin Rosskam's. We went from there to the Koppells and got home at

11. I was upset and scolded E because Paul Rosenfeld began kissing her before all the people at the Stettheimers and I thought it put her in a bad light and she should not have allowed it to go on. The result of it all was we got upset and neither of us could sleep.

Mon., Nov. 4
New York

Fine day but felt rotten. Took E with me to a publisher's lunch—Harcourt Brace. Went to see [Henry A.] Moe. Margaret Mayorga came at 5:30 and we sat in the room talking until 7. She very beautiful. E came and we went to the Blue Ribbon and then to the revival of the play Charlie's Aunt—very innocent and healthy slapstick.[114] All the streets jammed with cheering and booing partisans of Roosevelt and Wilkie.

Tues., Nov. 5
New York

Election day and the city suddenly very quiet. Went to the Plaza to lunch with my literary agent Chambrun and got some money from him. Worked and in the evening went about in the crowds with E. We went to Democratic headquarters[115] and to Times Square, then to our hotel room and the radio. The shouting and din kept us awake most of the night.

Wed., Nov. 6
New York

Pretty flat after election and saw no one. Tried to work but got little done. Went to see Moe, of Guggenheim, about South American trip, but got nothing definite. The town very quiet after the hulabaloo but I sense a general feeling of satisfaction about results. Most people seem to feel safer in going on with FDR.

Thurs., Nov. 7
New York

Had a batch of letters to get off so did not do much real work. Had to go to a meeting Author's League and speak there. Karl came in, looking very trembly. Afraid he is discouraged and blue. Helen Laird[116] came and we all drank together, Helen telling of her courtship by Teddy Dreiser. She looking very chic. Her sweetheart is the young painter son of my boyhood chum Herman Hurd. Karl, E and I dined together.

Fri., Nov. 8
Washington, D.C.

Worked in the morning and then E and I went to Washington with Ed Rosskam. I spoke there at "The Book Store" at 8:30. E went to Baltimore where her father had just been operated for cataracts on his eyes. It was declared successful. She got back to Washington for speech. Saw Ernestine Evans, Ellis Hoffman and others.[117] Speech went O.K. Afterwards we sat about drinking and hearing Washington gossip until 1 a.m.

Sat., Nov. 9
New York

Got up late in Washington and went to see Herbert Feis in State Department, about the South American trip. Then went with E, Roy Stryker and a clever South Carolina woman to lunch. E went again to Baltimore and I went to a reception at the Book Store.[118] Later a little woman poet came to talk of her problems. Got the 6 p.m. train and E got on at Baltimore.

Sun., Nov. 10
New York

Worked on a short story for Reader's Digest. E and I went for a walk, to Mary Emmett, none of her new young men about. Joe Girsdansky came in and, after drinking, we all went to dine and then to the horse show.[119] I thought the animals very beautiful but the whole effect rather too snobbish and soon grew tired of it. It was a shock to see the parade of big death dealing war machines on display.

Mon., Nov. 11
New York

Finished a short story—Tim and General Grant.[120] Went to get a phonograph and records by which to study Spanish.[121] It cost $50.00. We went to Paul's and he cooked a fine dinner himself in his little apartment. Margaret Marshall was there (The Nation) and we had good talk. We came home in the rain. Sad Armistice day.

Tues., Nov. 12
New York

A dark rainy day. Put in a good morning at work. In the p.m. studied Spanish. No adventures. In the evening Stanley and Margaret Young came and we went to the Blue Ribbon, where we sat eating and talking for several hours. Young is dissatisfied with a novel he has written and was blue but cheered up during the evening. Later E could not sleep.

Wed., Nov. 13
New York

A cold rainy day. I did a good morning on the book. Carlos Davila came and talked over going to South America. Went to Lippincott's but was a day off on dates. Went to a big cocktail party and met the German novelist [Lion] Feuchtwanger and also Somerset Maugham. Maugham a small stuttering man and Feuchtwanger a curiously ugly little man. Met many interesting, many silly people.

Thurs., Nov. 14
New York

So much mail that I got no work done. Went to see Frank Lloyd Wright's exhibition at Modern Museum. Frank not changed—same kingly man. Exhibition beautiful. Went to Lippincotts who are another publishing house hot on my new book. Tramped about in rain. Put in 2 hours on Spanish. Went to Ben Brenner's to see old movie Samoa.[122] The machine wouldn't work so sat for hours while they tinkered with it.

Fri., Nov. 15
New York

Cold and rainy but I got in a long morning of work and then went off to lunch at Cafe Royal with Dr. Joe. We went then to see Chaplin's The Great Dictator and were both made very sad to find it dull.[123] It seemed patched together—did not say anything—the old Chaplin gift seemingly quite gone. I wanted to weep.

Sat., Nov. 16
New York

After working went to Mary Emmett to find a quotation from Mid-American Chants.[124] Went to old book stores. E and I took a train and went to Croton-on-Hudson to Max Eastman's. We dined there and spent the night. They have a beautiful place overlooking the Hudson.

Sun., Nov. 17
New York

Spent the day with the Eastmans and Max gave me his book on Stalin. Francis Hackett and wife came.[125] I had not seen them for 15 years. Koppell came with his wife who is pregnant. We walked in the hills and talked until 6:30 and returned to the city with the Hacketts.

Mon., Nov. 18
New York

Worked in the a.m. but, all the time, had on my mind the talk with Scribner's. There are several publishers after the book I am writing. I felt that Scribner's had done practically nothing for me. I guess I put the whole story to them in a pretty strong way. We had it out for an hour and Mr. Scribner came across with a fine offer on the new book.

Tues., Nov. 19
New York

Did little work. This matter of settling the matter of publishers has got me down. Went to lunch with one—Koppell, of Alliance Books, a grand fellow. At 4 went to N.B.C. to rehearse for an interview, over the radio with Ted Weeks of Atlantic.[126] Don't take much to him. We dined at Century Club and had our performance at 10:30. Did not like doing it.

Wed., Nov. 20
New York

Did big morning's work. Went with Stanley Young to the Players to lunch.[127] Got proposal from Scribner's. Dictated letters, plan of child's book. Went then to Mary Emmett's and sat drinking and talking until 8. Went then to dine at Ticino's. Jack Noel, daughter—Mary and E. Left them and came to hotel—weary. Did Spanish and then to bed.

Thurs., Nov. 21
New York

E stayed at home and we spent most of the day loafing. At 4 went to the Century Club to have a talk with Robert Littell about South America—for Reader's Digest.[128] Went to a cocktail party at Stettheimer's. Went to dine at Galantières. Very flat all day.

Fri., Nov. 22
New York

Ill all day—a touch of flu or just weariness—from seeing too many people, excitement of deciding on publisher, etc. Got very generous offer from Scribner's but will go to Harcourt Brace. Feel more at home with the fellows there. Post man came for interview[129] but spent most of the day loafing and studying Spanish.

Sat., Nov. 23
New York

Ill all day—with a cold. Stayed in room and studied Spanish, keeping the phonograph going all day and evening.

Sun., Nov. 24
New York

Still laid up with a cold and infection so no work. In the p.m. Stanley Young and Frank Morley[130] came to talk over closing contract for memoirs and child's book I want to do. They stayed 2 hours and we seem to have arrived at a satisfactory understanding—I having definitely decided to leave Scribner's because of their bad work on my last three books.

Mon., Nov. 25
New York

In all day and ill. Could do no work. Studied Spanish and read Borrow.

Tues., Nov. 26
New York

Beginning to shake out of my let down but did not work. It has turned cold. Got sore at Eleanor because she stayed at Mary's party from 5 to 10. It was absurd and amusing but [I] was lonely for her.

Wed., Nov. 27
New York

Busy day. Did a lot of work, writing at my best. Photographer came to shoot me. Had a writeup in the Post.[131] Went to the Savoy[132] to a party for Senora De La Palencia, a very lovely Spanish woman.

Thurs., Nov. 28
New York

News piece about me in New York Post, giving this address, brought a storm of people, beggars, poets, broken actors, all day long. Worked well and went to a lunch in Rockefeller Center. Saw many people. Phone jangled all day. Karl came, looking a bit down on his luck but very charming. We dined and he told wonderful stories.

Fri., Nov. 29
New York

Work in the morning and letters and Spanish lesson in the p.m. A young man, Mr. Politis from Greece,[133] came with translations of verses and stories of mine in Greece. Went in the evening to Brooklyn to speak at Academy of Music on a writer's life. E flew to Washington and lunch with Mrs. Roosevelt, flying back in the evening.

Sat., Nov. 30
New York

Grey winter day with flurries of snow. Good morning of work. Went to lunch with E and Davila—the Algonquin—saw Paul and Lewis there. Dictated letters. Went to French Hospital to see Mrs. Davila. Went to dine with E at Mary Vorse's—Jones Street. Palencia there.

Sun., Dec. 1
New York

A grand day with E in our hotel room—the breakfast at the hotel across the street and the eager Greek waiter—then the long quiet day together and a lot of Spanish study. We went finally to Mary Emmett and took her to dine. She seemed very lonely. Alas she is now completely surrounded by gadflies who are holding her up.

Mon., Dec. 2
New York

Cold and windy. Worked all day—at the book in the morning and with Miss Van Deusen, dictating on the book in the p.m.[134] E and I dined together and then I spent the whole evening at the Spanish study.

Tues., Dec. 3
New York

Good morning of work and then to Century Club with Bob Littell. Went to book stores. Electrician from Camden, Ohio, came and touched me for $7.00. Dined with E and went to Koppell's at nine. Wells, young James Roosevelt, Isaac Don Levine, Morris Ernst all sitting in a group and solving world problems. Wells has a curiously cheap something about him. Once wrote well. Being a world thinker has damned him.[135]

Wed., Dec. 4
New York

Cold bleak day. I had done too much drinking at the Koppell party and was no good but did get a long part of the new book dictated in the p.m. Stayed in all day. We dined in the room and I went off to bed early. A half wasted day, due to dissipation.

Thurs., Dec. 5
New York

Did a short story but then was taken suddenly very ill. Had to give up lunch and dinner engagement. Evidently got some bad food, probably spoiled orange juice for breakfast. My illness made me very weak. No work. Cold and snowing outdoors.

Fri., Dec. 6
New York

Still suffering from the attack of indigestion and little work done. Tina came and I dictated new story—also part of book—Crushed Artist.[136] In the evening took August Derleth and his secretary to dine.[137] Heard great tales of his doing five, six, and even seven books a year.

Sat., Dec. 7
New York

Did not work too well. Took a walk in the sunshine, going to old book stores on 4th Avenue. The Spanish teacher came and we had a two hour session—E getting in on it.[138]

At 7 went to Roberto Rendueles, Spanish liberal in Davila office.[139] Charming man with a beautiful American wife. Both are connected with radio. Delightful evening.

Sun., Dec. 8
New York

Did a chapter on the book of memoirs and then spent the rest of the day with E. We went to Florine Stettheimer's to see her new painting of Wall Street.[140] There was a large crowd. Dined in a Japanese restaurant with the Russian sculptor Archipenko and his wife.[141] Studied Spanish.

Mon., Dec. 9
New York

Suddenly knocked over by an attack of flu—so that I was no good and could not work. Very discouraging. I did however have the girl in and dictated letters for an hour. Had to stay in the room all day.

Tues., Dec. 10
New York

Wasted day. Down with flu and no good.

Did however take a Spanish lesson. Otherwise the day a sheer waste.

Wed., Dec. 11
New York

No good—laid up all day with flu—just a little work on Spanish—
nothing else.

Thurs., Dec. 12
New York

Still laid up with the flu but better. However had to spend the day in the
room studying Spanish and reading.

Fri., Dec. 13
New York

Did no work—still weak from flu—but did take Spanish lesson. Spent
the day on Simon and Schuster's Letters from Great Men.[142]

Sat., Dec. 14
New York

Better but overdid. Wrote for 2 hours, but perhaps got at it too soon.
    Had a bad night with no sleep.

Sun., Dec. 15
New York

Out of the hotel for the 1st time since this illness. Miss Madrigal came to
give a Spanish lesson and while it was going on Ferdinand Schevill came
in. We all sat singing Spanish songs while Miss Madrigal played her
guitar. Ferdinand and E went off to a cocktail party at Max Schuster's
and I went off to bed. Did a little work in the a.m.

Mon., Dec. 16
New York

Pretty good morning's work on book of memoirs—the day cold and
rainy. I took Roberto Rendueles to lunch. A very sweet real person, a
Spanish gentleman. Rosskam came to talk of a novel he was writing and
of marital troubles. Went, guest of Mary Emmett, to see Ethel Barrymore
in "When the Corn is Green"—good acting but the play damn nonsense.[143]

Tues., Dec. 17
New York

Busy day—long morning of work. Took long Spanish lesson. Spent evening with Ferdinand Schevill. We went and sat in the Algonquin and Ferdinand talked of national affairs.

Wed., Dec. 18
New York

Phone at 8. Mother Copenhaver died in the night. A busy day, packing to go home—the shock to E terrible. She is standing up to it.

Had a conference with Mrs. Meloney of This Week and we took train at 7:30.

Thurs., Dec. 19
Marion

The house at Marion stunned, the center of all life here gone. Everyone wanders about like dead people—Mr. Copenhaver a wrecked boy—telegrams and flowers, all of the terrible necessary arrangements for such a time. The house flooded with people.

Fri., Dec. 20
Marion

The savage and barbaric long waiting to bury Mother Copenhaver. Christianity is like communism, it would be all right but for the Christians.

There is too much softness and indecision everywhere.

The house here filled with people, coming to call. I stay upstairs.

Sat., Dec. 21
Marion

Another dreadful day of waiting, my nerves on edge . . . the uncertainty about Randolph[144]—the flood of people—the waiting, waiting. Eleanor keeping busy and standing up to it remarkably well. The days however gorgeous and the country lovely as though nature were waiting to welcome Mother.

Sun., Dec. 22
Marion

A very beautiful day, as though nature were welcoming Mother. They read my short piece at the Church. For some reason all but the red haired preacher seemed vulgar. The vulgarity of the anxious concealment of the ground at the cemetery was terrible.

During the whole performance I played an imagined game of croquet with Mother.

Mon., Dec. 23
Marion

The day full of the question as to whether Mary [Emmett] should go or stay. Purely a matter of good taste. Finished a long Foreword. Drove Channing, Father and Mary to the farm and took John's Christmas. In the evening saw Mary off. Randolph came in at Tri-City Field at 7:30. We all sat up late.

Tues., Dec. 24
Marion

No Christmas preparation. I got back to work. The house filled with conferences among Mother's children—so many problems to be solved. In the p.m. was so overcome with sudden sadness that it produced a kind of blind dumbness.

Wed., Dec. 25
Marion

Got back to doing a little work on the book. Then we all went to Bob's for a Christmas dinner. It was a wet misty day. Walked with Henry and Katharine by the lake. People kept coming in all evening.

Thurs., Dec. 26
Marion

Worked in the morning. The family again occupied all day with conferences and getting things cleared about Mother's estate. I escorted them about from bank to court house, etc. Randolph and Henry making scarfs on the loom. It is a good thing that they are all so busy.

Fri., Dec. 27
Marion

Rain all day. Worked in the morning. Henry and Randolph wove me a muffler. It was decided among Mother's children that Katharine should run the business. At 4:30 E and I left, by train, for Knoxville—a warm rainy night.

Sat., Dec. 28
Knoxville

Came here with E who had to attend a meeting. It rained all day. We were in a let-down after the business at home. E gone all day. I was so [flogged?] I couldn't work so devoted the day to letters. Went to an old

book store where I got a copy my Triumph of the Egg at a low price.
Spent the rest of the day studying Spanish.

Sun., Dec. 29
Marion

Dark and rainy all day in Knoxville. I stayed working and writing letters
in the hotel room until 3 p.m. when we took the train for Marion. E and I
were both in a sag from the tense days at home, after Mother's death.

Mon., Dec. 30
Marion

I have been taking electric treatments for my sinus. Went there. Worked
on the book. Things went pretty well but it was again a cold wet day. I got
$1500.00 in travelers checks against the possibility of the South Ameri-
can trip.

We all spent the evening playing cards.

Tues., Dec. 31
Marion

A good day of work. We all went off to Ripshin in the p.m. where I paid
for the new farm wagon and left money with John to carry on during my
absence. Everything fine there and John doing good work. My little dog
very happy to see me which made me glad.

1 9 4 1

Wed., Jan. 1
Marion

Spent the day answering letters about Mother's death for E and others of the family. Drove to farm to get books for Ned Brown, agent in Hollywood.¹ Got additional story off to Mrs. Meloney of This Week. A cool clear cloudy day and E still in a great mess as executor for Mother's estate.

Thurs., Jan. 2
Marion

Got back to the book. The day very wet and thick. Eleanor flying about all day with all these affairs to be cleared up. I kept doing errands and driving the others about. Two silly pretentious women came in and spoiled the evening.

Fri., Jan. 3
Marion

The entire day spent in the rain with a photographer—a German—Walter Sanders of Life. Many photographs taken, mostly with other people, in the print shop, my study at Mother's, in the drugstore, at the farm. E left for Bluefield to get Chicago train and I took train for New York at 8:45.

Sat., Jan. 4
New York

Arrived back at Royalton at 12. Some hours getting settled in a new room 807. Some phone calls almost at once but was tired and did not try to work. John Emerson took me to dinner, with one of his women friends—undistinguished—and then I came back here. He seems quite his old self, the manic depressant thing seemingly quite gone, at least for the time.

Sun., Jan. 5
New York

Very cold—with bitter wind. Worked well. Miss Madrigal came at 2 and had good Spanish lesson. Met Ferdinand Schevill at John Emerson's room, the St. Regis. Don't think the two men took to each other. Ferdinand went away, after several nasty cracks about the Germans by John, he not knowing Ferdinand was one, and John and I went to see Mary Loos.[2] She looks like Anita but tall. Do not think she has Anita's brains. John and I dined and went to see the Kaufman-Hart George Washington Slept Here.[3] I thought it very dull.

Mon., Jan. 6
New York

Pretty good day. It was very cold. Worked some on the book in the morning and dictated in the p.m. Then to The Lambs, to dine with John Emerson and to see "Life with Father," a really fine and very amusing show.[4] John Emerson—my oldest friend—seemed very feeble and unwell but, at least for the time, has escaped from the manic depressant state he was formerly in.

Tues., Jan. 7
New York

Madrigal came and had good Spanish lesson. Slight attack of flu again but will not tell E. Drank a good deal which seemed to help. Bitterly cold. Went to Rendueles to dine. Roberto's old Spanish father there. Stout, charming old man, speaking English with difficulty—God seeker—has been every kind of religious convert. Much talk of God. Very little work done this day.

Wed., Jan. 8
New York

Pretty sick and blue all day. The war on my nerves. Pretty lonely for E. Couldn't work. Had also slight attack of flu. The day a dead loss.
   Stupid.

Thurs., Jan. 9
New York

The whole day in the room recovering from flu. I could not work. In spite of my illness I was too restless to be quiet and my brain kept churning away all day.

Eleanor in Chicago. She will return to Marion and then come here. I am very lonely for her.

Fri., Jan. 10
New York

The flu passing off so I wrote all right and then dictated a long time in the p.m. Then with Ferdinand to the Blue Ribbon and a long talk and beer. I was very restless, wanting E to be with me very much. Slept very little— nothing fit to read. The newspapers get worse and worse.

Sat., Jan. 11
New York

Not much good. Very lonely for E. Stayed about in the room all day but did little work. Went to dine with John Emerson—less depressing but saw with him a very depressing play—"Arsenic and Old Lace"—an insane family innocently indulging in murder—murder made into a farce.[5]

The strange thing is that it is a great success.

Sun., Jan. 12
New York

Good morning's work. I went to lunch with Stanley Young and saw Lewis Galantière and Marc Connelly.[6] Went to see the woman about the boat to Chile. It is uncertain. Went to Louise Rosskam whose man has run off South with another woman. I sat with her until 11. A bitter cold day.

Mon., Jan. 13
New York

Coldest day yet—10 above. Worked pretty well. Jim Boyd took me to the little club where I used to go with Frank Crowninshield.[7] Miss Van Deusen came and I dictated. Ferdinand came and we went to the Blue Ribbon. Fortunately he goes off home early so I got into bed in good time. Am hating New York. Want a warm place.

Tues., Jan. 14
New York

A big day of work as I did the whole of the radio play for the Free Company.[8] Then did a long Spanish lesson and to the Rendueles, off to dinner at Rockefeller Plaza.

Wed., Jan. 15
New York

Fairly slaughtered by the worst head and chest cold yet. In bed all day.

Thurs., Jan. 16
New York

Still helpless with the cold and in bed.

Fri., Jan. 17
New York

Ill in bed all day.

Sat., Jan. 18
New York

Still ill.

Sun., Jan. 19
New York

Still ill. Wasted day.

Mon., Jan. 20
New York

Eleanor arrived on early morning train. Had bum day and no work. Still in grip of cold.

Tues., Jan. 21
New York

The cold still on me, so no good. Did no work but, in the p.m., did dictate the little radio play, Above Suspicion. E had typhoid shot and was very ill.

Wed., Jan. 22
New York

E very ill from shot all day. I was better but still unable to work. Got passage for South America fixed for February 15th. Miss Madrigal came to give Spanish lessons.

Thurs., Jan. 23
New York

A little work done but cold still hanging on. However did go out to dine—then had bad evening.

Fri., Jan. 24
New York

No work again—cold and snowy outside. Took long Spanish lesson. Was told could not get boat to South America until February 15.

Sat., Jan. 25
New York

Cold getting better. However the writing turned out badly. Snowing outside. Wrote a lot of letters and in the evening E and I went out to dine at the Blue Ribbon.

Sun., Jan. 26
New York

We slept very late. Miss Madrigal came and I took lessons in Spanish verbs. E went out to a benefit show for actors' relief with Mary Emmett, who came in from a Cleon Throckmorton party rather drunk and fell on our bathroom floor.

Mon., Jan. 27
New York

Worked in the a.m. Took E and Roberto Rendueles to lunch. It snowed hard all day. Rosskam came. Dined out with E. My cold not quite cleared up. Packing to leave.

Tues., Jan. 28
New York

Took Spanish lesson in the morning, packed, went to council meeting Author's League, did letters. Left New York for Marion at 7:30.

Wed., Jan. 29
Marion

No snow here—cold and grey. Got unpacked, saw people, paid income tax. Dined at Bob's and went to see Andy. Feeling a bit less blue and worthless.

Thurs., Jan. 30
Sumter, S. C.

Left Marion, after breakfast, for Florida, going via Mt. Airy, Salisbury, Charlotte and on to Sumter in South Carolina, where I spent the night. Day clear and sunshiny. The day full of thoughts of E and memories of days down here with her.

Fri., Jan. 31
Jacksonville

Up quite early but did not take long drive, loafed along enjoying the sun. Many Cars on the road. Missing E as I always do, when she is not along. Stayed the night at Hotel Seminole—Jacksonville.

Sat., Feb. 1
Tampa

After the flu and cold the driving tired me so that I fairly ached with weariness, when I got here. Got a good room in Hotel Thomas Jefferson, dined and, at once, to bed and to sleep . . . all in.

Sun., Feb. 2
Tampa

Bad luck. The flu caught me again and I had to lay up all day in the hotel.

Mon., Feb. 3
Tampa

In bed with flu—reading Plutarch's Lives and studying Spanish.

Tues., Feb. 4
Tampa

Still down with flu—Plutarch and Spanish.

Wed., Feb. 5
Tampa

For the 1st time up and about, although still unable to work.

Thurs., Feb. 6
Tampa

Got into touch with a Mrs. Cortina here and had an interview with her regarding the chance to live temporarily in a Spanish family.[9] It rained hard all day.

Fri., Feb. 7
Tampa

Cold and clear. Did a good day's work on the book, drove out, studied Spanish and in the evening took Mr. and Mrs. Cortina to dine at Ybor City in a Spanish restaurant.

Sat., Feb. 8
Tampa

The most beautiful day yet here but in the p.m. it grew cold and rained. This west coast weather very tricky. Worked and then went exploring the town and suburbs and early to bed because of the cold and rain.

Sun., Feb. 9
Tampa

Dark and cold all day, so stayed in my room, working and studying Spanish. Was to have dined with a Spanish family—the Cortinas—but called it off to work. Got an article out of Mrs. Cortina.

Mon., Feb. 10
Tampa

A big celebration, in honor of a mythical pirate, one Gasparilla—presumed to have once made his headquarters here—dense crowds, the whole an imitation of the New Orleans Mardi Gras, floats, etc. Cold and clear. Walked about in the crowds and did a good deal of work in the hotel room.

Tues., Feb. 11
Tampa

Finished off the piece about Spanish Americans. A big crowd of middle class men in a park discussing God's intent toward man. A barefooted old man with a long beard, running through the streets, a sign on his breast, "The Cross is the Mark of the Beast." In the room studying Spanish. The young Spanish-Italian working man, Cortina, to dine and to a Spanish movie at Ybor City. Understood some of the talk.

Wed., Feb. 12
Louisville,
[Georgia]

Drove from Tampa to a town Louisville, in South Carolina.[10] Picked up a Georgia Cracker who drove part way for me. He had been Florida cowboy, commercial fisherman, truck driver. He was curiously self-conscious and apologetic about his lack of education.

Thurs., Feb. 13
Salisbury, N.C.

Drove here today, all day through the rain. Could have made Marion by hard driving but on account of wet roads too dangerous. Saw one bad wreck.

Fri., Feb. 14
Marion

A clear cold day—no snow for the trip through the hills and over Fancy Gap. Got to Marion at noon and found Eleanor there and waiting. There was a heavy mail waiting for me.

Sat., Feb. 15
Marion

Beautiful clear day but I took the day off and rested after long trip. Stayed in bed most of the day.

Sun., Feb. 16
Marion

Spent the day clearing up accumulated mail. A very clear beautiful day— soft and warm. Did no work.

Mon., Feb. 17
Marion

Got a little work done and sent off an article to Reader's Digest. Went to visit Funk in the evening. A heavy snow fell during the night.

Tues., Feb. 18
Marion

Really got to work again on the book. In the p.m. went to Abingdon to arrange for passport, for South American trip. Spent the evening with Funk.

Wed., Feb. 19
Marion

Did another piece for the book in the a.m. and went to Ripshin in the p.m. Everything at the farm O.K. Very cold.

Thurs., Feb. 20
Marion

Still another piece for the book. In the evening went to dine at Bob's. Still very cold.

Fri., Feb. 21
Marion

Worked on a new piece for the book. Fighting a cold. Spent the evening with Funk.

Sat., Feb. 22
Marion

The house full of people. Channing here and the children everyhere. A bit low, fighting off a cold, In the evening gave a men's dinner for six men and we sat talking until 10.

Sun., Feb. 23
On train

We got off from Marion at 3:20 p.m. Channing spent the day with us and my room was crowded all day so that I did no work.

Mon., Feb. 24
New York

Got into New York early and went to the Royalton. Had many people to see before getting off for South America. Roberto says tickets O.K. Passports came O.K. Got a few letters off and ran about town seeing people. Lunched with Roberto.

Tues., Feb. 25
New York

Went to see A. Caprile on Park Avenue, who gave me letters to several South American people. Went to Cardenas at Daily News building,[11] Reader's Digest. Digest turned down my piece.

Wed., Feb. 26
New York

We moved to Mary's house and had a party, about 20 people. Later 10 of us dined together at Grand Ticino, and E got suddenly sick. Again ran about seeing people. Had to phone Marion for police record. Got $450 from This Week.

Thurs., Feb. 27
New York

Closed up deal with Viking Press, buying back plates, copyrights, etc., to
6 books—cost $1993.00 borrowed money. Now control copyright on all
but Winesburg and Story Teller.[12] Karl came, also Jim Boyd. We all went
to Lewis Galantière and then to dine at Rendueles.

Fri., Feb. 28
At sea

Got aboard Santa Lucia, Grace Line at 11 a.m. and sailed at 12.[13] A cold
day with a heavy wind and snow. Thornton Wilder and Freda Kirchwey
aboard.[14] The sea got so rough that everything in the room flew back and
forth across the cabin.[15]

Notes

Notes to 1936

1. Eleanor Copenhaver Anderson, Anderson's wife since 1933, is referred to throughout the diary simply as "E." Anderson and Eleanor were staying at Rosemont, her family home in Marion, Virginia, where they invariably vacationed over the Christmas holidays.

2. Dr. U. G. Jones was an eye, ear, nose, and throat specialist in Johnson City, Tennessee. Anderson suffered greatly in the mid- and late-1930s from chronic sinus trouble. His winter trips during this period to Texas, Arizona, and Mexico represented attempts to alleviate for a while the pain of winter in the northern climate.

3. Laura Lu Scherer Copenhaver, Eleanor's mother, whom Anderson invariably addressed as "Mother" after he married Eleanor. Anderson and Mrs. Copenhaver were very close friends; and he valued her criticisms of his writings during the 1930s.

4. Apparently a trivial family spat. Eleanor's diary entry for January 1 reads: "Bad start— big fight with Sherwood over family, puppy, nothing."

5. Anderson's proposal for a closer and more supportive relationship among artists, especially through regular exchange of correspondence, which he was setting down in a letter to Theodore Dreiser. For the letter, see *The Portable Sherwood Anderson*, ed. Horace Gregory (New York: Viking Press, 1949), pp. 606–12.

6. Charles H. ("Andy") Funk, Marion attorney, was Anderson's close friend and is mentioned frequently in the diary as "Funk" or "Andy." The two men annually made a quantity of wine with grapes from Ripshin, Anderson's Grayson County farm.

7. In the early months of 1936, Anderson was actively gathering material for a projected four-volume history of the Civil War, with emphasis on the implications of the war for the beginnings of industrialism. The project was never completed.

8. Joe H. Wyse, resident highway engineer for Smyth and Grayson counties from 1933 to 1938; Wyse and Anderson were good friends.

9. *Kit Brandon*, Anderson's novel about bootlegging activities in Southwest Virginia, would be published by Scribner's on October 9, 1936.

10. January 2 was Thursday, not Wednesday.

11. Jasper ("Jap") Deeter and his repertory group from the Hedgerow Theatre near Philadelphia were touring several cities in the South. Anderson knew Deeter and many of his group well. The dramatic version of *Winesburg, Ohio* had been part of the repertory at Hedgerow since opening on June 30, 1934.

12. John Anderson, Sherwood's younger son, an artist; and Mary Chryst Anderson, wife of Sherwood's elder son Robert Lane Anderson.

13. Anderson's daughter Marion ("Mimi") Anderson Spear, and her husband Russell Spear, living at Madison, North Carolina.

14. Anderson was traveling with Eleanor to a conference of industrial young women, which she participated in as part of her work for the National Board of the YWCA.

15. See *Kit Brandon*, pp. 240–42.

16. Marcus Wilson Jernegan, *The American Colonies, 1492–1750* (1929).

17. Roger Sergel was a close friend of Anderson from Chicago, head of the Dramatic Publishing Company.

18. John Anderson and David Greear, young artist protégé of Anderson's.

19. James F. Birchfield, Abingdon, Virginia, newspaperman, who was editor-manager of the *Washington County Forum*, a newspaper published by Robert Lane Anderson and Sherwood Anderson from 1935 to 1939.

20. Burt Dickinson, Marion attorney and judge, former mayor of Marion, close friend of Anderson; and Anderson's son Robert Lane Anderson, frequently referred to in the diary as "Bob." "Culbert" is probably Denny C. Culbert, son of W. F. Culbert, a prominent Marion citizen who owned and operated the Culbert limestone quarry near town.

21. "A.F." is presumably Andy Funk; and "E.T." is presumably J. Emmett Thomas, prominent Marion citizen and democratic politician. In 1936 Thomas owned and operated a mill at Mt. Carmel in Smyth County.

22. Eleanor's brother Randolph Copenhaver, an air force doctor.

23. Jacques Chambrun, Anderson's literary agent in New York.

24. Anderson's farm and summer home twenty miles south of Marion in the mountains of Grayson County, near Troutdale, Virginia.

25. For this letter, see *Letters of Sherwood Anderson*, ed. Howard Mumford Jones and Walter B. Rideout (Boston: Little, Brown, 1953), p. 345. Ralph Church was a friend of Anderson from California who studied at Oxford and was later professor of philosophy at Cornell.

26. An obscure reference.

27. The mid-winter meeting of the Virginia Press Association, held January 17 and 18 at the John Marshall Hotel in Richmond.

28. L. Preston ("Pat") Collins was a Marion attorney and member of the Virginia House of Delegates, later lieutenant governor of Virginia from 1946 to 1952. Frank Lemmon was a Marion oil distributor and prominent figure in the Chamber of Commerce.

29. Dr. Toyohiko Kagawa, a popular lecturer, was headline news when he spoke before packed houses in Richmond during the January 16 to 18 period.

30. Mark Ethridge was a newspaperman, for many years publisher of the *Louisville Courier-Journal*. Vic Flanagan and her husband Roy, a political writer for the *Richmond News Leader*, were friends of Sherwood and Bob Anderson. Annabelle Morris Buchanan, a prominent resident of Marion, organized the White Top Folk Music Festivals, 1931 to 1936. Maury Maverick was a U.S. congressman from Texas and later mayor of San Antonio.

31. Channing and May ("Mazie") Copenhaver Wilson, Eleanor Anderson's brother-in-law and sister, who lived in Baltimore.

32. Anderson spoke at Latrobe Hall, Johns Hopkins University. After he spoke, his one-act play "Mother" was presented by four actors from the Playshop, a University dramatics club.

33. N. Bryllion Fagin, professor of English at Johns Hopkins, who had published *The Phenomenon of Sherwood Anderson* (Baltimore: Rossi-Bryn Company, 1927).

34. Mary Pratt Emmett, widow of Burton Emmett, wealthy advertising man and collector

who had provided some of the money used by Anderson to purchase the *Smyth County News* and the *Marion Democrat* in 1927. After Emmett's death in 1935, Mary continued to provide Anderson financial assistance and frequently lived or traveled with the Andersons.

35. The Andersons were staying in Chicago with their friends Roger and Ruth Sergel at 4830 South Kenwood.

36. Percy Wood was on the staff of the *Chicago Tribune*. Anderson was reading "Percy's book" in manuscript; and Wood was seeking Anderson's help in finding a publisher. Apparently the book was never published.

37. Lloyd Lewis, Chicago newspaper columnist and writer on the Civil War. Anderson knew his book on Sherman (1932). Ferdinand Schevill, professor of history at the University of Chicago and longtime close friend of Anderson.

38. Frank Knight was a professor of economics at the University of Chicago. For a fuller autobiographical account of Anderson's annoyance with Sandburg on this occasion, see "The Sandburg," *Sherwood Anderson's Memoirs: A Critical Edition*, ed. Ray Lewis White (Chapel Hill: University of North Carolina Press, 1969), pp. 466–69.

39. American poet, wealthy and prominent resident of Santa Fe.

40. In Eleanor's diary for this date, she says, "Met Majal Claflin, old friend of Sherwood's from Winesburg House. Now making tin." The "Winesburg House" is presumably the boarding house in Chicago where Anderson wrote *Winesburg, Ohio*.

41. Lynn Riggs was a playwright, whose play *The Lonesome West* was playing in repertory in 1936 at the Hedgerow Theatre, along with *Winesburg, Ohio*. Alice Corbin Henderson had been associate editor of *Poetry: A Magazine of Verse* from 1912 to 1916, after which she moved to Santa Fe because of having contracted tuberculosis.

42. Melvin T. Solve, professor of English at the University of Arizona; and Paddy J. Walsh, professor of mathematics at the University of Arizona, whom Anderson had met in Tucson in March 1932.

43. Broadway star of musical comedy, famous for her "torch song" delivery. Holman had played Belle Carpenter in *Winesburg, Ohio* at Hedgerow in 1934.

44. Confederate cavalry officer in the Civil War. Some of Mosby's exploits are recounted in *Kit Brandon*. Alfred Weathersmythe, a character in the novel, is represented as the grandson of one of Mosby's men.

45. William Edward Dodd, *Lincoln or Lee: Comparison and Contrast of the Two Greatest Leaders in the War Between the States* (1928); *A Cycle of Adams Letters, 1861–1865*, ed. W. C. Ford (1920).

46. *Modern Times*, according to Eleanor's diary.

47. See *Kit Brandon*, p. 308.

48. Former world's champion trick rider and roper and, with his horse Comanche Spot, a western film star.

49. Governor of Minnesota from 1931 to 1936, whom Anderson had met in 1934. Olson died on August 22, 1936, while still in office.

50. Bill Matthews, publisher of the *Star*, a Tucson daily newspaper.

51. A night club.

52. Malachi Hynes, according to Eleanor's diary.

53. Play by Zoë Akins, derived from the novel by Edith Wharton.

54. The Walshes gave Anderson a hat as a parting gift.

55. Uvalde, in southwest Texas west of San Antonio.

56. White Rock is a well-known brand of bottled water.

57. Anderson's closest friends in New Orleans for many years included Marc and Lucille

Antony, James and Dorothy Feibleman, Julius and Elise Friend, and Elma Godchaux. He visited them frequently in the 1930s. Marc Antony was an interior designer with interests in theater, art, and literature. James Feibleman, later chairman of the philosophy department at Tulane, authored a number of books on philosophy. Julius Friend was a wealthy business-man (family cotton business) and author who had been an editor of the *Double Dealer* in the 1920s. Elma Godchaux, sister of Lucille Antony, published a novel, *Stubborn Roots*, in 1936. Eleanor wrote in her diary on March 21, "Amazing how long this group have adored and stuck to Sherwood."

58. Harvey Perkins was a doctor of Preventive Medicine, then attached to Tulane Univer-sity. His wife's name was Barbara, not Dorothy.

59. Dorothy Feibleman, not the "Dorothy" Perkins of the previous entry.

60. Play by Edward Chodorov, based on "The Silver Mask," a story by Hugh Walpole.

61. The mother of Lucille Antony and Elma Godchaux.

62. Jeff and Lillian Feibleman, distant relatives of Jimmy Feibleman.

63. New Orleans newspaperman, novelist, and historian, author of *Father Mississippi* (1927), *Fabulous New Orleans* (1928), and *Old Louisiana* (1929).

64. *Stubborn Roots* (1936).

65. Who had taken leave in 1935 from her position in the theater department at Vassar to serve as National Director of the Federal Theatre Project until 1939.

66. Anderson had invited Roger Sergel to join him in Birmingham for a trip to Macon, Georgia.

67. Aaron Bernd, of 468 Broadway, Macon, had been a friend of Anderson since 1931. "Aaron's house" was a house in the country owned by Bernd, which he allowed Anderson to use while staying in Macon. Anderson once described Bernd as "a dealer in cattle hides with a mind."

68. After several months together, Anderson and Eleanor had parted in Birmingham at 7 a.m. on April 2, he to drive to Macon, she to take the train for Chattanooga.

69. Sue Myrick, newspaperwoman of the *Macon Telegraph*.

70. Margaret Mitchell, author of *Gone with the Wind* (1936).

71. I cannot identify any "Fletcher McCoy" who was on the Duke faculty in 1936. Possi-bly Anderson refers to William Fletcher McCord, a graduate student in psychology at Duke.

72. At Hungry Mother Park, just north of Marion. This new park, built by the Civilian Conservation Corps (CCC), would be dedicated on June 13, 1936.

73. The *New Yorker* published "Nice Girl" on July 25, 1936. Anderson's literary agent in London was Curtis Brown.

74. May Scherer, sister of Laura Lu Copenhaver and for many years dean of Marion College. "Aunt May" lived with the Copenhavers and was a favorite aunt of Eleanor's.

75. Anderson was stopping at the Hotel Rueger.

76. Play by Ferenc Molnar, part of the repertory at Hedgerow Theatre since 1929.

77. Jasper ("Jap") Deeter established the Hedgerow Theatre in 1923 in Moylan-Rose Valley near Media, Pennsylvania. A dramatic version of *Winesburg, Ohio* had been playing in repertory at Hedgerow since its opening on June 30, 1934. Anderson enjoyed visiting at Hedgerow frequently and formed close friendships with Deeter and many of the large group of actors and actresses there. Among the group mentioned in the diary for April 17 are Joseph Taulane and Catherine ("Katy") Rieser, who played George and Elizabeth Willard in *Winesburg, Ohio*. Rose Schulman, mentioned in the next entry, played Belle Carpenter in *Winesburg*.

78. Richard Houghton Hepburn's *Behold Your God*, an "economic satire," had its pre-miere at Hedgerow on April 21, 1936. Anderson was attending a rehearsal.

79. Wharton Esherick, sculptor in wood, and his wife Letty lived in the country west of Hedgerow at Paoli, Pennsylvania. Priscilla ("Pussy") Buntin, later Mrs. Emile Gauguin, was a former secretary of Anderson's, working in 1936 as business manager of the WPA Pennsylvania Art Project.

80. Miriam ("Mims") Phillips was one of Anderson's closest friends at Hedgerow. Harry Sheppard played Dr. Parcival in *Winesburg, Ohio*.

81. *The Mask and the Face*, by Luigi Chiarelli, adapted from the Italian by Somerset Maugham, in the Hedgerow repertory since July 5, 1930.

82. Shakespeare's *Twelfth Night* had been in the Hedgerow repertory since January 6, 1934.

83. Anderson was attempting a dramatization of his story "Hands," from *Winesburg, Ohio*, eventually called "Man Has Hands."

84. The world premiere of this play by Maria M. Coxe took place at Hedgerow on May 23, 1936. Anderson attended some of the rehearsals.

85. Anderson's *Triumph of the Egg*, dramatized by Raymond O'Neil.

86. Ferd Nofer, who played Tom Willard in *Winesburg, Ohio*.

87. Daughter of Wharton and Letty Esherick, who had played Helen White in *Winesburg, Ohio* at Hedgerow.

88. Anderson mentions taking "amital" several times in the diary; properly spelled "Amytal," it was a drug commonly prescribed in the period for nervous insomnia.

89. By Dreiser and Erwin Piscator, in the Hedgerow repertory since American premiere April 20, 1935.

90. "John" is Anderson's son, visiting from Washington, D.C. *Plum Hollow*, a drama of folk life in the Kentucky hills, written by Alvin Kerr from the story by Jean Thomas, had premiered at Hedgerow on June 15, 1935.

91. Oklahoma author and labor leader whom some of the Hedgerow players had met in Oklahoma City in late 1935.

92. See letter to Laura Lu Copenhaver, in *Letters*, ed. Jones and Rideout, pp. 350–52.

93. Maxwell Perkins, Anderson's editor at Scribner's since 1933.

94. *Like Falling Leaves*, by Giuseppe Giacosa, in the Hedgerow repertory since November 7, 1930.

95. The Andersons usually stayed when in New York with Mary Emmett at 54 Washington Mews. Eddie and Alice Wolf of Melfa, Virginia, were close friends of Mrs. Emmett. Ashley and Ethel Miller were Washington Mews neighbors.

96. Yeremya Kenley ("Y.K.") Smith and his wife Julie lived at 622 West 137th Street. It had been at Y. K. Smith's apartment in Chicago that Anderson first met Ernest Hemingway in the spring of 1921.

97. Novel published by Anderson in 1925.

98. Jacques Chambrun, whose office was at 745 Fifth Avenue.

99. Dr. Joe Girsdansky and his wife Ann were close friends of the Andersons. Leane Zugsmith was a Kentucky-born proletarian author: *Goodbye and Tomorrow* (1931), *The Reckoning* (1934); and her husband Carl Randau was a journalist and president of the Newspaper Guild from 1934 to 1940. The Cafe Royal was at 188 Second Avenue, a common haunt of Anderson's.

100. Eleanor noted in her diary for May 14, "Cocktails with Max Perkins. Fell completely for him. Like an overgrown country boy with hat too big."

101. Dr. Buford Jennette Johnson was a close friend of Mazie and Channing Wilson; a Johns Hopkins Ph.D., she published several books on child psychology and child development. She had been professor of psychology at Johns Hopkins in the 1920s and in 1936 was

supervising an experimental nursery school, at which Mazie Wilson also taught, on the Johns Hopkins campus.

102. Well-known stage and film actor, who played Jeeter Lester in *Tobacco Road*.

103. John Anderson recalled in 1982 that in 1936 he was working as "studio assistant" in the Special Skills Division of the Resettlement Administration, "grinding lithographic stones, looking after supplies, mounting exhibits, and helping out generally."

104. In a letter, Anderson identified the two women as "Miss Thomas and Miss Rinke." Eduard C. Lindeman was a prominent liberal who taught at the New School for Social Research, Columbia, Temple, and elsewhere. In the late 1930s he was frequently a consultant on social, educational, and labor problems. On May 20, Anderson was annoyed by Lindeman's conversation and, to be perverse, represented himself as a reactionary.

105. In December 1931 Anderson had transferred the ownership of the Marion newspapers, valued at $15,000, to his son Robert Lane Anderson, with the agreement that Bob would pay $5,000 each to Mimi and John prior to January 1, 1940. Anderson viewed this transaction as his principal legacy to his children.

106. *Battle Hymn*, historical drama about John Brown, by Michael Blankfort and Michael Gold, produced by the Federal Theatre Project at Daly's Sixty-Third Street Theatre.

107. New York stage and Hedgerow Theatre actress.

108. Mary Emmett's country place on the Hudson near Nyack, New York.

109. Paul Rosenfeld, New York author, journalist, literary and music critic. His several books include *Musical Chronicle* (1923); *Port of New York* (1924); and *Discoveries of a Music Critic* (1936). After 1918, Rosenfeld was a close friend of Anderson and had paid for the latter's first trip to Europe in 1921.

110. An article on Jasper Deeter and his Hedgerow Theatre, later published as "The Good Life at Hedgerow" in *Esquire* for October 1936.

111. Thomas Wolfe, *The Story of a Novel* (1936).

112. Town several miles north of Nyack on the Hudson River.

113. Katharine Van Meier of Stillwater, Minnesota, sister of Eleanor Anderson and Mazie Wilson.

114. "The Good Life" was the current title being used by Anderson for one of a series of efforts to write an autobiography during the 1930s. Earlier he had used the title "I Build My House"; and by mid-June 1936 he had changed the title to "Rudolph's Book of Days." Later, working more concentratedly in 1939 and 1940, he had largely completed his posthumously published *Sherwood Anderson's Memoirs* (New York: Harcourt, Brace and Company, 1942) by the time of his death on March 8, 1941.

115. Gertrude Stein, *The Autobiography of Alice B. Toklas* (1933).

116. Possibly Bruce Rogers, well-known book designer.

117. This anti-war play by Irwin Shaw (1936), advertised as "the thrilling drama that startled the world," was enjoying a successful run at the Ethel Barrymore Theatre, 243 West Forty-seventh Street.

118. Madge Jenison, bookwoman and author (*Sunwise Turn: A Human Comedy of Bookselling* [1923]). Anderson had first known her about 1915 in Chicago.

119. Photographer Alfred Stieglitz and his wife, the painter Georgia O'Keeffe, were close friends of Anderson. Dr. Leopold Stieglitz, at 1040 Park Avenue, was a younger brother of Alfred Stieglitz.

120. The party was at 12 East Tenth Street, home of attorney Charles H. Studin, who gave frequent parties for writers and artists. Guests mentioned by Anderson include V. F. Calverton, Marxist literary critic, author of *The Liberation of American Literature* (1932) and

editor of *The Modern Quarterly*; Max Eastman, social and literary critic, a founder and editor of *The Masses* and *The Liberator*; and Edmund Wilson, prominent literary critic. "Paul" is, as usual in the diary, Paul Rosenfeld.

121. Anderson refers to the leftist political leanings of the guests mentioned.

122. Karl Anderson, older brother of Sherwood and prominent painter, lived at Westport, Connecticut.

123. Maud Tousey Fangel, socialite of 61 West Ninth Street, was a good friend of Karl Anderson.

124. Deeter was preparing to stage a revised version of the dramatic *Winesburg, Ohio*. Arthur Barton had collaborated with Anderson on the earlier version first staged at Hedgerow in June 1934.

125. Gene Fowler was a well-known journalist and prolific author of popular biographies; two of his books were very popular in the mid-1930s, *The Great Mouthpiece: A Life Story of William J. Fallon* (1931) and *Timber Line: A Story of Bonfils and Tammen* (1933). Both were reprinted several times.

126. J. J. Scherer, prominent Lutheran clergyman and citizen of Richmond. Eleanor's "Uncle Jay" was a brother of her mother Laura Lu Copenhaver.

127. John Sullivan, a neighboring farmer at Troutdale, served Anderson for many years as caretaker at Ripshin.

128. In addition to the main house at Ripshin, Anderson also had built a log cabin on Ripshin Creek, where he regularly wrote on summer mornings.

129. The newly built Hungry Mother Park near Marion.

130. *America Through the Short Story*, ed. N. Bryllion Fagin (1936). George Cook, a Marion attorney, had two daughters, Blanche and Mary.

131. One of the few places in the diary where Anderson refers to his wife Eleanor as other than simply "E." He persistently misspelled her name as "Elenore."

132. Anderson had in mind an evening's entertainment of one-act plays, including *Triumph of the Egg*; *They Married Later*, recently written in New York; and *Tobacco Market*, in the planning stages.

133. Major Sullivan, son of John Sullivan.

134. Small farm community near Ripshin.

135. During the summer of 1936, Anderson was working on a segment of his autobiography tentatively titled "Rudolph's Book of Days" or "Cousin Rudolph." Earlier in 1936 (see diary entry for May 27), he had called the project "The Good Life." On July 22, 1936, Eleanor wrote in her diary, "Sherwood says he has never had such a good time in [his] life as with new book, now named Cousin Rudolph."

136. For Anderson's tribute sent to the Tass Agency, see *Letters*, ed. Jones and Rideout, p. 355. Anderson had read extensively in the works of Maxim Gorki early in life.

137. One of the periodic "blow-ups" in Anderson's relationship with Mary Emmett, which fluctuated between gratitude for her substantial financial support and extreme annoyance at having her around all the time.

138. David Greear.

139. Max Schmeling, an eight-to-one underdog, knocked out Joe Louis in the twelfth round at Yankee Stadium.

140. Edmund Wilson, *Travels in Two Democracies* (1936).

141. Anderson drove Eleanor to Camp Merrie-Woode, at Sapphire, North Carolina, for the Southern Industrial Girls Conference sponsored by the YWCA. Young women attending the week-long camp were workers in cotton mills and cigarette factories in the South.

142. Louisiana-born journalist and novelist whom Anderson had known in New Orleans in the mid-1920s.

143. The French Broad River.

144. Flora Thomas was maid-of-all-work at Rosemont and Ripshin.

145. Probably Catherine ("Katy") Rieser, of the Hedgerow Theatre group.

146. Jean Brown of Washington, D.C.

147. Mazie Wilson brought word to Eleanor that Mrs. Copenhaver was suffering from advanced hardening of the arteries.

148. A passage of twenty-seven words is here omitted.

149. Bascom E. Copenhaver, Eleanor's father.

150. Anderson, Eleanor, and David Greear drove to Hedgerow for the premiere July 10 of the "new" version of the dramatic *Winesburg, Ohio.*

151. Anderson was planning to publish a collection of plays, later published as *Plays: Winesburg and Others* (New York: Charles Scribner's Sons, 1937).

152. Flora Thomas the maid had been dismissed, a subject of some dispute within the family.

153. Anderson is speaking of Paul Rosenfeld.

154. Ralph Roeder, *The Man of the Renaissance. Four Lawgivers: Savonarola, Machaivelli, Castiglione, Aretino* (1933).

155. So-called because Anderson's artist friend Lucile Swan spent the summer of 1927 there, painting.

156. Robert Williams, a Smyth County native, had worked for Anderson on the Marion newspapers and would succeed B. E. Copenhaver as superintendent of Smyth County schools in July 1937. He later served as executive director of the Virginia Education Association.

157. Friend and former college classmate of Bob Anderson from Lebanon, Pennsylvania.

158. Neighboring farmer.

159. Marc and Lucille Antony from New Orleans.

160. Fred Wescott is a character in the fictionalized autobiography Anderson was currently working on, *Cousin Rudolph*. Fred Wescott also appears in a later unpublished novel, *How Green the Grass.*

161. Doris, Flora, Ruby, Virginia, etc., are "mountain girls" employed to do housework at Ripshin.

162. Anderson and Paul Rosenfeld, who frequently visited Ripshin during summer vacations, had developed a serious split over basic political dogma.

163. Y. K. Smith and his wife Julie had arrived from New York on August 2 for a visit at Ripshin.

164. Under pressure of so many guests, Eleanor wrote in her diary for August 3, "Should I give up job and salary or be dead tired all the time?"

165. John Anderson, the younger son.

166. A passage of nine words is here omitted.

167. Probably James F. Birchfield, Abingdon newspaperman, although Anderson knew other Birchfields in Marion.

168. The annual White Top Folk Music Festival, held on White Top Mountain near Ripshin beginning in 1931.

169. For this letter, see *Letters*, ed. Jones and Rideout, pp. 358–61.

170. George H. Engeman had first visited Ripshin in August 1934. For an interesting

account of his earlier visit, see *The Sunday Sun*, August 26, 1934, magazine section, pp. 4−5.

171. *The Children's Hour*, by Lillian Hellman; *Paths of Glory*, by Sidney Howard, from the novel by Humphrey Cobb.

172. The Barter Theatre is in Abingdon, Virginia.

173. Cary Ross, described earlier in the diary (July 27) by Anderson as the "son of a rich Knoxville banker," and the others mentioned were from Knoxville. John Moutoux, a newspaperman from the *News-Sentinel*, was planning an article on Anderson. His article, "Week-Ending with Sherwood Anderson," was published on August 30.

174. Joe Louis knocked out Jack Sharkey in the third round at Yankee Stadium.

175. Anderson was preparing an introduction for his volume, *Plays: Winesburg and Others*, published in 1937.

176. Mrs. Betty S. Anderson, a neighbor.

177. The standard summer late afternoon recreation at Ripshin was croquet, at which Anderson prided himself on his skill.

178. Clara Schevill was Ferdinand's late wife.

179. Anderson was having trouble keeping his writing of an introduction for his book of plays distinct from the impulse to write his memoirs. One section of the *Memoirs* (1942) is called "A Robin's Egg Renaissance."

180. Muckraking journalist, author of *The Autobiography of Lincoln Steffens* (1931). Steffens had died on August 9, 1936.

181. Nick Carter, Sr., was a radio writer for an advertising firm in New York. His first wife Helen Scherer had been Eleanor's first cousin. Evelyn and Mary Sprinkle were daughters of Dr. O. C. Sprinkle, a pharmacist at City Drug in Marion. Mary Sprinkle was a teacher at Marion High School; and Evelyn Sprinkle would become Nick Carter's second wife. Anderson had boarded with the Sprinkles in their house on Sheffey Street for awhile in the early 1930s.

182. On June 19, 1936, Anderson had applied for a pension as a Spanish American War veteran. He was given a physical examination on August 28 at the VA Facility in Roanoke, Virginia. On October 19, he was awarded a pension of twenty dollars per month for "being 10% disabled," effective June 19, his date of application. In October 1937 his pension would be raised to thirty-five dollars per month.

183. A Negro camp meeting held annually on the top of Iron Mountain, between Marion and Ripshin.

184. Mr. and Mrs. Wright were both employees of the Bank of Marion.

185. Visitors from Pennsylvania, Letty Esherick of Paoli and Priscilla Buntin of Philadelphia. Mary Emmett also arrived back at Ripshin on August 31.

186. This is the second major "blow-up" of Anderson's relationship to Mary Emmett in 1936 (see diary entry and note for June 19).

187. Clinton Hartley Grattan, *The Three Jameses, a Family of Minds* (1932).

188. Anderson had received six copies of his new novel from Scribner's on September 25; the official publication date was October 9, 1936.

189. Edwin P. O'Donnell, *Green Margins* (1936).

190. Because of the break with Mary Emmett, the Andersons were staying at the Royalton Hotel rather than as earlier at 54 Washington Mews. Beginning in October 1936 the Royalton was Anderson's "regular" hotel in New York for the rest of his life.

191. Anderson was a guest on WABC's 11:00 a.m. program, "Magazine of the Air."

192. The beginnings of a never-published book, to be called *How Green the Grass*, which Anderson continued to work on through 1937. Fred Wescott, the character whom Anderson had been writing about in the summer of 1936 for *Cousin Rudolph*, reappears in *How Green the Grass*.

193. Anderson refers to Harlan Logan, who became editor of *Scribner's Magazine* in 1936 and its publisher in 1937; publication was suspended in 1939.

194. "The Story-Teller's Job," *The Book Buyer*, December 1936, p. 8.

195. Lüchow's Restaurant was at 110 East Fourteenth Street. George Jean Nathan was a well-known dramatic critic, formerly co-editor (with H. L. Mencken) of *The Smart Set* and *The American Mercury*; also one of Anderson's fellow editors on *The American Spectator*.

196. Not published.

197. *The Theatre of the Moment* (1936). Nathan had presented a copy to Anderson the day before.

198. Anderson was one of 5,200 to see this fight at the Hippodrome Theatre, at Sixth Avenue and Forty-third Street, near the Royalton. He was very interested in the career of Joe Louis.

199. The Algonquin Hotel, earlier famous as a gathering place of authors, at 59 West Forty-fourth Street, across from the Royalton.

200. Tommy Smith, Manuel Komroff, and Edwin Justus Mayer had all been associated with the Liveright publishing firm, Anderson's publisher from 1925 to 1933. Smith was editor in chief; Komroff was production supervisor; and Mayer's *Firebrand* had been produced by Horace Liveright on Broadway in 1924.

201. Journalist, author, playwright; Hecht and Anderson had been close friends twenty years earlier in Chicago.

202. An impression of Joe Louis, published in *Signatures* (Winter 1937-38): 303-8. Anderson was obviously intending to use the famous nickname "Brown Bomber"; he also misused "boom" for "bomb" in other contexts. See Charles E. Modlin, "Sherwood Anderson and Boxing," *The Winesburg Eagle* 9, no. 1 (November 1985): 3.

203. Probably *And Stars Remain*, by Julius J. and Philip G. Epstein, at the Guild Theatre.

204. A club at 57 East Fifty-fourth Street.

205. B. W. Huebsch had been Anderson's publisher beginning with *Winesburg, Ohio* in 1919 and continuing until 1925, when Anderson went to Liveright. Huebsch had joined the newly founded Viking Press in 1925.

206. Russian-born novelist (*Babel* [1922], *The New Candide* [1924]). Cournos also translated a large number of books from Russian to English.

207. Drama by Edwin Denby and Orson Welles, adapted from the French, produced by the Federal Theatre Project at Maxine Elliott's Theatre, with Joseph Cotten.

208. Luise Sillcox was executive secretary of the Authors League of America; Barrett H. Clark was a Canadian born actor, director, and drama critic (*A Study of the Modern Drama* [1925], *Oedipus or Pollyanna* [1927]).

209. Jerome N. Frank, attorney at 285 Madison Avenue, later judge of the United States Circuit Court of Appeals, Second Circuit, New York. Anderson had known Frank in the early 1920s in Chicago and later when he was one of the young New Deal lawyers working for Henry Wallace at the Agriculture Department in the early 1930s.

210. See entry and note for June 3, 1936.

211. James Rorty, American author (*Where Life Is Better: An Unsentimental American Journey* [1936]), reviewed *Kit Brandon* in *Advance*, November 1936, pp. 25-26. Rorty had

gone with Anderson and others to the White House in 1932 to protest mistreatment of the "bonus army."

212. See entry and note for August 28, 1936.

213. Eugene O'Neill's play, which had been part of the Hedgerow repertory since July 25, 1925.

214. *Cast up by the Sea*, by Virginia Farmer and Stephen Leacock, had been in the Hedgerow repertory since April 30, 1924. *Shore Acres*, by James A. Herne (1893) and *The Old Homestead*, by Denman Thompson (1887) were popular sentimental dramas of Yankee rural life.

215. Drama by Simon Gantillon, which had its American premiere at Hedgerow on August 17, 1936.

216. Harold L. Ickes had been President Roosevelt's secretary of the interior since 1933. Anderson presumably is referring to one of Roosevelt's campaign speeches in New York on October 28.

217. See "Belief in Man," *New Masses*, 25th Anniversary Number, 21 (December 15, 1936): 30.

218. W. W. Norton, publisher of *The New Caravan* (1936), gave a party at 1 Lexington Avenue to introduce contributors to the press. Anderson's contribution was "Harry Breaks Through," pp. 84–89.

219. Editor of *The Colophon*.

220. Drama by John C. Moffitt and Sinclair Lewis, adapted from Lewis's novel, produced by the Federal Theatre Project at the Adelphi Theatre. This drama, on the dangers of fascism, had opened simultaneously on October 27 in eighteen cities.

221. Morris L. Ernst and Alexander Lindey, attorneys at 285 Madison Avenue. Ernst was a prominent liberal, involved especially in anti-censorship causes.

222. "Why I Write" was published in the *Writer*, December 1936, pp. 363–64.

223. Eleanor Anderson was working very actively to help ensure the re-election of President Roosevelt.

224. An editor at Random House and earlier Anderson's editor at Liveright.

225. That is, something about getting *Winesburg, Ohio* staged in New York.

226. John Emerson, actor, playwright, motion picture producer, and husband of Anita Loos, had begun life as Clifton Paden and was a boyhood friend of Anderson in Clyde, Ohio. Anderson had worked briefly for Emerson's production company in New York in 1918.

227. Drama by Bella and Samuel Spewack, at the Cort Theatre, 138 West Forty-eighth Street.

228. The Ziegfield Follies, with Fannie Brice, at the Winter Garden Theatre, 1634 Broadway.

229. *Kit Brandon* was published by Hutchinson in London in 1937.

230. Editor of *Story: The Magazine of the Short Story*.

231. Mary Emmett, Catherine Rieser, Eddie and Alice Wolf, [Ralph?] Thompson, Elmer Adler.

232. The Lambs, club at 128 West Forty-fourth Street.

233. Rev. Harry Frederick Ward, of Union Theological Seminary, was much involved in peace movements and liberal causes; and Francis J. McConnell was Methodist bishop of New York City.

234. Editor of *The Saturday Review of Literature*.

235. The *New York Times* National Book Fair, held November 4 through 19 at the

International Building in Rockefeller Center. Anderson was only one of many celebrity writers who spoke at the fair.

236. Drama about Napoleon's imprisonment, by R. C. Sherriff and Jeanne de Casalis, at the Lyceum, 149 West Forty-fifth Street, with Maurice Evans as Napoleon.

237. At 50 Central Park South.

238. The New Yorker Hotel at Eighth Avenue and Thirty-fourth Street.

239. Poet and editor of the Paris literary magazine *transition*.

240. At Charles Studin's; see entry and note for June 3, 1936.

241. Henry Morgenthau, Jr., Roosevelt's secretary of the treasury since 1934.

242. Roosevelt's secretary of labor since 1933. The Andersons and Eleanor's mother were in Tampa for the AFL convention.

243. Mary Heaton Vorse, leftist author of novels, including *Strike—A Novel of Gastonia* (1930).

244. Possibly Charles Rumford Walker; see entry and note for May 26, 1937.

245. The sailors had been jailed for picketing during a maritime strike.

246. Dr. Hamilton Holt was president of Rollins College from 1925 to 1949.

247. Gardner ("Pat") Jackson, champion of liberal causes, held various minor federal offices during the New Deal period. Stark Young, author and drama critic, and Frost had been at one time together on the faculty at Amherst and disliked each other.

248. Ellwood Cecil Nance, a Disciples of Christ minister, published several religious books with small presses, including *From Dust to Divinity* (1935).

249. Recently appointed ambassador to Sweden from the Spanish Republican government.

250. William P. Mangold was an editor of the *New Republic* and was associated with many liberal movements in the 1930s.

251. William Green, since 1924 president of the AFL.

252. Palencia was pleading the cause of the Spanish Republicans. She had also recently spoken at Madison Square Garden.

253. Marquis W. Childs was at the time a reporter for the *St. Louis Post-Dispatch*; Herbert Little was a reporter for the *Washington News*.

254. Josephine Pinckney was a South Carolina poet and novelist, whom Anderson had met in 1931 at the Southern Writers' Meeting at the University of Virginia. Dubose Heyward was a South Carolina author, best known for his novel *Porgy* (1925), later dramatized by himself and his wife Dorothy in 1927, and the basis of George Gershwin's opera *Porgy and Bess*. Anderson later revised his opinion of Heyward and wife.

255. In early December newspapers were filled with speculation that King Edward would abdicate his throne in order to marry Mrs. Wallis Simpson, a divorced American socialite. After more than a week of suspense, the abdication was announced on December 10.

256. Eleanor had to report on the convention to the National Board of the YWCA.

257. Odum and Phillips Russell were professors at the University of North Carolina at Chapel Hill. Paul Green, also of Chapel Hill, was a noted playwright (*In Abraham's Bosom* [1927], *Hymn to the Rising Sun* [1936]).

258. Novelist, whose best-known works were *Drums* (1925) and *Marching On* (1927).

259. Gustavus Myers, *The History of the Great American Fortunes* (1910).

260. The Federal Theatre Project was considering a production of *Winesburg, Ohio* in Chicago.

261. Anderson was amused that local gossip had created for him "a big affair with Leona Lincoln," a local beauty from a prominent family.

262. Barrett H. Clark, director of Dramatists Play Service, wanted Anderson to send plays

which DPS could "publish and handle the amateur rights of." Anderson was working over his one-act plays *Mother* and *They Married Later* to send to Clark.

263. Funk's woodworking shop, adjacent to his house a few doors from Rosemont, was a favorite gathering place for Funk, Anderson, and their cronies. The shop was sometimes called "The Funk Institute."

264. B. E. Copenhaver, Eleanor's father, owned a farm just north of Marion.

265. Ferd Nofer, Jasper Deeter, and Miriam Phillips, visitors from the Hedgerow Theatre.

266. Restaurant on Main Street in Marion, owned by Walter Wyatt.

267. Eleanor Wilson, young daughter of Mazie and Channing Wilson and Eleanor Anderson's namesake, was referred to in the family as "Little Eleanor" or "E-2."

268. The view from the top of Walker Mountain, north of Marion, is one of the most spectacular in southwest Virginia.

269. Eleanor's first cousin, son of Laura Lu Copenhaver's sister, Katharine Scherer Cronk.

270. Town northeast of Marion in Wythe County, Virginia.

271. Town southwest of Marion in Smyth County.

272. Waldie Van Eck's Dutch translation of *Kit Brandon* would not be published until 1947.

Notes to 1937

1. Anderson frequently mentions working on "Green Grass" during the latter part of 1936 and throughout 1937. This unpublished and apparently unfinished manuscript, now in the Newberry Library, was eventually titled *How Green the Grass*. The major characters are Fred and Rudolph Wescott, both of whom Anderson had also been using as characters in *Rudolph's Book of Days* earlier in 1936.

2. Pen name of Olive Tilford Dargan, author of poetic dramas, poetry, and prose (*Call Home the Heart* [1932], *A Stone Came Rolling* [1935]).

3. Marvin J. Anderson had in 1919 formed the Marion Publishing Company, which published the *Smyth County News* and the *Marion Democrat*. In 1921, he sold the papers to Arthur L. Cox, who in turn sold them to Sherwood Anderson in 1927. In 1937, Marvin Anderson had been for several years an agent of the Jefferson Standard Life Insurance Company. John Reed was an American journalist and revolutionary whom Anderson had known in Chicago between 1910 and 1920. Reed's posthumously published *Ten Days That Shook the World* (1926) is an eyewitness account of the Bolshevik Revolution in Russia.

4. Gordon W. Copenhaver lived until 1971.

5. See entry and note for March 20, 1936.

6. Wealthy United Fruit Company heiress and anthropologist who wrote several books on archeology in Honduras, Costa Rica, and elsewhere. See entry for March 11, 1937.

7. The Andersons had spent most of January and February 1935 vacationing at Corpus Christi and Brownsville, Texas. In 1937, they were renting a place at Yacht Beach Court, 2700 Rincon Street, Corpus Christi.

8. Dr. Henry Van Meier, Eleanor's brother-in-law, a physician in Stillwater, Minnesota.

9. Van Wyck Brooks, *The Life of Emerson* (1932).

10. Although Anderson did not write anything in his diary on this date, he wrote to Roger Sergel of "Grey skies, a grey sea and a grey heart."

11. James Boswell, *Journal of a Tour to the Hebrides with Samuel Johnson, LL.D.* (1785).

12. Donald Culross Peattie, *Green Laurels: The Lives and Achievements of the Great Naturalists* (1936).

13. Anderson was still attempting to write an introduction to the collection of plays to be published in 1937, and still having trouble keeping it separate from his "memoirs" project. Eleanor wrote in her diary on February 28, "Sherwood . . . dictated preface. Really his feeling about writing, how he started, etc. It's good, but I can hear [Clifton] Fadiman saying that he is retelling *Story Teller's Story*."

14. Marquis James, *Andrew Jackson, the Border Captain* (1933).

15. Roger and Ruth Sergel from Chicago.

16. Author of *Green Margins* (1936).

17. An article on Burton Emmett, published as "Friend," *PM*, No. 34 (1937): 2–4.

18. See page 361, note 6.

19. British drama by Ronald Gow and Walter Greenwood, adapted from Greenwood's novel.

20. Roark Bradford was the author of stories based on Negro folklore, whose *Ol' Man Adam an' His Chillun* (1928) was adapted by Marc Connelly in *The Green Pastures* (1930). T. S. Stribling was a Tennessee-born writer whose most ambitious work is his trilogy *The Forge* (1931), *The Store* (1932), and *Unfinished Cathedral* (1934).

21. By Ludwig Marcuse.

22. Frances Anne ("Fanny") Kemble, highly successful nineteenth-century Shakespearean actress, first published her *Records of Later Life* in 1882.

23. Eleanor's friend and fellow YWCA worker.

24. Julian Harris was the editor of various Southern newspapers and son of Joel Chandler Harris. Adolf Ochs (d. 1935) had published the *Chattanooga Times* beginning in 1878 and *The New York Times* beginning in 1896.

25. Anderson described the play as "on textiles, a kind of panorama of the industry done partly in songs and chants" (See entry and note for October 5).

26. L. E. Gordon was superintendent at the Virginia-Lincoln Furniture Corporation, a large Marion-based industry of which Charles C. Lincoln, Jr., was president.

27. Published by Scribner's September 9, 1937, as *Plays: Winesburg and Others*.

28. 54 Washington Mews, Mary Emmett's home.

29. An "authentic story of the Russian Revolution narrated in English by Max Eastman," at the Filmarte Theatre at 202 West Fifty-eighth Street.

30. The Triborough Bridge, connecting Queens, the Bronx, and Manhattan, was completed in 1936.

31. In Flushing Meadows, being prepared for the New York World's Fair of 1939 to 1940.

32. Lucille Charles at the Columbia Broadcasting Company.

33. *Power*, a production by the Living Newspaper unit of the Federal Theatre Project, an exposé of the electric light and power industry.

34. Labor play about a sit-down strike in an automobile factory, by John Howard Lawson, at the Bayes Theatre, 224 West Forty-fourth Street.

35. Labor violence in Hershey, Pennsylvania, between strikers of the recently-formed United Chocolate Workers' Union and outraged non-strikers and local citizens.

36. Eleanor's air force doctor brother, just returned from duty in the Philippines.

37. A passage of five words is here omitted.

38. Margaret Fry, a stenographer.

39. Dr. Henry Van Meier, Eleanor's brother-in-law from Stillwater, Minnesota.

40. Motion picture version (1937) of the Pearl Buck novel, starring Luise Rainer.

41. Maury Maverick was a freshman congressman from Texas. Herbert Feis was adviser on international economic affairs at the State Department. For Herb Little, Marquis Childs, and Gardner ("Pat") Jackson, see diary entries and notes for November 21 and 27, 1936.

42. W. Curtis Bok, wealthy Philadelphia judge, author, and later a justice of the Pennsylvania Supreme Court. Bok, son of philanthropist Edward Bok, did his own interior decorating as a hobby.

43. At the St. James Theatre, 246 West Forty-fourth Street, starring Maurice Evans. See entry for May 6.

44. The Ringling Brothers and Barnum and Bailey Circus.

45. Van Lingle Mungo was the pitcher for Brooklyn.

46. The Grand Ticino Restaurant, 228 Thompson Street, is mentioned several times in the diary. Frank Blum is probably Francis ("Frank") Blum, second wife of the artist Jerome Blum.

47. Special matinee at the Empire Theatre for the Stage Relief Fund.

48. English adaptation by Arthur Wilmurt of the French play by Andre Obey, which opened at Hedgerow on April 21., 1937.

49. Comedy by Lennox Robinson, which would open at Hedgerow on May 3, 1937.

50. The Knox Hat Company, 417 Fifth Avenue.

51. Anderson collected $249.15 in royalties due for Russian translations of his books.

52. Henry Allen Moe, secretary general of the Guggenheim Foundation.

53. Ernest Boyd, Irish-born critic and author, had been one of Anderson's fellow editors at *The American Spectator*. Erich Posselt, of Arrowhead Press in 1937, was associated in the 1930s with several firms which acted as agents for foreign rights and/or published "collector's editions" of minor works of well-known authors. Posselt pursued Anderson for material without success. He also edited *On Parade* (1929), a collection of Eva Herrmann's caricatures in which Anderson appeared.

54. Anderson had gone to Wells College, where his friend J. J. Lankes, the woodcut artist of Hilton Village, Virginia, was temporarily on the faculty. Lewis Galantière, critic and translator from the French (*The Goncourt Journals* [1937]), was a long-time friend.

55. Charles Harris Whitaker was at Wells to lecture under the auspices of the Lecture Club.

56. Brooklyn won this game five to one over Cincinnati, not the Pittsburgh Pirates.

57. Carl Hubbell is in the record books for "most consecutive games won." He won twenty-four straight games (sixteen late in the 1936 season plus eight at the beginning of 1937).

58. Comedy by Jean Ferguson Black, on this date a special performance for the Stage Relief Fund at the Morosco Theatre, 217 West Forty-fifth Street.

59. Maurice Long, wealthy laundry owner in Washington, D.C., and close friend of Anderson prior to Long's death in 1931. Rebecca B. Treves, wife of Dr. Norman Treves, had written Anderson in 1936 praising *Kit Brandon*, telling him that Maurice Long had been a mutual friend, and expressing a desire to meet him.

60. An unfinished manuscript, now in the Newberry Library, dealing with Anderson's trip in 1932 as a delegate to the World's Congress Against War in Amsterdam; it should not be confused with "Delegation," dealing with Anderson's going to Washington in August 1932 with the so-called "Writer's Delegation" to protest the treatment of the bonus marchers. The latter was published in the *New Yorker* in 1933.

61. Hit comedy, adapted by Robert Sherwood from the French of Jacques Deval.

62. Gordon ("Mickey") Cochrane, who was later elected to the Hall of Fame for his performance with the Detroit Tigers from 1925 to 1937, suffered a fractured skull in this game.

63. Cleon Throckmorton was an artist and scene designer for many New York stage productions. Charles Rumford Walker and his wife Adelaide, like Mary Heaton Vorse, were

radical members of the literary community. The Walkers had gone into Harlan County, Kentucky, in 1931 with Theodore Dreiser's "writer's delegation" to hold hearings on the mistreatment of striking miners. Anderson had declined an invitation to join them.

64. Russell and Mimi Spear were struggling to establish themselves as publishers of the *Madison Messenger* in North Carolina.

65. Longchamps Restaurants had several locations in New York City.

66. Author James T. Farrell had recently returned from Mexico, where he had met Leon Trotsky, the exiled Soviet revolutionary. This dinner party was the first meeting between Anderson and the younger Farrell, who greatly admired Anderson's work. Farrell wrote of this occasion in *Perspective*, Summer 1954, pp. 83–88.

67. Eleanor had attended Bryn Mawr for graduate work from 1918 to 1920; she received there a certificate in social work before joining the YWCA in 1920.

68. This story had appeared in Anderson's collection *Death in the Woods* (1933).

69. See entry for July 26, 1937.

70. John Sullivan's daughter, who worked as a housemaid at Ripshin.

71. "Personal Protest," *Canadian Forum*, August 1937, pp. 168–69.

72. Anderson was preparing to attend the Writers' Conference at the University of Colorado, Boulder, from July 26 to August 10.

73. John Anderson had invited his wife-to-be, Eleanore Jubell, to be a guest at Ripshin during early summer 1937. The "green house" was a guest house, near the main house at Ripshin.

74. The women from Marion College, a Lutheran women's school, regularly went on outings to Ripshin in the Spring. "Big June" was an annual homecoming celebration held in rural Grayson County.

75. Two small guest houses near the main house at Ripshin. They would be rebuilt as permanently roofed structures and their outside walls covered with bark.

76. *How Green the Grass.*

77. John Bitter, a young musician.

78. A passage of seventeen words is here omitted.

79. Cornelia Lane Anderson, Anderson's first wife and the mother of his three children.

80. Herbert Little worked for the *Washington News*. Ruby Black was Washington correspondent for United Press; her book *Eleanor Roosevelt* appeared in 1940.

81. Eddie and Alice Wolf lived at Melfa, Virginia, when not in New York.

82. At Camp Merrie-Woode, Sapphire, North Carolina.

83. Anderson had appealed to the Viking Press to take less than fifty percent of money received for reprinting stories which had originally appeared in books published by B. W. Huebsch.

84. "A Moonlight Walk," which Anderson had tried unsuccessfully to sell earlier with the title "Mrs. Wife," sold to *Redbook* for $750 and was published in December 1937. Eleanor described this story (July 6, 1937) as "a story Mother doctored up, renamed, and made Sherwood send off." See Hilbert H. Campbell, "Sherwood Anderson and His 'Editor': The Case of 'A Moonlight Walk,'" *Papers of the Bibliographical Society of America* 79 (Second Quarter 1985): 227–32. "Two Lovers" was published in *Story*, January–February 1939, pp. 16–25.

85. The fight in Chicago in which Joe Louis first won the heavyweight crown from Jim Braddock.

86. Orlie Stamper was the proprietor of a garage on the main street in Troutdale. Since Ripshin had no telephone or radio, the Andersons used the phone at the garage; and Anderson went there to listen to boxing and baseball on the radio.

87. David and John Greear.

88. See page 354, note 105.

89. Gerald Gordon, from New Orleans, had worked briefly for Anderson when he was running the Marion newspapers. Anderson said elsewhere that Gordon "didn't do well" and was an "impossible egotist."

90. Robert Porterfield, proprietor of the Barter Theatre in Abingdon.

91. George Daugherty was a life-long friend, whom Anderson had first known in Springfield, Ohio, and with whom he had worked for many years at the Critchfield Advertising Agency in Chicago. Scott Smith also worked at the Critchfield Agency.

92. Fort Hays Kansas State College.

93. Town just west of Hays in Ellis County, Kansas.

94. Presumably Anderson's mistake for *Saratoga*, released by MGM in July 1937. Anita Loos and Robert Hopkins wrote the screenplay for this motion picture, which starred Clark Gable and Jean Harlow.

95. Colorado State College, Greeley.

96. Anderson would be in Boulder at the University of Colorado until August 11. He participated as "General Adviser" at the Writers' Conference there. Among the "leaders and consultants" attending, were in addition to Anderson, were poet John Crowe Ransom, novelist Evelyn Scott, editor Whit Burnett of *Story*, W. M. Raine, T. H. Ferril, Marian Castle, novelist Ford Madox Ford, poet and novelist John Peale Bishop, playwright Margaret Mayorga, Howard Mumford Jones, William M. John, Lenora Weber, and Brewster Ghiselin. Anderson was to deliver two lectures (July 29 and August 10), assist with daily workshops, and participate in "round table" discussions on July 28 and August 6.

97. Anderson's slip; he went for the evening to the home of Edward ("Ted") and Natalie Davison. Davison, poet and faculty member at Boulder, was a principal among the conference organizers. Kenneth Davenport was at Fort Hays Kansas State College, where Anderson had lectured three days earlier.

98. Anderson's topic was "The Impulse to Write."

99. Major league second baseman, mostly at St. Louis, from 1915 to 1937; elected to the Hall of Fame in 1942.

100. The "drama woman" was Margaret Mayorga. Thomas Thompson, mentioned also in the July 29 entry, was a student at the conference. Anderson was reading the manuscript of a novel Thompson had written.

101. Robert Morss Lovett, critic, professor of English at the University of Chicago, longtime friend of Anderson.

102. Anderson and his wife dined with Dr. Valentine Fisher. Ted Davison apparently had some aspiration to be president of the university.

103. Joseph Cohen, University of Colorado professor.

104. Charles Milton Perry, since 1923 head of the Department of Philosophy at the University of Oklahoma.

105. Anderson is referring to a 1931 incident in Harlan involving Theodore Dreiser, when local officials propped a toothpick against his door one night to trap him in a charge of immorality and thus discredit his attempts to aid the striking coal miners.

106. John Sullivan's father.

107. Probably "Listen, Hollywood!" published in *Photoplay*, March 1938, pp. 28–29.

108. Letty Esherick and probably Hilda Worthington Smith, who was associated with the summer program at Bryn Mawr for women industrial workers.

109. Daughter of Nick Carter and his late wife Helen Scherer Carter, Eleanor's cousin.

110. Joe Louis defeated Tommy Farr at Yankee Stadium.

111. W. Lynn Copenhaver was President and Cashier of the Bank of Marion.

112. Joe Fowler.

113. A painting by Arthur G. Dove, a major modernist painter of the "Stieglitz Group."

114. Bruner Sullivan, son of John Sullivan.

115. Novel by John Peale Bishop (1935).

116. Anderson was seeking an increase in the twenty-dollar monthly pension he had been getting since 1936. The pension was increased to thirty-five dollars effective October 4, 1937.

117. Min Price owned the farm bordering Ripshin on the west side.

118. Towns in Grayson and Wythe counties.

119. Anderson's mistake for *You Can't Have Everything*, at the Lincoln Theatre in Marion, starring Alice Faye.

120. *Textiles*, in *Contemporary One-Act Plays*, ed. William Kozlenko (New York: Charles Scribner's Sons, 1938), pp. 1–22.

121. The Sunday magazine of the *Richmond Times-Dispatch* for Sunday, October 3, had published Anderson's "The Younger Generation," pp. 3, 6, 12.

122. Frank Copenhaver was part-owner of the Piggly-Wiggly Market in Marion, a Democratic politician, and one of Anderson's closest friends in Smyth County. John D. Lincoln was the son of Charles Lincoln, Sr., prominent Marion businessman. "Mrs. Swift" is unidentified.

123. A North Carolina-born writer of short stories, novels, and plays.

124. Author of several volumes of regionally published verse.

125. Anderson was seeking an increase in the disability pension of twenty dollars a month that he had been granted in 1936 for his service in the Spanish-American War. He was being aided by John Paul Cullen of the Veterans Administration, whom he had recently met at the Writers' Conference in Colorado. Although both Anderson and Cullen were hoping for an increase to fifty dollars, Anderson was notified on November 10, 1937, that an increase to thirty-five dollars a month was being granted.

126. Material being written at this time for the *Book of Days* would become part of Anderson's posthumously published *Memoirs* (1942). For Maurice Long, see entry and note for May 20, 1937.

127. Raymond Anderson, brother of Sherwood and Karl. Karl and Ray both lived at Westport, Connecticut.

128. Hemingway had been enraged by Eastman's review of *Death in the Afternoon*, called "Bull in the Afternoon," *New Republic*, June 1933, pp. 94–97. The well-publicized "fight" between the two men took place on August 11, 1937, when they met by accident in Perkins' office at Scribner's.

129. *From These Roots: The Ideas That Have Made Modern Literature* (1937).

130. The American Labor Party, founded in 1936, would represent the "balance of power" in the November 2 city election, in which Mayor Fiorello LaGuardia was re-elected.

131. Armstrong captured the featherweight (not flyweight) championship from Petey Sarron.

132. One of a series of government reports (1936 to 1940), called *Violations of Free Speech and the Rights of Labor*, the proceedings of a U.S. Senate Committee on Education and Labor, chaired by Robert M. LaFollette, Jr.

133. Russell Potter was the associate director of extension at Columbia University, and Walter Pack was a prominent photographer.

134. One of the best of the short stories left unpublished at the time of Anderson's death; published in *Tomorrow*, March 1946, pp. 28–32.

135. Heywood Broun, prominent New York columnist and critic, first president of the Newspaper Guild.

136. Burton Rascoe, prominent newspaper columnist, editor and critic, whom Anderson had first known when Rascoe was literary editor of the *Chicago Tribune* in the period before 1920. Rascoe's son had committed suicide.

137. Anderson visited Pirie McDonald, photographer at 576 Fifth Avenue, to have his picture made for the National Institute of Arts and Letters, to which he had been elected early in 1937. Hendrick Van Loon was an author and popularizer of encyclopedic subjects, including *The Story of Mankind* (1921).

138. In a letter to Laura Lu Copenhaver on Thursday, November 11, Anderson reported that Eric J. Devine was exhausted in the attempt to care for Faulkner, who had been drunk for two weeks. The "doctor" was Joe Girsdansky. They hoped to get Faulkner started for Mississippi on November 11. See *Sherwood Anderson: Selected Letters*, ed. Charles E. Modlin (Knoxville: University of Tennessee Press, 1984), pp. 213–14.

139. Margaret Mayorga, playwright and anthologist, who had been at the Colorado Writers' Conference with Anderson.

140. Drama by Rachel Crothers about the Oxford Movement, playing at the Plymouth Theatre, 236 West Forty-fifth Street, with Gertrude Lawrence.

141. *The No'Count Boy, White Dresses*, and *The Man Who Died at 12 O'Clock* had first played at Hedgerow on August 28, 1929.

142. *Ralston's Ring: California Plunders the Comstock Lode*, by George D. Lyman (1937).

143. For Pinckney and Heyward, see entry and note for November 29, 1936.

144. Thomas J. Tobias was secretary of the Poetry Society of South Carolina, before which Anderson lectured.

145. Novelist (*The Delectable Mountains* [1927]).

146. Gerald W. Johnson, close associate of H. L. Mencken and editorial writer for the *Baltimore Evening Sun*; author of biographies and historical studies (*Andrew Jackson* [1927], *America's Silver Age* [1939]).

147. George H. Engeman, reporter for the *Baltimore Sun*, who had more than once visited Anderson at Ripshin. See entry and note for August 14, 1936.

148. Anne Miller's Restaurant was at 46 West Eighth Street.

149. The Fasig-Tipton Company's Forty-third annual Old Glory Horse Auction, at Squadron "A" Armory, Ninety-fourth Street and Madison Avenue.

150. At Eighth Avenue and Fiftieth Street.

151. George Borrow, English Victorian author of *Lavengro* (1851) and *The Romany Rye* (1857), was one of Anderson's favorite authors.

152. Published in Anderson's *Memoirs* as "Pick the Right War."

153. Novelist (*The Wave* [1929]) who had been with Anderson at the Colorado Writers' Conference.

154. Keen's Chop House, 72 West Thirty-sixth Street.

155. At the Mercury Theatre, 110 West Forty-first Street, with Joseph Holland and Orson Welles.

156. Leftist writer, author of *Red Virtue: Human Relationships in the New Russia* (1933).

157. Of this incident, Eleanor Anderson recalled in 1949 that "We were talking about the South, noting that when you were too liberal they never blamed you for the liberal sentiment

or act, but found some extraneous point. Without thinking, I said to Tom that I had heard the week before in North Carolina that he was Jewish." Mrs. Anderson's remark threw Wolfe into a tantrum; he continued his attack by publicly insulting Anderson on December 17 at the Brevoort Hotel.

158. The well-known critic, satirist, and wit, who had been in Spain as a newspaper correspondent.

159. Comedy, dramatized by Brian Doherty from the novel by Bruce Marshall.

160. The Bamboo Forest Restaurant, 115 Waverley Place.

161. William E. Woodward, South Carolina-born author of "debunking" histories, such as *Meet General Grant* (1928); Helen Woodward was also an author (*Queen's in the Parlor* [1933]).

162. Norman Treves, M.D., and wife Rebecca, at 120 East Seventy-eighth Street. See page 363, note 59.

163. Edward Dahlberg was an essayist, stylist, contentious critic of American life and letters (*Bottom Dogs* [1930]).

164. Possibly *The Fireman's Flame*, musical melodrama by John Van Antwerp, at the American Music Hall, 141 East Fifty-fifth Street.

165. Dramatization by John Steinbeck of his novelette (1937), at the Music Box, 239 West Forty-fifth Street.

166. Barney Gallant's Bar and Restaurant, 86 University Place.

167. Saxe Commins, an editor at Random House, and his wife Dorothy.

168. Dr. Joe Girsdansky.

169. Joe Taulane.

170. Jack's Sandwich Shop, 14 West Forty-third Street.

171. Comedy by Arthur Kober, at the Lyceum Theatre, 149 West Forty-fifth Street.

172. Painter and illustrator for several magazines and newspapers, including *Vogue*, *New York Tribune*, and *Masses*. In 1937, he was doing murals for the Department of Justice.

173. Gladys Ficke, artist, wife of Arthur Davison Ficke, Iowa-born poet.

174. See entry and note for December 1, 1937.

175. *The Outward Room* (1937).

176. John Marin, American painter of the "Stieglitz Group."

177. Muralist, later on the faculty at Antioch College.

178. Clifford Odets' play about a prizefighter, at the Belasco Theatre, 115 West Forty-fourth Street.

179. The party was to raise money for the Spanish Loyalist cause.

Notes to 1938

1. The Mathieson Alkali Works, a major Smyth County industry since 1895. The CIO, or Congress of Industrial Organizations, was a federation of labor unions founded in 1935 by John L. Lewis.

2. Arthur B. Copenhaver was a brother of Bascom E. Copenhaver.

3. See entry and note for May 23, 1937.

4. Three hundred seven artists and sculptors were represented in the annual exhibition of American painting and sculpture at the Art Institute of Chicago.

5. Son of Roger and Ruth Sergel.

6. Charner M. Perry was assistant professor and secretary in the Department of Philosophy at the University of Chicago. See entry for February 25, 1938.

7. For Wood and Knight, see entry and notes for January 27, 1936.

8. A passage of sixteen words is here omitted.

9. A residence hall at 1414 East Fifty-ninth Street.

10. The Byrne Advertising Agency was at 35 East Wacker Drive.

11. Anderson was looking for Arnold Gingrich at 919 North Michigan Avenue.

12. Marco Morrow, long-time friend of Anderson from the advertising agency days in Chicago. Since 1919, Morrow had worked for Capper Publications in Topeka, Kansas. Eleanor had been staying at the Palmer House, while working in the Chicago office of the YWCA at 59 East Monroe Street.

13. Annetta Dieckmann.

14. A picture of Dr. Van Meier on snowshoes, identified only as "Country Doctor," appeared on page 13 of Life for February 7, 1938.

15. Laura Lu Copenhaver joined the Andersons in Memphis for a trip to visit Randolph Copenhaver at Kelly Field in San Antonio, Texas.

16. Thomas Zechariah ("Tom Mooney") was confined to San Quentin for more than twenty years after being convicted of murder in 1917. "Free Tom Mooney" became one of the liberal rallying cries of the 1930s. He was visited at San Quentin by Anderson, Dreiser, and other authors. Anderson's piece appeared in his Memoirs as "You Be the American Zola."

17. Rascoe and Hecht, both newspapermen, were friends of Anderson in his early Chicago days. Anderson is writing for his Memoirs.

18. Mary Emmett and her friend Winona Allen, who would travel with the Andersons into Mexico.

19. Painter and photographer who lived near New Iberia, Louisiana. When Anderson and Eleanor visited Hall in his restored antebellum home in 1935, Eleanor thought him "the weirdest person I ever saw." The section of Anderson's memoirs dealing with Hall is fragmentary.

20. As many as ten thousand workers, mostly Mexicans, were being exploited in the sixty pecan nut shelling plants in San Antonio. Julius Seligman was president of the National Pecan Shellers of America. Later in 1938 Seligman and other plant owners screamed loudly when the Fair Labor Standards law was passed, mandating a twenty-five cent per hour minimum wage nationally.

21. The Andersons were probably at San Luis Potosi.

22. Diego Rivera, noted Mexican painter and muralist. Eleanor noted on February 27 that "Sherwood [is] so sick of constant boosting of Rivera he won't look at a mural."

23. Anderson was writing about his older sister Stella (d. 1917) for his Memoirs.

24. For the Memoirs.

25. Lena Strackbein.

26. Betty Kirk and Lena Strackbein, newspaperwomen in Mexico City.

27. Emily Barksdale was an educator and author who published a novel, Stella Hope, in 1907. The Spanish couple was Manuel del Castillo Negrete and his wife.

28. Tepoztlán, just south of Mexico City.

29. Prominent newspaper editor from Raleigh, North Carolina, who had been secretary of the navy under President Wilson and who served as FDR's ambassador to Mexico from 1933 to 1941.

30. Marjorie Griesser, who in later years worked for the Viking Press.

31. J. V. Noel and his family.

32. Eric Reuhle, according to Eleanor's diary.

33. Arthur Barton had collaborated with Anderson on a dramatic version of Winesburg,

Ohio in 1933. Although Anderson had decided fairly early in the relationship that he wanted nothing more to do with Barton, he was trapped by a contract he had signed, agreeing to share royalties. The "Barton mess" continued to cause trouble for Eleanor long after Anderson's death.

34. Well-known Polish-born dancer.

35. Published in *Household Magazine*, August 1939, pp. 4–5.

36. William Spratling, a prosperous silversmith from Taxco, had been a young professor of architecture at Tulane when Anderson first knew him in New Orleans in the mid-1920s. Spratling and William Faulkner had produced in 1926 a satire on the New Orleans literary community called *Sherwood Anderson and Other Famous Creoles*. In 1938, Elizabeth Prall, Anderson's third wife, had long been living in Spratling's house, a fact which caused Anderson to decline Spratling's invitation to visit Taxco. Spratling discusses this chance Acapulco meeting with Anderson in *File on Spratling* (1967), his autobiography.

37. Lázaro Cárdenas, president of Mexico, 1934 to 1940, had just expropriated foreign-owned oil companies.

38. *Bringing Up Baby*, with Katharine Hepburn.

39. The story "sent off" was not "Mexican Night," which Anderson continued to work on (see March 29). The one "sent off" is apparently referred to by Eleanor in her diary when she says (March 27): "Sherwood wrote thing for *Nation* on Fascism which I tried to get him not to send."

40. "An Impression of Mexico—Its People" was published in *Southern Literary Messenger*, April 1939, pp. 241–42.

41. Robert M. Coates, *The Outlaw Years* (1930), a history of the Natchez Trace pirates.

42. Eleanor left to attend the National Convention of the YWCA in Columbus, Ohio.

43. By Evan Shipman (1935).

44. In mid-1938, Eleanor would become head of the Industrial Section of the National YWCA.

45. Mrs. Copenhaver was going to Warrenton, in northern Virginia, taking rugs from her crafts business to a show there. John Anderson was driving her and her husband to the show.

46. Southwestern State Hospital has been located in Marion since 1887. Dr. Joseph R. Blalock had become superintendent on February 1, 1938, replacing Dr. George A. Wright, who had resigned as of December 1, 1937.

47. Moses E. Sparks was fined by Justice William Birchfield because, according to the *Smyth County News*, "some 14 otherwise sound Marion citizens gave up some $6 each for a few knick-knacks."

48. Carnegie High School, founded in 1931, was the first black high school in the Marion area. Anderson had spoken at the dedication of the school on November 6, 1931. Located on Iron Street in Marion, the school was closed in 1965 because of integration.

49. Henry Armstrong took the welterweight title from Barney Ross.

50. Small town in the southern part of Wythe County, which is east of Smyth County and northeast of Grayson.

51. Previously the only access to this room was from the kitchen; the new door was put in so that the room wouldn't seem like "servant's quarters" when used for guests like Mary Emmett.

52. Anderson by this time had pretty much abandoned at a "half done" stage his enthusiasm of the previous summer, a novel called *How Green the Grass*. At this point he begins another novel, *A Late Spring*, which he worked on during the summer of 1938, but also

eventually abandoned. Both books survive only as fat stacks of holograph manuscript in the Anderson Collection at the Newberry Library.

53. A farewell dinner for Joe H. Wyse, the resident highway engineer for Smyth and Grayson counties since 1933, who was being transferred to Bedford County (see June 18).

54. A passage of twelve words is here omitted.

55. Eleanor's birthday was June 15, not June 14 as implied by this entry.

56. The Mathieson Alkali Works.

57. Annetta Dieckmann of the Chicago office of the YWCA.

58. As usual in late June, Eleanor went to the Conference of Southern Industrial Girls at Camp Merrie-Woode, Sapphire, North Carolina.

59. Joe Louis successfully defended his heavyweight title against Max Schmeling at Yankee Stadium. Anderson, as usual, went to Orlie Stamper's garage in Troutdale to listen to the fight on the radio.

60. Jack Scherer was Eleanor's cousin.

61. Both Laurel Creek and Fox Creek are near Ripshin.

62. On the phonograph.

63. Anderson accompanied Eleanor to the Okoboji Business and Industrial Girls Conference, at the YWCA Camp, Milford, Iowa.

64. Then a popular dance band leader.

65. Warren Nelson, teacher of labor problems, School for Workers in Industry, University of Wisconsin.

66. W. A. Steele, of the Owensboro Ditcher and Grader Company, Owensboro, Kentucky. Anderson had earlier handled Steele's advertising program for many years.

67. Eleanor accepted the position of head of the National Industrial Division of the YWCA. Earlier she had been working at what amounted to one-half time, allowing her time for extended travel or vacations with Anderson, such as the winter trips to the Southwest or the summers at Ripshin. Anderson was highly dependent on being with Eleanor during these years; and his sadness here is prophetic of the drastically reduced amount of time she had to spend with him during the remainder of his life.

68. *A Late Spring.*

69. Jonathan Daniels was the son of Josephus Daniels, ambassador to Mexico. He was his father's successor as editor of the Raleigh, N.C., *News and Observer* and also served the Roosevelt administration in various capacities, including presidential press secretary. Anderson was reading his *Southerner Discovers the South* (1938).

70. At Ohio University in Athens, Ohio. She submitted her thesis, "An Inquiry into the Life of Sherwood Anderson as Reflected in His Literary Works," in 1939.

71. William C. Stewart had been managing editor of *Today*, for which Anderson had written several articles in 1934. In 1938, he was working for the McNaught Syndicate.

72. Melvin Solve, head of the English Department at the University of Arizona, and his wife Norma.

73. A passage of five words is here omitted.

74. The story which, after expansion and revision, was published as "Pastoral" in *Redbook*, January 1940, pp. 38–39, 59. In progress of writing and revision the story had three different titles: "The Writer"; "The Most Unforgettable Character I Have Ever Known (He Was A Letter Writer)"; and "Pastoral."

75. Marietta ("Bab") Finley, in 1938 Mrs. Vernon Hahn, had been a reader for the Bobbs-Merrill Company in Indianapolis and one of Anderson's closest friends and most frequent correspondents in the period before 1920. She had provided substantial financial

assistance to support his children while they were growing up. Marvin Copenhaver was associated with Vance Hardware Stores, which had several branches in the region, including one in Marion.

76. Mrs. Betty S. Anderson, a neighbor.

77. A father-daughter-suitor problem.

78. See the letter to George Freitag in *Letters*, ed. Jones and Rideout, pp. 403-7. Eleanor wrote in her diary for August 18, 1938, "Sherwood came up from his cabin this morning wistful and in a glow. Why couldn't everything like this last so perfectly? He was working well, liked the people, etc.—but of course everything has to end. Why can't we hold the now?"

79. During the last two and one-half years of his life, Anderson tinkered off and on with the notion of producing, from his own writings and his own experience, a kind of "text-book" which would be of help to younger writers. The plan was never far advanced. The fragments of the project left at the time of his death have been edited and published by Sister Martha M. Curry, in *The "Writer's Book" by Sherwood Anderson* (Metuchen, New Jersey: Scarecrow Press, Inc., 1975).

80. J. M. Flanagan, new resident highway engineer for Smyth and Grayson counties, who had replaced Joe H. Wyse, a particular friend of Anderson, on July 1 (see entries for June 8 and 18).

81. Edgar P. Copenhaver, a brother of Bascom E. Copenhaver, lived at Rural Retreat in Wythe County.

82. Not further identified.

83. Young writer (*The Outward Room* [1937]), who later taught literature at New York University.

84. Anderson had changed the working title of his *Late Spring* project to "Men and their Women" and had changed the form to a "series of tales," modeled on *Winesburg, Ohio*.

85. Mrs. Copenhaver employed women in the area to make quilts, rugs, canopies, etc., for Rosemont Crafts Industries, a business she ran out of her home in Marion.

86. Mrs. Charles P. Greer, a Troutdale neighbor, died September 6 in Homeland Hospital, following surgery.

87. See August 27, 1936, for mention of "young" Nick Carter's father, Nick Carter, Sr.

88. "Book III," or the third story in the "series of tales" in *Men and Their Women*, was to include the characters Sidney and Henry Bollinger (see entry for September 25). The section is fragmentary and apparently represents Anderson's final attempt to work on *Men and Their Women*.

89. Fries, in Grayson County, is a textile milling town. Fries' Textile Plant and the surrounding company town were established around 1900 by Col. F. H. Fries.

90. Eleanor wrote on September 26 that "Sherwood [is] very blue—says he thinks it's the fall when he remembers each year his father going off and leaving his mother with no money for food or anything."

91. See entry and note for March 4, 1938.

92. St. John Ervine's play, actually titled *The First Mrs. Fraser*, had opened at Hedgerow on September 12, 1938.

93. Drama by Walter Harlan, which would have its American premiere at Hedgerow on March 2, 1939.

94. At the Mercury Theatre.

95. Thomas Wolfe had died on September 15.

96. Margaret Marshall, literary editor of *The Nation*.

97. Drama by Leslie and Sewell Stokes, at the Fulton Theatre with Robert Morley.

98. See entry and note for January 14, 1936.

99. Drama by Clare Boothe, at Henry Miller's Theatre, 124 West Forty-third Street.

100. Picture based on the book *Memoirs of a Cheat*, by Sacha Guitry, at the Fifth Avenue Playhouse, 66 Fifth Avenue.

101. A farewell party for Dreiser, who moved from New York to Los Angeles on November 25.

102. Lucile Swan and her former husband Jerome Blum, both artists, had been very close friends of Anderson and Tennessee Mitchell in the period around 1920. For Edward Dahlberg, see entry and note for December 9, 1937. Charles Olson was a young poet and critic, later influential theorist of poetry (*Projective Verse* [1950]). Dahlberg was a great admirer of Anderson's work and presented to him on this date a copy of *Bottom Dogs* (1930) with a long adulatory inscription. The Margarita Restaurant was at 116 East Fifty-ninth Street.

103. Iowa-born novelist, whose *Long Remember*, about the Battle of Gettysburg, was published in 1934.

104. Auction held annually by the Fasig-Tipton Company at Squadron "A" Armory, Ninety-fourth Street and Madison Avenue. Anderson had also attended on November 24 and 25, 1937.

105. Eleanor's YWCA friend.

106. A passage of three words is here omitted.

107. "W. F." may be Waldo Frank or William Faulkner, but the reference is obscure. In spite of Anderson's enthusiasm here for his "new theme," late 1938 was one of his lowest and most discouraging periods.

108. Drama by Lucy D. Kennedy, which had its world premiere at Hedgerow on May 16, 1938.

109. At the home of Mazie and Channing Wilson.

110. At 211 West Tenth Street. Earlier in 1938, Mrs. Angel had introduced herself by letter and sought Anderson's support for unrestricted Jewish immigration.

111. New York Gallery at 509 Madison Avenue, maintained by Alfred Stieglitz from 1929 to 1946 for the showing of modern American artists and photographers.

112. "Cruch" is Joseph Wood Krutch, for many years a drama critic for *The Nation*.

113. Drama by Robert Sherwood, *Abe Lincoln in Illinois*, at the Plymouth Theatre with Raymond Massey.

114. Betty Anderson had been formerly an associate of Eleanor's in the YWCA.

115. In 1938, Anderson had been gathering photographs of several of his friends to hang in a bedroom at Ripshin. He obtained a photograph of Stieglitz by Dorothy Norman.

116. Long-time managing editor of *The New Republic*.

117. Frank Fallon, a Roanoke florist, was a friend of Anderson.

118. Anderson's friend suffered from serious asthma.

119. Dr. Willis Sprinkle, son of Dr. O. C. Sprinkle, lived on Park Street. See entry and note for August 27, 1936.

120. Helen Stallings was the wife of playwright Laurence Stallings, of Yanceyville, North Carolina. D. Cohn is possibly David L. Cohn, Southern-born cultural journalist-historian.

Notes to 1939

1. Douty, a representative of the Textile Workers Organizing Committee, wanted to ask Anderson's advice about establishing a pro-union newspaper at Front Royal, Virginia, where the American Viscose Corporation was planning to open a new plant.

2. A high school teacher in Springfield, Ohio, at the time Anderson attended Wittenberg Academy (1899–1900). He once described her as "the first person to really introduce me to literature." She actually outlived Anderson and died on May 8, 1941.

3. Clyde grocer, boyhood friend of Anderson.

4. Dale Carnegie, *How to Win Friends and Influence People* (1936).

5. Anderson was to be "Resident Lecturer in Creative Literature" at Olivet College during January 1939, a chair earlier held by Ford Madox Ford. Joseph Brewer, Olivet's progressive president from 1934 to 1944, introduced experimental methods and many cultural activities to what had been earlier a traditional school with strong religious emphasis.

6. Robert G. Ramsay was registrar and dean of men at Olivet; Glenn Gosling and Charles E. Parkinson taught English and biology, respectively.

7. George Rickey, then a young painter on the Olivet faculty, later an important sculptor.

8. Davis Baker, business manager of Olivet College, and his wife Helen ("Penny") Baker.

9. Muriel E. Smith.

10. Anderson's address, "A Writer's Conception of Realism," was published as a pamphlet by Olivet College in 1939 and reprinted in *The Sherwood Anderson Reader*, ed. Paul Rosenfeld (Boston: Houghton Mifflin Company, 1947), pp. 337–47.

11. Carrow DeVries was a young writer from Wyandotte, Michigan, who worked as a policeman. He had first approached Anderson by correspondence in 1935. Virginia M. Shull and Alice Armfield taught English and modern languages, respectively, at Olivet.

12. "Joe's Boys" was the name of a house on Main Street in Olivet, rented by Glenn Gosling, Charles Parkinson, and George Rickey.

13. Frank D. Fitzgerald was governor of Michigan from 1935 to 1937, and again after January 1, 1939, until his death on March 16, 1939.

14. Anderson's sojourn at Olivet College proved to be very pleasant and restorative; and he returned several times in the remaining two years of his life. The experience also gave him the idea that a "solution" for him might be to attach himself to such a college for seven or eight months of each year.

15. Dr. John Philip Schneider was a longtime professor of English at Wittenberg. Sergius Vernet was research engineer of the Antioch Industrial Research Institute.

16. Dr. Manmatha N. Chatterjee, professor of social science at Antioch.

17. Young muralist on the faculty at Antioch College. He had corresponded with Anderson since 1933.

18. Highly popular musical revue produced by garment workers of Labor Stage, Inc., 106 West Thirty-ninth Street, already in its second year. Anderson went again to see the revue on October 12, 1939, and on May 1, 1940.

19. Cournos' name does not appear on anything which could be called a "Belmont book." But since he was hard up and doing hack work, he may have been employed by Columbia University Press to rewrite the memoirs of ninety-year-old former U.S. Congressman Perry Belmont, which appeared in 1940 as *An American Democrat: The Recollections of Perry Belmont.*

20. Prominent playwright (*The Adding Machine* [1923]; *Street Scene* [1929]) and New York regional director of the Federal Theatre Project.

21. Early 1920, while working on *Poor White* and trying his hand at painting.

22. Dr. Marion Souschon, a prominent surgeon with an office in the Whitney Bank Building, had taken up painting only five years earlier.

23. Phoebe Sours was assistant registrar, Fred Witkop alumni secretary, and Laura Marshall instructor in physical education, all at Olivet College.

24. "I Live A Dozen Lives" in October 1939 issue, p. 58.

25. Banker, businessman, prominent citizen.

26. Not identified.

27. Steve Coombs was a young man whom Anderson had met in Camden, Ohio, in 1934. Coombs had written recently to Anderson seeking advice about personal problems. J. R. Collins was assistant cashier of the Bank of Marion.

28. Phyllis Steele Hill, daughter of Anderson's old advertising client W. A. Steele of Owensboro, Kentucky. She had met Anderson in 1921 in Owensboro. In 1939 as Mrs. Fred Clark Hill of Chicago, she was seeking Anderson's criticism of her writing efforts.

29. On the editorial sold to *American Magazine*, see entry and note for March 25, 1939. "The Letter Writer" is the story published as "Pastoral" in *Redbook*, January 1940, pp. 38–39, 59. See entry and note for August 5, 1938. The $1500 "offer" for the story was, however, from *Reader's Digest*, not *Redbook*.

30. Charles Glenn was Frank Copenhaver's partner in operating the local Piggly Wiggly grocery store. The visitor, who admired Anderson's work and wanted to meet him, was from the headquarters of Piggly Wiggly in Atlanta.

31. Anderson was worried because he had been approached by a man from the Department of Justice about the nature of his connection with the World Committee Against War and Fascism, an organization headed by Henri Barbusse and Romain Rolland. Anderson's name appeared on the organization's letterhead as a member of its executive committee, although he does not seem to have participated in, or even to have understood, the activities of the organization.

32. The New School for Social Research (founded 1919), at 66 West Twelfth Street.

33. At the Forrest Theatre, 226 West Forty-ninth Street, starring Eddie Garr. This dramatization of Erskine Caldwell's novel by Jack Kirkland enjoyed one of the longest Broadway runs of all time; in 1939 it was in its sixth year of production.

34. Henry T. Volkening, of Russell and Volkening, Inc., Literary Agents, 522 Fifth Avenue, who had taught English with Wolfe at New York University. On April 8, 1939, Anderson had written Volkening a letter about an article on Wolfe the latter had published in the *Virginia Quarterly Review*.

35. Luise Sillcox was executive secretary of the Authors' League of America, Inc. Jules Romains was a prominent French novelist, poet, and playwright. The Downtown Gallery was at 113 West Thirteenth Street. "Les Amis de William Carlos Williams" was a literary society founded by Ford Madox Ford in early 1939. Anderson described his annoyance with the occasion in a letter to Cummings the next day. See *Selected Letters*, ed. Modlin, pp. 231–32.

36. Novelist (*The Daughter* [1938]) and wife of the painter Henry Varnum Poor.

37. Anna Brooks, Mary Emmett's recently employed maid.

38. Horace Kallen was a German-born professor at the New School for Social Research and author of many books of liberal and idealistic social commentary. Gene's Restaurant, at 71 West Eleventh Street, was near the New School for Social Research.

39. Juan Negrin.

40. Rose Butler, YWCA associate of Eleanor's. They dined at Chez Victor Restaurant, 305 East Fifty-seventh Street.

41. Tallulah Bankhead in Lillian Hellman's *Little Foxes*, at the National Theatre, 208 West Forty-first Street.

42. Anderson had earlier met and liked George L. Ridgeway and his wife at Wells College. Anderson had been invited to speak at Wells by J. J. Lankes, his friend the Virginia woodcut artist, then on the Wells faculty.

43. Bascom E. Copenhaver, Eleanor's father, visited to attend the World's Fair.

44. Alice and Eddy Wolf lived at Melfa, Virginia.

45. Author, who wrote using the pseudonym "Henrie Waste" (*Philosophy: An Auto-biographical Fragment* [1917], *Love Days* [1923]); sister of the painter Florine Stettheimer.

46. María Luisa Bombal, Chilean writer, published "En Nueva York con Sherwood Anderson" in *La Nacion*, October 8, 1939, p. 3. The newspaper man from Puerto Rico was R. Torres-Mazzoranna.

47. Norman and Rebecca Treves, of 170 East Seventy-eighth Street. See entry and note for May 20, 1937.

48. Brokerage House at 120 Broadway.

49. Anna Brooks and Miss Keener were both domestic helpers at 54 Washington Mews.

50. Fairs were held in lower Manhattan June 28 to 30, 1938, and June 13 to 18, 1939, by the North American Committee to Aid Spanish Democracy. Anderson published "The Fair" in the *Second Annual Village Fair Almanac*.

51. Author from Salto, Uruguay.

52. See entry and note for May 24. At this time Anderson met several Central and South American writers, who were in New York for the World's Fair.

53. *The Hot Mikado*, a "Negro version" of the popular Gilbert and Sullivan operetta, with Bill (Bojangles) Robinson, at the Broadhurst Theatre.

54. Margaret Forsyth and Dorothy McConnell, daughter of Methodist Bishop Francis J. McConnell, were officers of the YWCA.

55. The Brass Antique Shoppe, 32 Allen Street.

56. From Santiago, Chile; former president of Chile and in 1939 director of Editors' Press Service, 220 East Forty-second Street, New York.

57. Mrs. M. C. Migel of 71 East Seventy-first Street; her country home was in Monroe, New York.

58. The Blue Bowl Restaurant at 157 East Forty-eighth Street.

59. One of Anderson's several unpublished manuscripts about the character Talbot Whittingham.

60. A man named Tom Safford, from Hollywood, came to Washington Mews looking for another Emmett family, stayed on to talk with Anderson.

61. Movie based on Franz Werfel's play *Juarez and Maximilian* and Bertha Harding's book *The Phantom Crown*, at the Hollywood Theatre, with Paul Muni and Bette Davis.

62. An exhibition and sale of paintings and sculpture by black artists at the Salon of Contemporary Art, 143 West 125th Street. Richard Bennett was a stage and film actor, and father of three well-known film actresses: Constance, Barbara, and Joan Bennett.

63. "Father and Son," based on Anderson's memories of his father Irwin Anderson, was published in *Reader's Digest*, November 1939, pp. 21–25, as "Discovery of a Father." While in process, the story also had the titles "Unforgotten" and "A Certain Night."

64. *Out of the South* (1939), which Green had recently sent Anderson as a gift.

65. Anderson took a number of his books from Ripshin as a kind of lending library to the Southern Industrial Girls conference at Sapphire, North Carolina, to which he accompanied Eleanor (June 21 to 29).

66. Professor of economics at Amherst College and founder of the Consumer's Union.

67. Joe Louis and Tony Galento fought in Yankee Stadium.

68. Of the Children's Bureau, U.S. Department of Labor.

69. In a letter, Anderson described Burnham as "an old friend . . . some twenty years older than I." Not further identified.

70. Anderson had returned for the Olivet Writers' Conference (July 16 to 29). In addition to Anderson, the 1939 Conference Staff included John Peale Bishop, Padraic and Mary Colum, Karl Detzer, literary agent Nannine Joseph, Katherine Anne Porter, Carl Sandburg (who failed to appear), and scenario writer Hagar Wilde. Anderson refers to a memorial service for Ford Madox Ford, who had participated in previous Olivet conferences.

71. Parliaments were "joint discussions between staff members and Conference members on questions of general interest."

72. Anderson means *Reader's Digest*, which published "Discovery of a Father" in November 1939.

73. Anderson read the tribute to Dreiser from *Horses and Men*, "Man in the Brown Coat" from *Triumph of the Egg*, and "Tandy" from *Winesburg, Ohio*.

74. Critic Edmund Wilson and wife, who were spending a weekend in Chicago. This gathering was at Schevill's place, not "at Sergels."

75. Ferdinand Schevill had presented Anderson with cloth to have a suit tailored. "Parky" is Charles E. Parkinson, whom Anderson had met at Olivet in January.

76. Stephanie Kratovil was from Chicago; she later wrote Anderson to apologize for starting a fire in his car with cigarette ashes. See next entry. Anderson refers metaphorically to Detzer's lecture on Wednesday evening.

77. Anderson wrote to several of his correspondents in the summer of 1939 that he was now deliberately "devoting" himself to short stories.

78. The $1500 mentioned in entry for July 19, minus agent's commission.

79. Virginia Thomas, Greear's fiancée; later his wife.

80. Davis Baker and his wife Helen ("Penny"), like Glenn Gosling, were friends of Anderson from Olivet Collge.

81. Daughters of the Reverend J.J. Scherer, brother of Laura Lu Copenhaver.

82. Nearby towns in southwest Virginia.

83. Mr. and Mrs. Roy Lancaster from Allison's Gap, Virginia.

84. Colonel (later Major General) Guy Blair Denit was a surgeon in the U.S. Army; his wife Virginia was the daughter of B. Frank Buchanan, Marion native who had served as lieutenant governor of Virginia from 1918 to 1922.

85. A reference to U.S. Senator Harry F. Byrd, head of the Democratic "machine" in Virginia politics.

86. "Fred Griffith's World," the "dream story" mentioned on August 24 and 25, was sent to Jacques Chambrun, the literary agent, on September 2.

87. John Cronk was Eleanor's first cousin, whom Anderson did not like.

88. Whom Anderson had met at Olivet College in January.

89. Anderson had talked to Glenn Gosling about a possible collaboration on the "Writer's Book" project. See entry and note for August 21, 1938.

90. Town on the line between Grayson and Carroll counties in southwest Virginia.

91. Hitler launched his attack on Poland on September 1; Great Britain and France declared war on Germany two days later.

92. Stanley Young, an editor at Harcourt, Brace and Company and principal in-house editor for the posthumously published *Memoirs* (1942).

93. Anderson was preparing to speak at Roanoke College in Salem, Virginia; and at Princeton, not Cornell.

94. Centeno, Princeton professor, had translated Anderson's *Dark Laughter* into Spanish in 1931.

95. Published as "Here They Come," in *Esquire*, March 1940, pp. 80–81. While working

on the piece, Anderson attended the trotting races at Lexington, Kentucky, September 25 to 29, 1939.

96. Satirical cartoonist for liberal and radical publications; Young had been on the staff of *Masses* when Anderson first knew him in Chicago.

97. Anderson had been invited to address a convocation opening the academic year at Roanoke College. Author Pendleton Hogan, who was present, wrote a lengthy account of the occasion for *Winesburg Eagle* 5, no. 2 (April 1980), pp. 1–4; 6, no. 1 (November 1980), pp. 1–5.

98. Joe Louis defeated Bob Pastor in Detroit.

99. Published in the *Saturday Review of Literature*, December 9, 1939, pp. 13–14.

100. Pleasant Hill, revived as a conference center in recent years.

101. Dave and Hanley Bohon, who had run a prosperous mail order business from Harrodsburg.

102. "Sherwood Anderson, Writer-Railbird, Offers Study in Incongruity As He Follows Fall Trots," *Lexington Leader*, September 28, 1939, pp. 1–2.

103. Literary agent Jacques Chambrun had recently written Anderson, requesting material which would be suitable for *This Week*, the Sunday magazine section of the *New York Herald-Tribune*. *This Week* magazine was edited by Mrs. William Brown Meloney.

104. Including "Here They Come," the piece on trotting horses for *Esquire*.

105. Adele Day, of Hollywood, was an admirer of Anderson's writing.

106. Anderson sent "Why Not Oak Hill?" to his agent on October 6; it was published in *This Week* with the title "From Little Things" on February 11, 1940, p. 2, and republished as the first section of *Home Town* (1940).

107. Mrs. Emmett was consulting a Dr. Locke in Williamsburg, Ontario, Canada.

108. "So You Want to Be a Writer" sold to the *Saturday Review of Literature*. See entry and note for September 25, 1939.

109. See entry and note for February 8, 1939.

110. Prominent critic and interpreter of broad social and cultural issues (*Technics and Civilization* [1934], *The Culture of Cities* [1938]).

111. Mrs. Untermeyer remembers this occasion in her autobiography, *Private Collection* (1965).

112. Maurice R. Werner lived at 1245 Madison Avenue. "Cummings" is presumably E. E. Cummings.

113. Tony's Restaurant had locations at 57 West Fifty-second Street and at 112 East Fifty-second Street.

114. Stewart's Cafeterias had several locations in New York.

115. Anderson spoke on "Man and His Imagination" under the auspices of the Spencer Trask lectures at Princeton.

116. Morrow was Anderson's close friend and associate when both worked in Chicago advertising agencies. In 1939, Morrow was with Capper Publications in Topeka. Roger Baldwin was director of the American Civil Liberties Union.

117. Judge George A. Bartlett had granted Anderson his divorce from Tennessee Mitchell in Reno in 1924. Margaret ("Monte") and Dorothy were the judge's daughters. Caples was a friend from Anderson's days in Reno, 1923 to 1924.

118. Brownie Lee Jones and Helen Bridge, executives in the San Francisco branch of the YWCA. Anderson accompanied Eleanor to California for an extended tour in her capacity as head of the industrial section of the YWCA. She was featured at the fourth annual North-

ern California industrial Week-end Conference sponsored by the San Francisco YWCA on November 11 and 12.

119. Partner with Theodore Lilienthal in the San Francisco bookstore, Gelber, Lilienthal, Inc., which had published Anderson's *Modern Writer* in 1925.

120. "Why Not Oak Hill," retitled "From Little Things" when it was published February 11, 1940.

121. Holger Cahill.

122. Not identified.

123. See "Sherwood Anderson—Interviewed: From Him, Many Laughs; But Little Information," by Stanton Delaplane, *San Francisco Chronicle*, Sunday, November 12, 1939, p. 6.

124. Published as "Backstage with A Martyr," *Coronet*, July 1940, pp. 39–41.

125. Of the *San Francisco Chronicle*.

126. Relatives of Eleanor's mother, Laura Lu Scherer Copenhaver.

127. Also of the *Chronicle*.

128. The Bohemian Club was, and is, an organization of politically conservative businessmen.

129. Dr. Lin Yutang, popular Chinese-born philosopher, lecturer, and author. One of his popular books was *The Importance of Living* (1937).

130. Radical author (*Red Virtue: Human Relationships in the New Russia* [1933]).

131. "San Francisco At Christmas," published in "This World" section of the *Chronicle*, Sunday, December 24, 1939, p. 19.

132. The Andersons dined with Carrie Church, secretary at the Fresno YWCA, at the Paris Cafe in West Fresno.

133. Author (*Gentlemen Prefer Blondes* [1925]), playwright, screenwriter; wife of producer John Emerson, who as Clifton Paden had been a fellow Clyde, Ohio, resident and boyhood friend of Anderson.

134. Not further identified.

135. Published posthumously in *Yale Review*, Summer 1941, pp. 750–58.

136. Another daughter of Judge George A. Bartlett of Reno.

137. For John Emerson, see entry and note for November 3, 1936; in 1939, Emerson had succumbed to a manic-depressive illness and was confined to a sanitarium. A section of Anderson's *Memoirs* (1942) dealing with Emerson is titled "Money! Money!" (pp. 113–19).

138. "Man and His Imagination" was published in *The Intent of the Artist*, ed. Augusto Centeno (Princeton: Princeton University Press, 1941), pp. 39–79.

139. Paddy Walsh and Melvin Solve were professors at the University of Arizona. See entries for February and early March, 1936, which Anderson spent in Tucson.

140. Clifford and Helen Dowdey.

141. Anderson had talked with Aldous Huxley in Los Angeles, where the latter was working as a screenwriter. Anderson thought Huxley hypocritical for satirizing the same industry that paid him a large salary.

142. Sophie Chantal Hart, who had taught English at Wellesley College from 1892 to 1937, lived in retirement in Tucson, where she served on the Executive Board of the local YWCA.

143. Randolph Copenhaver.

144. Published as "Maury Maverick in San Antonio," *New Republic*, March 25, 1940, pp. 398–400.

145. A Paramount production, U.S. Army versus the Indians, with Preston Foster, Ellen Drew, and Andy Devine.

146. Lois Cook of San Benito, Texas, who married Randolph Copenhaver in 1940.

147. The Andersons couldn't spend the winter in the Southwest, as they had from 1935 to 1938, because of Eleanor's heavy job responsibilites in New York.

148. See entry and note for July 3, 1940.

149. Published in *Memoirs* (1942) with the sub-title, "Taking Eleanor to the Room Where I Wrote *Winesburg*" (pp. 277–80).

Notes to 1940

1. Published posthumously in *Decision*, August 1941, pp. 8–15.

2. The prominent Glass family of Lynchburg owned both the *Daily News* (morning) and the *Daily Advance* (afternoon). Carter Glass served in the U.S. Senate from 1924 until his death in 1946.

3. Rosskam edited Anderson's *Home Town* (1940) for Alliance Book Corporation; Stryker was chief, Historical Section, Division of Information, of the Farm Security Administration, which supplied the photographs for *Home Town*.

4. See pp. 336–40 in the original Huebsch edition (1924). See also Charles E. Modlin, "'In a Field': A Story from *A Story Teller's Story*," *Winesburg Eagle* 8, no. 2 (April 1983): 3–6.

5. John Rogers, Jr., at 16 East Eleventh Street.

6. Drama written by Clare Boothe, at the Plymouth Theatre, 236 West Forty-fifth Street.

7. Mr. and Mrs. Sanford Wendel of Los Angeles.

8. Playwright who lived at 419 East Fifty-seventh Street, author of *A Proud Woman* (1927), *Heavy Traffic* (1928), *The Season Changes* (1936), and other plays.

9. The National Institute of Arts and Letters.

10. Of the English department.

11. "Legacies of Ford Madox Ford," published in *Coronet*, August 1940, pp. 135–36.

12. At the Music Box, 239 West Forty-fifth Street.

13. A section of Anderson's *Memoirs* dealing with John Emerson, called "Money! Money!" when the book was published posthumously in 1942. See diary entry for December 3, 1939.

14. Konrad Bercovici, the Rumanian writer, wrote stories of European gypsy life and of life in New York on the Jewish East Side and in other "foreign" quarters of the city. Robert Nathan was a New York-born novelist, prolific author of books of satirical fantasy.

15. Arthur Davison Ficke, Iowa-born poet, whom Anderson had first known in Chicago in the period before 1920.

16. Henry Armstrong retained his welterweight title by knocking out Pedro Montanez in the ninth round at Madison Square Garden.

17. Henry G. Koppell, head of Alliance Book Corporation, which published Anderson's *Home Town*.

18. The Marshall Restaurant at 70 Lafayette Street.

19. For *Home Town*.

20. In an address book from this period, Anderson wrote, "Winesburg play. Hamilton. 1430 Broadway." Not further identified.

21. A popular film which had been running for five months at the World Theatre, 153 West Forty-ninth Street.

22. A Farm Security Administration photographer.

23. Aubrey Williams was head of the National Youth Administration, a WPA project. Mrs. Roosevelt delivered the closing address at a conference called by Williams, "to consider the special problems of unemployed young women," a topic of particular interest to Eleanor Anderson in her YWCA position.

24. Photographer and editor from 1938 to 1948 of *Twice A Year*, a journal of aesthetic and social concerns.

25. The March 11, 1940, issue of *Life*, in a short illustrated feature story on Nathan (pp. 52–54), included a picture of Anderson and Nathan in Club 21.

26. At the Booth Theatre, 222 West Forty-fifth Street, with Eddie Dowling and Julie Haydon.

27. Benjamin Lewis's liquor store at 5985 Broadway.

28. Grosz had lived in the United States since 1933, an expatriate from Hitler's Germany.

29. Satirical novelist, critic, and painter; founder of the vorticist movement in art.

30. Denys Wortman, of 288 West Twelfth Street, a well-known cartoonist for the *New York World Telegram and Sun* and United Features Syndicated Papers in the 1930s and later.

31. Polish-born novelist who lived in New York; his books were written in Yiddish or German, and most were translated into English. *The Nazarene* (1939) presents Jesus as the last and greatest Jewish prophet.

32. Lyon Sharman, *Sun Yat-sen, His Life and Meaning: A Critical Biography* (1934).

33. Denis Tilden Lynch, *"Boss" Tweed: The Story of a Grim Generation* (1927).

34. The Hotel Winthrop was at Lexington Avenue and Forty-seventh Street. Mrs. Copenhaver and the Van Meiers were in New York to attend the flower show at New York Botanical Gardens.

35. At 80 West Fortieth Street.

36. Sidney R. Fleischer was an attorney at 220 West Forty-second Street.

37. Philip Moeller, playwright and prominent producer and director for the Theatre Guild, lived at the Hotel Navarro, 112 Central Park South.

38. Easter fell on March 24 in 1940, not March 17.

39. Comedy written by James Thurber and Elliott Nugent, at the Cort Theatre, 138 West Forty-eighth Street.

40. At 2107 Broadway.

41. For Anderson's earlier contacts with Isabel de Palencia, see diary entries and notes for November 22 and 24, 1936.

42. At the Hudson Theatre, 141 West Forty-fourth Street.

43. An organization of newspapermen who had been foreign correspondents. Anderson spoke on country newspapers.

44. Bessie Beatty, secretary to PEN Club, American center, had written Anderson on March 8 that Robert Nathan, new president of PEN, was inviting Anderson as a guest to dinner at the Algonquin on March 28 at 7:30.

45. See entry and note for July 24, 1938.

46. Ferenc Molnar's play, at the Forty-fourth Street Theater, 224 West Forty-fourth Street, also with Ingrid Bergman and Elia Kazan.

47. Comedy directed by Marcel Pagnol, at the World Cinema.

48. Eugène Jolas was editor of *transition*, the avant-garde literary journal; James Johnson Sweeney was associate editor.

49. Photographer Bourke-White was Caldwell's former wife; they collaborated on several books, such as *You Have Seen Their Faces* (1937). Caldwell was located at the Hotel Pierce, 2 East Sixty-first Street.

50. Apparently the entries for April 5 and April 6 both describe activities for Friday, April 5. Entry for April 7 describes Saturday, April 6. Entry for April 8 catches up two days, Sunday and Monday, April 7 and 8.

51. "We Are All Small-Towners," published June 16, 1940, p. 2.

52. A passage of eleven words is here omitted.

53. The novelist, then living in North Carolina.

54. An Alfred Hitchcock film derived from the novel by Daphne du Maurier, starring Laurence Olivier and Joan Fontaine.

55. T. Edward Hambleton of Stevenson, Maryland.

56. Robert Booth was Mary Emmett's butler.

57. The Commodore Hotel at Lexington Avenue and Forty-second Street.

58. The Game Cock Cafe, 14 East Forty-fourth Street.

59. See entry and note for Febuary 8, 1939.

60. Emily Clark (Mrs. Edwin Swift Balch), author and reviewer, lived at 455 East Fifty-first Street; her best-known book was *Innocence Abroad* (1931). Oliver St. John Gogarty was an Irish-born physician and author (*I Follow St. Patrick* [1938], *Going Native* [1940]).

61. Frederick Jackson Turner, *The Frontier in American History* (1920).

62. Dr. Eugenia Ingerman of 27 Washington Square North.

63. John Rood, from Athens, Ohio, was featured in a show at the Georgette Passedoit Gallery, 22 East Sixtieth Street.

64. This "book" exists only as an eleven page manscript in the Newberry Library Anderson collection.

65. On May 22, Peter Kihss published "Sherwood Anderson Fooled in One of His Protests" in the *New York World Telegram*, p. 7.

66. This program, "Tonight's Best Story," was a Tuesday evening feature on New York station WHN.

67. "The Dance Is On" was not published in *This Week* but by *The Rotarian* in June 1941, after Anderson's death.

68. Croton-on-Hudson, north of New York City in Westchester County.

69. Editor, with Alfred M. Bingham, of the journal *Common Sense*, which had sought contributions from Anderson in the mid-1930s.

70. Wife of Princeton professor Augusto Centeno.

71. Probably Hugh J. Rhyne, Lutheran clergyman and president of Marion College, which was next door to Rosemont, the Copenhaver family home.

72. "Miss Belle" Sprinkle, wife of Dr. O. C. Sprinkle.

73. Hitler's armies had attacked an almost defenseless France on June 5. As the Germans neared Paris, Italy declared war on France and England. The French armies surrendered by June 22, 1940.

74. John Anderson introduced his father to the potter Edwin Scheier and his wife Mary. The Scheiers had built a kiln and started a pottery enterprise at a place called Old Glade, between Marion and Abingdon, Virginia. Anderson liked the Scheiers' work, purchased several pieces, and at one time offered them space for a kiln at Ripshin farm. Scheier later taught at the University of New Hampshire and developed a national reputation.

75. At Crumpler, North Carolina.

76. Dr. J. Hamilton Scherer, of the Medical College of Virginia at Richmond, was the son of Luther Scherer, brother of Laura Lu Copenhaver.

77. Harry M. Daugherty was U.S. attorney general from 1921 to 1924, under Presidents Harding and Coolidge.

78. As in 1939, Anderson was at Olivet College for the Writers' Conference, July 14 to 27. In addition to Anderson, the 1940 conference staff included John Peale Bishop, Padraic and Mary Colum, literary agent Nannine Joseph, Katherine Anne Porter, Carl Sandburg, juvenile fiction writer Leroy W. Snell, playwright John Van Druten, and Robert Penn Warren.

79. Much-published Pennsylvania poet (*Factories with Other Lyrics* [1915], *Ballads and Lyrics* [1925]).

80. Mrs. Marion Judd of Fanwood, New Jersey.

81. Professor of English at the University of Michigan, Ann Arbor.

82. Anderson refers to Archibald MacLeish's controversial article, "Post-war Writers and Pre-war Readers," *New Republic* 102 (June 10, 1940): 789–90.

83. Stanley Young was encouraging Anderson to publish his memoirs with Harcourt Brace.

84. See "A Good Time Was Had by All," *PM's Weekly* 1, No. 8 (August 11, 1940): 40. A review of Henry Beetle Hough's book *Country Editor*. *PM's Weekly* was the weekend supplement to *PM*, a recently established New York daily newspaper; the *PM* referred to in note to March 11, 1937 was a different publication, a slick magazine of the advertising community.

85. Anderson's niece, who for part of the summer of 1934 had worked at Ripshin as his secretary. Dave Greear had made a sculpture of her head.

86. Nathan ("Nat") Dickinson, a brother of Burt, was employed by the Virginia-Lincoln Furniture Corporation of Marion.

87. Published in the revised *Memoirs* (1969) as "I See Grace Again," pp. 294–304.

88. See entry and note for July 3.

89. Greer Williams was living near Sugar Grove for the summer; later in 1940 he was in Washington working for the U.S. Public Health Service.

90. Published in Anderson's *Memoirs* (1942) as "All Will Be Free," pp. 254–58.

91. A passage of six words is here omitted.

92. Anderson's *Memoirs*.

93. Published in *Memoirs* (1942) as "Old Mary, the Dogs, and Theda Bara," pp. 306–14.

94. Published in the revised *Memoirs* (1969), pp. 534–37.

95. James A. ("Doc") Thompson was owner of the City Drugstore in Marion. Will Birchfield was a trial justice in Marion. Billy Vines worked for the Norfolk & Western Railroad. The others, except Stager, are identified in earlier notes.

96. Bruner Sullivan, son of John Sullivan; see entry and note for September 14, 1937.

97. A passage of ten words is here omitted.

98. "Big Fish" was retitled "Stolen Day" when it was published in *This Week*, April 27, 1941, pp. 6, 23.

99. Leona Gross, who worked for Mrs. Copenhaver as housekeeper at Rosemont. Leona's brother Jones Gross, mentioned in the next entry, was gardener and handyman for the Copenhavers.

100. A passage of four words is here omitted.

101. Published as "Truly's Little House" in revised *Memoirs* (1969), pp. 504–7. Trealy G. Walls lived just "up the creek" from Ripshin. Anderson misspelled the name as "Treely," which was further transformed to "Truly" in the printed memoirs.

102. Both Kenneth Snider and Beattie Gwyn were prominent Marion businessmen. Both were at one time in the automobile business; and Gwyn later started Gwyn Distributing Company, a beer-distributing business.

103. B.E.'s brother, at Rural Retreat, Virginia.

104. Dr. M. M. Brown, Marion veterinarian and former mayor of Marion.

105. Eleanor's father would undergo a cataract operation on November 8, 1940.

106. A passage of twenty-one words is here omitted.

107. Anderson spoke at the University of Michigan. Seager's farm was at Onsted, Michigan, in neighboring Lenawee County.

108. Anderson spoke to the Detroit English Club at the Masonic Temple.

109. Comedy by Lawrence Langner and Armina Marshall, at the Morosco Theatre, 217 West Forty-fifth Street.

110. *The Trojan Horse,* by Christopher Morley, at the Millpond Theatre, Roslyn, Long Island.

111. *I Must Have Liberty* (1940).

112. M. Lincoln Schuster, partner in the publishing firm Simon and Schuster.

113. *Cabin in the Sky,* a musical fantasy, from the book by Lynn Root, was at the Martin Beck Theater, 302 West Forty-fifth Street. Miss Dunham, a well-known dancer, was making her acting debut as Georgia Brown in *Cabin in the Sky.*

114. *Charley's Aunt,* farce by Brandon Thomas, at the Cort Theatre, with Jose Ferrer.

115. At the Biltmore Hotel, Madison Avenue and Forty-third Street.

116. A young actress from Portland, Oregon, who had earlier played Louise Trunion in *Winesburg, Ohio* at the Hedgerow Theatre; she was seeking Anderson's help in finding work on the New York stage.

117. Ernestine Evans was a journalist, editor, and author, whom Anderson had first known in Chicago between 1910 and 1920. After 1930 she was for many years an editor at the J. B. Lippincott Company; I cannot identify Ellis Hoffman.

118. As author of the recently published *Home Town.*

119. The National Exhibition Horse Show at Madison Square Garden.

120. Published in *Sherwood Anderson Reader,* ed. Rosenfeld, pp. 846–50.

121. Anderson was studying Spanish to prepare for his planned tour of several South American countries in early 1941.

122. *Moana,* a 1926 Robert J. Flaherty documentary about life in Samoa. Benjamin Brenner was a liberal politician from Brooklyn, a New York State assemblyman, and later a justice on the New York State Supreme Court.

123. A satire on Hitler, at the Astor Theatre, Broadway and Forty-fifth Street.

124. Anderson's book of poems, published by John Lane in 1918 and reprinted by B.W. Huebsch in 1923.

125. Hackett had been editor of the *Friday Literary Review* of the *Chicago Evening Post* before leaving Chicago to become associate editor of the *New Republic* from 1914 to 1922. A prominent reviewer of new American Books, including Anderson's, he was also a biographer and novelist. Eastman's book was *Stalin's Russia* (1940).

126. Edward A. Weeks, editor of the *Atlantic Monthly,* had earlier worked for the Horace Liveright publishing firm. Anderson elsewhere described his radio appearance as "a 15 minute talk about life in American small towns."

127. The Players Clubhouse at 16 Gramercy Park.

128. Littell was associate editor of the *Reader's Digest,* which Anderson hoped would help support his planned trip to South America, in return for articles he would submit to the journal about his experiences.

129. William O. Player, Jr., who published "Sherwood Anderson Hopes—and Wonders" in the *New York Post* on November 27.

130. Both of Harcourt, Brace.

131. See entry and note for November 22.

132. The Savoy-Plaza Hotel, Fifth Avenue and Fifty-ninth Street.

133. M. J. Politis, of National Herald, Inc., 106 West Forty-seventh Street.

134. Justina Van Deusen, referred to in December 6 entry as "Tina," was working for Anderson as a stenographer.

135. H. G. Wells was visiting New York. Isaac Don Levine was a Russian-born journalist and author (*The Russian Revolution* [1917], *Red Snake* [1932]).

136. About a boyhood incident, published in *This Week*, May 18, 1941, pp. 12, 17, as "I Was a Bad Boy"; in *Memoirs* (1942) with title "Experiments"; and in revised *Memoirs* (1969) with title "Significant Days."

137. Prolific regional author from Sauk City, Wisconsin. At this meeting he gave Anderson a copy of his *Country Growth* (1940).

138. Anderson was being tutored in Spanish by Margarita Madrigal of 90 Bank Street.

139. That is, the Editors' Press Service, of which Carlos Davila was director.

140. Florine Stettheimer devoted herself between 1929 and her death in 1944 to four large paintings celebrating New York City: *Cathedrals of Broadway*; *Cathedrals of Fifth Avenue*; *Cathedrals of Wall Street*; *Cathedrals of Art* (unfinished).

141. Alexander Archipenko, Russian-born pioneer modernist sculptor, who had settled in this country in 1923. In late 1940, he had recently moved his studio from Chicago to 624 Madison Avenue, New York City.

142. *A Treasury of the World's Great Letters*, ed. M. Lincoln Schuster (1940).

143. *The Corn is Green*, drama by Emlyn Williams, at the National Theatre, 208 West Forty-first Street.

144. Eleanor's brother Randolph Copenhaver, who was in Alaska.

Notes to 1941

1. Brown, with whom Anderson had been corresponding since October 1940, was attempting to interest movie studios in some of Anderson's books, including *Kit Brandon*.

2. Daughter of Anita Loos's brother Clifford Loos.

3. At the Lyceum Theatre, 149 West Forty-fifth Street.

4. Drama by Howard Lindsay and Russell Crouse, from the book by Clarence Day, at the Empire Theatre, 1430 Broadway.

5. Written by Joseph Kesselring, at the Fulton Theatre on Forty-sixth Street, with Boris Karloff.

6. Playwright, best known for *The Green Pastures* (1930). This was Anderson's first meeting with Connelly.

7. Editor from 1914 to 1935 of *Vanity Fair*, for which Anderson had written extensively in the late 1920s.

8. James Boyd, mentioned in the previous entry, had formed the Free Company to combat foreign propaganda, by having prominent authors write radio plays about basic American freedoms. Plays contributed by Marc Connelly, Paul Green, Robert E. Sherwood, and others were broadcast by the Columbia Broadcasting Company in 1941. Anderson's play, *Above Suspicion*, a play about freedom from police persecution, was not completed before his death. The Free Company (probably Boyd) completed the play. It was broadcast "not . . . as his own work, but as a tribute to his memory." A collection of these plays, including *Above*

Suspicion, was published by Dodd, Mead in 1941 with the title *The Free Company Presents*. . . .

9. While in Tampa, Anderson enjoyed a very pleasant acquaintance with Mary Cortina, who taught Spanish at the University of Tampa, and her husband Joseph Cortina.

10. Louisville is in Georgia, not South Carolina.

11. A. Caprile, Jr., was an Argentinian who worked for the *Reader's Digest*. Editor's Press Service, of which the Chilean Carlos Davila was director, was in the Daily News Building at 220 East Forty-second Street. Edward Cardenas worked for Editor's Press Service.

12. The rights to all Anderson's books published prior to 1925 had belonged to the Viking Press since B. W. Huebsch joined the firm in 1925; in 1941, almost all the books had been long out of print. The transfer of plates, copyrights, etc., to Eleanor Anderson was completed in 1942.

13. Anderson and Eleanor boarded the Santa Lucia at Pier 58 on West Sixteenth Street and occupied Stateroom 41. Their destination was Valparaiso, Chile, via the Panama Canal. Anderson planned to spend three or four months studying and writing about small town life in Chile, the Argentine, and Peru.

14. Editor of *The Nation*; see her article on Anderson's death in *The Nation*, March 22, 1941, pp. 313–14.

15. The end of the diary. According to Eleanor's recollection, Anderson became ill almost immediately and was taken off the ship on March 4 and removed to Gorges Hospital, Panama Canal Zone, where he died at 5:40 p.m. on Saturday, March 8. After several days delay, Eleanor brought his body back to New York on the Santa Clara, another Grace Line ship. She was met in New York on March 24 by Karl Anderson, Paul Rosenfeld, Mary Emmett, Stanley Young, and Roberto Rendueles, all of whom joined her for the overnight train journey back to Marion, arriving March 25. "Aunt May" Scherer had made the arrangements for a funeral at Rosemont, Eleanor's family home; and Anderson was laid to rest in Round Hill Cemetery overlooking the town of Marion on March 26, 1941.

Bibliography

Works by Sherwood Anderson

Windy McPherson's Son. New York: John Lane Company, 1916.
Marching Men. New York: John Lane Company, 1917.
Mid-American Chants. New York: John Lane Company, 1918.
Winesburg, Ohio. New York: B. W. Huebsch, 1919.
Poor White. New York: B. W. Huebsch, 1920.
Triumph of the Egg. New York: B. W. Huebsch, 1921.
Many Marriages. New York: B. W. Huebsch, 1923.
Horses and Men. New York: B. W. Huebsch, 1923.
A Story Teller's Story. New York: B. W. Huebsch, 1924.
Dark Laughter. New York: Boni and Liveright, 1925.
The Modern Writer. San Francisco: Gelber, Lilienthal, 1925.
Sherwood Anderson's Notebook. New York: Boni and Liveright, 1926.
Tar: A Midwest Childhood. New York: Boni and Liveright, 1926.
A New Testament. New York: Boni and Liveright, 1927.
Hello Towns. New York: Horace Liveright, 1929.
Nearer the Grass Roots and Elizabethton. San Francisco: Westgate Press, 1929.
Alice and the Lost Novel. London: Elkin Mathews and Marrot, 1929.
American County Fair. New York: Random House, 1930.
Perhaps Women. New York: Horace Liveright, 1931.
Beyond Desire. New York: Liveright, 1932.
Death in the Woods. New York: Liveright, 1933.
No Swank. Philadelphia: Centaur Press, 1934.
Puzzled America. New York: Charles Scribner's Sons, 1935.
Kit Brandon. New York: Charles Scribner's Sons, 1936.
Plays: Winesburg and Others. New York: Charles Scribner's Sons, 1937.
A Writer's Conception of Realism. Olivet, Michigan: Olivet College, 1939.
Five Poems. San Mateo, California: Quercus Press, 1939.
Home Town. Edited by Edwin Rosskam. New York: Alliance Book Corporation, 1940.

Sherwood Anderson's Memoirs. New York: Harcourt, Brace and Company, 1942.

Collections, Letters, and Critical Editions

The Buck Fever Papers. Edited by Welford Dunaway Taylor. Charlottesville: University Press of Virginia, 1971.

France and Sherwood Anderson: Paris Notebook, 1921. Edited by Michael Fanning. Baton Rouge: Louisiana State University Press, 1976.

Letters of Sherwood Anderson. Edited by Howard Mumford Jones and Walter B. Rideout. Boston: Little, Brown and Company, 1953.

Letters to Bab: Sherwood Anderson to Marietta D. Finley, 1916–33. Edited by William A. Sutton. Urbana and Chicago: University of Illinois Press, 1985.

The Portable Sherwood Anderson. Edited by Horace Gregory. New York: Viking Press, 1949; revised edition, 1972.

Return to Winesburg: Selections from Four Years of Writing for a Country Newspaper. Edited by Ray Lewis White. Chapel Hill: University of North Carolina Press, 1967.

Sherwood Anderson: Selected Letters. Edited by Charles E. Modlin. Knoxville: University of Tennessee Press, 1984.

Sherwood Anderson: Short Stories. Edited by Maxwell Geismar. New York: Hill and Wang, 1962.

Sherwood Anderson's Memoirs: A Critical Edition. Edited by Ray Lewis White. Chapel Hill: University of North Carolina Press, 1969.

The Sherwood Anderson Reader. Edited by Paul Rosenfeld. Boston: Houghton Mifflin Company, 1947.

The Teller's Tales. Edited by Frank Gado. Schenectady, N.Y.: Union College Press, 1983.

The "Writer's Book" by Sherwood Anderson: A Critical Edition. Edited by Martha Mulroy Curry. Metuchen, N.J.: Scarecrow Press, 1975.

Index